In Conversation
A Writer's Guidebook

Second Edition

MIKE PALMQUIST, *Colorado State University*

BARBARA WALLRAFF

Content for multilingual writers contributed by
EMILY SUH, *Texas State University*

 bedford/st.martin's
Macmillan Learning

Boston | New York

For Bedford/St. Martin's
Vice President, Editorial, Macmillan Learning Humanities: Edwin Hill
Executive Program Director for English: Leasa Burton
Executive Program Manager: Stacey Purviance
Marketing Manager: Vivian Garcia
Director of Content Development, Humanities: Jane Knetzger
Senior Developmental Editor: Rachel Goldberg
Senior Content Project Manager: Gregory Erb
Senior Workflow Project Manager: Jennifer L. Wetzel
Production Supervisor: Brianna Lester
Senior Media Project Manager: Allison Hart
Senior Media Editor: Barbara G. Flanagan
Composition: Lumina Datamatics, Inc.
Text Permissions Manager: Kalina Ingham
Text Permissions Researcher: Elaine Kosta, Lumina Datamatics, Inc.
Photo Permissions Editor: Angela Boehler
Photo Researcher: Krystyna Borgen, Lumina Datamatics, Inc.
Director of Design, Content Management: Diana Blume
Text Design: Diana Blume and Laura Shaw Design, Inc.
Cover Design: William Boardman
Cover Image: Yippa/Moment/Getty Images
Printing and Binding: RR Donnelley

Printed in China
1 2 3 4 5 6   24 23 22 21 20 19

For information, write:
Bedford/St. Martin's, 75 Arlington Street, Boston, MA 02116

ISBN 978-1-319-15777-7 (Student Edition)
ISBN 978-1-319-25444-5 (Student Edition with Exercises)

Acknowledgments
Acknowledgments and copyrights appear on the same page as the text and art selections they cover; these acknowledgments and copyrights constitute an extension of the copyright page.

How to Use This Book

In Conversation is divided into six color-coded parts, with advice and examples for every stage of the writing process.

1 Part 1, Join the Conversation, helps you recognize yourself as a writer and develop critical thinking skills.

2 Part 2, Work with Genre and Design, introduces you to common types of documents and guides you in composing and designing, whether for a course assignment or on your own.

3 Part 3, Conduct Research, instructs you in how to find, evaluate, and manage your sources and avoid plagiarism.

4 Part 4, Draft Your Document, helps you move from research to a full-fledged draft, with attention to thesis statement, argument and evidence, organization, and synthesizing source materials.

5 Part 5, Revise and Edit, focuses on making your writing stand out, with strategies for writing clearly, correctly, and skillfully.

6 Part 6, Document Sources, explains how to cite your sources correctly in four different documentation systems—MLA, APA, *Chicago*, and CSE—with dozens of model citations and full-page tutorials.

To learn more about a topic, follow the cross-references. These yellow arrows lead you to related information in other parts of the book.

How Can I . . .

- Find a broad topic quickly? See the **Brief Contents** (inside front cover).
- Look up specific writing, research, or design advice? See the **Detailed Contents** (inside back cover).
- Learn how to design my document? See the **Genre Design Gallery (G)** for real-world models, helpful annotations, and handy checklists.
- Resolve a sticky writing problem? See the yellow **Writer to Writer boxes** for succinct advice on tough situations.

- Learn the difference between "affect" and "effect"? See **Frequently Confused, Misused, and Abused Words** (p. G-1) to clear up confusion about easily misspelled or misunderstood words.

- **Define terms my instructor uses?** See the **Glossary of Terms** (p. G-7) to understand important grammar, writing, research, and design terminology.

- Interpret my instructor's feedback on my essay? See the **Common Revision Symbols and Notations** (p. C-1) to learn what those marks mean.

- **Get advice for multilingual writers?** See the **Help for Multilingual Writers menu** below for topics of special interest to students whose first language is not English.

- **View a student model?** See the menu of **Models and Advice for Student Writing** below for examples of other students' work.

Preface

Imagine two writers, one living a few city blocks from the Atlantic Ocean and the other living 2,000 miles away in the Rocky Mountains. Imagine they're collaborating on a complex project, meeting face-to-face only rarely, and coming from very different starting points. Barbara has spent more than three decades as a professional editor, including many years as a senior editor at *The Atlantic*, while Mike has worked almost equally long as a college professor and before that as a professional writer.

Given our backgrounds, we haven't agreed on every aspect of writing and researching, or on every point of style. We certainly don't agree on how to write the possessives of proper nouns ending in "s." And that's fine. We both recognize that respectable opinion varies about plenty of things related to writing. In fact, many of the "Writer to Writer" discussions in this book grew out of our disagreements.

Fortunately, we agree on the important issues. From the start, we agreed that this book should be brief yet comprehensive; that it should approach writing from a rhetorical perspective; and that, despite its brevity, it should not sacrifice the details and examples that can help writers find their way through their most critical writing challenges. We also agreed to avoid the typical teacher-to-student stance used so often in textbooks. Instead, we've approached this book as experienced writers seeking to share what we've learned with other writers.

We recognize, of course, that many readers will not think of themselves as writers. We'd point out, though, that they write frequently: on social media, in email and text messages, for school publications, for personal blogs or journals. Our goal is to help our readers draw on their experiences with writing—and with conversation more generally—to write clearly, effectively, and compellingly.

This book, *In Conversation*, is the result. Practical and highly visual, it answers the questions that come up throughout our writing and research processes. This second edition offers more coverage for multilingual writers, new real-world examples, and stronger attention to authenticating sources. Here's hoping that you — like the many instructors and colleagues who have given us helpful feedback — find it a valuable guide to writing in the twenty-first century.

New to this Edition

- ⊕ **New content for multilingual writers.** New sections throughout

> **27.5 Use Articles Artfully** ⊕
>
> The words *a*, *an*, and *the* are **articles**. (The term comes from the Latin *articulus*, meaning "part," or in this case, specifically a "small connecting part.") *A* and *an* are called **indefinite articles**,

Part 5 support students whose first language is not English. Look for this icon to find all of our new coverage, from count versus noncount nouns and phrasal verbs to question word order and common spelling rules.

- **A version with exercises, for more student practice.** *In Conversation 2e with Exercises* contains 55 sets of exercises on common style, grammar, punctuation, and mechanics issues. Answers to odd-numbered questions in the back of the book give students a chance to self-check.

- **Critical attention to evaluating and authenticating sources in the era of "fake news."** A revised Chapter 7 arms students with the tools to assess bias, pop information bubbles, and seek alternative points of view.

- **More coverage of analysis.** A reorganized Chapter 12, Support Your Main Point, addresses analytical writing as well as argumentative writing, with specific information on causal analysis, data analysis, and trend analysis.

Features of the Book

- **A framework of writing as conversation, emphasizing the rhetorical situation, genre, and design.** *In Conversation* grounds writers in a deep understanding of their purpose, audience, and context. This emphasis has shaped the examples we use, the issues we highlight in our "Writer to Writer" features, and the genres and design strategies we discuss, particularly in the Genre Design Gallery in Part 2.

- **A Writer to Writer approach.**
More than 45 conversational
"Writer to Writer" boxes
help writers gain a nuanced
understanding of issues
ranging from context to
composing processes to
points of disagreement
about style, grammar, and
mechanics. Talking *as* writers

> **Writer to Writer**
>
> ***Can you use an essay in more than one class?*** Reusing an assignment for more than one class, often referred to as self-plagiarism, is generally frowned on by writing instructors. If you wrote a term paper in one class and then turned it in for a grade in another, you wouldn't learn anything new about conducting research, developing an argument, considering your readers, and so on.
>
> On the other hand, if you've written previously about a topic that still intrigues you, you might ask your instructor if you could build on your earlier work. Similarly, if you're working on a new topic that is relevant to two of your current classes, you might talk with your instructors about completing a more ambitious project for both classes.

to writers, we use these brief boxes to offer advice and answer questions such as "Is it okay to use contractions?" or "Help! How can I write a paper under pressure?"

- **A striking visual approach that pays special attention to genre and design.**
Taking a cue from the vibrant world of social media, our eye-catching visual approach features annotated models from various genres, from traditional academic essays to multimodal essays, infographics to articles. The Genre Design Gallery showcases real student writing and published work from a variety of disciplines.

- **Practical attention to the genres students compose in, especially argument.** Chapter 4, Choose Your Genre, gives writers the tools to work in a variety of genres, both inside the classroom and out. The Genre Design Gallery guides them in fashioning a variety of documents that communicate their points clearly and effectively.

- **Comprehensive coverage of information literacy.** Part 3 presents strategies for identifying, locating, and working with sources. We've paid a great deal of attention to how writers can acknowledge what others have written and create a space for their own contributions. We also discuss tools writers can use to produce effective, well-designed, accessible documents. We frame our discussions of working with information technologies not as a set of mechanical processes but as a set of choices shaped by rhetorical situation.

- **Attention to writing across disciplines, professions, and civic and political settings.** Because we hope that this book will be useful throughout a writer's life, we've included genres used in typical first-year writing courses and beyond to prepare students for their writing lives in the professional world.

- **A clear and conversational treatment of grammar, mechanics, and style.** Rather than presenting grammar and style as a set of hard-and-fast rules, Part 5 offers an accessible, thoughtful approach to issues that often vex writers. Annotated, student-friendly examples help students understand *why* grammar, style, and punctuation conventions have developed the way they have and what effects they have on an audience.

- **Practical tips on managing writing projects and information from sources.** Managing writing projects and organizing information from sources are especially difficult for writers who are just beginning to take on complex writing tasks as college students. Throughout *In Conversation*, we call attention to strategies writers can use to stay focused and keep track of information.

Besides sharing practical strategies to help with every stage of the writing process—from generating good ideas to polishing a final draft—this book also demonstrates how those strategies turn out. *In Conversation* is a clear, well-written guide to writing clearly and well. We hope you find it as enjoyable to read as we found it to write.

MIKE PALMQUIST, Colorado State University

BARBARA WALLRAFF, Independent Writing and Editing Professional

Acknowledgments

We are grateful to the many instructors who reviewed *In Conversation* during its development and shared their experience, ideas, and feedback with us:

Angelina Blank, SUNY Potsdam; Cheryl Caesar, Michigan State University; Polina Chemishanova, University of North Carolina at Pembroke; Daniel Compora, University of Toledo; Darren DeFrain, Wichita State University; Tom Deromedi, Mott Community College; Joshua Dickinson, Jefferson Community College; Regina Dilgen, Palm Beach State College–Lakeworth; Mike DuBose, University of Toledo; Jessica Enoch, University of Maryland; Jacqueline Goffe-McNish, Dutchess Community College; George Grella, University of Rochester; Joel Henderson, Chattanooga State Community College; Kristin Iacopelli, University of Toledo; Whitney Jacobson, University of Minnesota Duluth; Lisa Johnson, Casper College; Elaine Jolayemi, Ivy Tech Community College; Renee Krusemark, Northeast Community College; Rich Lane, Clarion University; Patrick Lewis, California State University, Northridge; Bronwen Llewellyn, Daytona State College; Elizabeth Long, College of Western Idaho; Leslie Lovenstein, University of Arkansas–Pulaski Technical College; Julia Mandel, Kent State University; Matt Messer, Tufts University; Tracy Ann Morse, East Carolina University; Van Piercy, Lone Star College–Tomball; Wanda Pothier-Hill, North Shore Community College; Jacob Ray, University of Toledo; Nancy Risch, Caldwell Community College and Technical Institute; Amy Schmidt, Delta College; Mary Ann Simmons, James Sprunt Community College; Daniel Stanford, Pitt Community College; Benjamin Steingass, University of Toledo; Steffanie Triller Fry, Purdue University Northwest; Jayne Waterman, Ashland University; Kathryn Winograd, Arapahoe Community College; Courtney Wright-Werner, Monmouth University; Savannah Xaver, University of Toledo.

In Conversation also benefited from the dedication and hard work of our Bedford/St. Martin's colleagues. Leasa Burton planted the seed of this book and of this partnership; her steady advocacy has been invaluable. Thank you to Edwin Hill, for continuing

Bedford's commitment to the discipline of composition; Stacey Purviance, for her energetic and capable leadership of the handbook team; Rachel Goldberg, for her always excellent editorial guidance and thoughtful collaboration; Gregory Erb, for his unflappable work as production editor; copyeditor Daniel Nighting, for his attention to detail; and marketing manager Vivian Garcia, for her enthusiastic support.

We are thankful to the many colleagues from the academic and publishing worlds who shared feedback as we worked on this book, particularly Nick Carbone, Sue Doe, Chris Neuwirth, and Richard Young. Special thanks to Emily Suh for ensuring that the book addresses the needs of multilingual writers and for drafting the exercises in *In Conversation with Exercises*. We also thank the many writers we've worked with in the classroom and in the workplace for their inspiration. We thank William Whitworth, who has also inspired us with his superb taste and love of good writing. Finally and most importantly, we thank our families—Jessica, Ellen, Reid, and Jim—for their constant support as we've worked on this book. Without their generosity, this book would not exist.

Bedford/St. Martin's puts you first.

From day one, our goal has been simple: to provide inspiring resources that are grounded in best practices for teaching reading and writing. For more than 35 years, Bedford/St. Martin's has partnered with the field, listening to teachers, scholars, and students about the support writers need. We are committed to helping every writing instructor make the most of our resources.

How can we help *you*?

- Our editors can align our resources to your outcomes through correlation and transition guides for your syllabus. Just ask us.

- Our sales representatives specialize in helping you find the right materials to support your course goals.

- Our Bits blog on the Bedford/St. Martin's English Community (**community.macmillan.com**) publishes fresh teaching ideas weekly. You'll also find easily downloadable professional resources and links to author webinars on our community site.

Contact your Bedford/St. Martin's sales representative or visit **macmillanlearning.com** to learn more.

Print and Digital Options for *In Conversation*

Choose the format that works best for your course, and ask about our packaging options that offer savings for students.

Print

- **Spiral-bound** To order the spiral-bound edition, use ISBN 978-1-319-15777-7.

- *In Conversation 2e with Exercises* To order the version with 55 exercises on grammar, style, punctuation, and mechanics, use ISBN 978-1-319-25444-5.

- A *Student's Companion to* In Conversation To order the supplement for Accelerated Learning Programs, use ISBN 978-1-319-33078-1.

Digital

- *Innovative digital learning space* Bedford/St. Martin's suite of digital tools makes it easy to get everyone on the same page by putting student writers at the center. For details, visit **macmillanlearning.com/englishdigital**.

- *Popular e-book formats* For details about our e-book partners, visit **macmillanlearning.com/ebooks**.

- *Inclusive access* Enable every student to receive their course materials through your LMS on the first day of class. Macmillan Learning's Inclusive Access program is the easiest, most affordable way to ensure all students have access to quality educational resources. Find out more at **macmillanlearning.com/inclusiveaccess**.

Your Course, Your Way

No two writing programs or classrooms are exactly alike. Our Curriculum Solutions team works with you to design custom options that provide the resources your students need. (Options below require enrollment minimums.)

- *ForeWords for English*   Customize any print resource to fit the focus of your course or program by choosing from a range of prepared topics, such as Sentence Guides for Academic Writers.

- *Macmillan Author Program (MAP)*   Add excerpts or package acclaimed works from Macmillan's trade imprints to connect students with prominent authors and public conversations. A list of popular examples or academic themes is available upon request.

- *Bedford Select*   Build your own print handbook or anthology from a database of more than 800 selections, and add your own materials to create your ideal text. Package with any Bedford/St. Martin's text for additional savings. Visit **macmillanlearning.com/bedfordselect**.

Instructor Resources

You have a lot to do in your course. We want to make it easy for you to find the support you need—and to get it quickly.

Teaching with **In Conversation** is available as a PDF that can be downloaded from **macmillanlearning.com**. In addition to chapter overviews and teaching tips, the instructor's manual includes sample syllabi, correlations to the Council of Writing Program Administrators' Outcomes Statement, and classroom activities.

Part 1

Join the Conversation

Part 1: Join the Conversation

Too many of us think that writing well requires a special set of skills and abilities. In fact, almost anyone can learn to write clearly and effectively with a moderate amount of effort. In this guidebook, you'll learn how to become a confident, effective writer by building on your already extensive understanding of how conversations work.

1. Understand Yourself as a Writer

2. Explore Conversations

3. Read Critically and Actively

01. Understand Yourself as a Writer

What does it mean to be a writer? In movies and books, writers are often portrayed as solitary souls, perhaps a bit prickly (if they write novels or short stories), possibly thoughtful and sensitive (if they write poetry), or even just a bit odd. Writers working as journalists are often shown in a passionate exchange with a colleague or an editor — probably on deadline and feeling pressure to meet it.

Most writers, of course, don't fit these stereotypes. Writers are normal, everyday people. In fact, most people you'll see today will be, at some point, writers. They'll post something to Facebook, Twitter, or Tumblr. They'll email a friend. They'll write a report for a class. They'll send a text message. They'll submit a proposal for a project. They'll write in a journal. They'll comment on an article or blog.

In short, they'll use writing to connect with others. Through writing, they'll engage in conversation about issues they care about. They'll use writing to share information and ideas or to advance an argument.

This book treats writing as an extension of the kinds of conversations we engage in on a daily basis. As you use this book, reflect on what you're likely to do, say, and hear in a typical conversation. More often than not, you'll find that the knowledge and skills you've developed through years of spoken conversation will help you communicate with others through writing.

1.1 Think of Writing as a Conversation

Imagine yourself at a party. When you arrived, you said hello to friends and found something to eat or drink. Then you walked around, listening briefly to several conversations. Eventually, you joined a group that was talking about something you found interesting.

If you're like most people, you didn't jump right into the conversation. Instead, you listened for a few minutes and thought about what was being said. Perhaps you learned something new. Eventually, you added your voice to the conversation, other members of the group picked up on what you said, and the conversation moved along.

1.1

Use Your Conversational Skills

Understanding how conversations work can help you become a better writer. Good writing, like good conversation, involves more than simply stating what you know. As writing scholars, notably rhetorician Kenneth Burke, have long argued, writing is a process that involves several activities:

- **Careful listening.** Reading critically is a key part of the writing process (see Chapter 3). It involves paying attention both to voices that seem familiar and comfortable and to those that seem unfamiliar, that challenge your understanding and perceptions, and that share ideas in surprising or unusual ways.

- **Reflection.** Just as you would listen politely and receptively in a face-to-face conversation to someone you've met for the first time, even if they speak in a way that you find new or even surprising, you'll want to reflect on the new ideas they present. You can learn more about writing to reflect on page 39, Sec. 4.1.

- **Exploration and discovery.** Writing is a process that builds on your reading and reflection in ways that prepare you to add your voice to the conversation.

- **A desire to share your ideas.** Your voice is important. Your perspective is worth sharing. Writing that emerges from thoughtful reflection and inquiry can help others advance their own thinking about an issue you've been exploring.

You already possess many of the skills that make for a good conversation, and you can use those skills in your writing. You can consider why you're interested in the conversation and why others are, too. And you can explore the contexts — physical, social, and cultural—that will shape how your document is written and read.

Today, many of us are as likely to engage in conversations through writing as through speaking. Some of us prefer a text message to a phone call. Some of us find email far more useful than meetings. And some of us keep up with friends through Facebook, Twitter, or Instagram more than we do in person.

You may not think of creating text messages, email messages, and social media posts as writing, yet it is. And the writing you've done in these settings can help prepare you for the writing you'll be asked to do in class or on the job.

Add Your Voice

Just as most people listen to what's being said before speaking up, most writers begin the process of writing about a topic by reading. Developing your contribution to a written conversation involves reading critically, reflecting on what you've learned, deciding what and how you want to contribute to the

Draft your contribution and share it with other members of the conversation.

Begin by reading about a topic or issue, just as you'd listen for a while before speaking.

Look for something new to share with the other participants in the conversation.

Think carefully about what you've read, just as you'd think carefully about what you'd just heard.

Writing is a form of conversation in which readers and writers share ideas about a topic or issue.

conversation, and drafting and sharing your contribution. In turn, others will read and respond to what you've written.

You can see this circular process of exchanges among readers and writers in a number of contexts. Articles in scholarly and professional journals almost always refer to previously published work. Letters to the editor in newspapers and magazines frequently mention earlier letters or articles. Comments on blog posts or tweets that respond to other tweets follow a similar pattern.

1.2 Understand Your Writing Situation

When people participate in a spoken conversation, they pay attention to factors such as why they've joined the conversation, who's involved in the conversation, and what's already been said. They also notice the mood of the people they're speaking with, their facial expressions and body language, and physical factors such as background noise. In short, they consider the situation as they listen and speak. Similarly, when writers engage in written conversation, they become part of a **writing situation**—the setting in which writers and readers communicate with one another.

The phrase *writing situation* is another name for *rhetorical situation*, a concept that has been studied for thousands of years. Viewing writing as a rhetorical act helps us understand how writers or speakers pursue their purposes; consider the needs and interests of their audiences; draw on sources; adapt to the conditions in which they address their audiences; and present, organize, or design their documents or speeches.

What you write about depends on your writing situation—your purposes, readers, sources, and context. In many cases, a writing assignment will identify or suggest these elements for you. If it doesn't, take some time to think about the situation that will shape your work.

Define Your Purposes and Roles

Writers join written conversations for particular **purposes**: to inform, to analyze, to convince or persuade, to solve a problem, and so on. In many cases, writers have more than one purpose, such as learning something about a subject while earning a good grade or a promotion.

To accomplish their purposes, writers adopt **roles** within a conversation. A writer might explain something to someone else, in a sense becoming a guide through the conversation. Another writer might advance an argument, taking on the role of an

1.2

Writing Purposes and Roles

Purpose	Role	Action
To share reflections on an individual, event, object, idea, or issue	Observer	Consider a topic by sharing what is learned through the process of reflecting on it.
To help readers become aware of the facts and ideas central to an issue	Reporter	Present information on an issue without adopting an argumentative or evaluative position.
To analyze and explain the origins, qualities, significance, or potential impact of an idea, event, or issue	Interpreter	Apply an interpretive framework to a subject and seek answers to an interpretive question.
To assess and help readers reach an informed, well-reasoned understanding of a subject's worth or effectiveness	Evaluator	Make judgments about an individual, event, object, or idea.
To make progress on understanding and developing a solution to a problem	Problem Solver	Identify and define a problem, discuss the effects of a problem, assess potential solutions, and offer a solution.
To convince, persuade, or mediate a dispute among readers	Advocate	Convince readers that a position on an issue is reasonable and well founded, persuade readers to take action, or mediate by bringing readers into agreement on how to address an issue.
To share new knowledge	Inquirer	Conduct research and other forms of inquiry.
To amuse readers	Entertainer	Write in an entertaining way in an attempt to maintain readers' interest (seldom a primary goal of academic or professional writing).

advocate for a particular approach to an issue. As in spoken conversations, these roles are not mutually exclusive. For example, a writer might create a website that both *informs* readers about the potential benefits of geothermal power and *argues* for increased reliance on this form of power.

Your purposes and roles will be shaped by your interests, experiences, knowledge, attitudes, values, and beliefs about the conversation.

Consider Your Readers

Just as writers have purposes, so do readers. Readers often want to learn about a subject, assess or evaluate ideas and arguments, or understand opposing perspectives. And like writers, readers are strongly affected by their own needs, interests, knowledge, experiences, values, and beliefs.

Your assignment might identify your readers, or audience, for you. If you are working on a project for a class, one of your most important readers will be your instructor. Other readers might include your classmates, people who have a professional or personal interest in your topic, or, if your project will be published, the readers of a newspaper, magazine, or website. If you are writing in a business or professional setting, your readers might include supervisors, coworkers, or customers.

Analyze Your Context

Writing is affected by a wide variety of contexts, including social, physical, technological, disciplinary, professional, cultural, and historical contexts.

- **Social contexts** shape the relationships between writers and readers. Are they friends? Strangers? Supervisor and employee? Instructor and student? Whatever the dynamic, social context will influence how writers and readers approach the writing situation.

- **Physical and technological contexts** affect both the kind of document you choose and the design of your document.

Where will you write? What writing tools will you use? Will your document be read in a quiet room, on a train, or in a coffee shop? Will your readers view it in print, on a tablet or phone, or on a large computer screen?

- **Disciplinary and professional contexts** are the shared experiences of members of particular disciplines, such as chemistry or sociology. Over time, members of a discipline develop consensus about how to report new findings, how to offer criticism of previous work in the field, and how to document sources.

- **Cultural and historical contexts** are a set of broader similarities and differences among writers and readers. The attack on the World Trade Center on September 11, 2001, is one example of a historical event that has strongly influenced much that has been written about terrorism in the popular press, in professional journals, and on the web. Similarly, widely shared cultural values—such as a belief in the importance of personal freedom—can shape writers' and readers' responses to arguments that support or run counter to those values.

Assess Potential Sources

In spoken conversations, speakers build on what has been said, often referring to specific ideas or arguments and identifying the speakers who raised them. Written conversations also build on earlier contributions. Writers refer to *sources*—or the work of other authors—to support their arguments, provide a context for their own contributions, or differentiate their ideas from those advanced by other authors. Writers also use sources to introduce new ideas, information, and arguments to a conversation. When writers refer to sources, they provide citations to indicate where the information comes from and to help readers locate the sources should they wish to review them.

As you analyze an assignment, determine whether you'll need to draw on information from sources such as magazine or journal articles, websites, or scholarly books. Ask whether you'll need to cite a certain number of sources and whether you're required to use a specific documentation system, such as the system created by the Modern Language Association (MLA) or the American Psychological Association (APA).

1.3

> You can read more about finding and using sources in Part 3 of this book.

Consider Genre and Design

Writers make choices about the type of document and the design of their documents largely in response to physical, social, and disciplinary contexts. They recognize that they are more likely to accomplish their purposes if their documents meet their readers' expectations, are designed to help readers understand ideas and information, and present their points clearly and effectively.

Genres are general categories of documents, such as opinion columns, scholarly articles, novels, and blogs. Genres typically develop to help writers accomplish a general purpose—such as informing readers or presenting an argument—within a specific context and for a certain audience. As the needs and interests of a community change, the genres used within that community evolve to reflect those needs and interests.

Document design is closely related to genre. In fact, the characteristic design of a particular type of document, such as the use of columns, headings, and photographs in a magazine article, can help you distinguish one type of document from another. Throughout this book, you'll find design treated as a central writing strategy.

> You can find in-depth discussions of genre and design in Part 2.

1.3 Manage Your Writing Processes

Writing is a lot like skiing. It's also a lot like teaching, coaching, managing a budget, and selling trucks. In fact, there are surprising similarities among these and other complex activities. The key factors that come into play—pursuing goals, acquiring and applying knowledge, considering strategies, and making decisions—are similar enough that the experiences of learning in other areas can help you gain new knowledge and skills as a writer.

1.3

Put in the Time and Effort

Another common theme among complex activities is the importance of practice. Musicians know that the more you practice, and the more often you receive useful feedback, the better you'll become. Seeking guidance from more experienced writers—including writing teachers, writing center consultants, and colleagues or supervisors—and then putting that guidance into practice are the keys to improving as a writer.

Adapt Your Processes

Most writing projects share some general similarities. You'll have a purpose, readers, and a context within which your writing will take place. You also might have a deadline, an expected

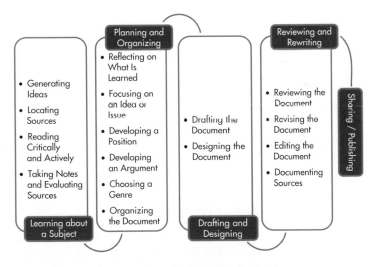

Writers can draw on a wide range of composing processes.

document length, and requirements for the kinds of sources you will use to support your argument.

Despite these similarities, it's rare to use every reading and writing process each time you write. In fact, you'll almost always find that some aspect of a writing project will distinguish it from the projects you've worked on in the past.

With these observations in mind, remember two things. First, because general types of writing projects share similarities, you can build on what you've learned from past projects. Second, because every project is likely to differ in some way from past projects, you'll want to adapt your processes to the specific needs of the project.

Draft and Revise: Repeat as Needed

Writing is anything but a step-by-step activity. You'll repeat tasks, rethink earlier decisions, and delete text that no longer works. In many cases, you'll write a first draft, revise it, think about it, ask for feedback, and revise yet again. If you don't like the outcome, you might reorganize your draft or take a break to learn more about your subject. Highly skilled and experienced professional writers do this regularly. At its heart, writing is a process of making judgments about whether you've done enough to accomplish your goals and deciding what to do when you feel you need to do more.

Understanding that writing involves constantly reenvisioning your document can help you avoid frustration. Learning more about an issue may lead you to rethink your position and refine your ideas. Rather than viewing this work as unnecessary and repetitive, you'll understand it as a natural and reasonable means of improving your contribution to the conversation.

1.4 Work with Other Writers

Writers frequently work together. A writer might seek advice about potential topics or ask for feedback on a draft. A writing instructor might direct students to work together to generate ideas, collect sources on a common topic, engage in peer review, and develop and refine arguments. An instructor or a manager might assign a group project.

Working with other writers draws on the same skills you use when you engage in any form of conversation—listening carefully, treating others with respect, and deciding how to make a useful contribution.

Generate Ideas Together

Common strategies for generating ideas with other writers include group brainstorming and role-playing activities.

Brainstorming. Group brainstorming draws on the differing backgrounds and experiences of the members of a group to generate ideas for a writing project. To engage in group brainstorming, follow these guidelines:

- Encourage everyone in the group to participate.

- Be polite.

- Build on one another's ideas.

- Generate as many ideas as possible.

- Take notes.

- Review the results and identify promising ideas.

Role-Playing. Role-playing activities are frequently used to generate and refine ideas. By asking the members of a group to take on roles, you can apply a variety of perspectives to a subject.

- **Appoint a "doubting Thomas."** Ask a member of the group to play the role of someone who demands evidence from a writer for every assertion.

- **Appoint a "devil's advocate."** Ask a member of the group to respond to a writer's arguments with reasonable counterarguments.

- **Stage a debate.** Assign speakers who represent different perspectives to argue politely with one another about an issue. Group members can adopt roles such as authors of the readings you've used in a class, political commentators or celebrities who have taken a strong stand on an issue, authorities on an issue, or people affected by an issue or event.

Collect Information Together

You may be asked to work together to collect, critically read, evaluate, and take notes on information from sources. Common collaborative activities for collecting and working with information include the following:

- Develop a search strategy for published sources (p. 105, Sec. 6.1).

- Assign responsibility for locating sources (pp. 107–114, Secs. 6.1 and 6.2).

- Assign responsibility for field research (p. 115, Sec. 6.3).

- Create shared annotated bibliographies (p. 47, Sec. 4.3).

- Share evaluations of sources (p. 125, Sec. 7.3).

- Share notes on sources (p. 36, Sec. 3.3).

Engage in Peer Review

Few experienced writers produce major documents without asking for feedback on their drafts. When peer review is designed effectively and treated seriously, it can provide valuable information about the clarity, organization, and design of a draft. Feedback from other writers can help you develop your main point or identify gaps in the reasoning and evidence you'll use to convince readers to accept your main point. It can also help you improve your writing process, which will benefit you long after you've completed your current project.

1.4

Getting Feedback from Other Writers

✔ **Be clear.** Let your reviewers know, for example, that you are struggling with the transition from one point to another or that you would appreciate feedback on your conclusion.

✔ **Be reasonable.** Don't expect your reviewers to spend more time making suggestions about a draft than you spent writing it. Ask for advice they can provide in less than half an hour of review.

✔ **Be prepared.** If you are asking the writer to comment on a printed draft, format it with double-spaced lines and wide margins. If you are providing a digital draft, make sure the reviewer can access, read, and comment on your file easily.

✔ **Be open to criticism.** Don't dismiss constructive criticism as a problem with the reviewer's comprehension. Even when the suggested revision isn't quite right, it might point to an area that needs attention.

✔ **Be willing to ask questions.** If you aren't sure what a reviewer's comments mean, ask for clarification.

✔ **Be willing to change.** If the feedback has merit, consider how you might revise your draft in response to it.

✔ **Be fair to yourself.** Don't feel obligated to incorporate every suggested change into your draft.

Ineffective feedback   **Effective feedback**

1.4

How would you feel if the only feedback you received on a 2500-word writing assignment was "nice job" or "needs work" or "unclear phrase"? How would you feel if the only feedback you received was on grammar?

> Maybe include some evidence that teachers don't always provide substantive feedback. Did you find any studies about feedback?

> Nice introduction!

> Are you being serious?

Too many high school students receive little or no feedback on their work — even on assignments that require literally hours and weeks of work. Most shrug it off and say, "What can you expect? The teacher is incredibly busy" or "It makes sense. It was just an assignment for a science class." But a growing number are asking for more. They want to improve as writers. They want to be prepared for college or a job. They want to see some return on their investment of time and effort.

> Awkward sentence! You might want to buy a better handbook.

> I wonder if you could support this claim with an anecdote from a student.

These students need to be heard. High school principals need to reward teachers who design good assignments and provide strong feedback. College and university teacher-education programs need to pay serious attention to writing theory, instruction, and practice. And teachers themselves need to recognize that it's never enough to read and grade an assignment. They need to see that feedback on writing is a critical part of the teaching process.

> This is way too confusing.

> I think you might want to introduce these ideas in a different order for greater impact.

Ineffective and **effective** feedback on a student's first draft

Giving Feedback to Other Writers

✔ **Be certain you understand the assignment.** Ask the writer to describe the draft's purposes and audience. Read the assignment sheet, if one is shared with you.

✔ **Be aware of any peer-review guidelines.** Use a rubric, if one is provided.

✔ **Be considerate.** Take your job seriously, and give the draft the time it deserves.

✔ **Be thorough.** To understand a draft's overall structure and argument, read it all the way through at least once before making any comments.

✔ **Be organized.** Take a few minutes to identify two or three areas most in need of work.

✔ **Be judicious.** Focus on the areas of the draft most in need of improvement. In most cases, changes that focus on bigger picture concerns such as purpose, readers, argument, and organization need to be addressed before lower-level concerns such as sentence structure and spelling.

✔ **Be specific.** Offer comments such as, "I found it difficult to understand your point in the second paragraph" and "Can you show the connection more clearly between this paragraph and the previous one?"

✔ **Be constructive.** Offer concrete suggestions about how the draft might be improved instead of simply pointing out what isn't working.

✔ **Be positive.** Identify places where the writer has succeeded, not just places that fall short.

✔ **Be responsible.** Review your comments before you give them to the writer.

02. Explore Conversations

Early work on a writing project involves "listening in" on conversations and choosing one to pursue. To begin this process, look for conversations that interest you and have room for new voices. Some written conversations address issues that have largely been settled, while others provide gaps in the conversation where new writers can share their ideas.

2.1 Generate Topics

A good topic is much more than an entry in an encyclopedia. It's a subject of debate, discussion, and discovery. Ideally, it's also something that interests and challenges you.

You can generate ideas about possible topics of conversation by using prewriting activities such as brainstorming, freewriting, blindwriting or dictating, looping, clustering, mapping, and using sentence starters. You can also discuss potential topics with others and conduct preliminary observations.

Brainstorm

Brainstorming involves making a list of ideas as they occur to you. This list doesn't need to consist of complete sentences—in fact, brainstorming is most successful when you avoid censoring yourself. Brainstorming sessions usually respond to a specific question, such as "What interests me about this project?" or "Why would anyone care about ____?" Although you're likely to end up using only a few of the ideas you generate, you can weed out the less promising ones later.

Freewrite

Freewriting involves writing full sentences quickly, without stopping and—most important—without editing what you write. You might set a timer and freewrite for five, ten, or fifteen minutes. Or you might decide to write until you've completed a set number of pages. Don't pause to consider whether your sentences are "good" or "bad," and don't pay attention to details such as spelling and grammar. If all of this work results in a single good idea, your freewriting session will have been a success.

Looping is another form of freewriting. During a looping session, you write for a set amount of time (five minutes works well) and then read what you've written. As you read, identify one key idea in what you've written, and then repeat the process with this new idea as your starting point. Repeat the looping process as needed to refine your ideas.

2.1

Writer to Writer

What if freewriting is too hard? If writing freely without editing feels too daunting, try blindwriting or dictating. Blindwriting is freewriting on a computer with the monitor turned off. Dictating involves speaking out loud. Most smartphones and tablets allow you to convert spoken words to text. These forms of freewriting can shift your focus from the text you've written so far, largely because you can do them without looking at the screen.

Cluster or Map

Clustering and mapping involve putting your ideas about a topic into graphic form. As you map out the relationships among your ideas, they can help you gain a different perspective on a topic. The process can also help you generate new ideas.

To cluster ideas about a topic, place your main idea at the center of a page. Jot down subcategories, causes and effects, or reasons supporting an argument around the main idea. Then create clusters of ideas that branch out from those key ideas. In these clusters, list groups of related ideas, evidence, effects, causes, consequences—in short, ideas that are related to your key ideas.

2.1

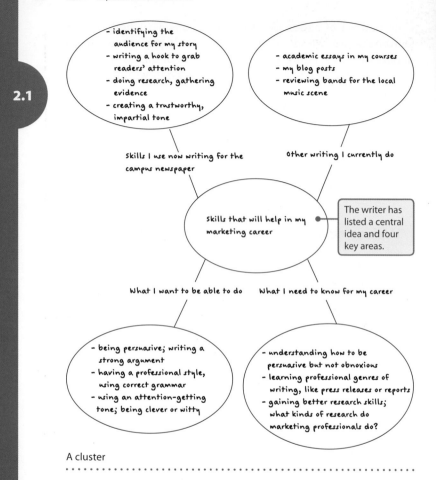

- identifying the audience for my story
- writing a hook to grab readers' attention
- doing research, gathering evidence
- creating a trustworthy, impartial tone

Skills I use now writing for the campus newspaper

- academic essays in my courses
- my blog posts
- reviewing bands for the local music scene

Other writing I currently do

Skills that will help in my marketing career

The writer has listed a central idea and four key areas.

What I want to be able to do

What I need to know for my career

- being persuasive; writing a strong argument
- having a professional style, using correct grammar
- using an attention-getting tone; being clever or witty

- understanding how to be persuasive but not obnoxious
- learning professional genres of writing, like press releases or reports
- gaining better research skills; what kinds of research do marketing professionals do?

A cluster

To map a topic, place your main idea at the top of a page. Then identify as many relationships as possible, such as related causes and effects, costs and benefits, or advantages and disadvantages. For example, if you are mapping a topic using causes and effects, treat each effect as a new cause by asking yourself, "If this happened, what would happen next?" Then use arrows to show the consequences. If you are mapping a topic using costs and benefits, show groups of costs and identify the relationships among them.

Use Sentence Starters

Sentence starters help you generate ideas by "filling in the blanks" in each sentence. They can also help you identify gaps—or conversational openings—in the conversation you're joining. There are nearly as many sentence starters as there are ideas about how to structure a sentence. You can make up your own or you can try some of the following.

2.1

Exploring Interests

I would like to understand [how / why / whether] ____ happened.

I want to know more about ____ so that I can ____.

I am interested in ____ because ____.

Explaining

There are three reasons this is [true / not true / relevant / important / essential]. First, ____. Second, ____. Third, ____.

The reason ____ is that ____.

Interpreting and Analyzing

This means that ____.

If we were starting over, we would ____.

It has always been the case that ____.

____ is significant because ____.

Understanding Causes and Effects

The root cause of this problem is ____.

This event happened because ____.

The goal was to ____, and the results are ____.

Predicting

Too often, we ____.

If we ____, then ____.

We would prefer that ____ is true, but we must recognize that ____.

Stating Beliefs

I believe ____.

We have to ____.

I want to ____.

Exploring Possibilities

If this is [true / happening / important], then ____.

We could ____.

How can we ____?

Evaluating

The most important aspect of ____ is ____.

This is better because ____.

Solving Problems

We can [change / improve / fix] this by ____.

Solving the problem of ____ would help by ____.

Reflecting

When I think about ____, I notice ____.

This reminds me of ____.

The most [memorable / striking / significant] thing about ____ is ____.

2.2

Be Flexible

Remember that your choice of a topic is subject to change. It's a starting point, not a final destination. As you learn about your topic, you might find that related topics are more appealing or more appropriate. You might even find that you need to rethink your choice completely.

Writer to Writer

When is it time to start over?   Writers frequently run into roadblocks that cause them to rethink their entire project. At the beginning of a project, it's not unusual to switch topics completely. Do so, however, only if it becomes clear that starting fresh will save you time and effort.

   If you do start over, don't throw away the effort you've already put in. Reflect on the problem you're facing and brainstorm or talk over how to sidestep it or solve it. Remember for future writing projects what led you to start over.

2.2 Focus on an Issue

Once you've chosen a topic, focus on a specific issue within it. Issues are points of disagreement, uncertainty, concern, or curiosity that are discussed by communities of readers and writers.

Get to Know the Conversation

Familiarize yourself with the conversation you are joining by looking for patterns in the information, ideas, and arguments you encounter in your sources.

- **Look for central concepts.** When several sources refer to the same idea, you can assume that this information is central to the topic.

- **Look for unanswered questions.** Sources that pose difficult questions are likely to give you important insights into the conversation.

- **Look for disagreements.** Some sources will explicitly disagree with other sources. Looking for these statements of disagreement can help you home in on the debates that are important to the conversation.

- **Look for recurring voices.** As you read sources, you might find that some authors write frequently about your topic or are frequently referred to by other writers. These authors might have significant experience or expertise related to the topic, or they might represent particular perspectives on the topic. Stay alert for these recurring voices.

Identify Useful Sources

Depending on your topic, some types of sources will be more useful than others. For example, if you're interested in a topic such as wind power or hydraulic fracturing (fracking), you might focus on government and industry websites, trade journals, newspapers, magazines, and blogs. If you're interested in a topic such as Shakespearean drama, books and articles in scholarly journals will be more useful.

2.3 Develop a Writing Question

Most writers use a *writing question* or *research question* to direct their efforts to collect, critically read, evaluate, and take notes on sources. Good writing questions are narrowly focused, allowing writers to collect information in time to meet deadlines. They can also be revised as writers learn more about an issue. It's best, at this early stage, to think of your writing question as a flexible guide.

Reflect on Your Disciplinary Context

As you generate ideas for a writing question, think about how your context might shape the questions you can ask. If you are writing a research report for a biology class, it's important to understand the kinds of questions biologists typically ask. The same is true for virtually every discipline and profession, since all have particular ways of asking questions and approaching information.

Disciplinary Questions

2.3

Discipline	Types of Questions	Examples
Humanities	Interpretive questions about literature, music, philosophy, rhetoric, and the arts	How did the acceptance of Manet's painting style open the door for Impressionism? What characteristics does Toni Morrison's character Amy Denver in *Beloved* share with Huck Finn?
Social Sciences	Questions about factors that affect human behavior	What is the significance of social-networking sites such as Facebook in modern-day protest movements? What factors contribute to a person becoming a mass murderer?
Sciences	"How," "what," and "why" questions about the natural world, including both the environment and living beings	What are the effects of exercise and diet on obesity among school-age children? What are the preventable causes of climate change?
History	"How," "what," and "why" questions about past events	What role did religion play in the American conservative movement of the twentieth century? Why did fascism ultimately fail in Italy in the 1940s?

Similarly, take into account the genres typically used within the discipline or profession. Books and longer reports are well suited to broader questions. Other genres—such as poster sessions, conference presentations, reports, and essays—are better suited to highly focused writing questions.

Consider Your Role

Your purpose and role as a writer will have a profound impact on your decisions about your writing question. Writers who inform their readers, for example, develop strikingly different questions than those who seek to persuade them to take action. A writer seeking to inform readers about the impact of fracking on air and water quality, for example, might pursue questions such as the following:

What are the effects of fracking on local air and water quality?

How have opponents of fracking characterized its impact on air and water quality?

What have recent scientific research studies indicated about the impact of fracking on air and water quality?

In contrast, had the writer sought to advocate a particular approach to the issue, the writing questions might have been the following:

In light of recent findings about the impact of fracking on air and water quality, should the U.S. government enact legislation to ban fracking?

Given scientific evidence that fracking has a negative effect on air and water quality, should the government establish regulations that might reduce or eliminate those effects?

Given the critical need to keep energy costs low, what steps should citizens and nongovernmental bodies take to encourage the responsible use of fracking?

The Relationship between Roles and Writing Questions

Purpose	Role	General Questions
To Inform	Reporter	What is known — and not known — about _____? How might we define _____?
To Create and Share New Knowledge	Inquirer	What causes _____? What are the effects of _____? What can [cure / repair / prevent] _____?
To Reflect	Observer	What are the implications of _____? How can we learn from the example of an individual or group? What can we gain from thinking about [an idea / a work of art / a work of literature / a performance / an event]?
To Evaluate	Evaluator	What conclusions have writers and readers already made about _____? What assumptions are shaping current thinking about _____? What are the best choices available for addressing _____? What are the relative strengths and weaknesses of _____?
To Analyze	Interpreter	What has occurred in the past that is relevant to _____? What causes _____? What are the effects of _____? Does the data suggest that _____ [is / is the result of] a trend? What is likely to happen [to / as a result of] _____? In what ways is _____ [similar to / different from] _____?

(Continued)

2.3

Purpose	Role	General Questions
To Solve Problems	Problem Solver	Why is _____ a problem? What is the best solution to _____? Why should we adopt _____ as a solution to _____?
To Convince, Persuade, or Mediate	Advocate	What are the origins of this argument? Who has made the best arguments about _____? What do the writers and readers involved in conversation about _____ want to [see happen / avoid happening]? How can we find common ground about _____?

Identify Gaps in the Conversation

Consider where you might offer something new to the conversation. You don't need to offer something that is radically new, nor do you need to change the direction of the conversation. But you should offer something of value to your readers. The following table uses an approach to newness developed by David Kaufer, Cheryl Geisler, and Christine Neuwirth.

Filling a Gap with Something New

Forms of Newness	Strategies
Newness by Aspect. Contributions related to experience or observation.	How can my personal experiences form the basis for a contribution to this conversation? How has my knowledge of this issue prepared me to offer something new? How can my investigations of this issue prepare me to share something new?
Newness by Analogy. Contributions based on comparison.	In what ways is this issue like a library? Like a church? Like a labor union?
Newness by Framework. Contributions based on application of methods from another discipline or profession.	How can an anthropological approach help us better understand this issue? A psychological approach? A legal approach?
Prize-Winning Newness. The least common form of newness.	What can I share that is truly new, game changing, or so unusual and surprising that it will gain my readers' attention?

Refine Your Writing Question

Once you've chosen your writing question, consider its scope and level of detail. If the question is too broad, ask yourself what part of the topic interests you most. If it's still too broad, ask yourself the question again. If your focus is too narrow, try to expand the topic to cover other factors, such as a larger geographic area or a longer time period.

2.3

Too Broad: How does the use of instructional technology in public education vary among industrialized nations?

Too Narrow: Do first-grade teachers prefer smartboards from Hitachi or Smart?

Balanced Focus: How can the use of tablets improve reading fluency among U.S. fourth-graders?

Specific question words can help you create a focused writing question. If you are interested in conducting an analysis, for example, you might use the words *what, why, when, where, who,* and *how.* If you are interested in informing readers about the goals or outcomes associated with a particular issue, you might use the word *would* or *could.* If the conversation focuses on determining an appropriate course of action, as would be the case if you were adopting the role of an advocate, the questions you generate are likely to use the word *should.*

You can also refine your writing question by calling attention to existing knowledge or assumptions that have been made around this issue.

Original Question

What should be done about steroid use by adolescent girls involved in competitive sports?

Alternative 1

Even though we know that universal drug testing of all athletes, younger and older, is difficult, what should be done about steroid use by adolescent girls involved in competitive sports?

Alternative 2

Given the lack of knowledge about the health consequences of steroid use, what should parents and doctors do about steroid use by adolescent girls involved in competitive sports?

2.3

As you refine your writing question, you might use conditional words and phrases such as the following:

Mix . . .	and Match
Although	we know that . . .
Because	it is uncertain . . .
Even though	it is clear that . . .
Given that	studies indicate . . .
In light of	recent events . . .
Now that	it has been shown . . .
Since	the lack of . . .
While	we cannot . . .

Another way to test your writing question is to conduct some preliminary searches in a library catalog or database or on the web. If you locate a vast amount of information in your searches, you may need to refine your question to focus on a more manageable aspect of the issue. In contrast, if your searches turn up empty, you may need to expand the scope of your writing question.

03. Read Critically and Actively

Reading critically means reading with a purpose. Unlike evaluating sources to see if they are suitable for your writing project (see Chapter 7), critical reading is a flexible process that takes place throughout your project.

3.1

3.1 Read with an Attitude

Whether you are looking for a topic or deep into your research, adopt a critical attitude. Accept nothing at face value; ask questions; look for similarities and differences among the sources you read; examine the implications of what you read; be alert for unusual information; and note relevant sources and information. Most important, be open to ideas and arguments, even if you don't agree with them. Give them a chance to influence your thinking.

Adopting a critical attitude means approaching sources with curiosity at every stage in the process. You'll note new information and mark key passages that provide insights into your subject. You'll take a more questioning stance as you determine whether sources fit into your project and are reliable. Later, as you draw conclusions about your writing question, you might take a more skeptical approach, becoming more aggressive in challenging arguments you've encountered. Remember that you are aiming to make a contribution. Don't hesitate to question the writers who have come before you. You should respect their work, but you shouldn't assume that their conclusions are the last word. Be prepared to challenge their ideas and arguments. If you don't, you'll simply repeat the ideas of others instead of advancing your own.

Read about assessing the appropriateness and credibility of sources in Chapter 7.

3.2 Read with Your Writing Situation in Mind

One way to get into the habit of reading critically is to approach a source with your writing situation in mind. Your purposes, role, readers, genre, and design provide a useful lens through which to consider a source.

Read a Source with Your Writing Situation in Mind

Reflect on . . .	By asking . . .
Your Purposes and Role	Are the information, ideas, and arguments in this source relevant to my writing question? Will they help me accomplish my purposes?
	Does this source present information, ideas, and arguments that make me reconsider my initial responses to my writing question?
	Does it provide new information, ideas, or arguments?
	Does it advocate for a certain response to the issue?
Your Readers	Would my readers want to know about the information, ideas, and arguments in this source?
	Would my readers find the source's information convincing or compelling?
	Would my readers benefit from a review of the argument and evidence presented in this source?
	How will my readers react to the argument and evidence presented in this source?
Genre	What type of evidence is usually provided in a document like mine?
	How are documents of this type typically organized? Can I find examples of effective organizational strategies in the sources I read?
Design	Does this source provide a useful model for designing my document?
	Will I be expected to provide charts, graphics, photographs, or other illustrations? If so, what can I learn from how illustrations are used in the source?
	Does this source help me understand how I might address the physical and technological contexts in which my document will be read?
Requirements and Limitations	If I find useful information in a source, will I be able to follow up on it with additional research? Will I have enough time to follow up on that information?
	How much information can I include in my document? Will my readers be looking for an overview or a detailed report?

3.3 Read Actively

Reading actively means interacting with sources. It involves skimming for organization and content, marking and annotating sources, and taking notes.

Skim for Organization and Content

Before investing too much time in a source, skim it. Skimming—reading just enough to get a general idea of what a source is about—helps you understand how a source is organized and whether it will be useful and relevant.

To skim most genres, use the following strategies:

- **Check the title** for cues about content.

- **Skim opening and closing paragraphs** for the purpose and scope of the document.

- **Skim captions** of photos and figures.

- **Check headings and subheadings** to learn about content and organization.

- **Read the first and last sentences** of paragraphs to identify the source's purpose.

- **Note illustrations,** such as photographs and other images, charts, graphs, tables, animations, audio clips, and video clips.

If you are skimming a longer document, such as a book or report, consider these additional strategies:

- **Check the table of contents** for a useful overview of the document's content and organization.

- **Check the index** to learn more about the content.

- **Check the glossary** for clues about the focus of the document.

- **Check the works-cited list** to learn about the types of evidence used in the document.

3.3

- **Check for pull quotes,** quotations or brief passages pulled out of the text and set in larger type elsewhere on the page.

- **Check for information about the author** to learn about the writer's background, interests, and purposes.

For a website or digital document, consider these strategies:

- **Scan for boldface, colored, or italic text.** Important information is often highlighted in some way on the page.

- **Check for links** to other sites to learn more about the issue.

- **Check the URL** to learn about the purpose of a website. Look for clues such as *.edu* for education, *.gov* for government, and *.com* for commercial and business sites.

- **Read the navigation menus** to see other content on the site.

Mark and Annotate Sources

Highlight or underline key passages so you can locate them easily later in your writing process. Write notes in the margin of print documents or use commenting tools on digital documents to keep track of your reactions and ideas. For instance, you might add a brief note explaining why you disagree with a passage or why you need to locate additional information.

Identify the Genre. Recognizing a source's genre will help you understand and question what you read in it. If you realize that a source is an opinion column, for example, you'll be less likely to be taken in by the use of questionable logic. If you are read-ing an annual report for corporate stockholders, you'll recognize that the writer's primary concern is to present the company in a positive light. If an article comes from a peer-reviewed scholarly journal, you'll know that it's been reviewed by experts in the field.

Identify Primary and Secondary Sources. Primary sources are either original works or evidence provided directly by an observer of an event. Try to read as many primary sources as possible so that you can come to your own conclusions about the issue. Primary sources include the following:

- essays, novels, short stories, poems, paintings, musical scores and recordings, sculpture, and other works of art or literature

- diaries, journals, memoirs, and autobiographies

- interviews, speeches, government and business records, letters, and memos

- reports, drawings, photographs, films, or video and audio recordings of an event

- physical artifacts associated with an event, such as a weapon used in a crime or a piece of pottery from an archaeological dig

Secondary sources comment on or interpret an event, often using primary sources as evidence.

Examples of Primary and Secondary Sources

Primary Sources	Secondary Sources
A play by William Shakespeare	An article that presents a literary analysis of the play
A recording or transcript of the statement made by the president	An interview in which a historian discusses the significance of the president's statement
The findings of a medical study concerning the benefits of strength training for women with osteoporosis	A website that reviews recent research about the prevention and treatment of osteoporosis

Identify Main Points. Most sources, regardless of their purpose, have a main point. Usually, the main point will be expressed in the form of a thesis statement (see Chapter 11). As you read critically, make sure you understand what the author of the source wants readers to know, accept, believe, or do as a result of reading the document.

3.3

Identify Reasons and Evidence. Once you've identified the main point, look for the reasons given to accept it. If an author is arguing, for instance, that English should be the only language used for official government business in the United States, that author might support his or her argument with the following reasons:

- The use of multiple languages erodes patriotism.

- The use of multiple languages keeps people apart. If they can't talk to one another, they won't learn to respect one another.

- The use of multiple languages in government business costs taxpayers money because so many alternative forms need to be printed.

Reasons make appeals to emotions, logic, principles, values, or beliefs (see p. 66, Sec. 4.8). As persuasive as a given reason might seem, it is only as good as the evidence offered to support it. In some cases, evidence is offered in the form of statements from experts on a subject or people in positions of authority. In other cases, evidence might include personal experience. In still other cases, evidence might include firsthand observations, excerpts from an interview, or statistical data.

Always consider where evidence comes from and how it is being used (see Chapter 7). If the information appears to be presented fairly, ask whether you might be able to use it to support your own ideas and try to verify its accuracy by consulting additional sources.

Identify New and Hard-to-Understand Information. Mark and annotate passages that contain information you haven't encountered before. You might be tempted to ignore information that's hard to understand. If you do, you might miss something that is critical to the success of your writing project. Instead, make a brief annotation reminding yourself to check it out later.

Identify Similarities and Differences. Look for similarities and differences among the sources you read. Note which writers agree

3.3

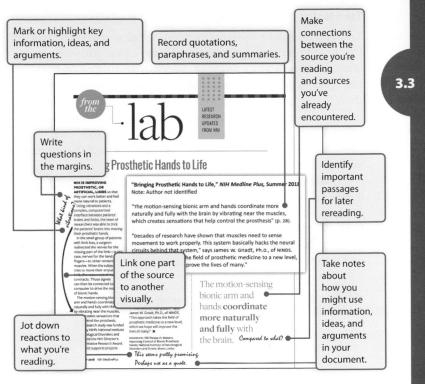

Marking and annotating a source

U.S. National Library of Medicine, *NIH MedlinePlus*, Summer 2018

with each other and which ones stake out contrasting positions. These notes can help you build your own argument.

Reread Promising Sources

As you work through your sources, you'll find that some are worth reading more carefully than others. When a source offers what appears to be good information, ideas, or arguments, spend extra time marking relevant passages and taking notes. Return to difficult passages later.

Take Notes

Taking notes has two benefits. First, it helps you keep track of the most important information, ideas, and arguments you've encountered in your sources. Second, and more important, taking notes helps you understand your sources more thoroughly than if you simply saved and highlighted copies of them. By paraphrasing or summarizing a source, for example, you force yourself to present passages from the source in your own words (see pp. 146–150, Sec. 9.3 and Sec. 9.4); you connect the source to what you already know.

Choose a method for taking notes—such as using note cards, a paper notebook, a word-processing program, web-based tools, or an app on a smartphone or tablet, for example—that reflects how you like to work with information. Learn about different methods by talking to other writers, your instructor, or a librarian, and then try a few of the most promising methods.

Learn more about quoting, paraphrasing, and summarizing in Chapter 9.

Part 2

Work with Genre and Design

Part 2: Work with Genre and Design

In this part of *In Conversation*, you'll find descriptions of important genres and advice for composing and designing them. The Genre Design Gallery showcases commonly used genres, with handy checklists and annotated visuals.

04. Choose Your Genre

In academic courses, you might be given an assignment that specifies the genre of the document you'll compose. If your assignment contains instructions such as *write an essay* or *create a website*, then you'll know that your instructor has a specific genre in mind.

Sometimes, however, you might be able to choose the genre you'll use to contribute to a conversation. In this case, choose a genre that reflects your understanding of your writing situation: what you hope to accomplish by writing and sharing a document, your understanding of your readers, the contexts in which your document will be written and read, and the sources you plan to use as you contribute to the conversation. The roles you plan to adopt—observer, reporter, interpreter, evaluator, problem solver, or advocate, among many others (p. 7, Sec. 1.2)—will also guide your decisions.

> ## Writer to Writer
>
> *How can I get to know genre conventions?* To immerse yourself in the design conventions of the type of document you're writing, consider looking for examples in that genre. You might have to search online or visit the library. Study the documents you like with an eye to their typefaces, colors, images, use of sidebars, and so on. Then use them as models, incorporating the design aspects you think are worth emulating.

4.1 Write a Reflective Essay

Writing to reflect is one of the most common activities writers undertake. At the beginning of almost every writing project, writers who adopt the role of *observer* (p. 7) spend time exploring and deepening their understanding of their subject. Reflection can also be the primary purpose for writing a document. In journals and diaries, writers reflect on a subject for personal reasons, often with the expectation that no one else will read their words. In more public documents — such as personal essays, memoirs, letters, and blogs — writers use reflection to share their thoughts in ways that benefit others.

Explore Your Subject

Reflective essays allow you to convey your thoughts about a subject with readers. You might reflect on a personal experience, an idea you've encountered in a book or a blog, a photograph or other object that holds meaning for you, a person you've met or read about, a troubling or inspiring conversation with a friend, or a recent event. In fact, you can reflect on almost anything. To get started, generate ideas by asking questions about your past or recent experiences, such as the following:

- Why is my favorite childhood memory so special to me?
- What recent news story annoys me the most?
- What is the last thing that made me laugh?
- What do I worry about most?
- What am I most proud of, and why?

You might brainstorm about the question (p. 18), freewrite (p. 18), or use techniques such as mapping and clustering (p. 19). Review what you've written and choose a subject that interests you.

Collect Details

Details are at the heart of most reflective documents. To collect details for a reflective essay, use the following strategies.

Conduct an Observation. Many reflective essays involve firsthand observation. Take notes as you observe. Later, freewrite or brainstorm about your subject: write down what you saw and heard, what you felt, even what you smelled. Provide as much detail as possible.

Learn more about conducting observations on p. 116 [Sec. 6.3].

4.1

Compare Your Subject with Something Else. Many subjects are best understood in relation to others. To find useful points of comparison, create a two-column log and record your reflections on the similarities and differences between the two subjects.

Discuss Your Ideas with Others. You can interview someone who is an expert on the subject or has been affected by it (see Chapter 6). You can also have conversations about the subject to learn what others think.

Learn more about conducting interviews on p. 115 [Sec. 6.3].

Learn More about Your Subject. Browse sources such as books, newspapers, and magazines to pick up bits of information that will add depth to your essay. See what's been written about your subject on news sites and in social media (see Chapter 6).

Tell Your Story

Most reflective writing—at least, writing that's interesting—tells a story. And every good story has a point. Your reflective essay should leave its readers with something to think about. Consider why your subject is meaningful to you, and think about how you can make it meaningful to your readers. The main idea of your reflective essay—the point of your story—should hold some significance for your readers. Ideally, after reading your essay, they'll continue to think about what you've written.

To create a story that engages your readers, consider the following elements.

- **Setting.** Where does your story take place? What is the setting like? How does the setting affect the story?

4.1

- **Character.** Who is involved in your story? What motivates them? What do they want to accomplish? What are their hopes and dreams?

- **Plot.** What happens in your story? In what order do the events take place?

- **Conflict.** Do the characters disagree about something? What do they disagree about? Why do they disagree?

- **Climax.** What is the defining event? What does the story lead the reader toward?

- **Resolution.** How is the conflict resolved?

- **Point of view.** Who is telling this story? A *detached observer* standing outside the action using third-person pronouns (*he, she, they*)? Or a *participant observer* sharing experiences and observations from a personal perspective using first-person pronouns (*I, me, we*)?

- **Dialogue.** What do the characters say to each other?

Even if you don't present your reflection as a traditional story, the elements of storytelling can help you shape your observations in a more concrete manner. Dialogue, for example, can help readers gain insight into how people are affected by or react to the subject. Point of view allows writers to reflect on a subject and make observations either from a distance or from up close.

Consider Genre and Design

For a reflective essay in an academic course, a simple design, with legible fonts, double spacing, and wide margins, is standard. Depending on your subject, integrating various types of media might enhance your reflection. In such a case, a multimodal essay would allow you to integrate images, animation, sound, and video to establish your points.

See the Genre Design Gallery to learn more about designing academic essays (pp. 86–87, Sec. G.1) and multimodal essays (pp. 90–91, Sec. G.3).

4.2 Write an Informative Article

Writers of informative documents, who adopt the role of *reporter* (p. 7), rely heavily on information obtained from written, media, and field sources. Many of the documents you encounter regularly are informative: newspaper and magazine articles, manuals, brochures, and books (including this textbook) allow writers to add information to conversations about a wide range of subjects. In writing-intensive courses, typical informative-writing assignments include essays, reports, and websites. You might also be asked to create articles, multimedia presentations, or posters.

Explore Your Interests

As you search for ideas, examine your daily life for inspiration. Consider personal interests and hobbies, your major or minor, your experiences in the workplace, and ideas you've encountered in your reading. Spend some time brainstorming or freewriting about these aspects of your life (p. 18, Sec. 2.1), and then review your notes to identify the areas that show the greatest potential. Select one or two that interest you most, and jot down your thoughts about what you already know and what you need to learn before you start writing.

Ask Questions about Promising Subjects. Before you begin examining sources closely, narrow your focus by determining which subjects interest you the most and which conversation you want to join. Ask questions such as the following.

- **Importance.** Why is this important? Who believes it is important? Why do they believe it is important?

- **Process.** How does _____ work? What steps are involved?

- **History.** What is the origin of _____? What recent events are related to it? What are the implications of those events?

4.2

- **Limitations.** What is limiting the use of _____? What has kept _____ from succeeding? What must happen before _____ is accepted?

- **Benefits.** Who benefits from _____? How do they benefit? Why do they benefit?

- **Advantages and disadvantages.** What are the advantages of _____? What are the disadvantages?

Gather Information

Informative articles tend to draw extensively on information from other sources and, to a lesser extent, on personal knowledge and experience.

Search for sources in library catalogs, in databases, and on the web. Visit your library to check out books and government reports, browse the shelves, and use the periodicals room. Not all information is created equal, and some sources will be more appropriate than others. Before you decide to use a source, assess its credibility and usefulness for your purposes (see Chapter 7).

Conducting interviews is another useful way to gather information for informative articles or essays. Interviews with experts in the field or individuals who have firsthand experience with an issue can add credibility and perspective to your document.

Learn more about collecting information through digital, print, or field sources in Chapter 6.

Present Your Main Point

In an informative article, the main point is usually presented in a straightforward fashion as a "lede," a single sentence or brief paragraph that opens the article and directs readers' attention to what you want them to learn about a subject. Consider how the following ledes about voter turnout among younger Americans direct readers' attention in a particular way.

> Increased turnout among younger voters in the last election suggests their growing desire to shape the state of politics in the United States.

Increased participation in politics by younger voters signals a significant shift in the political balance of power between younger and older Americans.

Regardless of the causes, the overall pattern of increasing voter turnout among younger voters should be cause for celebration among voters—young and old alike.

Although each of these ledes would provide a sound foundation for an informative article, the articles would have little in common. By focusing on distinctly different aspects of the subject, they require the writer to provide different supporting points and evidence.

Often, the lede in magazine and newspaper articles is a brief anecdote intended to grab readers' attention. Your lede will be shaped by what you've learned about your subject; your purpose; your readers' purposes, needs, and interests; your readers' knowledge and backgrounds; and the requirements and limitations of your writing project.

Develop Supporting Points and Evidence. Readers want more than a strong and intriguing main point—they want to know why they should accept it. If readers who are thinking about purchasing a car come across a lede such as "For many drivers, renting a car on an occasional basis is a cost-effective alternative to owning one," they'll want to know why renting could be a better choice. If readers interested in financing a college education read a lede such as "Today's college students have a wide range of options for reducing the overall cost of a college education," they'll want to know what those options are. To convince readers to accept your main point, you'll need to provide supporting points and offer evidence for each point.

For more on supporting points and evidence, see p. 171, Sec. 12.2.

Frame Your Information. After you've settled on the supporting points you want to make and the evidence you'll use to develop your ideas, spend some time thinking about how you'll put everything together for your readers. This will involve reflecting on how you set the tone for your essay in its introduction (Chapter 16), how you organize your essay (Chapter 13), and how you share your conclusions (Chapter 17).

 For more on organizing patterns, see p. 183, Sec. 13.1.

Consider Genre and Design

Design your article in a way that emphasizes key elements. By placing images, tables, charts, and figures in your draft, you can gain a sense of how the article will appear to readers. Sidebars and pull quotes (p. 80) can highlight important information for your readers. You can format your headings and subheadings and use colors to set a particular mood or break things down clearly. Using design as a composing element can help you anticipate how readers are likely to understand and respond to your article.

Learn more about designing informative articles on pp. 88–89, Sec. G.2, of the Genre Design Gallery.

The first stop for many of us looking for information is the web. Instead of writing an informative print article, you might choose to convey your information through a digital genre, such as a blog or an infographic on a website. Composing these genres requires many of the same steps described here — exploring a subject, gathering information, presenting your main point, developing supporting points, identifying evidence to back up those points, and framing your information. Consider whether your subject lends itself better to a different informative genre. If your issue is narrow and easy to convey visually, an infographic might work well. If your evidence makes use of images, audio clips, video clips, or links to other websites, or if your information includes bulleted lists or brief chunks of information, a website or a multimodal essay might be more effective.

See the Genre Design Gallery to learn more about designing infographics (pp. 96–97, Sec. G.6), multimodal essays (p. 90, Sec. G.3), websites (pp. 94–95, Sec. G.5), and blogs (pp. 98–99, Sec. G.7).

4.3 **Create an Annotated Bibliography**

Annotated bibliographies consist of a list of sources with complete publication information, usually formatted according to the rules of a documentation system such as the Modern Language Association (MLA) style (see Chapter 30) or the American Psychological Association (APA) style (see Chapter 31). Each entry in the bibliography is followed by a brief note, usually no more than three or four sentences long, that describes and offers comments about the source.

An annotated bibliography can serve not only as a useful record of your sources but also as a planning tool. You can note important information and ideas for use at a later point in your writing project, keep track of your reactions to sources, and call attention to connections among sources.

Consider Your Readers

The content, focus, and length of your annotations should reflect your purpose and the needs and interests of your readers. If you're preparing an annotated bibliography for a class, your instructor will most likely expect a clear description of the content of each source and some indication of how you might use the source. If you're using an annotated bibliography as a planning tool for a larger writing project, your annotations might highlight key information in a source, suggest how you can use ideas from the source, or emphasize relationships between sources.

Format the Bibliography Entries

Using the documentation system associated with the discipline you're working in (such as MLA style for a literature class), record all necessary citation information. Generally, you should gather the following information:

- Author(s); editor or translator, if applicable

- Title and subtitle; series information, if applicable

- Publication year; season, month, or date, as applicable

- Publisher or sponsoring organization

- Volume and issue number, if applicable

- Complete page numbers of the source

- Title of the website and its URL, if applicable

- Date you accessed a web source, if no publication date is available

See Part 6 (p. 363) for complete details on what to include for MLA, APA, *Chicago*, or CSE styles. Follow formatting guidelines, such as hanging indents and double spacing. Pay special attention to italics and punctuation. Alphabetize the entries by the authors' last names, and be consistent in formatting.

Here's an example of one writer's bibliography entry for a journal article, formatted in MLA style:

Widner, Christina. "Channeling Cruella De Vil: An Exploration of Proposed and Ideal Regulation on Domestic Animal Breeding in California." *San Joaquin Agricultural Law Review*, vol. 20, 2010, pp. 217–36.

Craft Your Annotations

The annotations in your annotated bibliography should help you make the most of the sources you've been gathering. A clear summary of the main idea of the source will be especially useful weeks or months later, when you might have forgotten the writer's finer points.

In addition to summarizing a source, you can also use an annotation to evaluate the relevance, evidence, timeliness, and comprehensiveness of the source as well as the biases of its author and publisher (see Chapter 7). Consider as well how you might use the source in your writing project. Ask whether it can provide you with useful evidence, whether it offers background information relevant to your document, or whether you might use it as a counterargument to a claim raised in another source.

Here is the student's annotation for that journal article on animal breeding:

Widner, Christina. "Channeling Cruella De Vil: An Exploration of Proposed and
    Ideal Regulation on Domestic Animal Breeding in California." *San Joaquin
    Agricultural Law Review*, vol. 20, 2010, pp. 217–36.

> After giving an overview of the problem of puppy mills and their origins after
> World War II, Widner discusses the federal Animal Welfare Act and how it fails to
> regulate puppy breeders adequately. Widner highlights successful legislation in
> California and other states and recommends more state inspectors, caps on the
> number of dogs a breeder can raise, and increased adoption of shelter dogs. I'll
> use this journal article to support my problem definition, showing how current
> legislation falls short. I'll use her recommendations for legal solutions to set up
> my solution to the problem.

Design Your Annotated Bibliography

Like academic essays, annotated bibliographies use double spacing, wide margins, and simple designs. They are intended to make the necessary information clear and accessible.

Learn more about **designing an annotated bibliography** on pp. 100–101, Sec. G.8, in the Genre Design Gallery.

4.4 Write a Rhetorical Analysis

Analysis involves adopting the role of *interpreter* (p. 7), helping readers understand the origins, qualities, significance, or potential impact of a subject. Rhetorical analysis focuses on one or more aspects of the rhetorical situation, including the writer's purpose, the audience's needs and interests, sources used in the document, and context. It often includes assessing how a writer presents a claim, connects to readers, frames the issue, and supports that claim with evidence and reasons. Rhetorical analysis is also useful for exploring the distinct cultural and linguistic qualities of a document and the contexts out of which

4.4

it emerges. A rhetorical analysis, as a result, can involve much more than simply summarizing and reflecting on what a writer is saying. It can address how the writer makes a point, presents sound reasoning, uses language and evidence, and appeals to readers; how the writer's work emerges from particular contexts, histories, and communities; and how the writer responds to a particular rhetorical situation.

Ask the Right Questions

Because rhetorical analysis scrutinizes the writing situation that shaped the creation and reception of a document, writers drafting a rhetorical analysis need to be comfortable asking a lot of questions: What is the writer's purpose? Who are the readers? How does the writer persuade or convince readers? How does the writer use evidence to support claims and reasons?

Conduct Research. When you write a rhetorical analysis, it's important to gather information about the author, publisher, and context of the document you're examining. Look into the author's background, purpose, values, and beliefs, and ask about other work written by the author. Consider where the document was published and the characteristics of likely readers. To learn about the author and publisher, look at copyright pages in journals and magazines, open the "About Us" pages on websites, and conduct web searches. To learn about likely readers and viewers, look for letters to the editor in a magazine or journal, see if any comments are provided on a website, or search for information about the publication's intended audience. You might be able to gain insights into readers' or viewers' prior knowledge of and interest in the subject as well as demographic information such as typical age, religion, gender, or geographical location.

You can also conduct research on the origins of the document you're analyzing and its effects on its audience. For example, a rhetorical analysis of the Declaration of Independence might focus not only on its content but also on the political, economic, and historical contexts that brought it into existence; reactions to it by American colonists and English citizens; and its eventual impact on the development of the U.S. Constitution.

Perform a Close Reading

Close reading is a form of critical reading (see Chapter 3) that focuses on the content, organization, and patterns within a written document. It is used extensively in the humanities as a means of analyzing both literary and nonliterary texts.

Identify the Claim. Read carefully and take notes on the main idea and supporting reasons. Identify the claim the writer is making—or, in the case of literary texts, the main idea of the work. Then consider your reaction to the claim and how it is presented in the document. Pay attention to both your objective and emotional responses to the claim.

Interrogate Reasons and Evidence. Look closely at the kinds of evidence offered by the writer. Are they convincing? What do they have in common? Does the author use statistics or numerical evidence to support a claim, or are anecdotes and narratives used to make a point? Consider the publication where the document appears. A rhetorical analysis of an article published in a scholarly journal on political science, for example, might rely more heavily on other scholarly articles and books than an analysis published in a popular magazine, which might use observation, interviews, and references to news articles or broadcasts.

Identify Appeals. As you examine the structure of an argument, look closely at the writer's use of appeals to logic, emotion, and character (p. 66, Sec. 4.8). These appeals are often referred to using the classic Greek terms *logos* (logic), *pathos* (emotion), and *ethos* (character). Courses that use these rhetorical concepts might also explore the notion of *kairos*, which refers to timing or opportunity. It is also common, in a rhetorical analysis, to ask whether the argument contains any logical fallacies, such as sweeping generalizations or questionable analogies (p. 68, Sec. 4.8).

4.4

Examine Style and Language. The writer's stylistic choices can have a major impact on how successful an argument is, so look closely at tone, figurative language, and organizing patterns. *How* the writer makes a point is sometimes as important as *what* the point is. Consider the writer's point of view and ask whether it is effective. Consider the use of language varieties and code meshing to gain insight into the writer's background. Examine how the use of metaphors, similes, or imagery affects how you read and respond to the document. If there are photos or other media in the document, ask yourself what they add to the argument.

Make an Interpretive Claim

Your interpretive claim is a brief statement that helps readers understand the overall results of your analysis. Draw on the research you've done and on your close reading of all aspects of the document to build your claim. Clearly convey the overall claim you want to make about the document—what it says and how well it says it, the kinds of evidence used to support the claim, the appeals used to reach readers.

Offer Evidence from the Document. Rhetorical analyses tend to rely on evidence from the document to support the interpretive claim and the reasons underlying it. If you are claiming that the writer betrays a certain political bias, show exactly where you see that bias in the document. Use evidence to provide examples and illustrations. If the document is particularly effective in its use of imagery or tone, provide examples that illustrate that technique.

Consider Genre and Design

Rhetorical analysis can take numerous forms, from scholarly articles and essays to blogs, websites, and even comics. For college courses, rhetorical analysis usually takes the form of an academic essay, but it can also appear as a newspaper or magazine article.

See the Genre Design Gallery to learn more about designing academic essays (pp. 86–87, Sec. G.1) and articles (pp. 88–89, Sec. G.2).

4.5 Create a Multimedia Presentation

Multimedia presentations, such as those created in Microsoft PowerPoint and Apple Keynote, are often used poorly and can result in a condition known as *PowerPoint boredom*. Fortunately, this is a curable condition. You can create multimedia presentations that engage and enlighten your audience, allowing them to follow your argument more easily and better understand complex ideas.

Plan Your Presentation

A strong multimedia presentation can accompany an oral presentation in front of a group of listeners, or it can function independently. If your presentation will supplement an oral presentation, the multimedia portion should highlight your points without stealing the show. Avoid reading slides aloud. Instead, use your slides to expand on or illustrate — not simply repeat — what you are saying. If the multimedia presentation serves as your only point of contact with your audience — that is, if it will be viewed on a computer, tablet, or smartphone — it needs to stand on its own. Make sure your slides convey your key points clearly and concisely in writing, since your audience will not be able to ask you questions. Test your slides by asking some friends to read a draft of your presentation. Observe their reactions to each slide, and ask them how you might improve the presentation.

Choose Your Sources

As you might do with a multimodal essay (p. 90, Sec. G.3), consider how various types of sources — such as images, audio clips, video clips, tables, and charts — can help you achieve your purpose. An image projected on a screen while you talk is more likely to complement your words than will a video clip, particularly one that has a sound track. On the other hand, a video clip can convey far more information. In all cases, make sure your sources will work within the time limits you face. A video clip might be compelling and highly persuasive, but if it is too long it will crowd out other points you want to make.

Keep your audience in mind as you choose your sources. Images and video clips that one audience might view neutrally might be considered offensive by another. If you are uncertain about the potential impact of a source, consult your instructor, a librarian, or a friend or classmate who might be similar to the audience you are trying to reach.

Compose Your Presentation

Your choice of composing tool will affect not only how you conceptualize your presentation but also the kinds of multimedia sources you can include and how they will appear. Conventional programs such as Microsoft PowerPoint and Apple Keynote offer the greatest flexibility in the types of sources you can include. They also offer a wide range of tools for linking to sites and media on the web. If you decide to use a less conventional program, such as Prezi (prezi.com) or Emaze (emaze.com), consider not only that program's capabilities, which might surprise and intrigue your audience, but also its limitations in handling various types of sources.

Look for program features that can help you during a presentation. The "presenter view" tools in conventional presentation programs allow you to see information that is not projected on the screen, such as notes on the current slide and small images of upcoming slides. These tools can remind you of important ideas that are related to but not displayed on the slide and can help you keep track of where you are in your presentation. Essentially, they serve the same function as the speaker's notes you might use during an oral presentation.

Learn more about designing multimedia presentations on pp. 92–93, Sec. G.4, of the Genre Design Gallery.

4.6 Write a Review

Writing a review involves adopting the role of *evaluator* (p. 7). Writers who adopt this role focus on reaching an informed, well-reasoned conclusion about a subject's worth or effectiveness and clearly conveying their judgments to readers. Writers typically evaluate a subject with one of three general goals: to determine whether something has succeeded or failed, to help readers understand how something might be improved or refined, or to help readers choose among alternatives. They form their conclusions by learning about their subject and considering how well it meets a given set of criteria—the standards or principles on which judgments are based.

4.6

Narrow Your Focus by Asking Questions

As you consider possible subjects for your evaluation, use the following questions to identify which ones capture your interest and best meet the needs of your assignment.

- **Importance.** Why do you think this is an important subject? Who else believes that it's important, and why?

- **Appropriateness.** What aspects of this topic lend themselves to evaluation? Do you have the resources and the time to learn about them and examine them closely?

- **Effectiveness.** Is _____ an effective response to _____? Is it designed well? Is it likely to produce the intended results?

- **Costs/benefits.** What are the benefits of _____? What are the costs? Are the benefits worth the costs?

Conduct Your Evaluation

An effective review is based on a clear understanding of your subject, a carefully chosen set of criteria, and well-supported judgments—first, about how well the subject of your review meets each criterion and, second, about the overall results of your evaluation.

Define Your Criteria. Criteria are the factors on which your judgments about a subject are based. In many written conversations, criteria are well established. Movie reviewers, for example, typically base their judgments on plot, characterization, cinematography, editing, and directing, while restaurant reviewers tend to use criteria such as the taste and presentation of the food, the attentiveness and courteousness of the waitstaff, the cleanliness and attractiveness of the restaurant, and the cost of a meal.

To keep your review brief and to the point—and, of course, useful for readers—focus on a limited number of criteria. Select criteria that are most relevant to your subject, your purpose, and the needs, interests, and backgrounds of your readers.

Identify Evidence. To identify evidence for your review, determine whether each criterion will rely on quantitative evidence (such as numeric data from surveys) or qualitative evidence (such as descriptive information from an interview). Then pinpoint potential sources of evidence by reviewing your initial research and any notes you've taken. Next to each criterion, list the evidence on which you'll base your judgments. If you find that you don't have enough evidence to support a thorough evaluation, look for more information.

Make Your Judgments. To make judgments about your subject, list your criteria and examine the evidence you've assembled. Write down your judgments in as much detail as possible so that you can draw on them as you draft your review.

The quality of your judgments depends not only on the number and kinds of criteria you've defined and the amount and types of evidence you've collected but also on your commitment to being fair and reasonable. If you're applying quantitative evidence to a small number of criteria, making your judgments might be a fairly straightforward process. However, if you're making multiple judgments on the basis of qualitative evidence, it might take significantly more time and effort to complete your evaluation. The challenge you face in making your judgments will also depend on the impact of your decision. For example, weighing which of three possible careers to pursue is of far greater consequence than comparing the features and costs of three video game systems.

Share Your Evaluation

The goal of a review is to share your judgment about a subject, often with the intention of helping readers make a decision. It's usually a good idea, then, to give readers a summary of your overall judgment — your verdict — in the form of a thesis statement (see Chapter 11). In some cases, you'll want to mention the criteria on which your judgment is based so that readers understand the thinking behind your evaluation.

4.6

Where you place your thesis statement depends largely on your understanding of your readers' needs and interests. Sharing your overall judgment at the beginning of the review allows readers to follow the logic of your evaluation process and better understand how the criteria and evidence relate to the overall result of your evaluation. However, if your overall judgment is likely to be seen as unusual or controversial, it might be more effective to share it later in the review, after allowing evidence to unfold in a way that helps readers understand the reasons underlying your conclusions.

Explain Your Criteria. Your readers should understand not only what your criteria are but also why you've selected them. In some cases, you can rely on general knowledge to supply the rationale for your choice of your criteria. If you were reviewing a new energy drink, for example, you could probably rely on a widespread understanding that taste is an important factor in the evaluation. Similarly, you wouldn't need to justify your use of nutrition and weight loss in a review of a diet program. In other cases, however, you should define your criteria explicitly. Your readers should understand how you've defined your criteria so that they can follow — and, ideally, accept — your evaluation.

Support Your Judgments with Evidence. Providing evidence to explain the reasoning behind your judgments helps readers accept your evaluation as valid and carefully thought out. Evidence can also help deepen your discussion of the overall results of your evaluation. Whether you draw your evidence from print, broadcast, or digital sources or from field research, be sure to identify your sources.

4.7

Be Fair. Provide a context for your review. By making it clear to your readers what you've evaluated, what you've considered during the evaluation process, and how you've approached the evaluation process, you can help them understand how and why you've come to your conclusions. If a reviewer has concerns about the size of a new phone, for example, she might point out that she has small hands or that she prefers to send texts using one hand. By providing context, you'll increase the likelihood that your readers will view your evaluation as sound and well supported.

Consider Genre and Design

The design of your review depends heavily on its audience and target publication. Take, for example, an article evaluating the health outcomes of two common treatments for ADHD. If it were published in a peer-reviewed academic journal, this article—like all others in the journal—would have a simple design and would include complete citation information for all references. If it were published on a website for parents with a child who has ADHD, the article would use features common to websites, such as colored headings, bulleted lists, images, and links to related sources.

See the Genre Design Gallery to learn more about designing academic essays (pp. 86–87, Sec. G.1), articles (pp. 88–89, Sec. G.2), and websites (pp. 94–95, Sec. G.5).

4.7 Write a Proposal

At its heart, a proposal is an attempt to address a problem. Not surprisingly, then, proposal writers take on the role of *problem solver* (p. 7). Their work involves calling readers' attention to a problem, discussing the nature and extent of the problem, and proposing a solution.

Explore Difficulties

A good problem-solving proposal begins with what educational philosopher John Dewey called a "felt difficulty"—the recognition that something isn't right. As you learn about an issue, you may find yourself wondering why something is the way it is, or perhaps you'll say to yourself, "That's not right." Treasure these early moments of recognizing a problem. If you feel that something isn't right, there's a good chance that a problem is near at hand.

As you search for felt difficulties in the world around you, consider the following potential areas:

4.7

- **Community.** What kind of difficulties have you encountered in your neighborhood? Have you been stuck in long lines at a bank or post office? Has the local food pantry been overwhelmed by an influx of new clients? Have you been bothered by the recent actions of local politicians or law enforcement officials?

- **Economy.** Are any of your friends or relatives having financial difficulties? Have you worried about what the future holds for you? For your family?

- **Work.** Do any issues at your workplace need to be addressed? Is the industry in which you work facing any challenges? Have you grown aware, through your course work or general reading, of difficulties facing people in your field of study?

- **News.** What have you read recently that surprised or worried you? What annoyed you or made you angry? What controversies have you noticed on the news or social media?

To begin turning a felt difficulty into a defined problem, jot down what doesn't feel right and then brainstorm or freewrite about it (p. 18, Sec. 2.1). If you have experience with the difficulty, reflect on it, discuss it with others, and find and review relevant published sources through your library or the web. (You can learn more about locating, collecting, and managing information in Part 3.)

Define the Problem

Some people define a problem with a particular solution in mind. As a result, their solution usually looks good in theory. But a solution based on a weak problem definition seldom works well in practice, and it is unlikely to convince readers. For this and other reasons, you should define your problem as clearly and accurately as possible.

4.7

You can define your problem by exploring situation and consequences, focusing on actions taken to accomplish a goal, or focusing on barriers to a desired outcome.

Situation/consequences. Explore the effects a problematic situation has on people or things. Ask yourself:

- What is the situation?

- What are the consequences? How severe are they? How long will they last?

- Who or what is affected?

Agent/goals/actions/results. Focus on actions that have unwanted results. Ask yourself:

- Who or what is the *agent* (the person, group, or thing that acts in a manner that causes a problem)?

- What *goals* does the agent want to accomplish?

- What *actions* does the agent carry out to accomplish the goals?

- What are the unwanted *results* of the agent's actions?

Goals and barriers. Identify goals, and ask what obstacles stand in the way of accomplishing them. Ask yourself:

- What are the goals?

- What barriers stand in the way of accomplishing the goals?

Each of these problem-definition strategies allows you to view a problem from a different perspective. Because your problem definition has powerful effects on the development of a solution to your problem, it can be useful to experiment with different ways of defining the problem.

Develop Solutions

If other writers have addressed this problem, explore the solutions they've proposed. Even failed solutions might have helped address some aspects of the problem. Create a list of potential solutions — both your own and those of other writers — and briefly describe them. Evaluate each solution by answering the following questions.

4.7

- How well does this solution address the causes and effects of the problem?

- To what extent does this solution address the needs of the people or things affected by the problem?

- What costs would be associated with this solution?

- What are the advantages and disadvantages of this solution?

Review your responses to the questions, and identify your most promising solutions. If you've identified more than one solution, ask whether the best features of each might be combined into a single solution.

Evaluate Your Solution. Most problems can be solved given unlimited time, vast sums of money, revisions to the laws of physics, or changes in human nature. If your solution requires any or all of these, however, your readers are likely to question its practicality. Before you start drafting your proposal, ensure that your solution is feasible by asking whether it can be implemented

- in a reasonable amount of time;

- with available funding;

- with available resources;

- given current knowledge and technology; and

- without causing additional problems.

Consider as well potential objections to your solution. You may be able to modify your solution to account for likely objections, or you may want to prepare an argument about why the trade-offs involved in accepting your solution are better than leaving things as they are.

4.7

Propose Your Solution

Your solution is what most readers will remember about your proposal. Once you've defined the problem, explain your solution fully, offering support for your ideas and considering your solution in light of promising alternatives.

Go into detail. Help your readers understand, in detail, how you would implement the solution, how much it would cost to put into effect, what effects the solution would have, and how you would judge its effectiveness in addressing the problem.

Provide support for your points. Your solution should offer a reasonable and thoughtful response to the problem, and it should be clear that your proposed solution is superior to alternatives. To identify support, list the key points you are making about your proposed solution. Then list relevant evidence below each point.

Address promising alternative solutions. Be sure to consider alternative solutions that are likely to occur to your readers. In proposing a solution to a problem, you are essentially making an argument that your solution is preferable to others. If your readers can think of alternatives, especially alternatives that might be less expensive or more effective than yours, they might wonder why you haven't mentioned them.

Consider Genre and Design

The design of your proposal will depend on your audience and where it will be published. Many workplace or government proposals use the simple, straightforward designs of academic essays, with headings, figures or photographs, tables, and captions. Proposals that will be published as newspaper or magazine articles or on the web will make use of colored text, bulleted and numbered lists, and links to sources and other related web documents.

4.8

See the Genre Design Gallery to learn more about designing academic essays (pp. 86–87, G.1), articles (pp. 88–89, G.2), and websites (pp. 94–95, G.5).

4.8 Write an Argument

Many people believe that an argument is effective only if it's won, that unless they *convince* others to agree with them or *persuade* them to take action, they've failed in their mission to make the world a better place. In fact, most written arguments aren't so much about winning or losing as about sharing the writer's perspective with others who are interested in an issue. That's why writers of argumentative essays, blog posts, or op-eds adopt the role of *advocate* (p. 7).

Choose an Issue

Arguments grow out of a belief that a choice must be made, a situation should be changed, or a mistake ought to be corrected. As you consider possible subjects, ask what bothers you. Ask what conflicts affect you, individually or as a member of a community. Look for an issue that matters not only to you but also to your readers.

Effective arguments are usually focused and narrow. Be wary of writing about something as broadly defined as climate change or ethics in politics. Instead, try to find a subtopic that you can manage in the space and time available to you.

Develop Your Argument

Creating an effective argument starts with knowing what you want others to believe (convincing) or how you want them to act (persuading).

Define Your Claim. Your *claim*, or thesis statement, is a brief statement that conveys the main point you want to make about your issue. In an argumentative essay or blog post, a thesis statement should be debatable, plausible, and clear.

- A debatable thesis statement is one with which readers can disagree.

- A plausible thesis statement appears at the very least to be reasonable and might be convincing or persuasive on its own.

- A clear thesis statement advances a claim that is easy to follow.

Keep in mind, however, that the extent to which you explicitly state your claim might vary according to your purpose and background. While many writers follow the Western academic tradition of presenting a well-defined claim, writers who are shaped by other cultural contexts might adopt a less direct approach, such as discussing the issue in a way that allows readers to move more slowly and reflectively in the writer's intended direction.

Learn more about defining your thesis statement on p. 166, Sec. 11.2.

Choose Reasons. Your argument will be effective only if you provide reasons to support your claim and back them up with evidence. To choose reasons, reflect on what your readers are likely to know about the issue, the kinds of questions they might have about it, and the conclusion you hope to share with them. Respond to questions such as the following by brainstorming, freewriting, clustering, or mapping (pp. 18–20).

- **Costs and benefits.** What costs and benefits are associated with accepting your claim? Are there monetary costs? Will valuable resources be wasted? Will human potential be wasted? Who or what will benefit? What form will these benefits take?

- **Personal experience.** What does your personal experience tell you is likely to happen if your main point is accepted and acted on? What does it tell you might happen if it is rejected?

- **Historical context.** What does history tell you is likely to happen (or not) if your main point is accepted? What does it suggest will happen if it is rejected?

4.8

- **Values and beliefs.** In what ways is your main point consistent with your values and beliefs and with those of your readers? In what ways is it consistent with larger societal and cultural values and beliefs?

Effective arguments make connections (sometimes called **warrants**) between a claim (or main point) and the reasons offered to support it. Sometimes readers accept a connection because they share the writer's values and beliefs, experiences, or knowledge of an issue. In other cases, readers accept a connection because the writer explains it effectively. This explanation (sometimes called **backing**) provides readers with information and analysis that can help them understand the connection.

Ask whether your reasons clearly connect to your thesis statement. If your readers' background and knowledge differ from yours, connections that make sense to you might not be clear to them.

Gather Evidence. Be sure to provide sufficient evidence for each of your reasons. Evidence can take the form of quotations, paraphrases, summaries, numerical data, and visual images. You can

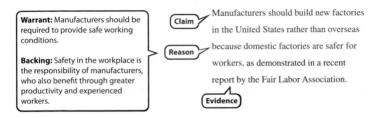

draw your evidence from written and media sources, personal experience, and field research you conduct yourself, such as interviews, observations, and surveys.

A writer arguing about the need to improve the U.S. health care system, for example, might draw on personal experience, interviews with friends and relatives, policy briefs from the American Medical Association, commentary by bloggers, reports issued by government agencies, and articles in popular and scholarly journals.

Learn more about gathering and using evidence in Chapter 12.

Appeal to Your Readers. The evidence you include should be strongly and clearly connected to your reasons. These connections, called **appeals**, help readers understand why a reason is appropriate and valid.

Appeals to authority ask readers to accept a reason because an expert or someone in a position of authority supports it. Evidence typically takes the form of quotations, paraphrases, or summaries of the ideas of experts, of political leaders, or of people who have been affected by an issue.

Appeals to logic ask readers to work through a set of propositions to reach a considered conclusion. You might use *deduction*, which moves from general principles to a conclusion:

Proposition 1 (usually a general principle)
Stealing is wrong.

Proposition 2 (usually an observation)
John stole a candy bar from the store.

Conclusion (results of deductive analysis)
John's theft of the candy bar was wrong.

You might also use *induction*, which draws conclusions from specific observations, often drawing on numerical data to reveal patterns. Induction is based on probability. Medical researchers, for example, typically observe large numbers of patients to assess the effectiveness and side effects of new medications.

Appeals to emotion ask readers to feel a particular way about an issue. Use this kind of appeal carefully. In scholarly articles and essays, emotional appeals are used infrequently, and readers of such documents are likely to ask why you would play on their emotions instead of making logical appeals or appeals to authority.

Appeals to principles, values, and beliefs rely on the assumption that your readers care about a given set of principles. Religious and ethical arguments are often based on appeals to principles, such as the need to respect God, to love one another, or to believe that all of us are created equal.

Appeals to character can be thought of as the "trust me" strategy, which commonly appears in celebrity endorsements. It is also in play when politicians refer to their military experience—when they say, essentially, "Believe me. I'm a patriotic person who has served our country." To use this kind of appeal, reflect on how your character, accomplishments, and experiences might lead your readers to trust you.

Consider Opposing Viewpoints

Considering opposing arguments, or **counterarguments**, allows you to anticipate questions and concerns your readers might have. Identify potential counterarguments by reviewing your notes to see how other members of the conversation have

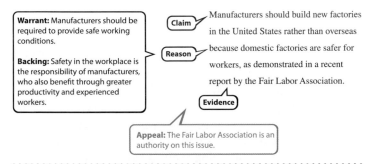

Warrant: Manufacturers should be required to provide safe working conditions.

Backing: Safety in the workplace is the responsibility of manufacturers, who also benefit through greater productivity and experienced workers.

Claim → Manufacturers should build new factories in the United States rather than overseas

Reason → because domestic factories are safer for workers, as demonstrated in a recent report by the Fair Labor Association.

Evidence

Appeal: The Fair Labor Association is an authority on this issue.

addressed the issue or by engaging in role-playing activities, such as *devil's advocate* (p. 13).

Acknowledging opposing points of view shows your readers that you are fair. It can establish common ground with readers who might otherwise disagree with you. You can qualify your concession by explaining that although part of a counterargument is sound, it also has weaknesses. This lays the foundation for explaining why your claim or reason is superior. Once you've addressed the main counterarguments, you can safely ignore minor ones.

As you draft your document, present your discussion of counterarguments using a reasonable and polite tone. You will gain little, if anything, by insulting or belittling writers with whom you disagree.

Check for Fallacies

Ensure the integrity of your argument by weeding out any **logical fallacies**, or errors in logic. Fallacies can undermine readers' willingness to accept an argument. Acquaint yourself with common fallacies, and then check that your argument does not fall victim to them.

Fallacies based on distraction attempt to divert readers' attention:

- A **red herring** is an irrelevant or distracting point. The term originated with the practice of sweeping a red herring (a particularly aromatic type of fish) across the trail being followed by a pack of hunting dogs to throw them off the scent of their prey. The question *Why worry about the rising cost of tuition when the government is tapping our phones?* is a red herring: government surveillance has nothing to do with increases in college tuition.

- **Ad hominem attacks** attempt to discredit an idea or argument by suggesting that a person or group associated with it should not be trusted. If you hear someone say that a proposed wind farm should be rejected because its main supporter cheated on her taxes, you're listening to an ad hominem attack.

- **Irrelevant history** suggests that something associated with an idea should disqualify it. You might hear, for instance, that an idea is bad because someone came up with it while they were drunk. Base your assessment of the idea on its strengths and weaknesses. Otherwise, you might as well say that an idea is sound because someone thought of it while they were sober.

4.8

Fallacies based on questionable assumptions often build seemingly strong arguments on a poor foundation. Once that foundation is removed, the argument falls apart.

- **Sweeping generalizations,** sometimes known as *hasty generalizations*, are based on stereotypes. Asserting that the rich are conservative voters, for example, assumes that everyone who is rich is just like everyone else who is rich.

- **Strawman attacks** oversimplify or distort another person's argument so it can be dismissed more easily. Just as a boxer can easily knock down a scarecrow, a writer who commits this fallacy might characterize an opposing position as more extreme than it actually is, or might refute obviously flawed counterarguments while ignoring valid objections.

- **Citing inappropriate authorities** can take several forms: citing as an authority someone who is not an expert on a subject, citing an authority who has a strong bias on an issue, suggesting that an individual voice represents broad opinion when that person's ideas are far from the mainstream, or treating paid celebrity endorsements as expert opinion.

- **Jumping on a bandwagon**, also known as *argument from consensus*, implies that if enough people believe something, it must be true. This type of argument substitutes group thinking for careful analysis.

Fallacies based on misrepresentation attempt to present limited or inaccurate information to readers.

4.8

- **Stacking the deck,** often referred to as *cherry-picking* or *suppressing evidence*, is the act of presenting evidence for only one side of an argument when sufficient evidence exists for an alternative argument.

- **Base-rate fallacies** are commonly found in arguments based on statistics. If you read that drinking coffee will triple your risk of developing cancer, you might be alarmed. However, if you knew that the risk rose from one in a billion to three in a billion, you might pour another cup.

- **Questionable analogies,** also known as *false analogies*, make inappropriate comparisons. They assume that if two things are similar in one way, they must be similar in others. For example, a writer might argue that climate change is like a fever, and that just as a fever usually runs its course on its own, so, too, will the climate recover without intervention.

Fallacies based on careless reasoning involve the use of faulty logic.

- **Post hoc fallacies,** formally known as *post hoc, ergo propter hoc* ("after this, therefore because of this") fallacies, argue that because one event happened before another event, the first must have caused the second.

- **Slippery-slope arguments** warn that a single step will inevitably lead to a bad situation. For instance, a common argument against decriminalizing marijuana is that using pot leads to the use of stronger narcotics.

- **Either/or arguments** present two choices, one of which is usually characterized as extremely undesirable. In fact, there might be a third choice, or a fourth, or a fifth.

- **Non sequiturs** are statements that do not follow logically from what has been said. For example, arguing that buying a particular type of car will lead to a successful love life is a non sequitur.

- **Circular reasoning**, also known as *begging the question*, restates a point that has just been made as evidence for itself. Arguing that a decline in voter turnout is a result of fewer people voting is an example of circular reasoning.

4.8

As you prepare to write a first draft, take another look at your main point, thesis statement, reasons, and evidence. Do they still make sense? Do they stack up well against competing arguments? Do they overlook anything obvious? Do they use appeals with integrity? Do you have enough evidence to meet the expectations of your intended readers? If you answer "no" to any of these questions, continue to develop and refine your argument.

Consider Genre and Design

In a college course, your argument will likely take the form of an academic essay. To reach a wider audience and include illustrations such as images, audio and video clips, and links, you might consider shaping your argument as a blog post, a multimodal essay, or a web-based article.

In many cases, the appeals you choose to make to your readers will suggest design elements that can enhance your argument. Photographs can strengthen (or serve as) an emotional appeal. Headings and subheadings can help readers follow your reasoning about an issue. Color and pull quotes can underscore appeals to values, beliefs, and principles by calling a reader's attention to shared assumptions and important ideas. Appeals to authority or expertise often present statistical data in the form of tables, charts, and graphs.

See the Genre Design Gallery to learn more about designing academic essays (pp. 86–87, Sec. G.1), multimodal essays (pp. 92–93, Sec. G.3), and blogs (pp. 98–99, Sec. G.7).

05. Design Your Document

Many writers think of designing a document as something that comes at the end of the writing process, after drafting, revision, and editing are complete. In fact, design can be a powerful tool as you plan and draft. By considering design early in your composing process, you can create a document that reflects your purposes, addresses your readers effectively, and takes advantage of the context in which it will be read.

5.1 Understand Design Principles

Before you begin formatting text and inserting illustrations, consider how the design principles of balance, emphasis, placement, repetition, and consistency can help you accomplish your goals as a writer.

Balance is the vertical and horizontal alignment of elements on your pages (p. 77). Symmetrical designs create a sense of rest and stability and lead the reader's eye to focus on a central part of a document. In contrast, asymmetrical—or unbalanced—designs suggest movement and guide readers' eyes across the page.

Emphasis is the placement and formatting of elements, such as headings and subheadings, so they catch your readers' attention. You can emphasize an element in a document by using a distinguishing color or font, by placing a border around it and adding a shaded background, or by using an illustration, such as a photograph, drawing, or graph.

Placement is the location of elements on your pages. Placing elements next to or near each other suggests that they are related. Illustrations, for example, are usually placed near the passages in which they are mentioned.

Repetition is the recurrence of elements throughout your document. As readers move from page to page, they expect navigation elements, such as page numbers, to appear in the same place. In addition, repeated elements, such as a logo or web

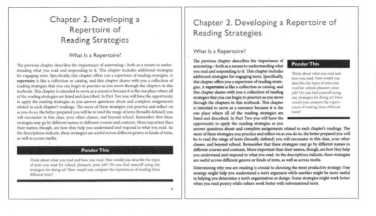

Symmetrical (left) and asymmetrical (right) layouts

Ellen Carillo

navigation menu, help establish a sense of identity across the pages of your document.

Consistency is the extent to which you format and place text and illustrations in the same way throughout your document. Treating each design element consistently helps your readers understand the structure of your document and locate the information they seek. A consistent design can also convey a sense of competence and professionalism to your readers.

Keep two other principles in mind: *moderation* and *simplicity*. An overly complex design can obscure important ideas and information. Using design elements moderately to create simple yet effective designs is the best approach.

5.2 Design for Your Writing Situation

Your decisions about design, from choosing appropriate fonts to presenting information in charts and tables to selecting compelling illustrations, can have powerful effects on how your readers react to your document.

Design for a Purpose

A well-designed document can help you:

5.2

- **Set a tone.** Establishing an emotional context is one of the most immediate benefits of good design. Drawing on the design principles of balance and placement, you can set a tone by using a particular color scheme, such as bright, cheerful hues, or by selecting photographs or drawings with a strong emotional impact.

- **Draw attention.** The design principles of emphasis and placement can call your readers' attention to central ideas and information. To highlight a definition or example, you might use borders or place the passage in a pull quote.

- **Convince or persuade readers.** The key to winning an argument is providing readers with appropriate, relevant evidence. Drawing on the principles of emphasis and placement, you can use illustrations, marginal glosses, pull quotes, and bulleted lists to help readers accept that evidence.

- **Clarify concepts.** Sometimes a picture really is worth a thousand words. A well-chosen, well-placed photograph, flowchart, diagram, or table can define a multistep process such as photosynthesis in far less space, and in many cases far more effectively, than a long passage of text. You can also identify the key elements of a complex concept with bulleted and numbered lists.

Design for Your Readers

A well-designed document does more than look pretty. It provides a context for readers and helps them understand what your document is trying to accomplish. It is also easy on the eyes: readers working with a well-designed document will not have to strain to read the text or discern illustrations.

Using images to create an emotional impact

Photo: ALFREDO ESTRELLA/AFP/Getty Images

Use document design to help readers do the following:

Understand the Organization of a Document. You can use headings and subheadings to signal the content of each part of the document. Keep in mind the design principles of emphasis and consistency: format your headings in a consistent manner that helps them stand out from other parts of the document (see below).

5.2

Locate Information and Ideas. Many longer print documents use tables of contents and indexes to help readers find what they are looking for. Websites typically provide a mix of menus and navigation headers and footers to help readers move around the site. When these navigation aids are integrated into pages, they are often distinguished from the surrounding text by the use of borders, shaded boxes, or contrasting fonts.

Recognize the Functions of Parts of a Document. If you include passages that differ from the main text of your document, such as sidebars (p. 80) and "For More Information" sections, help readers understand their function by designing them to stand out visually. For instance, web links are often underlined and formatted in a contrasting color.

Design to Address Genre Conventions

Understanding the design conventions of the type of document you plan to write will help you meet the expectations of your readers. Genres are characterized not only by distinctive writing styles, types of evidence, and organizing patterns but also by distinctive types of design. An article in a magazine such as *Time* or *Rolling Stone*, for example, is characterized by the

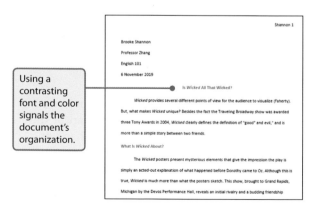

Using a contrasting font and color signals the document's organization.

Headings and subheadings in an essay

use of columns, headings and subheadings, pull quotes, and illustrations, while an academic essay is characterized by wide margins, double-spaced lines, and comparatively restrained use of color and illustrations. Your readers will expect your document to be similar in design to other examples of that genre. This doesn't mean that you can't depart from those conventions should the need arise, but it does mean that you should take their expectations into account as you design your document.

Learn more about the design conventions of commonly used genres in the Genre Design Gallery.

5.3 Use Design Elements Effectively

Get to know the range of design elements at your disposal as you design your document. These elements include fonts, line spacing, and alignment; page layout strategies; color, shading, borders, and rules; and illustrations.

Use Fonts, Line Spacing, and Alignment

Fonts, line spacing, and alignment choices are the most common design decisions made by writers. They are also among the most important, since poor choices can make a document difficult to read. The following examples provide an overview of the key features of fonts and the uses of fonts, line spacing, and alignment.

- **Left alignment** has a straight left margin and a "ragged right" margin; it is typically the easiest to read.

- **Right alignment** has a straight right margin and a ragged left margin.

- **Centered alignment** can make headings stand out.

- **Justified alignment** has straight alignment on both the left and right margins. It adds a polished look and can be effective in documents that use columns—but it also produces irregular word spacing and hyphenation, which can slow the reading process.

5.3

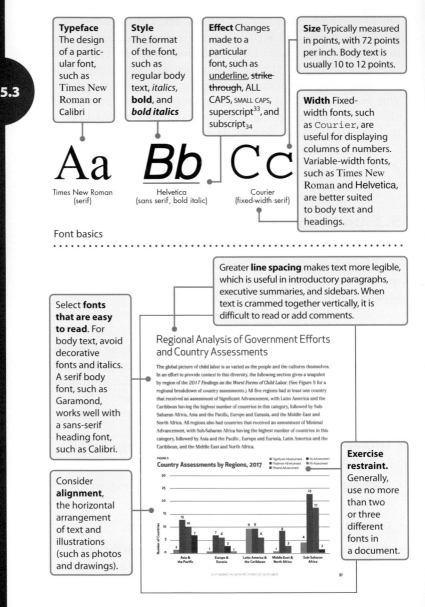

Typeface The design of a particular font, such as Times New Roman or Calibri

Style The format of the font, such as regular body text, *italics*, **bold**, and ***bold italics***

Effect Changes made to a particular font, such as <u>underline</u>, ~~strikethrough~~, ALL CAPS, SMALL CAPS, superscript[33], and subscript[34]

Size Typically measured in points, with 72 points per inch. Body text is usually 10 to 12 points.

Width Fixed-width fonts, such as Courier, are useful for displaying columns of numbers. Variable-width fonts, such as Times New Roman and Helvetica, are better suited to body text and headings.

Aa
Times New Roman (serif)

Bb
Helvetica (sans serif, bold italic)

Cc
Courier (fixed-width serif)

Font basics

Greater **line spacing** makes text more legible, which is useful in introductory paragraphs, executive summaries, and sidebars. When text is crammed together vertically, it is difficult to read or add comments.

Select **fonts that are easy to read**. For body text, avoid decorative fonts and italics. A serif body font, such as Garamond, works well with a sans-serif heading font, such as Calibri.

Consider **alignment**, the horizontal arrangement of text and illustrations (such as photos and drawings).

Exercise restraint. Generally, use no more than two or three different fonts in a document.

Regional Analysis of Government Efforts and Country Assessments

The global picture of child labor is as varied as the people and the cultures themselves. In an effort to provide context to this diversity, the following section gives a snapshot by region of the *2017 Findings on the Worst Forms of Child Labor*. (See Figure 9 for a regional breakdown of country assessments.) All five regions had at least one country that received an assessment of Significant Advancement, with Latin America and the Caribbean having the highest number of countries in this category, followed by Sub-Saharan Africa, Asia and the Pacific, Europe and Eurasia, and the Middle East and North Africa. All regions also had countries that received an assessment of Minimal Advancement, with Sub-Saharan Africa having the highest number of countries in this category, followed by Asia and the Pacific, Europe and Eurasia, Latin America and the Caribbean, and the Middle East and North Africa.

FIGURE 9
Country Assessments by Regions, 2017

Using fonts, line spacing, and alignment

Writer to Writer

Which are more readable, serif or sans-serif fonts?   A serif is the short line tailing off at the ends of strokes in certain typefaces, or fonts — like the body font used in this book. A typeface that features serifs is, of course, called a serif font; one that doesn't is sans serif.

You can find plenty of advice on the web about where to use various kinds of fonts. Yet even researchers who have studied the issue haven't reached any broad conclusions. So choose fonts that you like, that you find easy to read, that seem appropriate to your current purpose, and that look distinctly different from other fonts you plan to use in the same document. Mock up a page or so of your work that includes all your fonts. If you're satisfied with the way it looks, you're all set.

5.3

Lay Out Your Pages

Page layout is the placement of text, illustrations, and other objects on a page or screen. Successful page layout draws on a number of design elements, including white space, margins, columns, headers and footers, page numbers, headings, lists, captions, marginal glosses and pull quotes, and sidebars.

Use Color, Shading, Borders, and Rules

Color, shading, borders, and rules (lines running horizontally or vertically on a page) can increase the overall attractiveness of your document, call attention to important information, signal the organization of your document, announce the function of specific passages of text, and mark transitions between sections. Exercise restraint with these design elements. Avoid using more than three colors on a page unless the colors appear in an illustration. Be cautious about using multiple styles of rules or borders in a document.

5.3

Numbered and bulleted lists (not shown) display brief passages of related information using numbers or symbols (usually round "bullets"). The surrounding white space draws the eye to the list, while the brief content in each entry can make concepts or processes easier to understand.

Columns can improve the readability of a document by limiting the eyes' physical movement across the page.

Pull quotes highlight a passage of text — frequently a quotation — through the use of borders, white space, distinctive fonts, and colors.

White space — literally, empty space — frames and separates elements on a page.

Marginal glosses are short notes in a margin that explain or expand on text in the body of the document.

CANCER DETECTION

Racing Against Lung Cancer

...ging tools help patient in cancer fight

Headings and sub-headings identify sections and subsections, serve as transitions, and allow readers to locate information more easily.

Sidebars are brief discussions of information related to but not a central part of your document. Sidebars simplify the task of integrating supporting information into the body of the article.

...early 2016, Rhode Island ...esident Ted Simon had a ...ickle in his throat tha ...wouldn't go away. ...en the tickle turned into ...gh, he went to see his primary ...doctor.

The most common risk factor for lung cancer is cigarette smoking, as ...ll as exposure to radon, asbestos, and other types of dangerous chemicals. But like Ted, some patients with lung cancer don't have any risk factors.

in my lung, bone, ar Ted "I started drug shrunk my tumors levels for 18 month tumor reappearance scanning. When the growing again, we u to identify tumor cell in the bone and then contrast MRI to monitor cancer spread."

Ted added, "We di genotyping to see if a mutations appeared. We were lucky to find the appropriate mutation for a recently approved lung cancer medication. That treatment has kept tumors static for two months while we search for other options."

While Ted's stage 4 diagnosis has made treatment more complicated, imaging and diagnostic tools have helped him monitor the cancer as best as possible.

"Imaging and other diagnostic tools are a mainstay in our efforts to stay ahead of my cancer."

> "**Imaging and other diagnostic tools are a mainstay in our efforts to stay ahead of my cancer.**"
>
> - Ted Simon

...e diagnosis? Stage 4 lung ...er—advanced cancer that had ...dy spread to some other parts ...e body. ...st lung cancers do not cause ...toms until they have spread, but ...e people with early lung cancer do ...symptoms. Those include a cough ...does no go away or gets worse, ...hing up blood, and weight loss. ...was shocked to be diagnosed with ...nced lung cancer at age 60," Ted ...."I'm an avid runner. Never been ...oker. And I didn't have any other ...actors."

Following his diagnosis, Ted discovered his doctors had diagnostic tools that would help identify and track his cancer in important ways.

The first tool that helped diagnose Ted's condition was a simple chest X-ray. Ted was then referred to cancer specialists at the Dana-Farber Cancer Institute in Boston. They introduced him to imaging diagnostic tools that could help pinpoint more information about his cancer and its progress.

"PET scanning revealed tumors

Find Out More

▶ MedlinePlus:
https://medlineplus
html

▶ National Cancer In
https://www.cancer

▶ NCI Clinical Trials
https://www.cancer
cancer/treatment/c

▶ American Cancer S
https://www.cancer

Spring 2018   medline

Margins are the white space between the edge of the page or screen and text or graphics in your document.

Captions (not shown) describe or explain an illustration, such as a photograph or chart.

Headers, footers, and page numbers frame a page visually, appearing at the top or bottom of the page. They help readers find their way through a document.

Using page layout elements

. . . .

U.S. National Library of Medicine, *NIH MedlinePlus*, Spring 2018

5.3

GREAT FIGURES, AS KIDS

BY MARK HARTSELL   LIBRARY COLLECTIONS REVEAL THE
YOUNG LIVES OF MEN AND WOMEN
WHO HELPED SHAPE THE WORLD

Be consistent. Use the same colors for top-level headings throughout your document, another color for lower-level headings, and so on. Use the same borders and shading for sidebars. Don't mix and match.

Understand the effects of color. Some effects are physical. Bright yellow, for example, can tire your readers' eyes. Other effects are emotional. In many cultures, green is regarded as soothing because it is associated with nature and growth. Red, in contrast, is often associated with danger.

Call attention to important information. Color, borders, and shading can emphasize an illustration or an important passage of text by distinguishing it from the surrounding body text.

Signal the function of text. A colored or shaded background, as well as colored type, can be used to differentiate captions and pull quotes from body text. Rules can also separate columns of text on a page or screen.

Signal the organization of a document. In a long document, use a particular color for headers, footers, and headings. On a website, use the same background or heading color for pages in a section.

Using color, shading, borders, and rules
• •

Mark Hartsell, and the *Library of Congress Magazine*, September/October 2018, Volume 7, Number 5, pp. 18–19.

5.3

Use Illustrations

Illustrations can expand on or demonstrate points made in the text of your document. They can also reduce the amount of text needed to make a point, help readers better understand your points, and increase the visual appeal of your document.

As you work with illustrations, keep the following guidelines in mind:

- **Use an illustration for a purpose.** Illustrations are best used when they serve a clear function in your document. Avoid including illustrations simply because you think they might make your document look better.

- **Place illustrations near the text they illustrate.** Anchor illustrations as close as possible to the point where they are mentioned in the text. If they are not explicitly referenced (often the case with photographs), insert them where they will be most relevant.

- **Include a title or caption that identifies or explains the illustration.** Most documentation systems suggest distinguishing between tables and figures (other illustrations) and numbering tables and figures in the order in which they appear. Consult the documentation system you are using, such as MLA or APA, for specific guidelines on illustrations.

Mike Palmquist & Barbara Wallraff

Photographs, drawings, paintings, and sketches are frequently used to set a mood, emphasize a point, or demonstrate a point.

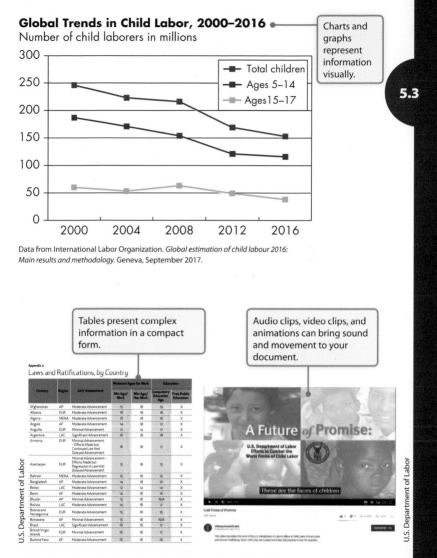

Global Trends in Child Labor, 2000–2016
Number of child laborers in millions

Charts and graphs represent information visually.

5.3

Legend:
- Total children
- Ages 5–14
- Ages 15–17

Data from International Labor Organization. *Global estimation of child labour 2016: Main results and methodology.* Geneva, September 2017.

Tables present complex information in a compact form.

Audio clips, video clips, and animations can bring sound and movement to your document.

Appendix 2.
Laws and Ratifications, by Country

U.S. Department of Labor

U.S. Department of Labor

Photographs, charts and graphs, tables, and multimedia

G

Genre Design Gallery ●————————————●

Essays may be the most common assignment in college courses, but a wide array of genres is available to you as a writer. Let your writing situation guide you as you choose what type of document to create and how to design it.

- **Academic Essays**
- **Articles**
- **Multimodal Essays**
- **Multimedia Presentations**
- **Websites**
- **Infographics**
- **Blogs**
- **Annotated Bibliographies**

G.1 Academic Essays

You're familiar with academic essays: formal and well thought out, carefully documented, and simply designed, with wide margins, readable fonts, and double-spaced lines. Yet writers can do far more with the design of essays than you might expect. You can use design elements such as fonts, color, shading, borders, and rules to help readers anticipate and more easily follow the organization of your essay. You can use tables, charts, and figures to let your readers understand and reflect on the information you include in your essay. If you are distributing your essay in digital form, you can link to related information, such as video clips, audio clips, animations, and data sets — or you can embed these materials directly in your essay. You can read more about how these design elements can help you in these areas in Chapter 5.

For a sample essay formatted in MLA style, see p. 394. For a sample essay formatted in APA style, see p. 429.

Checklist for Designing Academic Essays

✓ Cover page or essay header, depending on your instructor's preferences or the formatting requirements of the documentation style you are following

✓ Readable body font, such as 12-point Garamond

✓ Double-spaced lines

✓ Wide margins, at least one inch

✓ Consistent use of the documentation system you are following, for both in-text citations and end-of-essay references

✓ Headers or footers showing page numbers

✓ If used, headings and subheadings formatted in fonts and colors that distinguish them from the body text

✓ If used, illustrations labeled and placed either near relevant text or in an appendix, according to your instructor's preferences

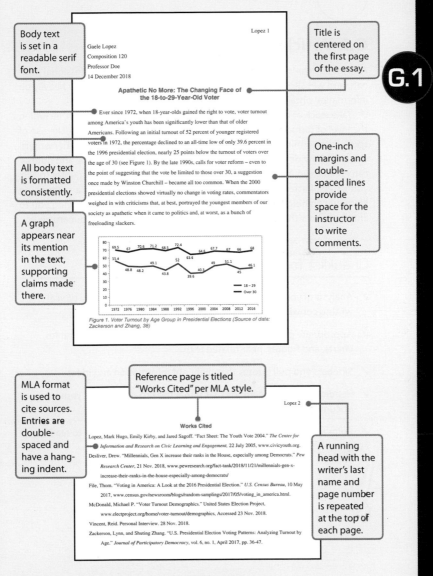

Body text is set in a readable serif font.

All body text is formatted consistently.

A graph appears near its mention in the text, supporting claims made there.

Title is centered on the first page of the essay.

One-inch margins and double-spaced lines provide space for the instructor to write comments.

Lopez 1

Gaele Lopez
Composition 120
Professor Doe
14 December 2018

Apathetic No More: The Changing Face of
the 18-to-29-Year-Old Voter

Ever since 1972, when 18-year-olds gained the right to vote, voter turnout among America's youth has been significantly lower than that of older Americans. Following an initial turnout of 52 percent of younger registered voters in 1972, the percentage declined to an all-time low of only 39.6 percent in the 1996 presidential election, nearly 25 points below the turnout of voters over the age of 30 (see Figure 1). By the late 1990s, calls for voter reform – even to the point of suggesting that the vote be limited to those over 30, a suggestion once made by Winston Churchill – became all too common. When the 2000 presidential elections showed virtually no change in voting rates, commentators weighed in with criticisms that, at best, portrayed the youngest members of our society as apathetic when it came to politics and, at worst, as a bunch of freeloading slackers.

Figure 1. *Voter Turnout by Age Group in Presidential Elections (Source of data: Zackerson and Zhang, 38)*

MLA format is used to cite sources. Entries are double-spaced and have a hanging indent.

Reference page is titled "Works Cited" per MLA style.

A running head with the writer's last name and page number is repeated at the top of each page.

Lopez 2

Works Cited

Lopez, Mark Hugo, Emily Kirby, and Jared Sagoff. "Fact Sheet: The Youth Vote 2004." *The Center for Information and Research on Civic Learning and Engagement,* 22 July 2005, www.civicyouth.org.

Desliver, Drew. "Millennials, Gen X increase their ranks in the House, especially among Democrats." *Pew Research Center,* 21 Nov. 2018, www.pewresearch.org/fact-tank/2018/11/21/millennials-gen-x-increase-their-ranks-in-the-house-especially-among-democrats/

File, Thom. "Voting in America: A Look at the 2016 Presidential Election." *U.S. Census Bureau,* 10 May 2017, www.census.gov/newsroom/blogs/random-samplings/2017/05/voting_in_america.html.

McDonald, Michael P. "Voter Turnout Demographics." United States Election Project, www.electproject.org/home/voter-turnout/demographics, Accessed 23 Nov. 2018.

Vincent, Reid. Personal Interview. 28 Nov. 2018.

Zackerson, Lynn, and Shuting Zhang. "U.S. Presidential Election Voting Patterns: Analyzing Turnout by Age." *Journal of Participatory Democracy,* vol. 6, no. 1, April 2017, pp. 36-47.

First page and works cited page of an academic essay

G.2 Articles

Articles appear in newspapers, magazines, scholarly and professional journals, and websites, among other publications. Typically, they rely heavily on information obtained from written, media, and field sources.

Take stock of the genre conventions in your target publication, including the level of formality (such as the use of contractions and slang), the use of specialized terminology (jargon), and references to the work of other writers. Consider how design elements, such as images, tables, charts, and figures, can enhance your article. By creating sidebars or inserting pull quotes (p. 80), you can call attention to key information. Using design as a composing element can help you view your draft as your readers will, allowing you to anticipate how they are likely to understand and respond to your article.

Checklist for Designing Articles

✓ Analysis of your target publication, focusing on its readers, typical writing conventions, and typical design conventions

✓ Appropriate placement of design elements, such as images, tables, charts, and figures, near related text

✓ Sidebars and pull quotes that highlight information and ideas

✓ Headings and subheadings that signal the organization of your document

✓ Color used to set a mood and indicate the function of text to readers

✓ Text set in columns for easy reading

The banner (title) at the top of the page contrasts with the text and the headlines for individual articles.

Images in the banner call attention to articles elsewhere in the newspaper.

Captioned photos add visual interest and information.

Newspaper article is formatted in columns.

Bylines are set in a bold sans-serif font to differentiate them from main body text.

Front page of a student newspaper

G.3 Multimodal Essays

Multimodal essays are characterized by their essay-like form and their use of multiple types of media. As essays, they present information in a linear sequence. As multimodal documents, they combine text with images, animation, sound, and video to establish a line of argument and support the writer's points.

Multimodal essays began appearing several years ago, most often on websites such as CNN.com and Salon. Increasingly, writing instructors are assigning multimodal essays, sometimes as original documents that incorporate images or media, and sometimes as extensions of more traditional print-based academic essays.

Multimodal essays can be created using a wide range of tools, including word-processing programs such as Microsoft Word, presentation programs such as Apple Keynote and Google Slides, mobile tools such as Adobe Spark Page, blogging tools such as Tumblr, website development tools such as Dreamweaver, and web-based tools such as WordPress or Wix.

Checklist for Designing Multimodal Essays

✓ Composing tools that are appropriate to your writing situation and design needs

✓ Consistent use of fonts, colors, shading, borders, and rules

✓ Larger fonts for headings and subheadings (such as 16-point Times or Verdana)

✓ Clear body font designed for on-screen reading (such as 11-point Calibri or Georgia)

✓ Appropriate placement of titles, text, and illustrations, with illustrations labeled and located near relevant text passages

✓ If used, transitions between pages (such as dissolves or page flips) that are quick and not distracting

✓ If used, background images and sounds that enhance rather than obscure the elements on each page

✓ Navigation tools such as "Next" and "Previous" buttons, links, menus, and tables of contents

Maximus Waste: A Food Waste Mockumentary

Columbia College Chicago's

First Year Seminar Honors Presents:

Curious Columbia's Food Waste Investigation

This year at Columbia College Chicago a group of the First Year Seminar Honors (FYSHN) students tackled the issue of food waste. After a thorough process of questioning, exploring, communicating, connecting, and evaluating everything to do with food waste, they have created a humorous documentary for public consumption. It is their goal to help spread awareness about the serious issue food waste in the world, as well as educate individuals about what they can do to create change.

A menu appears in the same location on each page.

A consistent look and feel is provided through the use of a common color scheme, font scheme, page layout, and page background image.

College Students vs. Food Waste

Every day students waste food. There is no question about it. In the US alone, about **30%** of college dorm food gets wasted. That accounts to **$48.2 Billion** worth of food that gets wasted every year. And it is not that students are not aware of the growing food waste trend, many simply feel that there isn't much for them to do about it.

For the past 14 weeks, I have observed students on on my campus every day as they go to eat at the University Center Dining Hall. Here students have a wide range of choices to their disposal. In this all-you-can eat buffet, students can get various foods that range from comfort food, to pizza, to ethnic food, and a deli. When students fill up their plates, they then go and charge the meal to their card. Students living within the University Center, or UC, get 15 meals a week while students living in other dorms have up to 150 meals throughout the semester.

Many students are aware of their own eating habits. Some of the students I spoke to claim that because of how much they pay, they feel they deserve to get as much food as possible from the dining hall. Many pile their plates full of food and eat very little. Others take samples from the different foods to see what they like and what they don't. All in all, the students all say that they are guilty of wasting food. A common consensus is that the food looks better than tastes.

The pages are designed in an attractive, uncrowded manner, with plenty of white space similar to a magazine ad.

Pages of a multimodal essay

• •

Maximus Waste: A Food Waste Mocumentary, http://www.foodwaste.cccwriting.org, Jack Dorst, Joe Erwin, Sarah Lemcke, Lia Miller, Carson Ruta

G.4 Multimedia Presentations

Multimedia presentations allow you to engage with your audience by choosing the sequence and duration of your slides. As you might do with a multimodal essay (p. 90, Sec. G.3), consider how images, audio clips, video clips, tables, and charts can help you achieve your purpose. If you are presenting in person, use gestures and movement to interact with your audience. Consider projecting images on a screen to complement your ideas while you talk, rather than a video clip with a sound track. If your presentation will be viewed on a computer, tablet, or smartphone, a video clip can provide more information and might be more effective in getting your points across to your audience.

Conventional multimedia presentation programs, such as Apple Keynote, Google Slides, Microsoft PowerPoint, Microsoft Sway, and OpenOffice Impress, organize presentations as a collection of slides ordered in a linear sequence from a cover slide to a closing slide. If you don't specify a particular layout, these programs use default slides consisting of a heading and a bulleted list. In contrast, a multimedia presentation program such as Prezi (prezi.com) allows you to create "zooming" presentations that can be useful for creative purposes such as digital storytelling.

Checklist for Designing Multimedia Presentations

✓ A multimedia presentation program that is consistent with your context, purpose, role, and audience

✓ Consistent use of fonts, colors, shading, borders, and rules

✓ Readable fonts for headings and subheadings

✓ A readable body font designed for viewing on a screen

✓ Minimal text for presenting information clearly

✓ If used, transitions between pages (such as dissolves or page flips) that are quick and not distracting

✓ If used, background images and sounds that enhance rather than obscure the elements on each page

✓ Multimedia elements used in moderation to advance your line of argument, not overwhelm viewers

EXAMINING LANGUAGE ACQUISITION IN INFANTS

G.4

Alex Harkins

LING1001

Title is formatted in a clear, eye-catching font.

The name of the presenter is clearly shown.

A multilevel bulleted list conveys key elements of the presenter's subject matter.

Fonts are large and easy to read.

The speaker uses the slides to support her presentation, rather than to take its place.

Is "baby talk" helpful or harmful?

A video clip provides visual interest and an expert's voice as evidence.

- Infant-directed speech (IDS)
- IDS has natural features that makes it helpful for language development:
  - Simpler vocabulary and sentence structure
  - Exaggerated pronunciation
  - Slower
  - Repetition (for example, "mama" and "night-night")
- Infants pay more attention to higher-pitched voices and sing-song tones
- Although simplified, "baby talk" is usually still slightly more advanced than a child's development

1:42 / 2:33

Slides from a multimedia presentation

Image provided by the National Science Foundation

G.5 Websites

Every day, we rely on the flexibility and engagement that websites offer, linking directly to related sites, providing access to video and audio files, and supporting communication among the website's readers and writers. This wealth of organization, navigation, and design options, however, raises significant planning, composing, and design challenges, including keeping your readers focused on reading your website instead of following links to other sites.

Writers typically design a website in the same way they design articles in a magazine, choosing a consistent color scheme, formatting headings and subheadings consistently across pages, and using borders, shading, and rules to help readers follow their argument. As in a multimedia presentation, writers must also address the placement and appearance of navigation menus and digital illustrations, such as audio and video clips, animations, and downloadable files.

Generally, a simple design is better. Don't try to cram too much on a single page, and place the most important information at the top. Readers often jump to another website if they don't easily find what they're looking for. Writers can develop their sites using websites such as Google Sites, Wix.com, and WordPress.com; web editors such as Dreamweaver; and even word-processing programs such as Microsoft Word.

Checklist for Designing Websites

✓ A readable body font designed for on-screen reading (such as 11-point Calibri or Georgia)

✓ Headings and subheadings formatted in fonts and colors that distinguish them from body text and signal their relative importance

✓ Information presented in brief, readable chunks, using bulleted and numbered lists whenever possible

✓ Color used to set a mood, highlight information, and help readers understand the function of text and illustrations on the site

✓ Moderate use of illustrations placed near the passages that refer to them

✓ Consistent and easy-to-use navigation tools, such as banners, menus, and icons on every page

✓ A home page that introduces the site's organization and content clearly

✓ Hyperlinks for all internal and external web references

✓ Opportunities for readers to engage with the site, such as email links, "Comments" buttons, and icons to share content on other social media platforms

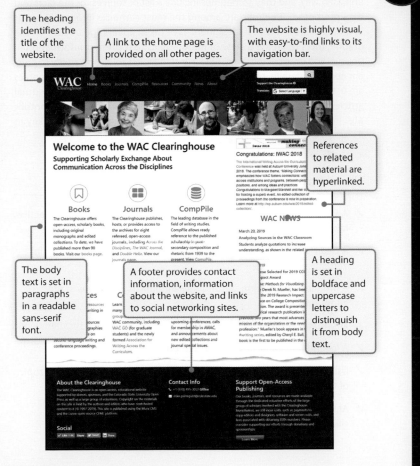

The heading identifies the title of the website.

A link to the home page is provided on all other pages.

The website is highly visual, with easy-to-find links to its navigation bar.

References to related material are hyperlinked.

The body text is set in paragraphs in a readable sans-serif font.

A footer provides contact information, information about the website, and links to social networking sites.

A heading is set in boldface and uppercase letters to distinguish it from body text.

Website

Mike Palmquist

G.6 Infographics

An infographic is a visual representation of a set of facts or data. As informative documents, infographics typically present information in a seemingly unbiased way, and they sometimes include a list of sources for the facts and data presented. Timelines are among the most common infographics, but in recent years innovative designers have taken advantage of easy-to-use graphic tools to create a slew of infographics that present information in unusual and unexpected ways. Because of their versatility and ability to present complex data in a format that is easy for readers to parse, infographics are useful in magazines and newspapers, on websites and blogs, in journal articles, and in a variety of other contexts. An infographic's design contributes in large part to its effectiveness, and a clear, cohesive design is key to its success.

Checklist for Creating Infographics

✓ An infographic template or tool that uses design principles for effective layout

✓ A clear, legible font designed for on-screen reading (such as 11-point Verdana or Georgia)

✓ A prominent, attention-getting title announcing the focus of the infographic

✓ Information presented in readable chunks, clearly labeled

✓ A legend that identifies icons or symbols used in the infographic

✓ Use of colors, icons, and images that set the mood or relate to the topic of the infographic

✓ At the footer of the infographic or elsewhere on your site, sources clearly cited or linked

Icons of water, non-perishable food, and other emergency supplies reflect the infographic's topic.

Slider bars indicate the percentage of U.S. residents who are prepared with each item.

The use of distinct colors (red for no, blue for yes) makes it easy to gauge how prepared U.S. residents are in each category.

MEASURING AMERICA

How Ready Are We?
Natural Disaster or Emergency Preparedness

To better understand the needs of first responders and other emergency workers, the 2017 American Housing Survey asks U.S. residents how prepared they are for disasters.

100 80 60 40 20 0 20 40 60 80 100

No   Yes

Emergency Water Supply
At least three gallons or 24 bottles of water for each person in the household.   58.6%
Not Reported

Nonperishable Emergency Food
Household has enough nonperishable food to sustain everyone in the household for three days.   81.3%

Prepared Emergency Evacuation Kit   52.9%

Emergency Meeting Location   36.5%

Communication Plan
The communication plan must include a contingency for the disruption of cell phone service.   26.4%

Evacuation Vehicle(s)
Vehicle(s) must be reliable and able to carry all household members, pets, and supplies up to 50 miles away.   91.0%

Evacuation Funds
If you had to evacuate your home for a safe place at least 50 miles away, do you have financial resources to meet expenses of up to $2,000?   75.6%

Generator Present
Asked of 1-unit buildings and multiunit buildings with 2 to 4 units.   18.7%

Access to Financial Information   80.8%

* Not reported: Households did not provide a response to this question.
Source: U.S. Census Bureau and U.S. Department of Housing and Urban Development, 2017 American Housing Survey.

United States Census Bureau
U.S. Department of Commerce
Economics and Statistics Administration
U.S. CENSUS BUREAU
census.gov

G.6

An infographic

U.S. Census Bureau

G.7 Blogs

Blogs are online forums that allow writers to present their opinions, observations, arguments, and reflections to a broad readership. They can consist of the contributions of a single writer, or they can draw on contributions from multiple writers. Blogs can be published and maintained by individuals or sponsored by news organizations, public interest groups, government agencies, corporations, and other organizations. When a blog is sponsored by an organization or a publication, the writer takes into account the purpose of the sponsor and the interests, needs, and backgrounds of readers who visit the blog.

Blog entries typically are brief and often present a personal perspective on an issue. However, because blogs have fewer length limitations than a piece in a newspaper, magazine, or journal might have, blog entries are more likely to rely on evidence from other sources than are opinion columns and letters to the editor. Their digital format enables them to use multimedia illustrations, such as video and audio clips or interactive polls, and to link to other sources. Because readers can respond publicly to a blog entry or link to it in their own blog, conversations can be extended over time and can involve readers and writers more actively.

Checklist for Designing Blogs

✓ A blog template that uses design principles for effective page layout

✓ Consistent use of fonts, colors, shading, borders, and rules

✓ Readable fonts for headings and subheadings and a readable body font designed for on-screen viewing

✓ A background that enhances rather than obscures the elements on each page

✓ Images, illustrations, and media used in moderation, so as not to crowd the page or overwhelm the reader

✓ Links to sources or relevant pages on your blog or elsewhere on the web

✓ Blog posts tagged by topic, so readers can find related information

✓ Opportunities for reader engagement through commenting, responding to polls, signing up for the blog feed, or sharing blog content via social media

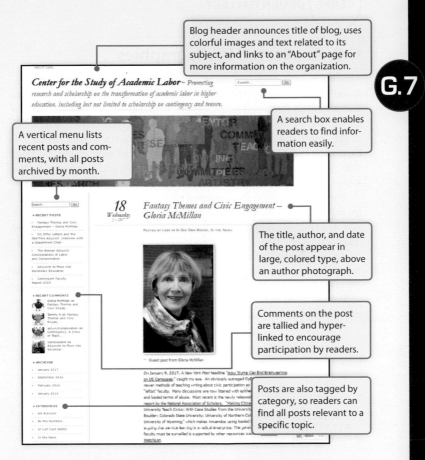

Blog header announces title of blog, uses colorful images and text related to its subject, and links to an "About" page for more information on the organization.

A search box enables readers to find information easily.

A vertical menu lists recent posts and comments, with all posts archived by month.

The title, author, and date of the post appear in large, colored type, above an author photograph.

Comments on the post are tallied and hyperlinked to encourage participation by readers.

Posts are also tagged by category, so readers can find all posts relevant to a specific topic.

A blog post

Colorado State University

G.8 Annotated Bibliographies

Annotated bibliographies can be useful tools as writers develop source-based essays. They consist of a list of sources with complete publication information, usually formatted according to the rules of a documentation system such as the Modern Language Association (MLA) system (see Chapter 30) or the American Psychological Association (APA) system (see Chapter 31). Each entry in the bibliography is followed by a brief note, usually no more than two or three sentences long, that summarizes and comments on the source.

If you are preparing an annotated bibliography for a class, your instructor will most likely expect a clear description of the content of each source and some indication of how you might use it. If you are using an annotated bibliography as a planning tool for a larger writing project, your annotations might highlight key passages, suggest how you can use information or ideas from the source, or emphasize relationships between sources. Sometimes an annotated bibliography will be the final result of your efforts, in which case your annotations should be written with the purposes, needs, interests, and backgrounds of your readers in mind.

Checklist for Designing Annotated Bibliographies

✓ A descriptive title that conveys the purpose of the bibliography

✓ Readable body font (such as 12-point Helvetica or Times New Roman)

✓ Double-spaced lines

✓ Consistent use of the documentation system you are following (such as MLA or APA)

✓ Complete citations formatted using hanging indents

✓ Informative annotations indented one inch

✓ Wide margins, at least one inch

Bellet, Benjamin W., Payton J. Jones, and Richard J. McNally. "Trigger Warning: Empirical Evidence Ahead." *Journal of Behavior Therapy and Experimental Psychiatry*, vol. 61, 2018, pp. 134–141. Science Direct, doi:10.1016/j.jbtep.2018.07.002

This experimental study by a group of Harvard researchers indicated that participants who were given trigger warnings prior to reading rated themselves and other readers as more likely to develop PTSD as a result of reading the passages. A significant limitation: the researchers excluded individuals who reported having experienced a "canonical stressor," such as rape or a natural disaster. This might be useful, but probably only for students who don't suffer from PTSD.

Holmes, Lindsay. "A Quick Lesson on What Trigger Warnings Actually Do." Huffington Post, 8 Aug. 2016, https://www.huffpost.com/entry/university-of-chicago-trigger-warning_n_57bf16d9e4b085c1ff28176d.

Holmes wrote this blog post in response to a welcome letter to incoming first-year students at the University of Chicago. The letter, written by the Dean of Students, stated that the university's commitment to academic freedom "means that we do not support so-called 'trigger warnings.'" Holmes argues that the letter reveals a "fundamental misunderstanding of triggering." There are several useful links in this article. It could be paired with the welcome letter to set up the discussion.

Rathje, Steve. "Do Trigger Warnings Help or Harm?" *Psychology Today*, 1 Aug. 2018, https://www.psychologytoday.com/us/blog/words-matter/201808/do-trigger-warnings-help-or-harm.

Rathje, a Ph.D. student in psychology at Cambridge University, reports on the study by Bellet, Jones, and McNally (see above). He views the exclusion of people who have been traumatized as a major limitation, noting that it is unclear that trigger warnings will lead people to avoid reading required course materials. He also notes the benefits for traumatized readers of being prepared for potentially disturbing content. This blog post might be useful for pointing out the limitations of the Harvard study.

G.8

Entries include all citation information the writer will need for the final document.

Annotations provide brief summaries of the purpose and content of the sources.

Citations are formatted according to the writer's documentation style (in this case, MLA).

Annotations are intended for the writer and the instructor. They indicate how and where the writer will use the source in the document.

Part 3

Conduct
Research

Hero Images/Getty Images

Part 3: Conduct Research

Focusing on early stages of a writing project, this part of *In Conversation* allows writers to understand and gain control over key research skills, including identifying and locating sources, evaluating sources, using sources in your writing, and avoiding plagiarism.

06. Collect Information

The primary challenge you will face as you do research won't be finding *enough* sources; it will be finding the *right* sources. To locate relevant, useful sources in library catalogs, in databases, and on the web, generate keywords and use basic and advanced online search strategies. To obtain your own primary sources (p. 32, Sec. 3.3), use field research methods such as interviews, observation, and surveys.

6.1 Search for Information with Digital Resources

To search for digital sources, generate keywords and use basic and advanced search strategies.

Generate Keywords and Phrases

Your writing question (p. 23, Sec. 2.3) can be a useful starting point for idea-generating techniques such as brainstorming and clustering (pp. 18–20, Sec. 2.1). In the following sections, consider how one writer used her writing question to generate a list of words and phrases to use in searches.

Understand Basic Searches

A basic search allows to you look for documents that contain a single word or phrase in the subject, title, text, and, in the case of databases, other parts of a database record. (See p. 109 in this section for more information about databases.) When you enter one or two words in the search field on Google or your library catalog, for example, you are conducting a basic search.

What should be done about **steroid use** by **adolescent girls** involved in **competitive sports**?

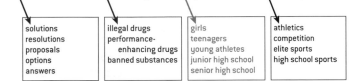

solutions	illegal drugs	girls	athletics
resolutions	performance-	teenagers	competition
proposals	enhancing drugs	young athletes	elite sports
options	banned substances	junior high school	high school sports
answers		senior high school	

Generating keywords

. . . .

6.1

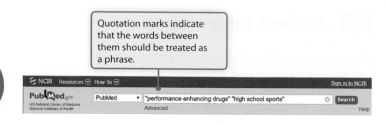

> Quotation marks indicate that the words between them should be treated as a phrase.

A simple search with phrases in the PubMed database

Basic searches can return large sets of results. To increase the odds that your results will be relevant to your subject, consider adding keywords, using exact phrases, and using wildcards.

Search for Exact Phrases. Sometimes the best way to locate information is to search for an exact phrase (see above). You can usually specify phrases in a basic search by using quotation marks.

Use Wildcards. Sometimes you're not sure what form of a word is most likely to occur. Rather than conducting several searches for *compete, competes, competitive, competition,* and *competitions,* for example, you can combine keywords into a single wildcard search. Wildcards are symbols that take the place of letters or strings of letters, expanding the scope of your search.

The most commonly used wildcard symbols are as follows:

* usually takes the place of one or more characters, such as compet*

? usually takes the place of a single character, such as wom?n

Understand Advanced Searches

Advanced search pages allow you to focus your searches in powerful ways using Boolean operators and search limits. Boolean operators specify whether keywords or phrases can, must, or must not appear in the results. The most common Boolean operators are AND, which finds sources that include both search terms; OR, which finds sources that include either term; and NOT, which finds sources that include one term but

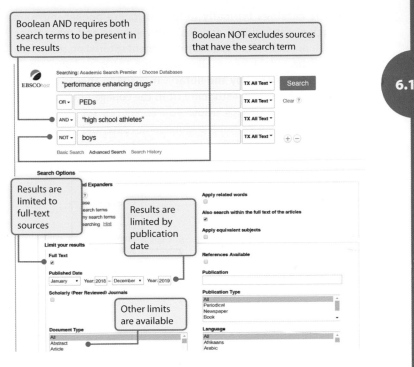

An advanced search in the Academic Search Premier database

. . . .

not the other. You can also limit your searches to documents that have particular characteristics, such as publication date, type of document, availability of full text (for databases) or, in the case of websites, the date on which a page on a website was last updated.

Search Library Catalogs

Library catalogs provide information about the print and digital materials in a library's collection. At a minimum, a catalog specifies the author(s), title, publication date, subject, and call number for each source in the library's collection. Often it will indicate the location of the source in the library and whether the source is available for checkout.

Online catalogs typically help you locate books; journals (although not individual articles); newspapers and magazines (although not individual articles); documents stored on microfilm or microfiche; videotapes, audiotapes, CDs, DVDs, and other multimedia items owned by the library; maps; and theses and dissertations completed by students from the college or university.

Most library catalogs allow you to search for sources by author(s), title, keyword, subject, publication date, and call number. You can also combine these types of searches.

Find subject categories by clicking on the call number of a source you are viewing.

Click on the subject entries in a catalog record to browse related sources by subject heading.

Some library catalogs allow visual browsing of book covers.

Searching by call numbers or subject headings

Writer to Writer

What if the library doesn't have a needed source? If the book or periodical you need isn't owned by your library, use interlibrary loan to borrow materials from another library. Most libraries allow you to request materials in person or on the web. You can learn how to use interlibrary loan at your library by consulting its website or a librarian.

6.1

Search Databases

A database allows you to search for sources that have been published on a particular subject or in a particular discipline regardless of whether the library has the sources in its collection. Although some databases, such as ERIC, MedLine, PubMed, and ScienceDirect, are available publicly on the web (p. 110), most are available only through library computers or a library website.

Databases vary in their purposes and areas of coverage. Depending on your topic, your college or university librarian can direct you to news and information databases, such as LexisNexis Academic and ProQuest Newspapers; subject databases, such as Academic Search Premier and ArticleFirst; bibliographies, such as Social Sciences Abstracts, which focus on particular professions or academic disciplines; citation indexes, such as Arts & Humanities Citation Index, which identify publications that have cited a particular source; and media databases, such as Artstor and AccessScience.

If the database you're using doesn't provide access to digital copies of the source, check your library's online catalog for the periodical title or request it through interlibrary loan (Writer to Writer box on this page).

To search for sources using a database, type keywords and phrases in the database's search fields. If you are conducting a basic search, the process will be similar to using a web search site (p. 110).

6.1

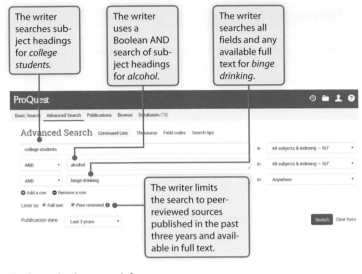

The writer searches subject headings for *college students*.

The writer uses a Boolean AND search of subject headings for *alcohol*.

The writer searches all fields and any available full text for *binge drinking*.

The writer limits the search to peer-reviewed sources published in the past three years and available in full text.

ProQuest database search form

Search the Web

Web search sites can help you sift through the vast amount of information available on the web. While web search is quick and easy, it has some drawbacks. The sources you find in a web search have not been carefully selected by librarians and editors, as is typically the case with the sources found through library catalogs and databases. Instead, sources found on the web can vary widely in quality, ranging from peer-reviewed articles in scholarly journals to blogs created by eighth-graders.

Web searches show what is available on publicly accessible websites, such as corporate, government, and educational sites. Few web search tools will provide access to information stored in databases that require visitors to log in with a password—for example, course materials in a learning management system such as Canvas or Blackboard. Similarly, web searches will not find information that is stored behind firewalls (security systems that limit access to authorized users).

Writer to Writer

Are all web search sites the same? Because most search engines index only a portion of the web, consider using more than one search engine. If you don't find what you're looking for on one, it doesn't mean you won't find it on another.

Common types of search tools include the following.

- *Web search engines* allow you to search for information on open websites and many social media sites. Leading search engines include Ask (ask.com), Bing (bing.com), DuckDuckGo (duckduckgo.com), Google (google.com), and Yahoo! (search.yahoo.com).

- *Meta search sites* provide results from several web search sites at the same time. These sites typically present a limited number of results on a single page. Meta search sites include Dogpile (dogpile.com), Yippy (yippy.com), and WebCrawler (webcrawler.com).

- *News search sites* allow you to conduct focused searches for current and archived news reports. You can find news on sites including Bing News (bing.com/news), Digg (digg.com), Google News (news.google.com), World News (wn.com), and Yahoo! News (yahoo.com/news).

- *Reference search sites* allow you to locate information that has been collected in encyclopedias, almanacs, atlases, dictionaries, and other reference resources. Leading reference search sites include Bartleby.com Reference (bartleby.com/reference), Encyclopedia.com (encyclopedia.com), *Encyclopaedia Britannica* (britannica.com), Information Please (infoplease.com), and Wikipedia (en.wikipedia.org).

- *Government search sites* provide access to information distributed through government agencies and institutions. Leading sites include GovSpot.com (govspot.com), USA.gov (usa.gov), the U.S. Government Printing Office Access (govinfo. gov), State and Local Government Directory (statelocalgov. net), and Canadian Government Search Engines (recherche–search.gc.ca).

- *Media search sites* provide access to nontextual information, including photographs, podcasts, and video. Established media search sites include Bing (bing.com/images and bing.com/videos), Google (images.google.com and www.google.com/videohp), Yahoo! (images.search.yahoo.com), and YouTube (youtube.com). FindSounds (findsounds.com) and Freesound (freesound.org) focus on audio.

Writer to Writer

Is it okay to use Wikipedia as a source?   One widely used reference site, Wikipedia (en.wikipedia.org), is collaboratively written by its readers. Because of its comprehensiveness, Wikipedia can serve as a useful starting point for research on a topic. However, because any reader can make changes to the site, it's best to double-check the information you find there. Once you get a good overview of the subject, you can continue your search for other, more reliable sources. It's also a good idea to find out whether your instructor will allow Wikipedia to be used as a source. For more information about the drawbacks of relying on wikis as authoritative sources of information, see p. 130, Sec. 7.3.

6.2 Search with Print Resources

Libraries contain significant collections of print resources designed to help you locate sources. Some of these resources provide information similar to that available in the databases discussed in the previous section, while others catalog information that is not available digitally.

6.2

Writer to Writer

What's wrong with using only databases and web search sites?
Using print resources to find sources has several benefits.

- *Some library reference resources are available only in print form.* While a growing number of print reference books have become available in digital formats, some are available only in print.

- *Print resources have longer memories.* Databases seldom index sources published before 1970, and they typically index sources only as far back as the mid-1980s. The web, which has existed only since the 1990s, does not provide access to many historical documents.

- *Print resources are more likely to include full-length works such as books.* In contrast, most databases focus on short works, such as articles in periodicals.

- *Entries in print indexes are easier to browse.* Databases support searching far better than they do browsing.

If your project has a historical component, print resources, such as bibliographies and indexes, are particularly valuable.

Use the Library Stacks

The library "stacks," or shelves, house the library's collection of bound publications. The classification systems used by most libraries — typically either the Library of Congress or Dewey decimal classification system — are subject based, which makes it easier to find materials on the same topic.

Use the Periodicals Room

Periodicals include newspapers, magazines, and scholarly and professional journals. A periodicals room — or journals room — contains recent issues for library visitors to browse. Many libraries also have a separate room for newspapers published in the last few weeks or months.

Writer to Writer

How can you browse the library effectively?   Because books on similar subjects are shelved together, you can browse the stacks to look for sources on your topic. For example, if your research takes you to the stacks for books about alcohol abuse, you're likely to find books about drug abuse, treatment programs, and codependency nearby. Browse the stacks in that same section; when you find a publication that seems useful, check the works-cited page for related works. The combination of browsing the stacks for sources and checking the works-cited pages of those sources can lead you to other publications relevant to your issue.

To ensure everyone's access to recently published issues, most libraries don't allow you to check out periodicals published within the last year, and they usually don't allow newspapers to be checked out at all. Older periodicals are sometimes placed in bound volumes in the stacks. Back issues of leading newspapers can often be found in full-text databases or in microfilm or microfiche, types of film containing miniaturized images of printed pages. You view these images using a microform reader, a projection unit that looks something like a large computer monitor.

Writer to Writer

How can you find out if your library has a certain periodical? Use the library catalog to conduct a title search for a periodical in the same way you search for a book. The catalog will show the call number of the periodical and, often, where it is located in the library.

6.3 Collect Information with Field Research

Some writers think of field research as a last resort for learning about an issue. If they can't find anything relevant in books, articles, newspapers, blogs, social media, or the broadcast media, then they might consider field research.

These writers misunderstand the value and power of field research. Far from being a good fallback position, field research is sometimes the best way to learn about an issue or collect information to support a position.

You can use field research to:

- bring new voices, experiences, and ideas into the conversation

- introduce a new perspective not found in published sources

- test a new idea or argument

- provide information on a topic so new that little or no authoritative information is available

- explore, through survey data, changes to established trends

- strengthen your argument with firsthand reports from people who have been affected by an issue

Conduct Interviews

Interviews — in which one person seeks information from another — can provide firsthand accounts of an event, authoritative interpretations of events and issues, and reactions to an event or issue from people who have been affected by it. Most interviews follow a question-and-answer format, but some more closely resemble a free-flowing discussion. You can conduct interviews face to face, over the telephone, via email, via Skype or FaceTime, and through text messaging or a chat program.

To conduct an interview:

- **Identify candidates.** Consider who can help you collect the information you need. Ask your instructor and classmates for suggestions. Then ask whether they can introduce you to those candidates.

- **Develop interview questions.** Develop questions that will require more than a yes or no answer and be prepared to ask follow-up questions.

- **Decide how — or whether — you will record the interview.** Because some people might be nervous about being recorded, be prepared to explain how you'll use the recording. Make them comfortable about the interview process.

- **Take notes.** Recordings can be lost through technical glitches. More important, taking notes allows you to save your thoughts about how you might use an interview in your document.

- **Analyze your interview.** Much as you would with any other source, approach the interview critically. Look for any new information or ideas. Look for statements that confirm or contradict information from other sources. Assess whether what was said is relevant and credible. Look for statements that provide context or that might help your readers better understand the issue.

Conduct Observations

Like interviewing, observing a setting can provide you with valuable information you would not be able to find in other sources.

To conduct an observation:

- **Decide what you should observe and how often you should observe it.** The biggest limitation of observation is that you can see only one thing at a time. Spreading yourself too thin will result

Writer to Writer

Should you clean up quotations from interviews or report exactly what was said? If you take a quotation from a printed source, even one that was originally spoken, you should either copy it exactly or put the changes you make inside brackets (see p. 144). But what about the normal stutters, mistakes, and missteps that creep in when we're speaking? If you're not using the original quotation verbatim, indicate through brackets how you have cleaned it up for clarity. The principles are:

- Consider whether the speaker's point is clear if you use an exact quotation.

- Consider whether meaningless clutter (especially "um's" and "uh's") is likely to distract your readers from the point.

- If you modify the quotation make sure the modified quotation says what the person meant to say.

- Don't make the person seem clumsier with language than is actually the case.

in fairly "thin" results. Then again, narrowing in too quickly can mean that you miss important aspects of the setting.

- **Determine whether you need permission to observe.** Seeking permission to observe someone can be complicated. People have expectations about privacy, but people can (and often do) change their behavior when they know they are being observed. As you consider whether to ask for permission, imagine yourself in the position of someone who is being observed. If you are still uncertain, ask your instructor for advice.

- **Conduct your observation(s).** Arrive early and review your planning notes. If you are recording the session, test your camera, recorder, phone, tablet, or computer. Take notes even if you're recording the session.

- **Analyze your observations.** Treat your observation notes or recording as you would any other source. Identify key features and patterns of behavior, identify key individuals and describe their actions, and look for unusual and surprising patterns and actions.

Conduct Surveys

Surveys allow you to collect information about beliefs, attitudes, and behaviors from a group of people. Typically, surveys help you answer *what* or *who* questions—such as, "Who will you vote for in the next election?" Surveys are less useful in obtaining the answers to *why* questions, because people seldom write lengthy, careful responses.

To conduct a survey:

- **Decide whom to survey.** If you're interested in what people in a specific group think about an issue, you could try to survey all of them. Most surveys, however, aren't given to everyone in a group. National polls, for instance, seldom survey more than one thousand randomly selected people, yet they are used to gauge the opinions of everyone in the country.

- **Develop your survey.** Start by evaluating the strengths and weaknesses of typical survey questions, as shown on page 120. Effective surveys are usually brief, are easy to complete, and include an explanation of the purpose of the survey. Good surveys also describe how results will be used and provide contact information.

- **Distribute your survey.** Surveys can be distributed via email, the web (using sites such as SurveyMonkey and SurveyGizmo), or social networking sites. Be prepared for low response rates. The sheer number of surveys people are asked to complete these days has reduced the public's willingness to respond to them. In fact, a good response rate for an online survey is 30 percent, while a good response rate for a survey conducted in a face-to-face setting, such as in class, is 50 percent or higher. That said, many professional pollsters find lower response rates acceptable.

- **Analyze your results.** Tabulate your responses in a spreadsheet program, such as Microsoft Excel or Google Sheets. Look for patterns in the data, surprising results, or striking differences. Keep in mind the need to ensure confidentiality for your respondents. A respondent might reveal, for example, that she is the only veteran in a particular writing class. If you find this kind of information, omit it from your report. In your final document, include a copy of your survey questions as an appendix.

Writer to Writer

How can you contact an expert or another well-known person?
Enlisting the help of experts and others you admire can be rewarding. Before reaching out, make sure you won't be wasting someone's time. If you're writing about the movement coordination disorder dyspraxia, you might learn that the actor Daniel Radcliffe has it. But you should contact him directly only if you are seeking specific information or a personal perspective. Otherwise, you can search online for "Daniel Radcliffe dyspraxia" to locate all the information you'll need.

If you decide to correspond with someone, determine how to get in touch. Actors, authors, musicians, and so on often have agents, part of whose job it is to field inquiries. Scholars, politicians, judges, and businesspeople are affiliated with institutions, where they have email addresses. While many academics are willing to respond to email, other well-known people are more likely to pay attention to mailed letters.

In your correspondence, clearly identify what you'd like the person to tell you and briefly explain why you're asking; mention your deadline if you have one; and make it easy for the person to respond by including your full contact information in your email or a stamped self-addressed envelope with your letter.

6.3

Election Survey

Thank you for completing this survey.

A 1. Did you vote in the last presidential election?   ☐ yes   ☐ no

2. I vote:

In every election	In most elections	In about half of the elections	Rarely	Never
☐	☐	☐	☐	☐

B 3. I have voted in the following types of elections (check all that apply):
   ☐ Regular local elections
   ☐ Special local elections
   ☐ Regular statewide elections
   ☐ National elections

4. Voting is a civic duty: ☐ true   ☐ false

C 5. All eligible voters should participate in local, state, and national elections:

Strongly Agree	Agree	Not Sure	Disagree	Strongly Disagree
☐	☐	☐	☐	☐

6. Please rate the following reasons for voting on a 1-to-5 scale, in which 5 indicates very important and 1 indicates not at all important:

	1	2	3	4	5
To be a good citizen	☐	☐	☐	☐	☐
To have a say in how government affects my life	☐	☐	☐	☐	☐
To support a particular cause	☐	☐	☐	☐	☐
To vote against particular candidates	☐	☐	☐	☐	☐

D 7. Please rank the following types of elections from most important (4) to least important (1):
   _____ Presidential elections
   _____ Statewide elections
   _____ Local (city and county) elections
   _____ Student government elections

E 8. Please tell us what influenced your decision to vote or not vote in the last election.

A Yes/no and true/false items divide respondents into two groups.

B Multiple-choice items indicate whether a respondent knows something or engages in specific behaviors. Because they seldom include every possible answer, be careful when including them.

C Likert scales measure respondents' level of agreement with a statement, their assessment of something's importance, or how frequently they engage in a behavior.

D Ranking forces respondents to place items along a continuum.

E Short-answer items allow greater freedom of response but can be difficult to tabulate.

Election survey

Use Correspondence

Correspondence includes any textual communication, such as letters, faxes, and email. Correspondence can also take place through the communication tools available on social networking sites such as Facebook.

Although many writers benefit from corresponding with experts, consider all the individuals who might provide information on your topic. If you are writing an article about the effects of recent flooding in the Midwest, you could write to relatives, friends, or even strangers to ask them about their experiences. Consider corresponding with staff at government agencies, corporations, and organizations, too.

Attend Public Events and View Broadcast Media

Public events, such as lectures, conferences, and public meetings and hearings, often provide writers with useful information. As with observations, you can record many public events by taking notes or bringing an audio or a video recorder. Be aware, however, that it is unethical to record events when you have been asked not to do so. If you are asked not to record an event, find out whether a transcript, podcast, or video recording of the event will be available.

07. Assess Your Sources

We live in a time where news reports and critical opinion pieces are often dismissed as "fake news." We regularly see news that truly is fake distributed widely via social media—either by people who are unaware that it's not based in fact or, worse, by people who make up information or promote conspiracy theories simply to divide and antagonize people. We often find it difficult to tell hoaxes from hard news. And we know that a large number of people get their news only from sources that reflect their political and cultural views.

As a writer, understanding how to find your way through the maze of real news, fake news, and deliberate deception is critical to the success of your writing project—and possibly to your success as a citizen.

7.1 Assess the Information in Your Sources

Begin by considering the purpose and publisher of a given source. If you're looking at an article or video from a news organization, such as CNN, Fox News, MSNBC, or National Public Radio, consider its bias. While each of these news organizations claims to be fact-based, fair, and balanced, their coverage of major events and issues can vary significantly. Understanding tendencies among the publishers of the sources you encounter can help you recognize how issues are framed, how facts are presented (or not), and how differing perspectives are considered (or not). Assessing bias on a website, podcast, blog, or social media page might be more difficult, especially if the origins of the content are unclear. As recent events have shown, social media sites struggle to balance the diverse needs, interests, values, and beliefs of hundreds of millions of users (billions, in the case of Facebook) with the need to reduce the spread of misinformation and disinformation, particularly in light of arguments about free speech and freedom of expression.

You can adopt several strategies to help verify the credibility of the information you encounter:

- **Routinely withhold judgment.** New and intriguing information attracts readers' attention, especially when it is consistent with readers' expectations and experiences or when it resonates with them emotionally. Some of the most widely circulated fake news over the past few years has been spread by people who were intrigued by something that seemed extraordinary.

- **Verify information.** Embrace the Russian proverb, "*Doveryai, no proveryai*"—trust but verify. Double-check every fact. Triple-check them. And then be open to new information that might lead you to check once again. You can verify information by looking at how it's reported in a variety of sources and through fact-checking sites such as Snopes.com, FactCheck.org, and PolitiFact.

- **Think critically.** Use your memory regarding facts that you've verified. Trust your evolving understanding of the issue. Reflect on what you are learning about the issue and, when you are uncertain about whether something you've read is credible, seek more information.

7.2 Pop the Information Bubble

Getting trapped in an information bubble—often referred to as a filter bubble or an echo chamber—is a common problem. We enter information bubbles when we turn only to information sources that are consistent with our values, beliefs, and experiences. For example, Americans who are politically conservative appear to be more likely to view Fox News than MSNBC, a news source that is widely viewed as politically progressive (the reverse is also true).

7.2

> Fox News, NBC News, and CNN report on the same event.

News organizations can frame events differently.

You can break out of an information bubble by using the following strategies.

- **Be skeptical**, even of sources you agree with. Develop a healthy skepticism about all news, and especially news distributed via social media. Put your skepticism into high gear every time you view a tweet or social media post, a politically oriented video on the web, or a campaign or issue ad.

- **Seek alternative perspectives.** Your understanding of an issue might be framed by repeated appeals to the same set of values and beliefs or by repeated use of similar types of evidence. Eventually, this framing might seem so reasonable that alternative viewpoints will seem uninformed. While it might be reassuring to hear news sources that you agree with, it can also decrease your willingness to consider other perspectives.

- **Consume news differently.** Change your viewing and reading habits. In the same way that you might strive to eat a balanced diet, balance your intake of information and ideas. It might be uncomfortable to spend time viewing news from sources that espouse values different from your own, but it's likely to help you write more effectively.

7.3

Checklist for Assessing the Credibility of a Source

✓ Approach sources with skepticism.

✓ Routinely withhold judgment or overly emotional responses to new information.

✓ Verify information. Check, double-check, and even triple-check information before you invest your trust in it.

✓ Seek alternative perspectives. Do your best to avoid life in an information bubble.

✓ Reflect on how the source fits your growing understanding of the issue.

7.3 Apply Evaluative Criteria

At the beginning of a writing project, you'll most likely make quick judgments about your sources. Skimming an article, a book, or a website might be enough to tell you that spending more time with the source would be wasted effort. Sources that appear more promising should be evaluated to determine how well they meet your needs as a writer.

Evaluate Relevance

Relevance is the extent to which a source provides useful information. To determine the relevance of a source, reflect on your purposes, role, and readers. Ask if the information, argument, and ideas will help you reach your goals. Your readers will expect information that meets their needs, too. If they want to read about video streaming services, for instance, pass up sources that offer only reviews of the latest shows and channels.

7.3

Evaluate Evidence

Evidence is information offered to support an author's reasoning about an issue (p. 65, Sec. 4.8). Evidence is connected to reasons through appeals to authority, emotion, principles, values, beliefs, character, and logic (p. 66, Sec. 4.8). It can also include measurements and observations, typically referred to as empirical evidence. As a writer, you should evaluate not only the kind of evidence used in a source but also the quality, amount, and appropriateness of that evidence. Insufficient evidence, for example, may indicate that the source is not credible. Ask the following questions about each source:

- Is enough evidence offered?

- Is the right kind of evidence offered?

- Is the evidence used fairly?

- Is the source of the evidence provided?

If you have doubts about the accuracy of evidence, verify it. If an author argues, for example, that a politician is untrustworthy because the merchandise sold by his campaign was made outside the United States, consult a fact-checking site.

Evaluate the Author

Evaluating the author might seem like an obvious move, but many sources, including websites and some social media posts, provide little or no information about the author. If the author is identified, such as in signed opinion columns in a newspaper or magazine, your evaluation might consider the author's experience; whether the author is politically conservative, liberal, or moderate; or whether the author is affiliated with an organization or known cause of some kind. Similarly, you might find it useful to know that a message published on a web discussion forum or in the comments section following an article was written by a recognized expert in the field. Ask the following questions about the author of a source:

- Is the author knowledgeable about the topic?

- What organization or organizations is the author affiliated with?

- How do the author's biases affect the information, ideas, and arguments in the source?

Evaluate the Publisher

A publisher is a person or group that prints or produces the documents—including books, newspapers, journals, articles, websites, or sound and video files—written by authors. Personal blog posts or sources obtained through field research have no publisher. Make informed judgments about publishers in much the same way that you evaluate authors by asking the following questions:

- What information can I learn about the publisher by searching on the web or reviewing a website's home page, "About Us" section, or other identifying information?

- How do the publisher's biases—as demonstrated in their mission statements, websites, or other published work—affect the information, ideas, and arguments in the source?

Evaluate Timeliness

The importance of how recently a source was published varies according to your writing situation. If you're writing an article on the use of superconducting materials in twenty-first-century mass transportation projects, you probably won't want to spend a lot of time with articles published in 1968. On the other hand, if you're writing about the 1968 presidential contest between Hubert Humphrey and Richard Nixon, sources published around that time will take on greater importance.

7.3

Evaluate Comprehensiveness

Comprehensiveness is the extent to which a source provides a complete and balanced view of a topic. Like timeliness, the importance of comprehensiveness varies according to the demands of your writing situation. If you are working on a narrowly focused project, such as the role played by shifts in Pacific Ocean currents on snowfall patterns in Colorado in the winter of 2008, comprehensiveness might not be as important as other evaluation criteria. However, if you are considering a broader issue, such as the potential effects of global climate change on agricultural production in North America, or if you are still learning as much as you can about your issue, give preference to sources that treat the issue fully.

Evaluate Genre and Medium

Genre and medium can help you understand the roles authors take on as they contribute to a written conversation. Understanding the typical characteristics of a genre, for example, can help you recognize whether the source will be appropriate and useful for your project. Similarly, considering how the medium—print, digital, or broadcast—shapes the manner in which authors typically share ideas with readers can help you make judgments about a particular source. Imagine, for instance, two articles on the health benefits of yoga, one published in *People* magazine and the other published in a medical journal. The former might be written by a general writer who is knowledgeable about yoga, and it might share personal anecdotes using a casual tone. The latter would likely be written by an expert researcher, and it would present empirical evidence and use specialized terminology. Both might be excellent articles, but the kind of information they offer will differ and the contribution they might make to your project will depend heavily on your purpose and role.

Evaluate Digital Sources

Because anyone can create a website, start a blog, contribute to a wiki, or post to a social network, a comments section, or an email list, approach these sources with more caution than you would reserve for sources that undergo a lengthy editorial-review process.

Websites and Blogs. To assess the relevance and credibility of a website or a blog, consider the following.

Check its domain (.com, .edu, .gov, and so on) to learn about its purpose and publisher:

.biz, .com, .coop	business	.mil	military
.edu	higher education	.name	personal
.gov	government	.net	network organization
.info	publications	.org	nonprofit organization

Check the title bar, page header, and page titles to learn about the site's purpose, publisher (p. 127), and relevance (p. 125).

Read the body text and review illustrations to evaluate relevance (p. 125), evidence (p. 126), and comprehensiveness (p. 128).

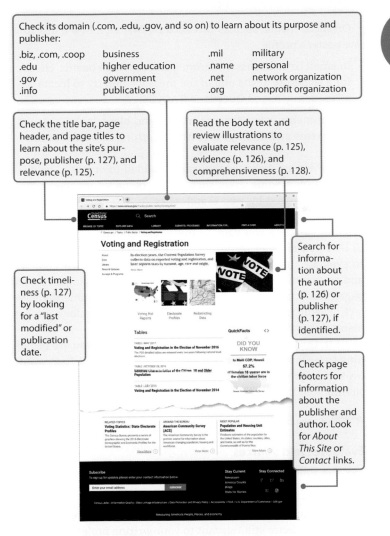

Check timeliness (p. 127) by looking for a "last modified" or publication date.

Search for information about the author (p. 126) or publisher (p. 127), if identified.

Check page footers for information about the publisher and author. Look for *About This Site* or *Contact* links.

Assess the relevance and credibility of a website or blog

. . . .

U.S. Census Bureau

Social Networking Sites and Discussion Venues. To assess the relevance and credibility of posts on these online venues, try to learn something about the author.

- On social media, such as Facebook or Twitter, follow a link to a poster's profile.

- In email lists, discussion forums, and message boards, check for a signature at the end of the message and try to locate a Frequently Asked Questions (FAQ) list.

- In comments lists following articles and blogs, look for signed comments and attempt to learn something about the author.

Wikis. Wikis are websites that can be added to or edited by visitors to the site. Some wikis, such as Wikipedia (en.wikipedia.org), are highly ranked by web search sites (p. 110, Sec. 6.1). Experts on an issue sometimes contribute to wikis and provide analyses that can help you gain an initial understanding of an issue or lead you to other resources. Unfortunately, it can be difficult to evaluate the credibility of wiki pages because their creators and editors might not be identified and because changes to wiki pages can occur quickly. Some entries, in fact, become the subject of "edit wars," in which edits to a page are undone almost instantly by those who disagree with the edits.

With this in mind, it is best to use wikis when you are beginning to learn about an issue. Avoid citing them as the "last word" on a topic because that last word might change before you submit your final draft.

Learn more about using wikis on p. 112, Sec. 6.1.

Evaluate Field Sources

Ask the following questions as you evaluate information collected through field research.

- Are the questions you asked in an interview, a survey, or correspondence still relevant to your writing project? Were they answered fully and honestly?

- Are the individuals you interviewed or corresponded with as qualified and knowledgeable as you expected?

- Is the information you collected in an observation still relevant? Are your observation notes as complete as you had hoped they would be?

7.3

- Did survey respondents have adequate time to complete the survey? Did they appear to expect their privacy would be maintained? Are the results consistent with results from similar surveys?

Learn more about field research on p. 115, Sec. 6.3.

08. Manage Your Sources

Even with a narrowly defined writing question, it's likely that your research will produce a large number of relevant sources. To make the most of them, decide how to save, organize, and keep track of your sources as you plan and draft your document.

8.1 Save and Organize Print Information

Print information can include any of the following:

- your written notes (in a notebook, on loose pieces of paper, on sticky notes, and so on)

- printouts from websites and databases

- articles sent through a library's interlibrary loan service

- printed drafts of your writing question, position statement, thesis statement, or outline

- books, magazines, newspapers, brochures, pamphlets, and government documents

- photocopies of articles, book chapters, and other documents

- letters, printed email messages, survey results, and so on

Rather than letting all this information build up in messy piles on your desk or stuffing it into your backpack, create a filing system to keep track of your print documents. Filing systems can range from well-organized piles of paper labeled with sticky notes to three-ring binders to file cabinets filled with labeled files and folders.

Writer to Writer

What's the best way to organize print sources? There's no single right answer. Regardless of the approach you take, keep the following principles in mind.

- **Make it easy to locate your print materials.** Decide whether you want to group material by topic, by date, by *pro* versus *con*, by type of material (web pages, photocopies, original documents, field sources, and so on), or by author.

- **Stick with your organizing scheme.** Using just one approach will make it easier to locate materials throughout your writing project.

- **Always include complete publication information**, even if you have to write it on the document yourself.

- **Record the date you located the material.**

- **Annotate each of your print materials.** A brief note indicating how it might contribute to your project can be helpful later, when the source is not as fresh in your mind.

8.2 Save and Organize Digital Information

As you save digital information, keep it organized. The simplest strategy is to save your work in a single folder using descriptive file names, such as "Interview Notes from Sean Burns, April 14." The single-folder approach might not work well for larger projects. Rather than scrolling through several screens of files, you might find it more efficient to create multiple folders to hold related files.

Download

Consider saving all of your digital sources on a hard drive, flash drive, or network-based service such as Box, Dropbox, iCloud, or OneDrive. Downloading sources allows you to open them

8.2

in a web browser or word processor at a later time. You can download web pages and images by using the save command (usually available through a browser's right-click or command-click menu). You can download from databases by marking and saving records returned by a search and by saving full-text documents.

Copy and Paste

You can copy text from relevant sources into a word-processing document or a notes tool such as OneNote or Evernote. Be sure to keep track of source information, such as the URL and the date you viewed a source, so that you can return to it if necessary and cite it appropriately.

Use Email

You can email yourself messages containing digital documents you've found in your research. Some databases allow you to email the text of selected records directly from the database. You can also use email as a "file folder" by sending messages to yourself that include copies of documents in the form of pasted text or attached files. A subject line such as "My Comp 110 Writing Project" enables you to sort your messages or search for the phrase *writing project* and easily view all of the information you've collected.

Photograph and Record

If you have a smartphone or a tablet, you can record conversations with others, record voice memos with ideas about your project, save videos, and take photos of sources you find in the periodicals room (p. 114, Sec. 6.2).

Save Bookmarks and Favorites

You can use a Bookmarks or Favorites list in your web browser to keep track of your sources. Remember, however, that websites can and do change. If you suspect that the page you want to mark might change before you complete your writing project, download or print it so that you won't lose its content.

Use Web Tools

Web clipping tools work with your browser as toolbars or "add-ons" and can be used to copy all or part of a web page. Leading free web capture tools include Diigo (diigo.com), PowerNotes (powernotes.com), and Zotero (zotero.org). Content curation tools allow you to create collections of sources and share them—individually or as a group. Scoop.it (scoop.it), for example, allows you to save, annotate, and easily revisit websites, blogs, and other online content. Leading, free content curation tools include Listly (list.ly) and Paper.li (paper.li).

Back Up Your Files

Replacing lost information takes time and effort. Avoid the risk of losing your research by taking the time to make copies of your digital files and downloads.

Writer to Writer

What should URLs look like in my document?   Here are two things to keep in mind:

First, if the citation style you're following allows it, delete "http://" or "https://" when "www" comes next. Those "http"s aren't really necessary, and they waste space. The version that begins with "www" will take readers to the correct site.

Second, it's good form to shorten very long URLs using a service such as bitly.com or tinyurl.com. Shortening URLs makes them more readable and saves space in your document.

8.3

8.3 Compile Bibliographies

A bibliography is a list of sources with complete publication information, usually formatted according to a documentation system such as those created by the Modern Language Association (MLA; see Chapter 30), the American Psychological Association (APA; see Chapter 31), or the Council of Science Editors (CSE; see Chapter 33) or found in books such as the *Chicago Manual of Style* (*Chicago*; see Chapter 32). As you take notes, use a working bibliography or an annotated bibliography to keep track of the sources you've consulted.

Create a Working Bibliography

A *working bibliography* is a running list of the sources you've explored and plan to use as you work on your writing project. Include as much publication information about a source as you can gather (see Part 6 for more on citations). As you explore your topic, collect sources, and evaluate them, you will add potentially useful sources and delete sources that are no longer relevant. Eventually, your working bibliography will become one of the following.

- A *works-cited* or *reference list* — a formal list of the sources you have referred to in a document

- A *bibliography* or *works-consulted list* — a formal list of the sources that contributed to your thinking about an issue, even if those sources are not referred to explicitly in the text of the document

Keeping your working bibliography up to date helps ensure that you will cite all the sources you use in your document — an important contribution to your efforts to avoid plagiarism.

Create an Annotated Bibliography

An *annotated bibliography* provides a brief note about each of the sources you've listed, in addition to its complete citation

Information You Should List in a Working Bibliography

Type of Source	Information You Should List
All Sources	Author(s) Title Publication year Medium consulted
Book	Editor(s) of book (if applicable) Publication city Publisher Series and series editor (if applicable) Translator (if applicable) Volume (if applicable) Edition (if applicable)
Chapter in an Edited Book	Publication city Publisher Editor(s) of book Book title Page numbers
Journal, Magazine, or Newspaper Article	Journal title Volume number or date Issue number or date Page numbers
Website, Blog Entry or Reply, Discussion Forum Post, Email Message, or Chat Transcript	URL Access date (the date you read the source) Sponsoring organization (if listed)
Field Research	Title (usually a description of the source, such as "Personal Interview with Jessica Lynn Richards" or "Observation of June Allison's Class at Tavelli Elementary School") Date (usually the date on which the field research was conducted)

8.3

information. These notes, or annotations, are typically just two or three sentences. The content, focus, and length of your annotations will reflect both your purposes for creating an annotated bibliography and the needs and interests of your readers.

An annotated bibliography is a useful tool even if it's not required. By turning your working bibliography into an annotated bibliography, you can remind yourself of important information, ideas, and arguments in your sources; record your reflections, evaluations, and analyses of each source; note your responses to your sources; and record your ideas about how the source might be used to advance your position on your issue.

8.3

For more on creating and designing an annotated bibliography, see p. 47 (Sec. 4.3) and pp. 100–101 (G.8).

> ## Writer to Writer
>
> ***Is there automated help for formatting citations?***   Microsoft Word includes an automated tool that will format your citations into any of a few common styles, including APA, *Chicago*, and MLA. You'll find an "Insert Citation" button in the "References" section of the full ribbon.
>
> A variety of other free citation help tools are available on the web. These tools require you to type the elements of each citation into a form — or else enter an identifier, such as DOI or PubMed number, that will allow the tool itself to extract citation information from the source. You can also generate citations in specific styles, such as APA, in many databases.
>
> Be aware that if you're entering the information yourself, the accuracy and formatting will be only as good as you make it. And keep in mind the usual warnings about relying on automatic processes that can't think. Be sure to proofread an automatically generated bibliography at least as carefully as one you prepared on your own, and check that its format matches the one your instructor wants you to use.

09. Use Sources Effectively

You can integrate information, ideas, and arguments from sources into your draft by quoting, paraphrasing, summarizing, presenting numerical information, and using illustrations. As you do so, make a point of distinguishing your ideas from those found in your sources.

9.1 Identify Your Sources

You should identify the sources of information in your document for several reasons. First, ethically, you are obligated to document the sources you use. Second, doing so allows you (and your readers) to recognize the boundaries between your ideas and those borrowed from sources. Third, it can help you strengthen your argument by calling attention to the qualifications or experiences of the person whose ideas you are incorporating.

Use Attributions and In-Text Citations

Whenever you quote, paraphrase, or summarize, distinguish between your ideas and information obtained through your sources by using attributions — brief comments such as "according to" or "as the author points out" — to alert your readers that the point is not your own. Sometimes referred to as *signal phrases*, attributions alert your readers that you are providing information from a source.

Writers who use MLA or APA documentation format also include citations — or acknowledgments of source information — within the text of their document to indicate where borrowed material ends. These citations, in turn, refer readers to a list of works cited or a list of references at the end of the document.

Note the following examples, which use attributions and in-text citations:

9.1

MLA Style

Antero Garcia argues, "Education reform is the best solution for fixing our public schools" (22).

"Education reform is the best solution for fixing our public schools" (Garcia 22).

MLA-style in-text citations include the author's name and exact page reference.

Attributions identify the author of the quotations.

APA Style

Antero Garcia (2019) has argued, "Education reform is the best solution for fixing our public schools" (p. 22).

"Education reform is the best solution for fixing our public schools" (Garcia, 2019, p. 22).

APA-style in-text citations include the author's name, publication date, and exact page reference.

As you acknowledge material you've found in your sources, be aware that the verbs in attributions can convey important shades of meaning. For example, there's quite a difference between writing that someone "alleged" something and someone "confirmed" something. The attributions you choose can play an important role in signaling the intent of an author and, in turn, can shape how your readers view the issue.

The form your attributions take will depend on your citation style. MLA recommends present tense ("the author points out"), while APA recommends past tense ("the author pointed out") or present perfect tense ("the author has pointed out").

Some Common Attributions

according to	confirmed	observed
acknowledged	declared	pointed out
affirmed	denied	remarked
alleged	described	reported
asked	disputed	said
asserted	emphasized	stated
assumed	expressed	suggested
believed	interpreted	thought
claimed	mused	wondered
commented	noted	wrote

9.1

For more about the differences in how MLA style and APA style use attributions, see p. 367 (Sec. 30.1) and p. 404 (Sec. 31.1).

Provide a Context

As you quote your sources, do more than simply place text between two quotation marks. Such "orphan quotations"—quotations dropped into a paragraph without any introduction—are confusing. Worse, paraphrases and summaries inserted without context can easily be mistaken for the writer's own work, leading to accusations of plagiarism.

To provide a clear context for your source information, establish why the quotation, paraphrase, or summary is reliable by identifying the source's credentials. In addition, indicate how it relates to your main idea and what it contributes to the point you are making. If you don't, readers will wonder why it's there.

> Understanding the root causes of binge drinking among college students is a challenging task. Aaron White and Ralph Hingson from the National Institute on Alcohol Abuse and Alcoholism note that "a broad array of factors influence whether a particular college student will choose to drink, the types of consequences they suffer from drinking, and how they respond to those consequences" (201).

Attribution identifies the source as experts.

MLA-style in-text citation identifies the page number of the quotation.

9.2 Quote Strategically

A well-chosen quotation can have a powerful impact on your readers' perception of your argument. Quotations can add a sense of immediacy by bringing in the voice of someone who has been affected by an issue. They can also lend authority to your argument by conveying the words of an expert. When you choose how much to quote, consider the length and complexity of the passage as well as the obligation to present ideas and information fairly.

Learn more about citation styles in Part 6.

Use Partial Quotations

Partial quotations can be anything from a single word to most of a sentence. They are often used to convey a well-turned phrase or to complete a sentence using important words from a source, as in the following example.

> On a visit to Silicon Valley, U.S. Secretary of Defense Ashton B. Carter said that the documents Edward J. Snowden leaked revealed "a difference in view between what we were doing and what people perceived us as doing" (Sanger & Perlroth, 2015, para. 4).

Quotation marks indicate the borrowed phrase.

Source information, including the authors, date, and number of the paragraph containing the quotation, is clearly identified per APA guidelines.

Use Complete Quotations

Complete quotations are typically used when the meaning of the passage cannot be conveyed adequately by a few words, as in the following example.

As I read Malala Yousafzai's book, *I Am Malala*, I found myself reflecting again and again on her observation, "We realize the importance of our voices only when we are silenced" (235).

> An attribution identifies the source of the quotation.

> Only the page number is needed in a parenthetical citation in MLA style.

Use Block Quotations

Block quotations are extended quotations (usually more than four typed lines) that are set off in a block from the rest of the text. In general, use a colon to introduce the quotation, indent the entire quotation one inch from the left margin, and include source information according to the documentation system you are using (such as MLA, APA, *Chicago*, or CSE). Since the blocked text indicates that you are quoting directly, you do not need to include quotation marks.

In her 2013 article, "What's Right with the Autistic Mind," Temple Grandin argues that we should look not only at what's wrong with the autistic mind but also what is right with it:

> Don't get me wrong. I'm not saying that autism is a great thing and all people with autism should just sit down and celebrate our strengths. Instead, I'm suggesting that if we can recognize, realistically and on a case-by-case basis, what an individual's strengths are, we can better determine the future of the individual—a concern now more than ever, as the rate of autism diagnoses reaches record levels. (para. 3)

> In block quotations, the citation information is placed after the period.

> A paragraph number is provided for an online source in APA style.

> Quotation marks are not used to enclose block quotations.

Writer to Writer

Should you use the first names of sources' authors? Documentation styles have different preferences for how to treat names of the authors of sources. The first time you refer to someone, MLA and *Chicago* advise you to include the first name or initials if that's known to be the person's preference: *Harriet Tubman, E. O. Wilson*. After that, use only the last name: *Tubman, Wilson*. This convention is common in journalism and other forms of nonfiction as well as academic writing.

In APA style, which is primarily used for academic writing in the social sciences, introduce sources by giving the author's last name and the year of publication of the source in the text: *Wilson (2012)*.

First names rarely come up in the scientific papers written in CSE style.

Modify Quotations Appropriately

You can modify a quotation—deleting unnecessary words or changing the tense of a word—so that it fits your sentence. For example, if you wanted to change a pronoun, you would use brackets to indicate the change.

Original Quotation:

"Every man takes the limits of his own field of vision for the limits of the world."

Quotation Modified Using Brackets:

Schopenhauer said that we all take "the limits of [our] own field of vision for the limits of the world."

> Brackets indicate a word that has been changed.

If a passage you are quoting contains a misspelled word or an incorrect fact, use the word "sic" in brackets to indicate that the error occurred in the original passage.

Quotation Modified Correctly Using "Sic"

"Donald Trump's interest in protecting the American steal [sic] industry strongly shaped his foreign trade policies" (Vincent 221).

Remember that writers have an obligation to quote sources accurately and fairly. You should indicate when you have added or deleted words, and you should not modify quotations in a way that distorts their meaning.

The most useful strategies you can use to modify quotations include using ellipsis marks (. . .) to indicate deleted words, using brackets [ ] to clarify meaning, and using "sic" to note errors in a source.

Learn more about integrating quotations into your document in Chapter 15. Learn more about quoting from interviews in the Writer to Writer box on p. 117 (Sec. 6.3).

Checklist for Integrating Quotations into a Document

✔ Identify the source of the quotation.

✔ Punctuate the quotation appropriately, enclosing the passage in quotation marks.

✔ Use ellipsis marks, brackets, and "sic" as necessary.

✔ Check each quotation against the source to be sure you aren't introducing errors or misrepresenting the source.

✔ Use transitions and attributions to integrate the quotation effectively into your document.

✔ Ensure that the source is cited in your works-cited or references list.

9.3

Writer to Writer

What verb tense should you use in attributions?   If your document uses MLA style, use present tense: *Alice Chen says.* . . . APA recommends that you use past or present perfect tense: *Alice Chen said* . . . or *Alice Chen has said.* . . .

If you're writing something that doesn't need to follow a documentation style, there's no rule about which verb tense to use for attributions, or signal phrases. We recommend using the past tense when you've given the quotation or paraphrase a "setting"—that is, if you've told readers when or where it was spoken or written:

> In a 2015 university commencement speech, Apple CEO Tim Cook said, "The sidelines are not where you want to live your life. The world needs you in the arena."
>
> Over lunch, Apoorva reminded us all . . .

You can also use the past tense if readers know that the writer or speaker is dead:

> Benjamin Franklin said, "An investment in knowledge pays the best interest."

Otherwise, use the present tense:

> She claims it's a major problem.
>
> Even Apple CEO Tim Cook says data tracking is "totally out of control."

If, however, you want to suggest that a setting for the quote exists but it's not relevant, use the present perfect:

> Even Apple CEO Tim Cook has said data tracking is "totally out of control."

9.3 Paraphrase

A paraphrase is a restatement, in your own words, of a passage from a source. Paraphrases can be used to support a point you make or to illustrate another author's argument about an issue.

Good writers rarely rely exclusively on quotations, so consider paraphrasing your sources as you take notes.

One of the challenges of paraphrasing is to avoid mirroring the source material too closely. You should do more than simply make minor changes to the words and sentence structure of a source. Another challenge is to avoid distorting the meaning of the source as you paraphrase.

9.3

Original Passage

"High school grades and test scores are not the only factors considered by colleges and universities in the admissions process. Other factors that influence college admissions decisions include high school rank, being an athlete, alumni connection, extracurricular activities, special talents, and other personal characteristics of applicants."

Source: William H. Gray III, "In the Best Interest of America, Affirmative Action Is a Must," p. 144.

Appropriate Paraphrase

William H. Gray III notes that, in addition to high school grades and standardized test scores, most colleges and universities make admissions decisions based on an applicant's participation in sports, involvement in extracurricular activities, personal qualities, talents, relations to alumni, and class rank (144).

Preserves the meaning of the original without replicating sentence structure and wording

Inappropriate Paraphrase

William H. Gray III notes that high school grades and test scores are not the only issues weighed by colleges and universities during college admissions decisions. Other factors that influence those decisions are high school rank, participating in athletics, connections to alumni, out-of-school activities, unique talents, and other personal qualities of applicants (144).

Does not differ sufficiently from original; uses the same sentence structure

Inappropriate Paraphrase

William H. Gray III notes that participation in sports and
involvement in extracurricular activities are among the
most important factors affecting college admissions
decisions (144).

Distorts the meaning of the original passage

Checklist for Integrating Paraphrases into a Document

✔ Identify the source of the paraphrased material.

✔ Compare the original passage with your paraphrase. Make sure not only
that you have conveyed the meaning of the passage but also that the
wording and sentence structure differ from those in the original
passage.

✔ Use transitions and attributions to integrate the paraphrase smoothly
into your document.

✔ Ensure that the source is cited in your works-cited or references list.

Learn more about integrating paraphrases into your
document in Chapter 15.

9.4 Summarize

A summary is a concise statement, written in your own words, of
information found in a source. Unlike paraphrases, which are about
as long as the text on which they are based, summaries are shorter
than the text being summarized. When you integrate a summary
into your draft, review the source to make sure your summary
fairly and accurately conveys the ideas in the original source. Be
careful, as well, to identify the source and include a citation.

Summarize an Entire Source

Writers frequently summarize an entire document. In some
cases, the summary might occupy one or more paragraphs or

be integrated into a discussion contained in one or more paragraphs. In other cases, the summary might be as brief as a single sentence.

Below, a writer summarizes a report that explores economic incentives for using thermal energy to generate electricity:

9.4

In 2014, the National Renewable Energy Laboratory published *Geothermal Exploration Policy Mechanisms: Lessons for the United States from International Applications.* This report provides an analysis of potential government incentives for developing new utility-scale geothermal electric projects. Report authors Bethany Speer, Ryan Economy, Travis Lowder, Paul Schwabe, and Scott Regenthal note that, while the United States has the largest installed base of geothermal power facilities in the world, growth has been slow over the past decade. To increase our reliance on this low-impact form of energy production, they recommend that the federal government formulate policies and offer economic incentives that address the most significant obstacles to growth: the high risks and high costs of drilling to locate reliable sources of geothermal energy.

The major recommendations from the report

The main point of the report

The author, title, and publication date are identified in the text, so parenthetical citation is not required for either MLA or APA style.

In contrast, the same writer offered a much briefer, "nutshell" summary of a related source:

In an article published in the journal *Renewable & Sustainable Energy Reviews,* Kewen Li and his colleagues (2015) analyzed the relatively slow growth of geothermal power and offered a framework for new development in this energy sector.

Following APA style, the publication date is identified in parentheses.

Summarize Specific Ideas and Information

You can also use summaries to convey key information or ideas from a source:

9.4

> The discussion of "Jails and Jailbirds" in Flexner's *I Hear*
> *America Talking* lists seventeen informal or slang words
> Americans have used for jails, in addition to the standard
> word "penitentiary,"[10] which was coined in Quaker
> Pennsylvania in the late 1700s.

Per *Chicago* style, a citation appears as a numbered footnote.

The summary identifies the author and specific source of the ideas.

Summarize a Group of Sources

It's common to read phrases such as "Numerous authors have argued . . ." or "The research in this area indicates that . . ." These kinds of collective summaries allow you to make a point briefly and with authority. They are effective particularly at the beginning of a document, when you are establishing a foundation for your argument, and they can serve as a transitional device when you move from one major section of the document to another.

When you are summarizing a group of sources, separate the citations with a semicolon.

> Several critics have argued that the young Beethoven
> had a profound effect on Mozart in his later years
> (Graulich 217; Sherman 78; Watters 33).

> The emergence of promising new drugs for hepatitis C
> has been well documented (Page, 2019; Richards, 2017;
> Vincent, 2018).

APA guidelines require including author and date information.

Per MLA style, the authors and page numbers are provided in parentheses.

Checklist for Integrating Summaries into a Document

✔ Identify the source you are summarizing.

✔ Ensure that you have summarized the source in your own words instead of stringing together a series of close paraphrases.

✔ Use transitions and attributions to integrate the summary smoothly into your document.

✔ Ensure that the source is cited in your works-cited or references list.

> Learn more about integrating summaries into your document in Chapter 15.

9.5 Present Numerical Information

Some arguments and ideas are bolstered by numerical information, such as statistics. You can present this information within your text, or you might use tables, charts, or graphs. Keep in mind that you still need to accurately and fairly present the numerical

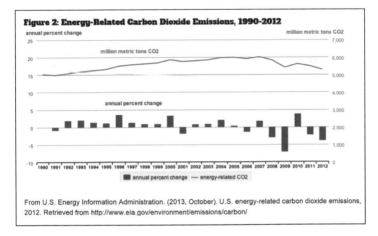

Figure 2: Energy-Related Carbon Dioxide Emissions, 1990-2012

From U.S. Energy Information Administration. (2013, October). U.S. energy-related carbon dioxide emissions, 2012. Retrieved from http://www.eia.gov/environment/emissions/carbon/

Chart on a website

information in your document and clearly identify the source of the information, just as you would for textual information.

For more information about using tables, charts, and graphs, see pp. 82–83 (Sec. 5.3).

9.6 Use Images, Audio, Video, and Animations

Including images in your print document and images, audio, video, or animation files in your electronic document can enhance its effectiveness. Use caution, however, when taking media from other sources. Simply copying it into your document might violate copyright rules (p. 153).

Writer to Writer

How should you integrate media sources in a digital document?
In a digital document, such as a website or a multimedia presentation, use the following approach for integrating media.

- Make a link between your document and a document that contains an image, sound clip, or video clip rather than simply copying the image and placing it in your document.

- If it isn't possible or appropriate to create a link to another document, you should contact the owner of the image, sound clip, or video clip for permission to use it.

As you do for the other sources you cite in your document, be sure to present images, audio, or video fairly and identify their authors or creators.

10. Understand and Avoid Plagiarism

Few writers intentionally try to pass off the work of others as their own. However, deadlines and other pressures can lead writers to take notes poorly and cite sources improperly. When this happens, it can damage the relationship you are trying to establish with your readers.

Citing sources is a rhetorical act that allows your readers to determine which of the ideas and information in your document are your own and which are drawn from your sources. If readers suspect you haven't acknowledged your sources, they may doubt your credibility, and they might even stop reading your document. Worse, submitting academic work that does not include proper identification of sources might result in failing a course or some other disciplinary action.

10.1 Understand Plagiarism

Plagiarism is a form of intellectual dishonesty. It involves either unintentionally using someone else's work without properly acknowledging where the ideas or information came from (the most common form of plagiarism) or intentionally passing off someone else's work as your own (the most serious form of plagiarism).

Plagiarism is based on the notion of "copyright," or ownership of a document or idea. Like a patent, which protects an invention, a copyright protects an author's investment of time and energy in the creation of a document. Essentially, it assures authors that when they create a document, someone else won't be able to steal ideas from it and profit from that theft without penalty.

10.1

> ## Writer to Writer
>
> *Isn't plagiarism simply another form of remixing?*   Plagiarism in academic writing differs in important ways from the kind of mixing and remixing that takes place in popular culture. While listeners enjoying a song on the radio might not be surprised to hear part of another song added to a mix, readers of an article in *Time* magazine or an academic journal expect that all passages from other writers will be cited properly. The authors of those passages do, too. Context matters, and in this case the context of academic writing differs significantly from that of popular culture.

Unintentional Plagiarism

In most cases, plagiarism is unintentional, and most cases of unintentional plagiarism result from taking poor notes or failing to use them properly. You are plagiarizing if you:

- Quote a passage in a note but neglect to include quotation marks and then later insert the quotation into your document without remembering that it is a direct quotation.

- Include a paraphrase that differs so slightly from the original passage that it might as well be a direct quotation.

- Don't clearly distinguish between your ideas and ideas that come from your sources.

- Neglect to list the source of a paraphrase, quotation, or summary in your text or in your works-cited list.

Although unintentional plagiarism is, by definition, something that the writer hasn't planned to do, it is likely to have consequences. Some instructors might require that an assignment be rewritten; others might impose a penalty, such as a lowered grade or failure on the assignment.

Intentional Plagiarism

Intentional plagiarism is a form of intellectual dishonesty and is taken very seriously. It can lead to academic penalties ranging from a reduced grade on an assignment to failure of a course to expulsion from school. Intentional plagiarism includes:

10.1

- Engaging in "patchwork writing," which involves piecing together passages from two or more sources without acknowledging the sources and without properly quoting or paraphrasing.

- Creating fake citations to mislead a reader about the sources of information used in a document.

- Copying or closely paraphrasing extended passages from another document and passing them off as the writer's original work.

- Copying an entire document and passing it off as the writer's original work.

- Purchasing a document and passing it off as the writer's original work.

Writer to Writer

Can you use an essay in more than one class?   Reusing an assign-ment for more than one class, often referred to as self-plagiarism, is generally frowned on by writing instructors. If you wrote a term paper in one class and then turned it in for a grade in another, you wouldn't learn anything new about conducting research, develop-ing an argument, considering your readers, and so on.

On the other hand, if you've written previously about a topic that still intrigues you, you might ask your instructor if you could build on your earlier work. Similarly, if you're working on a new topic that is relevant to two of your current classes, you might talk with your instructors about completing a more ambitious project for both classes.

10.2

10.2 Understand How to Avoid Plagiarism

To ensure your writing is an honest exchange of information, ideas, and arguments, you should carry out your research ethically. In general, you should:

- Acknowledge the sources used in your document. By doing so, you show respect for the work that others have done before you.

- Accurately and fairly represent the information, ideas, and arguments you've taken from sources—to ensure that you do not misrepresent that work to your readers.

- Provide citation information for your sources. These citations help your readers understand how you have drawn your conclusions and where they can locate those sources should they want to consult them.

These three rules are the essence of research ethics. Several strategies can help you research ethically and avoid unintentional plagiarism.

Conduct a Knowledge Inventory

When you are just beginning to learn about an issue, you might find it difficult not only to express your own ideas clearly but also to restate or reframe the information, ideas, and arguments you've encountered in your sources. You don't want to end up with a document composed of passages that have been copied without attribution or paraphrased too closely. Start with a knowledge inventory to gain insights into what you do and don't understand about the issue. Ask yourself three questions.

- What do you already know about the issue?

- What don't you know?

- What do you want to know?

Your answers can provide a starting point for brainstorming, collecting and working with sources, and planning. They can also serve as a guide for discussing the issue with others, such as your instructor, a librarian, or people who are knowledgeable about the issue. These discussions can help you determine the most productive ways to learn more about your issue.

10.2

Take Notes Carefully

Unintentional plagiarism occurs most often when a writer takes poor notes, such as direct quotations that are not enclosed by quotation marks, paraphrases that are too close to the original passage, and summaries that repeat a source's exact phrasing. Taking notes accurately and appropriately is the first — and arguably the most important — step in avoiding unintentional plagiarism.

As you take notes, keep the following guidelines in mind:

- Enclose every quotation in quotation marks.

- Look for notes that differ from your usual style of writing. If a note doesn't sound like your own writing, it probably isn't. Double-check the note against the original source.

- Ensure that every paraphrase differs in both wording and sentence structure from the original passage.

- Avoid creating summaries that are little more than a patchwork of sentences pulled from the original source.

- Include publication information about the source on every note.

- Double-check your notes to be sure that they are accurate and complete.

> **For more on quoting, paraphrasing, and summarizing, see Chapter 9.**

10.2

Writer to Writer

Do you always need permission to use source materials? If you do not plan to publish a course assignment online or in print, you generally can use material from another source without seeking permission. Remember, however, that in all cases you must still cite the source of the material you use.

Writers who plan to publish their work should seek permission to use material from a source if they want to quote a lengthy passage or, in the case of shorter works such as poems and song lyrics, a significant percentage of the source.

To seek permission to use a source, explain why and how you want to use it. Many authors and publishers allow academic use of their work but frown on commercial uses. When you contact an author or a publisher, include your name and contact information, the source you wish to use, your purpose in using it, and the context in which it will be used.

Cite Your Sources

Include a complete citation for each source you refer to in your document. The citation should appear both in the text of the document and in a works-cited or references list. In the body of your document, use author attributions to clearly distinguish information, ideas, and arguments drawn from your sources. Signal your use of information from sources with phrases such as "according to Reid Vincent" and "Jessica Richards argues" (p. 140, Sec. 9.1).

Writer to Writer

How can you tell what is common knowledge? Although crediting other authors for their work is important, some of the information you'll use will probably be common knowledge. Common knowledge is information that is widely known, such as the fact that the Declaration of Independence was signed in 1776. Or it might be the kind of knowledge that people working in a particular field use on a regular basis.

As you explore your topic, you will begin to identify what is generally known. For instance, if three or more sources use the same information without citing its source, you can assume that the information is common knowledge. If those sources use the information and cite the source, however, make sure you cite it as well.

10.2

Understand Why Writers Plagiarize

Although most plagiarism is unintentional, some students plagiarize deliberately. The most common reasons offered to explain intentional plagiarism—and steps you can take to avoid falling victim to its temptation—are listed below.

- **"It's easier to plagiarize."** Some people believe it takes less work to cheat than to create an original document. That's probably true—but only in the short term.

- **"I ran out of time."** Most writers occasionally find themselves wondering where all the time has gone and how they can possibly complete an assignment on schedule. If you find yourself in this situation, contact your instructor about a revised deadline. You might face a penalty for turning in work late, but it will almost certainly be less severe than the penalty for intentional plagiarism.

- **"I couldn't care less about this assignment."** It's not unusual to put off assignments that don't interest you. Rather than avoiding the work, try to approach the assignment in a way that interests you (p. 18, Sec. 2.1).

- **"I'm no good at writing."** A lot of people have doubts about their ability to earn a good grade in a writing course. If you lack confidence, seek assistance from your instructor, a campus writing center, a tutoring center, or a friend or family member.

- **"I didn't think I'd get caught."** Some students believe that they won't get caught plagiarizing. Most writing instructors, however, become familiar with their students' writing styles, and plagiarism detection software increases the likelihood that plagiarism will be detected.

- **"Everybody cheats."** Some people fear that if they don't plagiarize, they'll be at a competitive disadvantage. In fact, the number of students who plagiarize is actually quite low. Few students plagiarize intentionally, and those who do still tend to earn lower grades than their peers.

- **"This course is a waste of my time."** If you view a course as little more than a box that needs to be checked, it might seem reasonable to check that box with as little effort as possible. If you're caught plagiarizing, however, you'll most likely receive a reduced—or failing—grade for the assignment or the course. Instead of plagiarizing, talk with the instructor or an academic adviser about your lack of interest. You might find that the course actually has some relevance to your interests and career plans.

10.3 Understand How to Address Accusations of Plagiarism

If your instructor or supervisor expresses concerns about the originality of your work or your use of sources, ask for a meeting to discuss the situation. To prepare for the meeting:

- Review your document to identify passages that might have raised suspicions.

- Collect the sources and other materials you've used in your writing project.

- Collect materials you've written during the project, such as the results of brainstorming and freewriting sessions; organizational materials you've created, such as clusters, maps, and outlines; and rough and final drafts of your document.

- Reflect on your writing process.

During the meeting, listen to the concerns of your instructor before responding. It's natural to feel defensive about the situation, but try to understand why your instructor has concerns about your document. Take notes during the meeting, think carefully about what has been said, and respond as clearly as possible. Your instructor might have follow-up questions about the sources you've used, your writing process, or your draft.

10.3

If you find that you have engaged in unintentional plagiarism, ask your instructor for guidance about how to avoid it in the future. Ask, as well, what consequences you might face should it be determined that you have plagiarized intentionally.

If you and your instructor are unable to resolve the situation, you might face a disciplinary process. Learn as much as you can about the academic integrity policies at your institution.

Draft Your Document

Part 4: Draft Your Document

Working with sources and reflecting on what you've learned prepare you to draft your contribution to the conversation.

11. Define Your Thesis Statement

12. Support Your Main Point

13. Organize Your Ideas

14. Write Your First Draft

15. Use Sources to Accomplish Your Purpose

16. Write Effective Introductions

17. Write Effective Conclusions

11. Define Your Thesis Statement

Your main point is the foundation for your argument. Expressed first as a position and then as a thesis statement supported by reasons and evidence, it is shaped by your purpose, role, readers, genre, and knowledge of the conversation you've chosen to enter.

11.1 Take a Position

Writers take a position when they react to what they've learned, develop opinions about it, or decide to take actions because of it. When you're new to a conversation, your position is likely to be tentative and incomplete. As you learn more, your position will become more clearly defined and well thought out.

Let your writing situation guide you as you take a position on the issue or subject you've been reading about. Reflecting on how you are approaching the conversation will prepare you for the work of developing your thesis statement and, eventually, your draft.

Review Your Notes

The first step in taking a position is to reread your notes and consider what you've learned. During your review, do the following:

- List important information, ideas, and arguments that you've come across in your reading.

- Consider what interests you about those ideas and arguments.

- Review and elaborate on the ideas and arguments that you've come up with as a result of your own thinking about the subject.

When you complete your review, identify the ideas you would most like to address in your document.

11.2

Focus on Your Purposes and Roles

Just as your role as a writer has an impact on your writing question (p. 23, Sec. 2.3) so, too, will it shape your position. Adopting the role of *observer* (reflecting) or *interpreter* (analyzing) will lead to positions that differ significantly from those that might emerge from roles such as *problem solver* (defining or solving problems) or *advocate* (convincing or persuading).

Reflect on Your Readers

Consider whether taking a particular position will help you address your readers' purposes, needs, interests, knowledge, experiences, values, and beliefs. If you find that your position is not well aligned with your readers' concerns, revise it.

Draft a Position Statement

Decide on your position by brainstorming as you did early in your writing project. You need not write more than a sentence or two and you need not edit your preliminary position carefully. Focus, instead, on your overall take on the conversation and what you might want to say to the other readers and writers involved in it. Consider the following:

> Some of our coaches seem to be playing fast and loose with NCAA recruiting rules.

11.2 Draft Your Thesis Statement

To develop your thesis statement, think about how your position relates to the type of document you will write and to the information, ideas, and arguments you want to include. Then try out different ways of phrasing your thesis statement. As you develop each new version, try to predict how your readers will react to it.

Consider Genre

An effective thesis statement will suit the genre you plan to write (p. 6, Sec. 1.2). An academic essay generally contains a calm, clearly written statement of what you want readers to learn, believe, or do. A newspaper article presents information in a balanced and seemingly unbiased manner. An opinion column will be more assertive, and perhaps more entertaining, in its treatment of an issue.

Argumentative Academic Essay

- The university should ensure that its recruiting practices are in full compliance with NCAA regulations.

A strong but formal assertion

Informative Newspaper Article

- The university is taking steps to bring its recruiting practices in line with NCAA regulations.

A seemingly unbiased statement of fact

Opinion Column

- The university's coaches need to get their act together before the NCAA slaps them with sanctions.

A focus on opinion rather than primarily on facts and an informal tone

Identify Keywords

Begin developing your thesis statement by identifying important information, ideas, and arguments related to your position. When you first explored a conversation (see Chapter 2), you asked questions to learn about your subject. Review those questions and examine them for keywords and phrases. Then look through your notes to see how your sources address those questions or use those keywords and phrases. The following example shows a list of initial questions and the important information, ideas, and arguments a writer found in her sources.

Questions about how writing teachers respond *to* student work

What are the most common ways that teachers give students feedback *on their* written work?

11.2

Have different approaches *to* writing feedback *been studied? Are any proven to be more successful than others?*

Is written feedback *more effective than* oral feedback?

What is the goal *of feedback on* student writing?

What my sources say:

Feedback that makes observations is more valuable than feedback that evaluates whether writing is good or bad, successful or unsuccessful (Johnston para. 5).

Teacher feedback encourages students to do more than just improve their sentences; it helps them develop important habits of mind (Sommers para. 16).

What goes on in a successful classroom is far more than just "teaching writing"; it extends to what students learn about being citizens of the world (Sommers para. 19).

> The writer circled keywords and phrases in her initial questions about her subject and then identified sources that address those keywords and phrases.

Use the keywords and phrases you've identified in the various versions of thesis statements that you try out.

Draft Candidates

A powerful thesis statement can invite your readers to learn something new, suggest that they change their attitudes or beliefs, or argue that they should take action of some kind.

Consider how the following thesis statements reflect these three ways of focusing a position statement.

11.2

Position Statement

Teachers should take more classes about writing theory and classroom practice and participate in more professional development on the job.

Thesis Statement: Asking Your Readers to Learn Something New

Recent research on how teachers give feedback has identified students' most common writing problems and teachers' most common responses.

Thesis Statement: Asking Your Readers to Change Their Attitudes or Beliefs

When teachers give feedback on written work, they are communicating to students values and ideals that go beyond the classroom.

Thesis Statement: Asking Your Readers to Take Action

Parents should demand that school districts provide more research about and guidance for responding to student work.

Experiment with different approaches to determine which one works best for your writing situation. The thesis statement you choose should convey your position in a way that addresses your purposes and your readers' needs, interests, backgrounds, and knowledge of a subject. For example, if you're focusing on the causes of a problem, your thesis statement should identify those causes. If you're arguing for a particular solution to a problem, your thesis statement should identify that solution.

Hone Your Thesis Statement

A broad thesis statement has no bite. The following thesis statement is too broad; it makes an observation, but it goes no further.

11.2

Broad Thesis Statement

The feedback that teachers provide on written work has a big impact on students' development as writers.

To focus your thesis statement, ask what should be learned, what attitudes should be changed, or what action should be taken. Consider readers' likely responses to your thesis statement, and then attempt to head off potential counterarguments or questions.

Focused Thesis Statement

Because the feedback that teachers provide has a strong impact on students' development as writers, teacher training programs should incorporate best practices for responding to student writing.

Keep in mind that your thesis statement is a work in progress. Stay alert to new ideas and information that might change your position. Continue to refine or even substantially revise your thesis statement so that you can better frame the issue for your readers.

12. Support Your Main Point

Your readers will expect you to do more than simply present your main point as a thesis statement. They'll look for reasons and evidence to back it up.

12.1 Choose Reasons to Support Your Main Point

To choose reasons to support your main point, consider what your readers are likely to know about the issue, the kinds of questions they might have about it, and the conclusion you hope to share with them. Your reasons should be acceptable to your readers and consistent with your purpose and role as a writer (p. 166).

Readers should understand and, ideally, accept the connections you make between your main point and reasons. In argumentative writing, these connections are often referred to as *warrants* (p. 65, Sec. 4.8). Your readers might accept the connection because they share your values and beliefs or have similar experiences with and knowledge of the issue you are addressing; because you've explained it effectively; or because they're so familiar with the genre that it won't be necessary to explain the connection. For example, if you are writing a restaurant review, you won't need to explain why reasons such as "the food tastes great" and "the service is outstanding" support your main point that the restaurant is worth visiting.

12.2 Gather Evidence to Support Your Reasons

You can draw on a wide range of evidence to support your reasons. Your evidence might take the form of quotations, paraphrases, summaries, numerical data, and visual images. It might take the form of data from interviews, observations, and surveys. It might be drawn from your personal experiences. And it might emerge from analysis of your subject.

Use Search Tools and the Library

You can search for information in a wide range of published sources, including those found in libraries, the news media, on the web, and in social media. These sources can range from peer-reviewed scholarly and professional publications, such as books and journal articles, to news stories that are reviewed by professional editors, websites that promote everything from commercial products to social and political issues, and informal (and not necessarily well-considered) posts to social media sites such as Facebook and Twitter.

Conduct Field Research

Writers frequently use field research to learn about an issue and to produce evidence they can use to support their reasoning about a topic or issue. News reporters, for example, routinely interview people who know about or have been affected by an issue. Social scientists frequently use observation and surveys to collect information. And many writers use correspondence — in particular, email and other forms of messaging — to seek information from experts on an issue. Field research methods are often tailored specifically to a writing situation. Interview and survey questions, for instance, can be narrowly focused. As a result, information gathered through field research methods can be highly relevant to the main point and reasons you present in your document.

To learn about searching libraries, news media, social media, and the web and conducting field research, see Chapter 6.

12.3 Reflect on Your Reasons and Evidence

Reflection allows you to think deeply about a particular subject — in this case, your main point and the reasons and evidence you've assembled to support it. You might think about your main point in relation to your personal experiences. You might reflect on it in relation to what you've learned through your investigation of your conversation. You might try to understand it through the lens of story. However you choose to engage in reflection, you'll find that it offers the opportunity to connect what you learn through your reflections to what you already know, to gain insights that you had not yet considered, and to develop a deeper understanding of the subject.

12.4

As you reflect, keep track of your ideas through writing, dictating, clustering, mapping, or simply sketching your ideas on a piece of paper. The process of recording your ideas may lead you to engage in further reflection. As you read what you've written, you might find your thoughts heading in new directions.

12.4 Analyze Your Reasons and Evidence

Analysis is a structured form of reflection. Engaged in rigorously, it can help you draw conclusions about the origins, qualities, significance, or potential effects of a subject. A strong analysis requires a well-crafted interpretive question, a thorough understanding of your subject, and a rigorous and fair application of an appropriate interpretive framework. It also requires a clear understanding of your writing situation.

Your primary goal in analyzing your main point, reasons, and evidence is to help your readers understand the connections among them. In argumentative writing, these connections are often referred to as *appeals* (p. 66, Sec. 4.8). As you present your reasons and evidence, think about how to convey the connections you see by using appeals to logic, authority, emotion, character, principles, values, and beliefs. Consider as well, given your readers, whether to simply leave those connections unstated.

Establish Your Starting Points

Analysis typically begins with a question. If you've already developed a writing question, you can use it to carry out your analysis. If not, review the discussion in Chapter 2 (pp. 23–28, Sec. 2.3) about how to develop a writing question. Typically, writers assess their understanding of the subject or issue they are writing about before conducting their analysis.

12.4   Analysis involves applying an interpretive framework to your subject or issue. An interpretive framework is a set of strategies for identifying patterns that has been used successfully and refined over time by writers interested in a given subject area or a particular field. Writers can choose from specialized frameworks used in disciplines across the arts, sciences, social sciences, humanities, engineering, and business. A historian, for example, might apply a feminist, political, or cultural analysis, among others, to interpret diaries written by women who worked in defense plants during World War II, while a sociologist might conduct correlational tests to interpret the results of a survey. In a writing course, you'll most likely use one of the broad interpretive frameworks discussed here: trend analysis, causal analysis, data analysis, text analysis, and rhetorical analysis.

Seek a Fuller Understanding of Your Subject

If you've ever met people who don't know what they're talking about but nonetheless are certain of their opinions, you'll recognize the dangers of applying an interpretive framework before you thoroughly understand your subject. If you seek to enhance your understanding of your subject or issue, use *division* and *classification*.

Division breaks a subject into its parts and considers what each contributes to the whole. A financial analyst, for example, might examine the various groups within a company to understand what each group does and how it contributes to the overall value of the company. As you use division, you might find that a part is essential—or that it makes little or no contribution to the whole.

12.4

Classification places your subject — or each part of your subject — into a category, allowing you to discover how and to what extent your subject or a part of your subject is similar to others in the same category and how it differs from those in other categories. For example, if you are analyzing state representatives, you might place them in standard categories: Democrat, Republican, Libertarian, Green, and so on. Or you might create categories especially for your analysis, such as who voted for or against particular types of legislation. Identifying those similarities and differences, in turn, allows you to consider the subject, or its parts, in relation to the other items in your categories.

Classification and division are often used in combination, particularly when you want to consider similarities and differences among different parts of your subject.

Analyze Trends

Trend analysis is a frequently used interpretive framework. Trend analysis focuses on sequences of events and the relationships among them. It is based on the assumption that understanding what has happened in the past allows us to make sense of what is happening in the present and to draw inferences about what is likely to happen in the future.

To conduct a trend analysis, gather enough information to establish that a trend exists. If the information supports the presence of a trend, you can speculate about its causes, effects, and whether it will continue.

Be cautious with trend analysis. Some analysts seem willing to declare a trend on the flimsiest set of observations: when an NFL team wins the Super Bowl for the second year in a row, for instance, some sports writers are quick to announce the start of a dynasty. As you look for trends, cast a wide net. Learn as much as you can about the history of your subject, and carefully assess it to determine how often events related to your subject have moved in one direction or another.

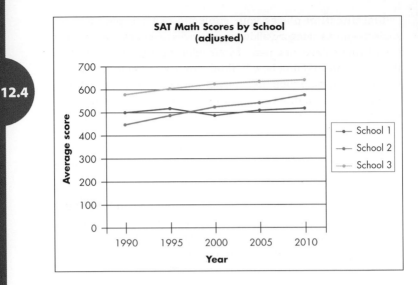

Trend analysis looks for patterns that hold up over time.

. . . .

Analyze Causes and Effects

Causal analysis focuses on the factors that bring about a particular situation. It can be applied to a wide range of subjects,
such as the Great Recession, the rise of terrorist groups, or
the impact of calorie restriction on longevity. Writers carry
out causal analysis when they believe that understanding the
underlying reasons for a situation will help people address
the situation and its likelihood of recurring or understand its
potential consequences.

In many ways, causal analysis is a form of detective work.
It involves tracing a sequence of events and exploring the
connections among them. Because the connections are almost
always more complex than they appear, it pays to be thorough.

- **Uncover as many causes as you can.** Effects rarely emerge from
  a single cause. Most effects are the results of a complex web

of causes, some of which are related to one another and some of which are not. Although it might be tempting, for example, to say that a murder victim died (the effect) from a gunshot wound (the cause), that would tell only part of the story. You would need to work backward from the murderer's decision to pull the trigger to the factors that led to that decision, and then further back to the causes underlying those factors.

12.4

- **Effects can also become causes.** While investigating the murder, for instance, you might find that the murderer was jumpy from the steroids he'd been taking in an attempt to qualify for the Olympic trials in weight lifting, that he had long been envious of the victim's success, and that he had just found his girlfriend in the victim's arms. Exploring how these factors might be related—and determining when they are not—will help you understand the web of causes leading to the effect.

- **Determine which causes are significant.** Not all causes contribute equally to an effect. Perhaps our murderer was cut off on the freeway on his way to meet his girlfriend. Lingering anger at the other driver might have been enough to push him over the edge, but it probably wouldn't have caused the shooting by itself.

- **Distinguish between correlation and cause.** Too often, we assume that because one event occurred just before another, the first event caused the second. We might conclude that finding his girlfriend with another man drove the murderer to shoot in a fit of passion—only to discover that he had begun planning the murder months before, when the victim threatened to reveal his use of steroids to the press just prior to the Olympic trials.

- **Look beyond the obvious.** A thorough causal analysis considers not only the primary causes and effects but also those that might appear only slightly related to the subject. For example,

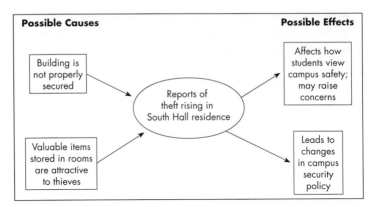

Causal analysis involves tracing connections among events.

you might consider how the murder affected not only the victim and perpetrator but also their families and friends, the wider community, an overburdened judicial system, and even attitudes toward Olympic athletes. By looking beyond the obvious causes and effects, you can deepen your understanding of the subject and begin to explore a much wider set of implications than you might have initially expected.

Analyze Data

Data analysis focuses on information, such as facts, observations, or statistics. Most of us analyze data in an informal way on a daily basis. For example, if you've looked at the percentage of people who favor a particular political candidate over another, you've engaged in data analysis. Analyzing numerical information related to your subject can help you better understand the subject and explore relationships among its parts.

To begin a data analysis, gather your data and enter the numbers into a spreadsheet or statistics program. You can use the program's tools to sort the data and conduct tests. If your set of data is small, you can use a piece of paper and a calculator. As you carry out your analysis, keep the following guidelines in mind:

12.4

- **Data can be descriptive.** If you conduct a survey (p. 118, Sec. 6.3), you can use the data to understand who completed the survey and how they responded. You can look at standard groupings, such as gender, age, race, ethnicity, and educational attainment.

- **Data can be categorized.** To classify the results of your survey, you might compare responses from different groups of respondents, such as various genders. You might look at each group's average level of agreement with a statement in your survey. Or you might use statistical techniques using spreadsheet programs or statistical programs such as Microsoft Excel or SPSS.

- **Data can help you understand relationships.** Correlation tests allow you to draw conclusions about your subject. For example, you might want to know whether support for proposed changes to graduation requirements increases or decreases according to GPA. A correlation test might indicate that a positive relationship exists — that support goes up as GPA increases. Be careful, however, not to confuse causation with correlation. Tests will show, for example, that as shoe size increases, so do scores on reading tests. Does this mean that large feet improve reading? Not really. The cause of higher reading scores appears to be attending school longer. High school students tend to score better on reading tests than do students in elementary school — and, on average, high school students tend to have much larger feet.

12.4

Take great care to ensure the integrity of your analysis. You will run into problems if you collect too little data, if the data is not representative, or if the data is collected sloppily. Similarly, you should base your conclusions on a thoughtful and careful examination of the results of your tests. Picking and choosing evidence that supports your conclusion might be tempting, but you'll do a disservice to yourself and your readers if you fail to consider all the results of your analysis.

Analyze Texts

Today, the word *text* can refer to a wide range of printed or digital works — and even some forms of artistic expression that we

Use of Social-Networking Sites	# surveyed	% who use social networking regularly
Gender		
Male	48	56%
Female	42	65%
Age		
16–20	20	85%
21–30	31	71%
31–45	28	46%
45+	11	27%
Education		
Some high school	12	35%
High school graduate	25	56%
Some college	34	65%
College graduate	16	64%
Graduate school	7	62%

Data analysis can involve assessing information from a variety of sources.

might not think of as documents. Texts open to interpretation include novels, poems, plays, essays, articles, movies, speeches, blogs, songs, paintings, photographs, sculptures, performances, websites, videos, television shows, and computer games.

Students enrolled in writing classes often use the elements of literary analysis to analyze texts. In this form of analysis, interpreters focus on theme, plot, setting, characterization, imagery, style, and structure, as well as the contexts — social, cultural, political, and historical — that shape a work. Writers who use this form of analysis focus both on what is actually presented in the text and on what is implied. They rely heavily on close reading of the text to discern meaning, critique an author's technique, and search for patterns that help them understand the text as fully as possible. They also tend to consider other elements of the wider writing situation in which the text was produced — in particular, the author's purpose, intended audience, use of sources, and choice of genre.

If you carry out a text analysis, keep the following guidelines in mind:

- **Focus on the text itself.** Although you will typically reflect on the issues raised by your interpretation, maintain a clear focus on the text in front of you, and keep your analysis grounded firmly in what you can locate within it. Background information and related sources, such as scholarly articles and essays, can support and enhance your analysis, but they can't do the work of interpretation for you.

- **Consider the text in its entirety.** Particularly in the early stages of learning about a text, it's easy to be distracted by a startling idea or an intriguing concept. Try to review the full text before focusing on a particular aspect of the text.

- **Avoid "cherry-picking."** Cherry-picking refers to the process of using only those portions of a text that support your overall interpretation and ignoring aspects that might weaken or contradict your interpretation. As you carry out your analysis, factor in *all* the evidence. If the text doesn't support your interpretation, rethink your conclusions.

 Read about the close reading that is often involved in text analysis in Chapter 3.

12.4

Analyze Rhetorical Situations

Rhetorical analysis focuses on the rhetorical situation (see p. 49) that shaped the creation of and response to a particular document. A rhetorical analysis, for example, might focus on how a particular document (written, visual, or some other form) achieved its purpose or on why readers reacted to it in a specific way.

 Read more about conducting rhetorical analysis on p. 49, Sec. 4.4.

13. Organize Your Ideas

A well-organized document allows readers to anticipate what will come next. Choose an organizing pattern that is appropriate to your writing situation. Then turn to mapping or outlining strategies to organize the reasons and evidence you'll use in your document.

13.1

13.1 Choose a Pattern

Organizing patterns provide an overall principle for arranging the reasons and evidence you plan to present in your document. Common organizing patterns include the following:

- **Chronology** The document's organization follows a sequence in which events occur over time. For example, you might focus attention on the events leading up to a recent election or during a certain time span.

- **Description** The document provides a point-by-point description of a subject, such as the typical architectural features of a suburb or the features of a new car. Description is best for documents that address physical spaces, objects, or people—things that we can see and observe—rather than theories or processes that are not visible.

- **Definition** The document lays out the distinguishing characteristics of a subject and then provides examples and reasoning to explain what differentiates it from similar subjects. A document defining *pride*, for example, might begin by stating that it is an emotion and then move on to explain why that particular emotion is not as harmful as many people believe.

- **Cause/Effect** The document is organized according to factors that lead to (cause) an outcome (effect). For example, you might identify the reasons behind a recent strike by grocery store employees or the health risks that contribute to heart disease.

- **Process Explanation** The document outlines the steps involved in doing something or explains how something happens. You might, for example, help readers understand the stages of nuclear fission or teach them what steps to take in the event of a meltdown in a nearby power plant.

- **Comparison/Contrast** The document identifies similarities and differences among the information, ideas, and arguments relevant to a subject. Documents that compare and contrast might use a point-by-point approach, in which the writer presents each relevant point individually and then analyzes how that point operates in the two items being compared. Or they might use a whole-by-whole approach, in which the writer addresses the first item in its entirety and then turns to the second item.

- **Pros/Cons** Ideas and information are organized to show support for and opposition to an argument or proposal. For example, a writer might organize an analysis of legislation calling for a ban on fracking by explaining why some groups support the legislation (pros) and others oppose it (cons).

- **Strengths/Weaknesses** The document examines positive and negative aspects of a subject, such as increasing federal funding for health care by instituting a national lottery. Documents using this organizing pattern typically work toward a conclusion stating that one or two considerations outweigh the others.

- **Costs/Benefits** The trade-offs associated with a subject, usually a choice or proposal of some sort, are considered in turn. For example, a document might discuss why the cost of implementing a particular educational initiative is justified (or not) by the potential for higher test scores.

- **Problem/Solution** The document defines a problem and discusses the appropriateness of one or more solutions. If multiple solutions are discussed, the writer usually asserts the merits of one solution over the others.

Choose an organizing pattern that reflects your purposes and role. If you're adopting the role of *reporter*, for example, you might select chronology, process explanation, or cause/effect. If you're adopting the role of *evaluator*, you're likely to choose strengths/weaknesses, costs/benefits, or comparison/contrast. If you're adopting the role of *advocate*, you might opt for an organizing pattern that is well suited to argumentation, such as pros/cons or problem/solution.

13.2

Keep in mind that a writer may use more than one organizing pattern in a document. For instance, a process explanation often works in tandem with chronology, since both present steps in a sequence. Similarly, a document using a problem/solution approach might also adopt a strengths/weaknesses pattern to evaluate potential solutions.

13.2 Create Maps and Outlines

Maps and outlines can represent the sequence in which your reasons and evidence will appear in your document. As you develop a map or an outline, consider how to present your reasons and the evidence you'll use to back them up. Later, use your map or outline as a plan for drafting your document.

Create a Map

Maps can help you explore sequences of reasons and evidence. For example, you might use a timeline to show how an argument builds on one supporting point after another. This use of maps is particularly effective as you begin to think about organizing your document, and it often relies on the organizing patterns discussed on pp. 183–185, such as chronology, cause/effect, comparison/contrast, costs/benefits, and problem/solution.

Here, a writer has mapped the reasons and evidence in an argumentative essay about U.S. reliance on private military corporations (PMCs) in its war on terror. Later, he'll use this map to develop an outline.

13.2

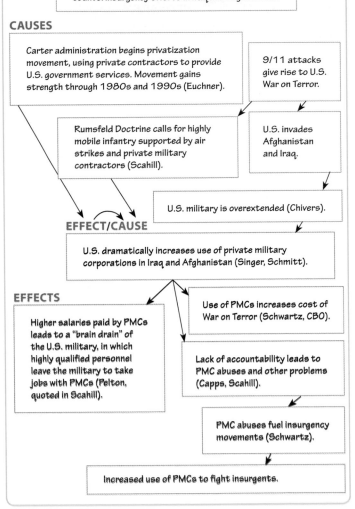

Thesis Statement: By relying heavily on PMCs to carry out military operations, the U.S. Department of Defense undermined its own counterinsurgency efforts in Iraq and Afghanistan.

CAUSES

Carter administration begins privatization movement, using private contractors to provide U.S. government services. Movement gains strength through 1980s and 1990s (Euchner).

9/11 attacks give rise to U.S. War on Terror.

Rumsfeld Doctrine calls for highly mobile infantry supported by air strikes and private military contractors (Scahill).

U.S. invades Afghanistan and Iraq.

U.S. military is overextended (Chivers).

EFFECT/CAUSE

U.S. dramatically increases use of private military corporations in Iraq and Afghanistan (Singer, Schmitt).

EFFECTS

Higher salaries paid by PMCs leads to a "brain drain" of the U.S. military, in which highly qualified personnel leave the military to take jobs with PMCs (Pelton, quoted in Scahill).

Use of PMCs increases cost of War on Terror (Schwartz, CBO).

Lack of accountability leads to PMC abuses and other problems (Capps, Scahill).

PMC abuses fuel insurgency movements (Schwartz).

Increased use of PMCs to fight insurgents.

Mapping an argument to trace causes and effects

· ·

Create an Informal Outline

Outlines can take many forms to show the structure of a document: a brief list of words, a series of short phrases, or even a series of sentences. You can use informal outlines to remind yourself of key points to address or of notes you should refer to when you begin drafting. In the informal outline shown here, each item represents a section the writer planned to include in an essay on attempts to limit coca production in South America.

---

1. Introduction—what is coca? where is it grown?

2. Cultural and economic importance of coca crop

3. Evo Morales's plan: "zero cocaine, not zero coca"

   • Benefits of the Morales plan

4. Brief history of other plans and their failures

   • U.S. "war on drugs"

   • aerial fumigation/coca eradication

   • alternative cropping

5. Conclusion supporting the Morales plan

An informal outline
. . . .

A thumbnail outline is another type of informal outline. In the following example, the writer identified the major sections in an essay and noted which sources could be used to provide background information and support the argument.

13.2

Intro
Introduce private military corporations as integral to U.S. military operations. Present the many costs of PMCs to be examined.

Section 1
Explain the history of PMCs, from the Napoleonic era to today. Focus on the post-9/11 era and how privatization of the U.S. military has increased in the last ten years. Key sources: interview transcripts from Brothers and Euchner.

Section 2
Discuss the frequent use of PMCs in Iraq and Afghanistan, as well as their diversified functions. Examine the distinction between PMCs and mercenaries. Key sources for background and argument: Scahill and Singer.

Section 3
Give examples of abuses and illegal acts by PMC contractors. Explain why contractors have not been convicted of crimes. Key sources for abuse evidence: Capps, Simpson, and Savage; key sources for lack of legal accountability: Singer, Yeoman, and Risen.

Section 4
Present the view that abuses by contractors undermine the image and goals of the U.S. military. Key sources: the Army Field Manual and the Congressional Research Service report.

Section 5
Discuss other "costs" of PMCs, in particular the amount of taxpayer money spent on them and the brain drain that occurs. Key sources: Stanger, Moshe, and Pelton.

Conclusion
Look at ways Americans can take civic action to end the overreliance on PMCs.

A thumbnail outline

Create a Formal Outline

A formal outline provides a complete and accurate list of the points you want to address in your document. Formal outlines use Arabic numerals, letters, and Roman numerals to indicate the hierarchy of information. An alternative approach, common in business and the sciences, uses numbering with decimal points:

13.2

```
I.
    A.
        1.
        2.
    B.
        1.
        2.
    II.
```

```
1.
    1.1
        1.1.1
        1.1.2
    1.2
        1.2.1
        1.2.2
2.
```

Writers use formal outlines to identify the hierarchy of information, ideas, and arguments. Create a formal outline to identify

- your main point and/or thesis statement,

- your reasons,

- the sequence in which those reasons should be presented,

- evidence for your reasons, and

- the notes and sources you should refer to as you work on your document.

The most common types of formal outlines are topical outlines and sentence outlines.

Topical outlines. Topical outlines present the topics and subtopics you plan to include in your research document as a series of words and phrases. Items at the same level of importance should be phrased in parallel grammatical form. In the following topical outline, the writer includes the thesis statement, lists the key points that will be made in the document, maps out the support for those key points, and uses a conventional system of numbers and letters.

13.2

Thesis statement: Although competitive sports can provide young female athletes with many benefits, they can also have negative effects, the worst of which is increasing drug use.

I.   Female Participation in Competitive Athletics
   A. Short history and current trends
   B. Understanding female athletes

II. Positive Impact of Competitive Athletics
   A. Physiological (Kane & Larkin)
      1. Reduced risk of obesity and heart disease
      2. Increased immune functioning and prevention of certain cancers
      3. Improved flexibility, strength, and aerobic power
   B. Psychological (Kane & Larkin)
      1. Improved self-esteem
      2. Enhanced mental health
      3. Reduced symptoms of stress, anxiety, and depression
   C. Sociological
      1. Expansion of social boundaries
      2. Teaches responsibility, discipline, and determination
      3. Education asset

III. Negative Impact of Competitive Athletics
   A. Physiological (Graham)
      1. Overtraining
      2. Eating disorders
      3. Exercise-induced amenorrhea and osteoporosis

Part of a topical outline

Sentence outlines. Sentence outlines use complete sentences to identify the points you want to cover. Sentence outlines typically serve two purposes.

- They begin the process of converting an outline into a draft of your document.

- They help you assess the structure of a document that you have already written.

When you've created your outline, ask whether it can serve as a blueprint for the first draft of your document. Taking the time to create an effective outline now will reduce the time needed to write your first draft later.

Thesis statement: Although competitive sports can provide young female athletes with many benefits, they can also have negative effects, the worst of which is increasing drug use.

I.   Society has been concerned with the use of performance-enhancing drugs among younger male athletes, but many don't know that these drugs are also used by female athletes.
    A.   Women began participating in sports in the mid-nineteenth century, although participation was not encouraged until recently. Millions of girls are involved in a wide range of physical activities and are participating in school-sponsored sports.
    B.   In response to the pressures of competitive sports, girls' steroid use has increased, and younger and younger girls are taking steroids.

II. Sports can benefit a girl's growth and development physiologically as well as psychologically and sociologically.
    A.   Participation in sports has a wide range of positive physiological effects on adolescent girls.

Part of a sentence outline

14. Write Your First Draft

14.2

To help your readers follow your argument, build on your efforts to organize your ideas, write effective paragraphs, use transitions to guide them through your document, and present your argument and ideas in a way that's easy to follow. Your first draft lays the foundation for additional drafts that will take shape as you refine your ideas.

14.1 Use Your Map or Outline

Your map or outline provides a framework you can use to draft your document. You can translate a bulleted list of items, for instance, into a series of brief sentences, or write paragraphs based on the key points in the map or outline. If you created a formal outline, you can use each main point as a topic sentence for a paragraph and each subpoint as a supporting sentence.

Check your outline to see whether you have presented your points effectively. Pay particular attention to the evidence you will use, checking whether you are

- providing enough evidence to support your points,

- relying too heavily on a limited number of sources, or

- relying too heavily on support from sources that favor one side of the conversation.

As you work on your document, you might find it necessary to reorganize your ideas or add evidence. Think of your map or outline as a flexible guide rather than a rigid blueprint.

14.2 Focus Your Paragraphs

Writers use paragraphs to present and develop a central idea. Paragraphs often have a topic sentence in which the writer makes an assertion, offers an observation, or asks a question. The rest of the sentences in the paragraph should elaborate on the topic. Aim for paragraphs that are focused, unified, and well developed. The following paragraph presents and supports one central idea:

14.3

> The central idea of the paragraph follows an initial question.

> Given the potential costs in justice and national security, why hire military contractors at all? Ironically, perhaps the most often cited reason for using private contractors is that using these corporations saves the taxpayer money because the government can hire them on an as-needed basis and does not have to pay for contractors' training, health care, or pensions. Professor Allison Stanger of Middlebury College challenges this notion in her 2009 book *One Nation Under Contract: The Outsourcing of American Power and the Future of Foreign Policy* when she points out that nearly all private contractors previously served in the military, meaning that many of them are receiving pension payments anyway. Stanger writes that "the federal government is effectively paying for the training and retirement of the contractors it hires, all appearances to the contrary, as well as paying double or triple the daily rate for their services." Therefore the Department of Defense would actually save taxpayers money by reversing the trend of privatization.

> The third and fourth sentences use evidence from a source.

> The final sentence draws a conclusion that supports the paragraph's central idea.

Depending on the complexity of your argument and the type of document you are writing, a single paragraph might be all you need to present a reason and its supporting evidence — or it might convey only part of your argument.

14.3 Organize Your Paragraphs

Effective paragraphs follow an organizing pattern, often the same one used in the document as a whole, such as chronology, description, or costs/benefits (p. 184). These common patterns help readers anticipate what you'll say. Readers who recognize a pattern, such as problem/solution, will find it easier to focus on your ideas and argument. Note how the following paragraph uses the problem/solution organizing pattern.

14.3

> The paragraph begins by restating the problem.

> The central idea of the paragraph is provided in the third sentence.

What can we do to help adolescent female athletes avoid illicit drug use? How can we help them avoid the pitfalls of competitive athletics? Parents, coaches, and the athletes themselves all play a crucial role in averting bad choices. First, parents and coaches need to be aware that performance-enhancing drugs are a problem. Some adults believe that steroid use is either minimal or non-existent among teenagers, but one early study concluded that "over half the teens who use steroids start before age 16, sometimes with the encouragement of their parents. . . . Seven percent said they first took 'juice' by age ten" (Dudley, p. 235).

> One part of the solution to the larger problem is provided.

> The fifth sentence provides evidence from a source to illustrate the nature of the problem.

Writer to Writer

What should you do if you've got writer's block?   There's a reason that staring blankly at the work you're trying to do has a name — it's pretty common. But don't give in. Try these strategies:

- **Eliminate distractions.** Switch off your phone and stay away from the internet. Turn off music, or play music you find inspiring. Get clutter off your desk.

- **Get up and move.** Take a walk, take out the trash, or do some jumping jacks. If you just need a brief recharge, do something physical that doesn't demand your full energy and attention as you mull over what you're writing.

- **Take a break.** If moving isn't enough, do something that will take your mind off your writing project altogether. Take a shower, call a friend, prepare a meal, do laundry.

- **Just write.** Write anything, preferably on your topic. You might even set a goal of writing a certain number of words in a certain period of time.

- **Write *to* someone.** If you were talking with a friend or mentor about your topic, what would you say? Would you start by asking questions? If so, write your questions down. Or perhaps you already have a plan, in which case imagine you're telling your friend what you want to say and then write that.

14.4

14.4 Create Transitions

Transitions help readers understand the relationships among sentences, paragraphs, and even sections of a document. They smooth the way and move the reader's eye along to what comes next.

No Transitions

There is no cost-effective way to store wind energy to provide electricity when the wind is not blowing. Wind generators and infrastructure to connect to the grid are expensive. Wind systems can harm wildlife such as birds, and in scenic areas many people dislike the way they look.

Inconsistent Transitions

First, there is no cost-effective way to store wind energy to provide electricity when the wind is not blowing. Another thing to keep in mind is that wind generators and infrastructure to connect to the grid are expensive. Also, wind systems can harm wildlife such as birds, and in scenic areas many people dislike the way they look.

14.4

Consistent Transitions

First, there is no cost-effective way to store wind energy to provide electricity when the wind is not blowing. Second, wind generators and infrastructure to connect to the grid are expensive. Third, wind systems can harm wildlife such as birds. And finally, in scenic areas many people dislike the way they look.

Transitions frequently appear as words and phrases, such as those used in the previous example. They can also take the form of sentences and paragraphs. Transitional sentences, such as the following, often appear at the end or beginning of paragraphs and serve to link two paragraphs.

The results of the tests revealed a surprising trend.

The outcome was far better than we could have hoped.

Transitional paragraphs, such as the following example, call attention to a major shift in focus within a document.

In the next section, we explore the reasons behind this surprising development. We focus first on the event itself. Then we consider the reasons underlying the event. Our goal is to call attention to the unique set of relationships that made this development possible.

Headings and subheadings can also act as transitions by signaling to the reader, through distinct formatting, that a new section is beginning. You can read more about formatting headings and subheadings later in this chapter.

As you create transitions, pay attention to the order in which you introduce new information and ideas. In general, it is best to refer to information and ideas that have already been introduced before introducing new information or ideas.

Introducing New Information First

Admissions staff look at the kind of courses students are taking, in addition to looking at grades.

Building on Information That Has Already Been Introduced

And it's not just grades that matter; admissions staff also look at the kind of courses students are taking.

The second example begins by referring to information from the previous paragraph, providing an effective transition to a new paragraph even as it introduces new information about additional college admissions criteria. In contrast, the first example leads with the new information.

14.4

Here are some common transitions and their functions:

To Help Readers Follow a Sequence	To Contrast
furthermore	however
in addition	on the other hand
moreover	nevertheless/nonetheless
next	despite
first/second/third	although/though
To Elaborate or Provide Examples	**To Signal a Concession**
for example	I admit that
for instance	of course
such as	granted
in fact	to be sure
indeed	**To Introduce a Conclusion**
to illustrate	as a result
To Compare	as a consequence
similarly	because of
in the same manner	therefore
like	thus
as in	for this reason

Writer to Writer

Is it okay to end a paragraph with a quotation?   Sometimes it is. Ask yourself whether you're being lazy by failing to analyze or comment on the quote and whether your point would be clearer if *you* said something more. But if the quotation is there because it makes your point better or more authoritatively than you feel you could, or if it serves as a comment on what you just said, feel free to use it as the final element of the paragraph.

14.5 Give Readers a Map

Think of maps as promises to your readers that help establish their expectations and convey your purposes for writing. You can use several strategies to give your readers a sense of where your document is taking them.

If you are working on an informative document, you might promise to explain the details of a complex issue to your readers. If you define a problem in your introduction, that definition signals that you will present a solution by the end of your document. If you begin with a surprising argument, you are promising to back it up with reasons and evidence that will intrigue your readers.

Build on Expectations

Like you, your readers are likely to be familiar with some of the more commonly used organizing patterns, such as strengths/weaknesses or comparison/contrast. Let their experiences work to your advantage. Try to provide what readers are likely to expect where they are most likely to expect it. This is not to say that your *content* ought to be exactly what they expect. Instead, focus on their expectations about structure, organization, and genre. If you've described the strengths of a particular object or argument, for instance, you can bet readers will expect you to discuss weaknesses before long.

Provide Signposts

The test of a well-organized document is whether readers can move smoothly through it without wondering, "Where did that come from?" As you draft, check whether your document is organized and designed consistently and predictably. You might find the following techniques useful in smoothing the way for your readers.

Provide Forecasts and Cross-References. A forecast—a type of transitional sentence (p. 195, Sec. 14.4)—prepares your readers for a shift in the focus of your document. A forecast at the end of a major section might say, "In the next section, you can read about. . . ." Cross-references tell your readers that they can find related information in another section of the document or let them know that a particular issue will be addressed in greater detail elsewhere. On a website, forecasts and cross-references might take the form of small images, flags, or links such as "Continue" or "Next."

14.5

Use Headings and Subheadings. You can help your readers keep their place in your document by using headings and subheadings. Your formatting should distinguish between headings (major sections) and subheadings (subsections).

Use a Menu. If you are writing a digital document such as a website or a multimodal essay, you can add a menu on the side, top, or bottom of your pages that readers can see as they work through your document.

Pay Attention to Design Principles. As you draft your document, follow the principles of effective design. Using a readable body font that is clearly different from the headings font, for example, can improve readability significantly. Similarly, breaking out information using bulleted and numbered lists, providing descriptive page headers or footers, and integrating illustrations effectively into your text can greatly enhance readability. If you are drafting a digital document, keep in mind the uses of digital illustrations.

You can read more about design in Chapters 4 and 5.

14.5

Writer to Writer

Help! How can I write a paper under pressure?   Let's say your paper is due in twenty-four hours and you're only getting started. Not good. But don't just begin frantically writing one sentence after another.

- Start by thinking carefully about your topic. It shouldn't be too narrow (for instance, the contributions of custom postcard printing to the Utah economy in 1989) or too broad (the history of postcards).

- Make the topic something that you care about and that will be easy for you to research — perhaps because it's a long-standing interest of yours or because you've already written about it (p. 155, Sec. 10.1).

- If your paper needs to include a minimum number of sources, ask where can you gather them quickly. Ease of research can help determine your topic.

- Sketch a rough outline for yourself: What do you want your readers to learn from your document? How can you interest them at the outset? What do you want them to be thinking about when they finish?

- *Now* start writing.

- Stick with your plan. If doing so seems impossible, do the best you can to solve the problems that arise and keep following your plan.

- If you manage to get only partway through what you wanted to write by the deadline, turn in what you've written anyway. It will demonstrate that you put *some* effort into the assignment, and it might earn a better grade than the failing grade you'll get if you turn nothing in.

- Think specifically about what you'll need to do differently for your next paper to achieve a more satisfying result.

Of course, you'll learn more and write a better paper if you give it as much time as it needs. And your instructor can tell if what you've turned in was written in a hurry. Writing is like that: it tells people things about you that you haven't said and might not be aware of. Try to have your writing tell readers mostly good things about you.

15. Use Sources to Accomplish Your Purpose

How you use information from sources can have a powerful effect on your readers. A well-placed quotation can lend authority to your argument. A concise summary of a recent study can reframe a reader's understanding of an issue. A striking image or video can bring an issue to life in a way that text alone cannot.

Sometimes, the sources you choose will lend themselves to particular purposes, such as making an argument or reflecting on an event. The strategies discussed in this chapter can be applied across most types of documents.

15.1 Introduce an Idea

You can use a quotation, paraphrase, or summary to introduce an idea or argument to your readers. Note how the following quotation frames a debate about funding for public transit as a battle between community activists and a state legislature concerned about dwindling revenue.

> "The Speaker of the House and her ideological lackeys have rejected every reasonable attempt to make progress on this issue," said Alicia Garcia, spokesperson for A Road Less Traveled, which is sponsoring a state referendum on their mass transit plan. "Our only option is to turn to the people of the state."
>
> If Garcia and backers of Referendum C are successful, . . .

The highlighted phrases place the blame for the problem on the legislature.

In contrast, the following quotation frames the debate as a question of how best to spend scarce state funds.

> "In the past decade, funding for road construction in real dollars has declined by 12.2%," said Nathan Sanders, chair of the House Special Committee on Transportation. "Referendum C, if passed, would further erode that funding by shifting state dollars to light rail." As the state considers the merits of Referendum C, opponents of the measure have . . .

> The highlighted phrases call attention to the financial challenges faced by the state.

15.2 Contrast Arguments

You can use source information to illustrate the nature and intensity of disagreements around an issue. The following example uses partial quotations (p. 142, Sec. 9.2) to highlight differences in proposed solutions to a problem.

> Solutions to the funding shortfall for road construction range from traditional approaches, such as raising taxes on fuel, to more radical solutions, such as basing taxes on miles driven. Advocates of increased fuel taxes, such as Vince Richards of Common Cause Colorado, argue that the approach "is a proven and widely accepted practice" (A2). Those in favor of the mileage tax argue, however, that it is "a solution that fairly shifts the costs to those who benefit most from public roads" (Rumskalla 23).

Consider how contrasting ideas and arguments will affect your readers. Paraphrase and summary can help you express complex ideas concisely. Quotations can help you convey the emotional qualities of an author's position on an issue.

15.3 Provide Evidence

Unsupported assertions amount to little more than a request for a reader's trust. Even when the writer is eminently trustworthy, such arguments are flimsy and easy to dismiss. In contrast, providing evidence to support your assertions makes your argument more convincing. Note the differences between the following passages.

Unsupported Assertion

Consumers are showing a greater awareness of the public good in their buying choices.

> No evidence is provided to support the writer's assertion.

Supported Assertion

Consumers are showing a greater awareness of the public good in their buying choices. According to Nielsen's Global Survey on Corporate Social Responsibility earlier this year, 55 percent of global online consumers across sixty countries indicated a willingness to pay more for products and services from companies that are committed to positive social and environmental impact.

> A summary of the study's results provides evidence for the assertion.

Visual sources can also lend support to an assertion. For example, a claim about the unintended consequences of military action might be accompanied by a photograph of a war-torn street or a wounded child.

15.4 Align Your Argument with an Authority

Aligning your argument with a subject matter expert, scientist, politician, or religious figure allows you to borrow someone else's credibility and status. Start by making an assertion and follow it with supporting information from a source, such as a quotation, paraphrase, or source summary.

> New developments in computers and robotics promise to bring about significant changes in both the workplace and daily life. "We are nearing the point where computers and robots will be able to see, move, and interact

naturally, unlocking many new applications and empowering people even more," said Bill Gates, co-founder and former chairman of Microsoft Corporation (qtd. in Titlow, Walters, par. 3).

15.6

> Bill Gates is a well-known authority on technology.

15.5 Define, Illustrate, or Clarify

Information from sources is often clearer and more concise than what writers might draft themselves. You can define a concept by quoting or paraphrasing a dictionary, encyclopedia, or informative article, or use an illustration to help readers understand a complex process, such as the steps involved in cellular respiration.

Writers also use information from sources to clarify statements:

Some studies have found connections between weight loss and coffee intake. Unfortunately, drinking a couple of cups of coffee each day won't necessarily lead to weight loss. In fact, notes Mayo Clinic certified dietitian Katherine Zeratsky, it could lead to weight gain. "Some caffeinated beverages, such as specialty coffees, are high in calories and fat," states Zeratsky. "So instead of losing weight, you might actually gain weight if you drink too many of these" (par. 8).

> A quotation from an expert clarifies the writer's statement.

15.6 Set a Mood

You can also choose quotations and illustrations to establish an overall mood for your readers. The emotional impact of images of a celebration at a sporting event, an expression of grief at a funeral, or a calming mountain vista can elicit certain reactions from your readers. Similarly, a striking quote, such as "The screams of pain coming out of that room will stay with me as long as I live," can evoke a specific mood.

15.7 Provide an Example

It's often better to *show* with an example than to *tell* with a general description. Examples provide concrete evidence in your document. Note how the writer of the following passage uses an example from a well-known television show to illustrate a point about Americans' relationship to the environment.

> In an early season of *Mad Men*, the Draper family ends a picnic by unashamedly shaking the trash from their blanket onto the grass. That scene suggests how far Americans have come, over the past half century, in terms of environmental responsibility. My friends and I all cringed watching that scene. In fact, I imagine the point of the scene was to make us cringe.

> A vivid example helps make the writer's point.

15.8 Amplify or Qualify

A writer might amplify a statement by providing examples from sources or qualify a statement by noting that it applies only to specific situations. Amplifications can expand the scope of your points, as in the following example about the dangers football players face when they add bulk.

> NFL offensive linemen who weigh less than 300 pounds are often described as "undersized," so it's no surprise that young football players are getting the message that bigger is better—and bulking up. Unfortunately, they're getting the wrong message. Asheley Skinner and her colleagues reported that a study of more than 8,000 high school football players showed that excess weight was not correlated with success. Worse, only 8 percent of high school linemen were considered to be at a healthy weight, while 21 percent were classified as "morbidly obese" (p. 924).

Qualifications, in contrast, allow you to narrow the scope of your statements, helping your readers understand your meaning. Note in the following example how the writer makes it clear that deaths related to weight gain are rare in football.

15.8

> While few high school football linemen suffer severe and immediate health consequences as a result of added weight, Skinner and her colleagues reported that weight gain during adolescence "may lead to the development of ongoing obesity that becomes even more severe when they no longer have the physical activity to compensate for caloric intake" (p. 926).

16. Write Effective Introductions

A good introduction provides a point of entry into the subject that catches readers' interest and leads smoothly into the main points. As you draft your introduction, consider how you might contextualize your issue and set up your main point. Many writers find that crafting an effective introduction is the most challenging part of drafting. If you run into difficulties, put your introduction aside and come back to it after you've made more progress on the rest of the document. There's no law that says you have to write the introduction first.

16.1 Frame the Issue

Your introduction provides a framework for your readers as they approach your topic. By calling attention to a specific situation, by asking a particular question, or by conveying a carefully chosen set of details, you can help your readers view the issue in a particular way. Consider, for example, the differences between two introductions to an essay about ensuring fair and open voting processes.

Introduction 1

In the face of yet another election forced into a recount, Florida found itself the subject of national scrutiny. Republican Rick Scott, the outgoing governor who had seen a safe lead in the state's Senate race dwindle to a virtual tie as late returns were tabulated, alleged that "unethical liberals" were trying to steal the election. He subsequently filed three lawsuits in an attempt to preserve his lead, including one that sought to exclude legally cast votes that had not been counted by the reporting deadline (conveniently, in a Democratically leaning county). In response, Scott's opponent, Democratic incumbent Bill Nelson, described Scott's actions as an effort "to stop every legal vote from being counted." He filed suit to extend the deadline for counting votes. The result? A feeding frenzy among news pundits, demonstrators arriving from out of state, and consternation among the voters of Florida.

Introduction 2

16.1

In the face of yet another election forced into a recount, Florida found itself at a cross-roads. Caught between feuding candidates, confronted with demonstrators (many of whom reportedly came from outside of the state), and concerned about the potential for violence, election officials went into action, trying not only to ensure a fair and open election process but also to avoid the kinds of mistakes that might lead to riots or worse. As tensions rose, election officials and their staffs worked into the night, counting votes in an attempt to meet deadlines, wondering which of the competing lawsuits would prevail, and worried that they were doomed to repeat the failed recount of the 2000 presidential election. The result? Additional lawsuits and, perhaps most notably, a further polarization of the American electorate.

The first introduction frames the issue as a conflict between Democrats and Republicans. The second introduction frames it as a crisis for election officials and, ultimately, for all Americans. While both introductions draw on the same basic information about vote counts, lawsuits, and allegations of election fraud, and while both will do a good job of introducing the essay, they point readers' attention onto different aspects of the subject.

You can frame your discussion by calling attention to specific aspects of a topic, including:

- the agent: a person, an organization, or a thing that is acting in a particular way

- the action: what is being done by the actor

- the goal: why the actor carried out the action

- the result: the outcome of the action

Introduction 2

In the face of yet another election forced into a recount, Florida found itself at a cross-roads. Caught between feuding candidates, confronted with demonstrators (many of whom reportedly came from outside of the state), and concerned about the potential for violence, election officials went into action, trying not only to ensure a fair and open election process but also to avoid the kinds of mistakes that might lead to riots or worse. As tensions rose, election officials and their staffs worked into the night, counting votes in an attempt to meet deadlines, wondering which of the competing lawsuits would prevail, and worried that they were doomed to repeat the failed recount of the 2000 presidential election. The result? Additional lawsuits and, perhaps most notably, a further polarization of the American electorate.

agent
goal

action

result

16.2

16.2 Choose an Introductory Strategy

Your introduction offers probably the best opportunity to grab your readers' attention. You can shape their understanding of your issue by choosing one of several introductory strategies.

State the Topic

Tell your readers what your issue is, what conversation you're focusing on, and what you'll add to the conversation, as in the following introduction:

> Artists and their artwork do not exist in a vacuum. The images artists create influence and in turn are influenced by the society and culture in which they are created. The artists and artworks of the Dutch Baroque period are no exception.

Establish the Context

In some cases, you'll want to give your readers background information about your subject or an overview of the conversation. Notice, for example, how writer Ben Fritz introduces a chapter in his book *The Big Picture: The Fight for the Future of Movies*, which discusses how the movie industry has changed in the twenty-first century:

16.2

> As Hollywood sought new sources of money in recent years to help fund the risky, original movies it wouldn't make itself, it didn't just look north to Silicon Valley. It also turned east, to China.

Lead with Your Thesis

If your research document presents an argument, evaluation, solution, or interpretation, use your introduction to get right to your main point. In other words, lead with a thesis statement, as in the following introduction.

> While the private tragedies of its central characters have public implications, William Shakespeare's *Julius Caesar* is more about personal struggles than political ambition. It is easy to see the play as one whose focus is the political action of public events. The title character, after all, is at the height of political power. However, the interior lives of Julius Caesar, Marcus Brutus, and their wives offer a more engaging storyline. Shakespeare alternates between public and private scenes throughout the play to emphasize the conflict between duties of the Roman citizenry and the feelings and needs of the individual, but it is the "private mind and heart of the individual" that the reader is compelled to examine (Edwards 105).

Define a Problem

If you are proposing a solution to a problem, begin your document by defining the problem. Note how this strategy is used in the following introduction to an academic essay.

Almost daily, headlines and newscasters tell us about athletes' use of performance-enhancing drugs. Indeed, stories of such drug use seem to grow in number each year, with investigations of possible steroid use by college football players, by major league baseball players, and even by Olympic gold medalists. It is easy to gain the impression that many adult athletes, particularly males, may be using drugs to improve their performance and physical appearance. What may be surprising and even shocking to most of us, however, is that these drugs, especially anabolic steroids, are increasingly used by adolescent athletes and that girls are just as likely as boys to be users.

16.2

Surprise Your Readers

Grab your readers' attention by telling them something they don't already know. It's even better if the information is shocking, unusual, or strange.

> What is the most common cause of hunger in the world? Is it drought? Locusts? Crop diseases? Nope. Most hunger in the world has absolutely nothing to do with food shortages. Most people who go to bed hungry, both in rich and in poor countries, do so in places where markets are filled with food that they cannot afford.

Ask a Question

Asking a question invites your readers to participate in the conversation. The following introduction encourages readers to consider the problem of steroid use by adolescent female athletes.

> What role is competitive sports playing in this dangerous trend? Why are some girls feeling the need to ingest performance-enhancing drugs?

Tell a Story

Everyone loves a story, assuming it's told well and has a point. You can use a story to introduce a subject to your readers, as student writer Caitlin Guariglia did in a reflective essay about a trip to Italy.

> Crash! The sound of metal hitting a concrete wall is my first vivid memory of Rome. Our tour bus could not get any farther down the tiny road because cars were parked along both sides. This, our bus driver told us, was illegal. He did not tell us, exactly; he grumbled it as he stepped out of the bus. He stood there with his hands on his hips, pondering the situation. Soon, people in the cars behind us started wandering up to stand next to the bus driver and ponder along with him. That, or they honked a great deal.

Provide a Historical Account

Historical accounts can help your readers understand the origins of a situation and how it has changed over time. A website focusing on relations between the People's Republic of China and Taiwan opened with this historical account:

> On February 21, 2000, the People's Republic of China (PRC) shocked diplomats and China scholars with its release of the white paper "The One-China Principle and the Taiwan Issue." In this eighteen-page document, the Chinese government outlined its case that, in keeping with the "One China" principle to which the United States and Taiwan had allegedly agreed, Taiwan is the rightful property of the People's Republic of China, and it revealed that it intended to use force if Taiwan did not move to reunite with the mainland.

Draw a Contrast

Drawing a contrast asks your readers to begin making a comparison. A writer began an essay about the role of cocaine in Bolivia's economy by contrasting what the word *cocaine* means to U.S. citizens and to South American coca farmers.

> To most Americans, the word *cocaine* evokes images of the illegal white powder and those who abuse it, yet the word has a completely different meaning to the coca farmers of South America.

Lead with a Quotation

A quotation allows your readers to learn about the issue from someone who knows it well or has been affected by it, as in the following introduction.

16.2

> "Without a few lucky breaks, we'd still be bagging groceries at Albertsons," says lead singer Rickie Jackson of the recent Grammy-winning band Soft Affections.

Preview Your Supporting Points

The most direct way of framing an issue and signaling the organization of your document is to provide a brief overview of your supporting points.

> This report will cover three approaches to treating cancer of the bladder: chemotherapy, a combination of chemotherapy and radiation, and surgical removal of the organ.

17. Write Effective Conclusions

Your conclusion provides an opportunity to emphasize your point and to share your final thoughts about the issue with your readers.

17.1 Reinforce Your Main Point

At a minimum, your conclusion should summarize the reasons you've offered to support your main point. You might echo your thesis statement (in different words) or, if your introduction didn't include an explicit thesis statement, you might state your main idea in your conclusion. Your goal should be to provide a clear indication of what you want someone to think, believe, or do as a result of reading your document.

Consider how the following conclusion calls attention to the impact of Bolivian president Evo Morales's vision for South American coca farmers.

> Through his bold program of "zero cocaine, not zero coca," Morales aims to improve the lives of Andean farmers and the economies of South American countries, while still remaining committed to controlling the illegal drug trade. Morales's example illustrates that it is time to work *with* coca farmers, rather than against them.

17.2 Select a Concluding Strategy

Conclusions that simply summarize a document, like the one shown above, are common — and sometimes effective, especially when the writer has presented complex concepts. But a conclusion can do much more than just restate your points. It can also urge your readers to continue thinking about what they've read, to take action about the subject, or to learn more about it.

As you draft, think about what you want to accomplish. You can choose from a range of strategies to write an effective conclusion.

Offer Additional Analysis

17.2

Extend your discussion of the issue by supplying additional insights. In a website about wind-generated electrical power, one writer concluded by linking wind power to the production of hydrogen gas.

> Another promising area—in terms of wind power's contribution to clean energy—is the role it can play in a "hydrogen economy." Because hydrogen gas, when burned, does not produce carbon dioxide (its only emission is water vapor), some legislators and environmentalists are looking to hydrogen as a replacement for fossil fuels. Generating hydrogen gas, however, requires power, and a number of plans to generate it rely on coal-powered plants. Wind-power advocates argue that wind turbines, instead, can supply the power needed to produce hydrogen gas. Recent government studies support this approach (International Renewable Energy Agency, 2018).

Speculate about the Future

Reflect on what might happen next, as this writer does in her essay about controlling the spread of malaria.

> Compounded by poor health care systems in many of the countries faced with malaria, the overall health effects of the disease can be severe. For countries with high rates of malaria and little funding available for expensive control strategies, DDT may continue to be the answer.

Close with a Quotation

Select a quotation that does one of the following:

- offers deeper insight into the points you've made in your document

17.2

- sums up the points you've made in your document

- points to the future of the issue

- suggests a solution to a problem

- illustrates what you would like to see happen

- makes a further observation about the issue

- presents a personal viewpoint from someone who has experienced the issue

This writer used a quotation from a personal interview to underscore her main point about the use of steroids among adolescent girls involved in competitive sports.

> In short, these athletes have not lost sight of the true objective of participating in sports—they know that their success is due to their efforts and not to the effects of a performance-enhancing drug. When asked what she would say to athletes considering steroid use, Melissa Alvarez said:
>
> > If you are training and doing your best, you should not have to use steroids. At the end of the day, it is just a game. You should never put your health at risk for anything, or anyone. It should be your top priority. (personal interview, September 26, 2018)

Close with a Story

Tell a story about the issue you've discussed in your document. The story might suggest a potential solution to the problem, offer hope about a desired outcome, or illustrate what might happen if a desired outcome isn't realized. This writer concluded his newspaper article by continuing a story he told in his introduction.

> So [Scott] struggles to get a foothold in the civilian work force. His brother in Boston lost his roommate, and early last month Scott moved into the empty bedroom, with his parents paying Scott's share of the $2,000-a-month rent until the lease expires on Aug. 31. And if Scott does not have a job by then? "I'll do

something temporary; I won't go back home," Scott said. "I'll be a bartender or get work through a temp agency. I hope I don't find myself in that position."

Close with a Question

Questions invite readers to consider the implications of the ideas explored in a document.

> In the end, we as voters and taxpayers must ask ourselves, who do we want to carry out U.S. defense missions abroad: those accountable to the U.S. military, or those beholden to private corporations?

Call Readers to Action

Make a recommendation or urge your readers to do something specific. For example, you might ask them to help solve a problem by donating time, money, or effort to a project. Or you might ask them to write to someone, such as a politician or corporate executive, about an issue. Calls to action ask readers to do more than simply accept what you've written; they ask readers to do something about it.

> The Stop Outsourcing Security Act, whose purpose is to phase out private military contractors, has been introduced repeatedly since 2007 and has died in Congress every time. Until we citizens demand accountability from the contractors and pressure our representatives to take action, we will continue to pay the needless costs — social as well as financial — that these profit-oriented companies exact.

Link to Your Introduction

This technique is sometimes called a "bookends" approach because it positions your introduction and conclusion as related ends of your document. The basic idea is to turn your conclusion into an extension of your introduction.

- If your introduction used a quotation, end with a related quotation or respond to the quotation.

- If your introduction used a story, extend that story or retell it with a different ending.

- If your introduction asked a question, answer the question, restate the question, or ask a new question.

17.2

- If your introduction defined a problem, provide a solution to the problem, restate the problem, or encourage readers to move on to a new problem.

Part 5

Revise and Edit

Part 5: Revise and Edit

Few writers create brilliant first drafts. The goal is to get your thinking out there where you can explore and develop it. Only once you're clear about what you want to share, in what order, is it worth crafting sentences carefully.

18. Revise Your Document

When you revise, you'll want to focus on how well your document responds to your writing situation, uses information and ideas to make a point, presents background or reasons, and uses evidence.

18.1 Focus on the Big Picture

Revising involves rethinking and re-envisioning what you've written. It tackles such big-picture issues as whether your draft suits your writing situation, your thesis statement is sound and well supported, you've properly integrated sources into your document, you've organized and presented your ideas clearly and effectively, and you've made good decisions about genre and design.

Consider Your Writing Situation

As you revise, ask whether your document achieves your purposes. If you want to inform readers about a particular subject, for instance, consider whether you've provided enough of the right kind of information and whether that information is presented clearly. If your goal is to convince or persuade your readers, ask whether you have chosen sound reasons and evidence and presented them as effectively as you can. You can also ask questions like these:

- Will my readers trust what I have to say? How can I establish my credibility?

- Will my readers have other ideas about how to address this subject? How can I convince them that they should believe what I say?

- Will my readers find the evidence I've provided consistent with their values, beliefs, and experiences?

Finally, think about the specific requirements of the assignment, such as length and number of sources. Evaluate your efforts to work around limitations, such as lack of access to information. Assess whether you've taken full advantage of your opportunities.

18.1

Consider Your Main Point

Ask yourself how well you are conveying your main point to your readers. First, check whether your thesis statement is phrased in a way that is compatible with the needs and interests of your readers. Second, ask whether the reasons that support your main point will help readers accept your thesis statement. As you make this assessment, keep in mind your primary role. For instance, if you've chosen the role of reporter, present facts that will allow readers to reach a conclusion without coming out and telling them what that conclusion should be.

Consider Your Use of Sources

Next, think about how you've used source information in your document. Review the amount of evidence you've provided and the appropriateness of that evidence for your purposes and readers. If you are making an argument about an issue, determine whether you've identified and addressed reasonable opposing viewpoints. As you review your use of sources, ask the following questions:

- Have you presented information, ideas, and arguments from your sources accurately and fairly?

- Are all quotations, paraphrases, and summaries accurate and appropriately documented?

- Have you introduced the work of other authors clearly? (For more information about attributions, see Chapter 9.)

Ask yourself, as well, whether you've identified the sources of the information, ideas, and arguments you use in your document in ways that capture the attention of your readers.

Neutral Attributions	Expressive Attributions
The author wrote . . .	In the author's opinion . . .
The author said . . .	The author denied this, noting . . .
The author stated . . .	In response, the author observed that . . .

18.1

It's also important to review your works cited or references list for completeness and accuracy. Remember that lack of proper documentation can diminish your credibility.

> Learn more about integrating sources in Chapter 9 and about documenting your sources in Chapters 30 through 33.

Writer to Writer

Aren't say *and* write *the only attributions you need?* Some writing coaches and, in particular, some journalists argue that there's little point in using any verbs of attribution other than *says, said, writes,* and *wrote.* After all, saying is saying — what else is there to say? Yet alternative verbs like *admit* and *claim* do a second job in addition to attributing an idea or quotation to its source: they indicate the stance of either the source or you, the writer. Consider the differences among these:

> *"I chopped up the bench for firewood," he said.* (This version is purely factual.)

> *He admitted that he chopped up the bench for firewood.* (*Admitted* implies that he considered what he did an offense.)

> *He claimed that he chopped up the bench for firewood.* (*Claimed* implies that he may or may not have chopped up the bench, or perhaps that he is proud of the action.)

Whenever you want to weave an extra layer of meaning into an attribution, look for a verb that will do the job.

Consider Organization

Your readers should be able to locate information and ideas easily. Ask whether your introduction helps your readers anticipate the organization of your document. Reflect on the appropriateness of your organizing pattern (p. 183, Sec. 13.1) for your purposes and your readers.

Make sure your document is easy to read. See if you need additional headings or subheadings (p. 199, Sec. 14.5). Check that your paragraphs are unified (p. 192, Sec. 14.2) and their structure is effective (see p. 193, Sec. 14.3). If you have several shorter paragraphs in a row, consider combining the ones that express similar ideas. If you have a number of longer paragraphs, break them up and add transitions. Finally, ask whether your conclusion leaves your readers with something to think about. The most powerful conclusions do more than just summarize what you've said.

Consider Genre and Design

If your assignment gave you a choice of genres, ask whether the genre you've selected is appropriate, given your purposes and readers. For example, would it be more effective to reach your readers via an informative website, an opinion column, or a brochure? Would publishing your document as a blog post or as a comment on a magazine or newspaper article work better? Regardless of the genre, make sure that you've followed the conventions associated with it, such as level of formality, accepted sources of evidence, and organization.

For more on genre choices and conventions, see the Genre Design Gallery beginning on p. 85.

Take a careful look at how you've designed your document (see Chapter 5). Does it resemble what your readers will expect? For example, if you're writing an academic essay, have you double-spaced your lines, used a readable font, and set wide margins? If you're creating a website, have you made it easy for your readers to find their way around? Have you formatted your headings and subheadings consistently? Have you used design principles and elements to achieve your purposes?

18.2 Revise Strategically

You can draw on several strategies for reviewing and improving your document. As you use them, keep track of your ideas for revision by writing comments on sticky notes or in the margins of print documents, by using the Comments tool in word-processing documents, or by creating a to-do list in your writer's notebook.

Save Multiple Drafts

Since you may not be happy with every revision you make, it's a good idea to make a new copy of your draft before every major revising session. You can add a number to your drafts' file names, such as Draft1, Draft2, and so on; add the date, such as Draft_April6 and Draft_April10; or use some other naming system that works for you.

Highlight Your Main Point, Reasons, and Evidence

As you revise, make sure that your main point (usually expressed as a thesis statement), reasons, and evidence are fully developed. An effective way to do this is to identify and examine each element in your draft, both individually and as a group of related points. For a printed document, use a highlighter, colored pens or pencils, or sticky notes. For a digital document, use a highlighting tool. If you are focusing on evidence, use different colors to highlight evidence from different sources (to help you check whether you are relying too heavily on a single source) or to differentiate the types of evidence you are using (such as quotations, paraphrases, summaries, and numerical data).

If you've relied too heavily on a particular source, your readers might wonder why they shouldn't simply read that source and ignore your document. If you've provided too little evidence, they'll question the basis for your conclusions.

Don't go looking for trouble. But if you have a nagging sense that there is a flaw in your argument or a weakness in your evidence, this is the time to take another close look at your document. Once you understand what's bothering you, you might find that you can solve the problem in a straightforward manner.

18.2

Challenge Your Assumptions

It's easy to accept ideas and arguments that you've worked so hard to develop. But what would a reader with fresh eyes think? Challenge your main point, reasons, and evidence by using one of the following strategies. Keep track of your challenges by using the Comment tool in your word-processing program.

- **Put yourself in the place of your readers.** Pretend that you are one of your readers. Ask yourself the questions they might ask. Imagine the concerns they might bring to your document. A reader interested in solving a problem might ask, for example, whether a proposed solution is cost-effective, is stronger than alternative solutions, or has unacceptable side effects. As you revise, take these questions and concerns into account.

- **Play devil's advocate.** A devil's advocate raises reasonable objections to ideas and arguments (p. 63, Sec. 4.8). As you review your document, identify your key claims and then pose reasonable objections to them. Can you refute them? Make note of these potential objections, and take them into account as you revise.

- **Play the "so what?" game.** As you read your document, ask why readers would care about what you are saying. By asking "so what?" questions, you can gain a better understanding of what your readers are likely to care about and how they might respond to your arguments and ideas. Jot down your responses to these questions, and consider them as you revise.

Scan, Outline, and Map Your Document

Use the following strategies to review the structure, organization, and design of your document:

- **Scan headings and subheadings.** Headings and subheadings should track the flow of your ideas. Ask whether the organization they reveal is appropriate for your writing situation and your role as a writer.

- **Scan the first sentence of each paragraph.** This quick reading can reveal points at which your ideas shift. Note these shifts, and think about whether they are appropriate and effective.

18.2

- **Outline your document.** Create a topical or sentence outline of your document (p. 189, Sec. 13.2) to assess its structure and organization. Sometimes called a reverse outline, this helps you identify the sequence of your points and the amount of space devoted to each aspect of your document. If you are viewing your document in a word-processing program, use the Styles tool to assign levels to headings in your document; then view it in Outline view.

- **Map your document.** Like an outline, a map (p. 185, Sec. 13.2) can help you identify the organization of your points and the amount of evidence you've used to support them.

For more on maps and outlines, see p. 185, Sec. 13.2.

Ask for Feedback

After you've spent long hours on a project, it can be difficult to recognize problems that your readers might have with your draft. You might read the same paragraph eight times and still fail to notice that the evidence you are using to support a point actually contradicts it. Ask for feedback on your draft from a friend, relative, colleague, or writing center tutor—anyone who will be frank as well as supportive. Be specific about the kinds of comments you're looking for. Hearing "it's just fine" from a reviewer will not help you revise. You can learn more about engaging in peer review in Chapter 1.

18.2

Checklist for Revision

✔ **Review your writing situation.** Does your document help you achieve your purposes? Does it address your readers' needs, interests, knowledge, and backgrounds? Is it well adapted to the context in which it will be read?

✔ **Consider your writing assignment.** Does your document address the writing assignment's requirements? Does it effectively work around limitations and take advantage of opportunities?

✔ **Evaluate the presentation of your ideas.** Does your document provide a clear and appropriate thesis statement? Do your reasons and evidence support your thesis statement, and are they consistent with your primary role as a writer?

✔ **Assess your use, integration, and documentation of sources.** Have you offered adequate support for your points, considered reasonable opposing viewpoints, integrated and acknowledged your sources, and distinguished between your work and that of other writers? Have you used some variety in your introduction and attribution of sources? Have you documented your sources appropriately?

✔ **Examine the structure and organization of your document.** Is the introduction clear and concise, does it convey your main point, and does it help your readers anticipate the structure of your document? Is the organization of the document easy to follow? Are paragraphs easy to read? Are transitions effective? Does the conclusion do more than just summarize the document?

✔ **Evaluate genre and design.** Does the genre you've created help you accomplish your purposes? Have you followed the style and design conventions associated with the type of document you've created?

19. Edit Your Document

The meaning of *editing* varies widely. Newspaper and magazine editors, for example, are involved in almost all aspects of developing and writing a document. Copy editors, in contrast, are involved only in the late stages of developing a document. In this chapter, we focus on editing as assessing the effectiveness, accuracy, and appropriateness of the words and sentences in a document.

19.1 Edit for Your Readers

Before you begin to edit, ask whether you should continue to revise your draft (Chapter 18). If you're uncertain about the document's organization or whether you've provided enough support for your argument, deal with those issues first. In the same way that you wouldn't start painting a house until you've finished building the walls, hold off on editing until you're confident that you're finished revising.

Focus on Accuracy

You risk damaging your credibility if you provide inaccurate information in your document. To reduce this risk, do the following:

- **Check your facts and figures**. Your readers might think that you're deliberately misleading them if you provide inaccurate information. As you edit, return to your original sources or your notes to check any facts and figures.

- **Check every quotation.** Look back at the original sources or consult your notes to ensure that you have quoted each source accurately. Make sure that you have noted any changes to a quotation with ellipsis marks or brackets and that those changes haven't altered the meaning of the passage (see pp. 144–145, Sec. 9.2). Be sure to cite each source both in the text and in a works-cited or references list (see Part 6).

19.1

Writer to Writer

Can you trust the internet on the spelling of names and unusual words? You already know not to believe everything you read on the internet. Still, there is a way to use it to check the spelling of proper names (*CocaCola* or *Coca-Cola* or *Coca Cola*?) and unusual (*phlebotomy*) or relatively new (*Ebola* or *ebola*?) words.

If you're checking a proper name, search for the product's or organization's website. That will almost invariably give only one spelling, and it will be the correct one. For other words, type your best guess into your search engine — say, *flebotamy*. If it returns "Showing results for *phlebotomy*," have a look at those results and see if they're what you want.

Relatively new words may be in flux. For example, for 30 years after the internet came into use, the name was generally capitalized, but more recently the trend has been toward lowercasing it, and now that's the way *internet* is usually rendered.

To confirm a new term like *Ebola* (often capitalized like the river near which the virus was discovered), go to Google News (news .google.com). Much of what is there has been professionally edited. Search for either version of *Ebola*; assess the quantity and quality of the sources that use each version of your term and decide which one seems most reliable.

You can also use this technique to check expressions you're unsure of. Is it *extract revenge* or *exact revenge*? Type in both versions, with quotation marks around them, one at a time, and see how many results the search engine tells you there are, as well as what the sources are. As of this writing, *exact* returns nearly 20 times more results than *extract*. *Exact* it is.

- **Check the spelling of every name.** Don't rely on spell checkers, which provide the correct spelling for only the most common or prominent names.

Focus on Economy

Editing for economy involves reducing the number of words needed to express an idea or convey information. You can often achieve greater economy in your writing by removing unnecessary modifiers, removing drab introductory phrases such as *there are* and *it is*, and eliminating stock phrases such as *last but not least* (see p. 275, Sec. 24.2). Editing for economy generally makes it easier for your readers to understand your meaning.

19.1

Focus on Consistency

Editing your document for consistency helps you present information and ideas in a uniform way. Use the following techniques to edit for consistency:

- **Treat concepts consistently.** Review your document for consistent treatment of concepts, information, ideas, definitions, and anecdotes.

- **Use numbers consistently.** Check the documentation system you are using for its guidelines on the treatment of numbers. Some recommend, for instance, that you spell out the numbers zero through nine and use Arabic numerals for numbers larger than nine.

- **Treat your sources consistently.** Avoid referring to some sources using first names and to others using honorifics, such as *Dr.*, *Mr.*, or *Ms.* Especially avoid referring to members of one gender by their first names and members of another gender by their last names. Also check that you have cited your sources appropriately for the documentation style you're using, such as MLA or APA (see Part 6). Review each reference for consistent presentation of names, page numbers, and publication dates.

- **Format your document consistently.** Repair any inconsistencies in your use of fonts, headings, and subheadings and in your placement and captioning of images, tables, charts, and other illustrations (see Chapter 5).

Focus on Style

Your readers will judge you—and what you have to say—not only on what you say but also on how you say it. Edit for matters of style by choosing the right words, using active and passive voice appropriately, adopting a consistent point of view, simplifying needlessly complex sentences, varying your sentence length and structure, providing transitions, and avoiding disparaging language (see Chapters 20–21).

19.2

Focus on Spelling, Grammar, and Punctuation

Poor spelling doesn't necessarily affect your ability to get your point across — in most cases, readers will understand even the most atrociously spelled document — but it does affect what your readers think of you. If you ignore spelling errors in your document, you'll erode their confidence in how knowledgeable you are. The same goes for grammar and punctuation. If your sentences have subject–verb agreement problems (see p. 288, Sec. 25.1) or don't use the right punctuation (see Chapter 28), readers might not trust you about other things. As you put the finishing touches on your document, keep a dictionary and a good grammar handbook (such as this one) close by.

Writer to Writer

Which dictionary should you use?   Some style manuals recommend that you consult them together with particular dictionaries. If the choice is left up to you, look for a dictionary that's up to date and widely used. Merriam-Webster's online dictionary (www.merriam-webster.com), among others, meets these criteria.

19.2 Edit Strategically

Thorough editing involves making several passes through your document to ensure that you've addressed accuracy, economy, consistency, style, spelling, grammar, and punctuation. The following tips can make that process both easier and more productive.

Read Carefully

As you've worked on your document, you've become quite familiar with it. As a result, it can be easy to read what you *meant* to
write instead of what you actually wrote. The following strategies can help you read with fresh eyes:

- **Take a break before you edit.**   If time permits, allow a day or
  two to pass before you begin editing your document. Taking
  time off between revising and editing can help you see your
  document more clearly.

- **Pause between sentences for a quick check.**   Avoid getting caught
  up in the flow of your document by pausing after you read
  each sentence. Slowing down can help you identify problems
  with your text.

- **Read aloud.**   Reading your document aloud can help you find
  problems that might not be apparent when you read it silently.

- **Read in reverse order.**   To check for problems with individual
  sentences, start at the end of your document, read the
  last sentence first, and then work backward through the
  document. To check for problems at the word level, read each
  word starting with the last one in the document. Disrupting
  the normal flow of your document can alert you to problems
  that might not stand out when you read it normally.

Mark and Search

Use the following marking and searching strategies to edit for
accuracy, economy, consistency, and style:

- **Mark your document.**   As you read, use a highlighter or the
  highlighting tool in your word-processing program to mark
  errors or information that should be double-checked.

- **Use the Find and Replace tools.**   Use your word-processing
  program to edit concepts, names, numbers, and titles for
  consistency and accuracy. If you are referring to sources

19.2

using a parenthetical citation style, such as MLA or APA, use the Find tool to search for an opening parenthesis. If you discover you've consistently misspelled a word or name, use the Replace tool to correct it throughout your document. Take care that you replace only what you want to replace with the correct substitute.

- **Use the Split Window tool.** Some word-processing programs allow you to split your window so that you can view different parts of your document at the same time. Use this tool to ensure that you are referring to a concept in the same way throughout your document or to check for consistent use of fonts, headings, subheadings, illustrations, and tables.

Writer to Writer

Can you trust spelling, grammar, and style tools? Word-processing tools that check spelling, grammar, punctuation, and style can help make editing a document quicker, but be aware of their limitations.

Spell checkers have two main weaknesses. First, they can't iden-tify words that are spelled correctly but misused — such as *to/two/too*, *cite/site/sight*, and *precede/proceed*. Second, spell checkers are ineffective when they run into words they don't recognize, such as proper names, technical and scientific terms, and unusual words. To compound this problem, spell checkers often suggest replacement words. If you accept suggestions uncritically, you may end up with a paper full of incorrect words and misspelled names.

The primary shortcoming of grammar, punctuation, and style checkers is inaccurate advice. Grammar- and style-checking tools can point out problems you may have overlooked, such as a subject–verb agreement mismatch that occurred when you revised a sen-tence. However, if you don't have a strong knowledge of grammar, punctuation, and style, inaccurate advice can easily steer you wrong.

For spelling advice, consult an up-to-date dictionary or news .google.com (see the Writer to Writer box on p. 232). If you have concerns about the suggestions you receive from the grammar-, punctuation-, and style-checking tools, consult the relevant part of this book.

Ask for Feedback

Two pairs of eyes are better than one. After you've edited your document, ask a friend, relative, or classmate to proofread it and to make note of any problems.

19.2

Checklist for Editing

✔ **Ensure that your document is accurate.** It's impossible to overemphasize this. Check facts and figures, quotations, and the spelling of names.

✔ **Edit for economy.** Strive to express your ideas and argument concisely yet clearly.

✔ **Ensure that your document is consistent.** Use concepts, numbers, and source information consistently. Check your document for consistent use of formatting and design.

✔ **Improve your style.** Strive for economy, use appropriate words, check your verbs, rewrite overly complex sentences, vary sentence length and structure to enhance meaning, and remove disparaging language.

✔ **Check for correct spelling, grammar, and punctuation.** Use your word processor's spelling, grammar, punctuation, and style tools; consult a dictionary and the grammar section of this book; and ask someone to proofread your draft.

---

20. Understand the Parts of a Sentence ⊕

To learn any new skill, it helps to understand the terminology. Just as your recipe will probably turn out better if you understand specialized cooking terms, such as *julienne* and *blanch*, knowing the meaning of terms such as *independent clause* and *subordinate clause* can help you can write clear, concise, effective sentences.

20.1 Identify Subjects ⊕

Almost every English sentence must include a **subject**—a noun or pronoun or phrase that the sentence is about:

> My friend is a chef.
>
> She cooks delicious food.

> *My friend* and *she* perform the actions of the sentences.

Some sentences have more than one subject:

> Even her breakfasts and snacks are divine.

> *Breakfasts* and *snacks* are both subjects in this sentence.

Subjects Can Be Implied

The exception to the rule is **commands**, which are also called verbs in the **imperative mood** (see p. 304, Sec. 25.3). The subject is always implied, and it is always *you*:

> [You] Please eat some more!

Occasionally, the subject will not look like a noun or a pronoun but will be a phrase taking on that role.

> Where I want to be is in the kitchen.

> The phrase *where I want to be* is the subject.

Subjects Can Be Placeholders

Generally, in English the subject comes before the verb. But in certain cases, mostly involving the **placeholders** *there* and *it*, the subject comes after. *There* or *it* stands in for the subject:

20.1

There are tasty leftovers in the kitchen.

> The subject is *leftovers; there* is holding its place; and the sentence is equivalent to but more idiomatic than *Tasty leftovers are in the kitchen.*

It is a good idea to eat them today.

> The sentence is equivalent to *To eat them today is a good idea.*

Placeholders occasionally hold the place of . . . nothing in particular:

It is raining.

Revising the sentence without the placeholder will usually make it stronger. (See p. 288, Sec. 25.1, and p. 316, Sec. 26.3).

✗ There are almond flour, buckwheat flour, oat flour, and amaranth flour, among others, that can be used to bake gluten-free cakes.

✔ Almond flour, buckwheat flour, oat flour, and amaranth flour, among others, can be used to bake gluten-free cakes.

Subjects Can Be Verbals

Sometimes the subject can look like a verb, even when it's not. **Verbals**, including infinitives (*to sleep, to dream*) and gerunds (*sleeping, dreaming*), may look like verbs but actually work as nouns or modifiers. They refer to the idea of the action rather than stating that a subject carries out the action.

Cooking with her always makes me hungry.

> *Cooking* is what this sentence is about, so it is the subject.

To watch her cook makes me hungry too.

> This sentence is about *watching*. In many cases, like these examples, gerunds and participles are interchangeable.

20.2 Identify Verbs 🌐

Every English sentence must include a *verb*:

✗ I hungry.

✔ I am hungry.

English has several kinds of verbs. **Action verbs** describe actions that the subject performs:

She cooks.

Linking verbs connect the subject to a word or phrase that describes that subject. The noun, pronoun, or adjective that follows the linking verb gives new information about the subject:

My friend is an excellent chef.

> *Is* links the noun *chef* to the noun *friend*, which the sentence is equating. *Is* is a form of the verb *be* — the most common English linking verb.

I become hungry when she tells me about her workday.

> *Become* links the information about getting *hungry* (an adjective) to the subject *I*.

These are linking verbs:

appear   be   become   feel   look   remain   seem   smell   taste   turn

Helping or **modal verbs** precede the kinds of verbs above to indicate tenses, emphases, moods, and degree of likelihood.

I do like to cook.

I could become a chef too.

My friend will advise me.

For more information about helping and modal verbs, see p. 299, Sec. 25.2.

20.3

Writer to Writer

What are phrasal verbs? A verb may include more than one word. A combination of words like *turn in* may look like a verb plus a preposition — but it's actually a **phrasal verb**, and *in* is a **particle** here, not a preposition. Prepositions (see p. 264, Sec. 23.3) have objects: *in* a pickle, *on* a sandwich.

Phrasal verbs, too, may have objects: *turn in* my paper, *turn on* the radio. On the page, the construction may seem identical to *turn* followed by a prepositional phrase: *turn in the giant slalom, turn on a red light*. But the meaning is different: what happened to the paper is that it was *turned in*; what happened to the radio is that it was *turned on*. What happened in the giant slalom is that the skier *turned*; what happened on the red light is that the car *turned*.

20.3 Recognize Clauses and Phrases ⊕

The idea of the **clause** — a group of words that contains both a subject and a verb — is fundamental to the English language. A **main clause** (or independent clause) conveys a complete thought and can stand alone as a sentence:

I play.

Most clauses contain not only a subject and a verb but other elements as well, such as **phrases**, or groups of words meant to be understood together:

I play in a band.

> *In a band* is a prepositional phrase that provides more information but needs a subject and a verb to make a sentence.

21. Choose the Right Sentence Structures

Sentences come in many flavors, and just as there are terms for literal flavors, like *chocolate* and *caramel*, there are terms for the structures of sentences. Different structures can convey a single idea to your readers, give equal weight to two or more ideas, or emphasize one idea over another.

21.1 Put Main Ideas in Main Clauses

I play in a band.

Simple ideas can be expressed simply. If the ideas are powerful, simple phrasing will only strengthen them by making clear that the power doesn't come from fancy wording but from the idea itself.

"Procrastination is the thief of time."—Charles Dickens

"Don't raise your voice. Improve your argument."—Desmond Tutu

"Nothing will work unless you do."—Maya Angelou

All the same, a series of simple main clauses, one after the other, sheds no light on any relationships that you perceive among the ideas or information you are sharing. To show relationships between ideas and information, it helps to have the full array of sentence structures at your command.

21.2 Give Multiple Ideas Equal Weight

When you join two or more main clauses in a single sentence, the result is a **compound sentence**. Compound sentences are good for presenting two or more related ideas and giving them equal emphasis:

┌ MAIN CLAUSE ┐   ┌──────── MAIN CLAUSE ────────┐
I play in a band, and I volunteer at the school radio station.

Be sure to put a comma between the main clauses of a compound sentence, and use a **coordinating conjunction** between them, or between the last two of them:

> I love both activities, but I need to give one of them up.
>
> I could quit the band, or I could quit the radio station.
>
> I don't have enough time to study, I never see my old friends, and I'm not even making money.

21.2

Conjunctions connect ideas and things and show relationships between them. English has two kinds of conjunctions — subordinating (see p. 243, Sec. 21.3) and coordinating. Coordinating conjunctions connect things to which you are giving equal rank or emphasis. For instance, *and* in the third example above says that all three things are true. *Or* in the second example presents the two things as alternatives. Coordinating conjunctions are an important little part of speech, and there aren't many of them. These are all the coordinating conjunctions:

> and   but   for   nor   or   so   yet

A compound sentence with no conjunctions or commas is likely to be an incorrect, hard-to-follow run-on (see p. 250, Sec. 22.2):

> ✗ I don't have enough time to study I never see my old friends I'm not even making money.

A compound sentence with commas but without a conjunction is likely to be an incorrect comma splice (see p. 250, Sec. 22.2):

> ✗ I don't have enough time to study, I never see my old friends, I'm not even making money.

If you don't want to include a conjunction in a compound sentence you've written, you can put semicolons (see p. 251, Sec. 22.2) between the clauses:

> ✔ I don't have enough time to study; I never see my old friends; I'm not even making money.

21.3 Emphasize a Main Idea over a Lesser One

A **complex sentence** contains a main clause plus one or more **subordinate**, or dependent, **clauses**. Like a main clause, a subordinate clause contains a subject and a verb. But unlike a main clause, a subordinate clause doesn't amount to a complete thought and so cannot stand on its own as a sentence. It is subordinate to, or dependent on, a main clause. Complex sentences are good for indicating which of two or more ideas is your focus.

MAIN CLAUSE

SUBORDINATE CLAUSE

My parents, who are both lawyers, find their careers fulfilling.

The focus of this sentence is on how the writer's parents feel about their careers. The subordinate clause *who are both lawyers* adds information that will give readers a fuller understanding of the main clause (*My parents find their careers fulfilling*).

The same information could be conveyed in a compound sentence, like this:

MAIN CLAUSE   MAIN CLAUSE

My parents are both lawyers, and they find their careers fulfilling.

But the emphasis is different. This version gives equal emphasis to the two parts of the sentence.

"Who are both lawyers," in this example, is a **relative clause**—one of two types of subordinate clauses. Both types introduce information that the writer wants to place in the background of the main clause. Relative clauses come after a noun or pronoun and supply information about it.

My mother works at a small firm that has just three lawyers.

That has just three lawyers is a relative clause about the noun *firm*; it relies on the main clause for its meaning.

Relative clauses begin with **relative pronouns**:

that   which   who   whom   whose

For more on *which* and *that*, see page 333, Sec. 28.1. For more on *who* and *whom*, see page 310, Sec. 26.1.

21.3

The other type of subordinate clause contains an independent clause but begins with a **subordinating conjunction**. A subordinating conjunction indicates that you're giving less emphasis to the idea in the clause it introduces than to the idea in the main clause.

```
┌─────── SUBORDINATE ───────┐ ┌─────── MAIN CLAUSE ───────┐
            CLAUSE
```
When I think about my future, I don't see myself as a lawyer.

> The subordinating conjunction *when* relegates the first clause to a supporting role in this sentence.

```
┌─────── MAIN CLAUSE ───────┐ ┌─── SUBORDINATE ───┐
                                     CLAUSE
```
I hope to be a music critic because I love music.

> The subordinating conjunction *because* turns *I love music* into a subordinate clause.

English has many subordinating conjunctions, the most common of which are these:

after	even though	unless
although	if	until
as	in order to	when
as if	provided that	whenever
as long as	since	where
as soon as	so that	whereas
as though	than	wherever
because	that	whether
before	though	while

A sentence that consists only of a subordinate clause feels incomplete and is an incorrect fragment (see p. 246, Sec. 22.1):

✗ Though I would love to make as much money as my parents do.

21.3

Usually, a fragment can be corrected by attaching it to the sentence before or after it:

✔ I hope to be a music critic, though I would love to make as much money as my parents do.

✔ Though I would love to make as much money as my parents do, I do not love the idea of becoming a lawyer.

> ## Writer to Writer
>
> *Is it okay to start a sentence with* **and, but, because,** *or* **since?** You've probably had instructors tell you that some of these are not okay as initial words, but they may have just been trying to prevent you from treating sentence fragments (see p. 246) as sentences. Many sentence fragments start with one of those words: "And justice for all." "But not really." "Because it was beautiful."
>
> But many perfectly good sentences (like this one) also start with these words. *And* and *but* are often used because the previous sentence was already long, and the writer decided for good reasons to break it in two. These coordinating conjunctions are connecting the idea in the new sentence with the idea in the previous one. With *because*, a writer may prefer to state the cause before the effect: "Because it was beautiful, I couldn't take my eyes off it."
>
> Because *since* can be a synonym for either *because* or *after*, starting a sentence with *since* can lead to confusion. Consider "Since the researchers have lost touch with their subjects, it's been impossible to follow up on the study's results." Is that "Because the researchers..." or "After [they] lost touch, it [became]..."? Revise sentences like this to make your meaning clear.

21.4 Combine Coordination and Subordination

A sentence with more than one main clause and at least one subordinate clause is called a **compound complex sentence**.

```
┌──────── MAIN CLAUSE ────────┐  ┌──── SUBORDINATE ────┐
                                        CLAUSE
The healthiest food is expensive because it is fresh, but
```

```
┌──────── MAIN CLAUSE ────────┐  ┌──── SUBORDINATE ────┐
                                        CLAUSE
people need healthy food whether or not they are rich.
```

It won't improve your writing to make a habit of constructing elaborate sentences. But it is good to be skilled at turning a group of short, closely related ideas into one compound complex sentence. In the example above, the writer uses one closely knit sentence to present a problem, give an explanation, and take a stand on an issue.

22. Write in Complete Sentences

Most of us use incomplete or ungrammatical sentences in spoken conversation. However, writing gives you a much better opportunity to convey exactly what you mean. Besides, readers can't generally give direct feedback to a writer, the way a listener can tell a speaker "I'm sorry, I don't understand what you just said." So writers are held to a higher standard. Readers who encounter poor sentences are likely to conclude either that you don't know what's correct or that you don't care about making yourself understood.

22.1 Turn Fragments into Full Sentences

Fragments are parts of sentences that the writer has punctuated as if they were complete sentences. The idea they're trying to express is incomplete.

✘ We start getting everybody up at six in the morning. Even the residents who want to keep sleeping.

✘ I saw the band Vogon Soup about three years ago when they were playing at Hooper's. And again the next year, when they put on a spectacular show.

Such careless use of fragments makes the writer seem unskilled. Often, all the writer needs to do to correct the problem is attach the fragment to the previous or next sentence:

✔ We start getting everybody up at six in the morning, even the residents who want to keep sleeping.

In other cases, it's easier or clearer or both to change the wording of the fragment so that it can stand on its own as a sentence:

✔ I saw the band Vogon Soup about three years ago when they were playing at Hooper's. I saw them again the next year, when they put on a spectacular show.

It is true that everyday speech is full of fragments, particularly in answer to questions—fragments like "Not me," "Over here," and "Because I said so!" Since fragments are conversational, you'll find them in dialogue in journalism and fiction, and you'll see and hear them regularly in advertising. But in academic writing, fragments suggest that the writer either doesn't know what a proper sentence is (see Chapter 21 for more about sentence structure) or couldn't be bothered to revise.

22.1

Watch Out for Subordinate Clauses

Subordinate clauses (see p. 242, Sec. 21.3) contain subjects and verbs, so some of them are easily mistaken for sentences. But they also contain a signal—a relative pronoun (see p. 243, Sec. 21.3) or a subordinating conjunction (see p. 243, Sec. 21.3)—that they aren't intended to be understood fully by themselves. They depend on a main clause for some of their meaning.

✘   ⌜———— SENTENCE ————⌝ ⌜———— FRAGMENT ————
Dinner is served at five sharp. Because the kitchen workers go off

⌜————————⌝
duty at six.

Because, a subordinating conjunction, makes sense only if it's understood in relation to the previous sentence. It turns the second sentence into a fragment. One way to correct the fragment is to connect the subordinate clause to the previous sentence.

✔   ⌜———— MAIN CLAUSE ————⌝ ⌜———— SUBORDINATE CLAUSE ————
Dinner is served at five sharp, because the kitchen workers go off

⌜————————⌝
duty at six.

✘   ⌜———— SENTENCE ————⌝ ⌜———— FRAGMENT ————
Vogon Soup has two alpha males. Who are the lead guitarist and

⌜————————⌝
the drummer.

> *Who* (when it's not asking a question) must be attached to something outside the clause, or else it creates a fragment.

✔ Vogon Soup has two alpha males, who are the lead guitarist and the drummer.

> The fragment is fixed by joining the two clauses.

22.1

In these examples, a comma between the clauses indicates that the subordinate clause is not essential to the main point of the sentence (see p. 242, Sec. 21.3).

Another way to correct fragments like these is to cut or change the wording that requires them to connect to another clause:

✔ Dinner is served at five sharp. The kitchen workers go off duty at six.

✔ Vogon Soup has two alpha males. They are the lead guitarist and the drummer.

Watch Out for Verbals

Verbals are infinitives (*to work*, *to play*) and -*ing* verb forms (*working*, *playing*) that look like verbs but are actually functioning as nouns or modifiers.

✘ We put out snacks in the evening. To keep the residents from going to bed hungry.

> *To keep . . .* doesn't express a complete idea.

✔ We put out snacks in the evening to keep the residents from going to bed hungry.

> Because the main point is that the staff members don't want the residents to go to bed hungry, no comma is needed between the clauses.

✘ All eyes were on Gordie. Prancing back and forth on stage as he played his guitar.

> Notice how incomplete the highlighted phrase feels without the previous sentence.

✔ All eyes were on Gordie prancing back and forth on stage as he played his guitar.

> The point is that Gordie's prancing riveted the audience, so no comma is needed before the modifier.

22.1

If you correct a fragment by attaching it to the previous or next sentence, make sure you haven't just turned it into a dangling modifier (see p. 263, Sec. 23.3):

✗ Prancing back and forth on stage, the audience couldn't take their eyes off Gordie.

✔ The audience couldn't take their eyes off Gordie as he pranced back and forth on stage.

For more on verbals as subjects, see page 237 (Sec. 20.1).

Watch Out for Fragments That Begin with Prepositions

Prepositions indicate direction (*into* the dining room), location (*near* the window), time (*before* dinner), or another characteristic (*except* me) and introduce an object (*dining room, window, dinner, me*). Together, a preposition and its object make up a **prepositional phrase**. Because these phrases lack a subject, a verb, or both, they must be attached to a main clause.

If you begin a sentence with a prepositional phrase, be sure to finish the sentence.

✗ After eating dinner so early. The residents have a long evening ahead of them.

✔ After eating dinner so early, the residents have a long evening ahead of them.

> Here the fragment is attached to the adjacent sentence.

When you attach a fragment to the sentence that follows, you should generally put a comma after it to help readers find the beginning of the main clause.

Watch Out for Fragments That Consist of an Example

✗ Vogon Soup plays some covers of other bands' music. Such as "Here Comes the Sun."

✔ Vogon Soup plays some covers of other bands' music, such as "Here Comes the Sun."

Generally, set examples off with a comma (see p. 330, Sec. 28.1) or a dash (see p. 349, Sec. 28.5).

22.2 Fix Run-On Sentences and Comma Splices

Run-on sentences and **comma splices** consist of two or more main clauses (each containing a subject and a verb, and each able to stand alone as a sentence) joined in a way that makes them ungrammatical and hard to follow. In a run-on sentence, the main clauses are just stuck together:

┌──────────── **MAIN CLAUSE** ─────────────┐ ┌────────────────────
✗ The band has just three other members they play different

───────── **MAIN CLAUSE** ─────────┐
instruments on different tracks.

In a comma splice, a comma — and only a comma — comes between the main clauses:

┌──────────── **MAIN CLAUSE** ─────────────┐ ┌────────────────────
✗ The band has just three other members, they play different

───────── **MAIN CLAUSE** ─────────┐
instruments on different tracks.

Run-ons and comma splices make the writer look sloppy. If you are prone to writing run-ons or comma splices, review the discussion of standard sentence structures that starts on page 240. To avoid problems with run-ons or comma splices, you need to be able to recognize main clauses. Once you can pick them out, solving the problems is simple. You have four options.

Use a Comma and a Coordinating Conjunction

You can join two main clauses that are roughly equal in importance by inserting a comma and a coordinating conjunction—*and,
but, for, nor, or, so,* or *yet*:

22.2

> The band has just three other members, but they play different
>
> instruments on different tracks.

For more on using commas with coordinating conjunctions, see
page 330, Sec. 28.1.

Use a Semicolon

This option also works well when the two clauses are of equal
importance. In a run-on, add a semicolon between the two
clauses. In a comma splice, replace the comma with a semicolon:

> The band has just three other members; they play different
>
> instruments on different tracks.

To clarify the relationship between the clauses, consider adding
a transition word or phrase (see p. 257, Sec. 23.2), such as *in
contrast* or *meanwhile*, to the second clause, followed by a comma:

> The band has just three other members; however, they play
>
> different instruments on different tracks.

Break the Sentence in Two

This option is most likely to work well if the two clauses are long
or involved.

✗ The band has just three other members — Steve, Buzz, and
   Eliot — and they play different instruments on different tracks.

✔ The band has just three other members — Steve, Buzz, and Eliot.
   They play different instruments on different tracks.

If the clauses are relatively short, as in the next example, the
result is liable to sound choppy and disjointed:

✗ The band has just three other members. They play different
   instruments on different tracks.

Subordinate One of the Clauses

This option works well if you decide that the idea in one of the clauses is more important than the idea in the other. Put the more important idea in the main clause and the lesser one in the subordinate clause (see p. 242, Sec. 21.3).

22.2

```
┌──────────── MAIN CLAUSE ────────────┐ ┌─────────────────────┐
```
✔ The band has just three other members, who play different

```
┌────── SUBORDINATE ──────┐
        CLAUSE
```
instruments on different tracks.

The writer's main point is that the band has just three other members.

23. Write Clear, Logical Sentences

Individual sentences, like whole essays and paragraphs, can be well or badly organized. They're well organized if readers can easily make sense of them and can understand how they relate (or don't) to the sentences before and after them.

23.1 Use Parallelism Logically

Parallelism means putting similar ideas or elements of a sentence in similar form. When you're presenting a series of items or making comparisons among them, the items should be of the same kind, and each of them should connect seamlessly to the rest of the sentence.

Make Elements in a Series Parallel

Many sentences contain series—lists of similar things, actions, or people.

> The nursing home residents' eyes light up when we set out chips, cookies, or brownies.

Series go wrong when the items in the list are mismatched—that is, not parallel.

> ✗ The residents talk with each other, doing crossword and jigsaw puzzles, and some of them read books.
>
> The highlighted phrases are not parallel.

To correct a mismatched series, make all the elements serve the same function in the sentence.

> The residents talk with each other, do crossword and jigsaw puzzles, and read books.
>
> The revised sentence lists the residents' activities in parallel form.

Sometimes items in a series are connected by *either . . . or* or *neither . . . nor*. These items should also take a parallel form.

23.1

✗ Many prefer either playing cards or to watch movies.

> *Playing* is not parallel with *to watch*.

Either form is correct; what's incorrect is the lack of parallelism. The sentence can be revised in either of two ways:

✔ Many prefer either playing cards or watching movies.

✔ Many prefer either to play cards or to watch movies.

Writer to Writer

Does parallelism apply to bulleted lists?   It certainly does. But by the time people writing bulleted lists get to the end of them, sometimes they've forgotten how their list started. So we read stuff like:

A first aid kit should include:

- Compression bandages
- Sterile gauze pads
- The adhesive tape you pack should be designed to stick to skin

Since the first two bulleted items are nouns — and since the list was advertised as consisting of things that ought to be in a first aid kit — the last item should be a noun, too.

- Adhesive tape designed to stick to skin

Compare Like with Like

When you make a comparison, present the items you're comparing in parallel form:

✗ That store's food prices are as expensive as a gourmet restaurant.

> *Prices* is not parallel with *restaurant*.

✔ Shopping for food in that store is as expensive as eating in a gourmet restaurant.

✔ That store's food prices are as expensive as the prices in a gourmet restaurant.

> The revised sentences match *shopping* with *eating* and *prices* with *prices*.

Comparisons can also fall short when writers fail to notice what they're actually comparing:

✘ Our state's food prices are higher than most other places.

> This sentence doesn't make sense, because it compares *prices* with *most other places*.

✔ Our state's food prices are higher than prices in most other places.

✔ Food prices are higher in our state than they are in most of the nation.

> The revised sentences compare *prices* with *prices* and *in our state* with *in most of the nation*.

Connect Elements in a Series to the Rest of the Sentence

Even a perfectly grammatical sentence can go wrong if the ideas don't align just right. This problem comes up when wording intended to connect a series of parallel items to the rest of the sentence doesn't apply to all of them:

✘ I listen to music before, during, and after I study.

> *I listen to music before I study* is fine, *I listen to music after I study* is fine, but *I listen to music during I study* is garbled.

✔ I listen to music before, while, and after I study.

> *I listen to music while I study* is fine.

✗ Sometimes we discover residents eating fries, subs, slices of pizza, milkshakes, beer, and wine that family members have smuggled in.

23.1

> People don't *eat* milkshakes, beer, and wine, so either this word or the series needs correction.

One way to solve a problem like this is to change the connection point so that all the items do make sense with it:

✔ Sometimes we discover residents with fries, subs, slices of pizza, milkshakes, beer, and wine that family members have smuggled in.

Another option with a long series like that one is to break it into two or more, each with its own connection point. Add a conjunction to the first series to show readers where it ends, and add another conjunction before the second or last series to show where it begins:

✔ Sometimes we discover residents wolfing down fries, subs, and slices of pizza and gulping milkshakes, beer, and wine that family members have smuggled in.

> *Wolfing down* applies to the food, and *gulping* applies to the drinks.

The principle that words must connect properly applies even to series of just two, anywhere in a sentence:

✗ I like music as much or more than my friends do.

✔ I like music as much as or more than my friends do.

✗ We try to make sure family members have a clear understanding and obey the rules.

✔ We try to make sure family members have a clear understanding of and obey the rules.

Or, even better than the previous sentence, because it's easier to follow:

✔ We try to make sure family members clearly understand and obey the rules.

Watch out for elements of a series that are liable to connect in ways you don't intend them to:

✘ Nurses and residents with dementia attend the morning exercise class.

> Do the nurses as well as the residents have dementia?

Such problems can usually be solved by changing the order of the elements in the series:

✔ Residents with dementia attend the morning exercise class with their nurses.

23.2 Let Readers Know Where Your Sentence Is Going

Just as drivers appreciate signs on the highway telling them what's coming up, readers appreciate signals about where a sentence is headed. Use these strategies to help readers anticipate and understand your writing.

Use Conjunctions and Transition Words

As you do at the paragraph level, use conjunctions and transition words (see p. 195, Sec. 14.4) to indicate where your sentences are heading in a new direction.

Put your signposts, particularly ones that signal a change, where they'll be most helpful—before your readers have started to lose their way:

✘ I love reading the band's tweets, checking out their links, and sharing them with friends. Some of my friends mainly use their phones to send photos and tweets about the band instead.

By the time readers get to the signposting word *instead*, they will have had to figure out for themselves that the writer is making a distinction between how he responds to the band and how his friends do.

✔ . . . But some of my friends mainly use their phones to send their own photos and tweets about the band.

Putting the signpost *but* at the beginning of the change in direction helps readers follow the writer's train of thought.

Start with information that readers will need to make sense of what follows. Long sentences are the most likely to leave readers feeling lost or misled. Suppose, for instance, a long sentence describes something that could have happened in your town yesterday but ends with the information that the event took place in Australia 150 years ago. Readers will probably wish they'd known that from the start.

Make sure, too, that readers will have no trouble understanding what any pronouns you use are referring to. Pronouns that come before their antecedents (see p. 314, Sec. 26.2, for more on pronouns and antecedents) are likely to be confusing:

✘ At every performance, when they jump onstage and start dancing as if they can't help themselves — as if their lives depended on dancing — fans show how the band energizes them.

Who are *they*? We don't find out until the last part of the sentence.

✔ At every performance, when fans jump onstage and start dancing as if they can't help themselves — as if their lives depended on dancing — they show how the band energizes them.

The revision puts *fans* at the beginning so we know who's jumping onstage.

Keep Related Ideas Together

Except in special circumstances, it would probably never occur to anyone to write anything like this:

> ✗ Mary, a nursing home resident I like a lot, was born in August. Her birthday is on the 18th of the month, and the year she was born was 1920.

23.2

A clear-thinking person would write, instead:

> ✔ Mary, a nursing home resident I like a lot, was born on August 18, 1920.

Sometimes writers do scatter bits of related information all over a sentence. In most cases, the result is not good:

> ✗ Mary founded the women's studies department after becoming a professor at Central University, but earlier, before she was married, she danced professionally and earned a degree in music in hopes of being a concert pianist.

Putting the different parts of Mary's life in chronological order will certainly help straighten this sentence out. Readers expect chronological events to be presented in time order. But even after the time order is straightened out, a couple of problems remain:

> ✗ As a young woman, Mary danced professionally and earned a degree in music in hopes of being a concert pianist, but after she married, she became a professor at Central University, founding its women's studies department.

First, most of the sentence is about Mary's professional life, so the mention of her marriage introduces a seemingly unrelated idea. The sentence would be better off without the mention of the marriage. Second, the sentence seems to say that she danced in hopes of being a concert pianist. The flip side of keeping related ideas together is keeping unrelated ideas apart.

✔ As a young woman, Mary danced professionally, and she earned a degree in music in hopes of being a concert pianist, but ultimately she became a professor at Central University, founding its women's studies department.

Chronology is not the only possible organizing principle. In the following draft of the sentence about Mary, the writer focuses on relationships between *ideas* rather than events in Mary's life:

✔ Mary was born on the day the United States ratified the Nineteenth Amendment to the Constitution, which gave women the right to vote — and this coincidence, she says jokingly, must have inspired her career at Central University as a professor and the founder of the women's studies department.

Keep related ideas together all the way down to the micro level. Put modifiers next to what they're modifying. Dropping them in carelessly looks just that — careless. Misplaced modifiers can even mislead readers.

Limiting modifiers such as *almost, barely, hardly, merely, nearly, only,* and *simply* are particularly liable to make trouble. Compare these sentences:

He *almost lost* all his friends.

He *lost almost* all his friends.

The first sentence says he didn't lose his friends; he *almost lost* them. The second sentence says he did lose *almost all* his friends.

Only I thought we needed money.

I *only* thought we needed money.

I thought we needed *only* money.

The first sentence means that no one but the writer thought money was needed. The second sentence means that the writer merely imagined the need for money. The third sentence means that the writer thought that nothing but money was needed.

Keep the Flow Moving Forward

23.2

A good sentence, like a good composition, builds toward its conclusion. The second most emphatic place in a sentence is the beginning. This is the natural spot to establish the connection, if there is one, between what you just said and what you are starting to say now:

> Forensic linguistics is the science of analyzing words to determine whether the person who spoke or wrote them committed a crime. One famous criminal who was caught with the help of forensic linguistics is Ted Kaczynski, the Unabomber, who from 1978 to 1995 killed three people and injured twenty-three.

The word *criminal* here ties in with *crime*, which ended the previous sentence.

Don't wait too long to get around to something that could possibly hold the reader's interest:

✗ On August 18, 1920, the day when a resident of my nursing home whose name is Mary was born, it also happened that . . .

✔ Women got the right to vote on August 18, 1920 — the very day when . . .

If your sentence contains a series, either make the series move forward chronologically (or backward chronologically, if there's a reason for doing so) or build it conceptually from smaller to bigger or from less to more impressive:

> On seemingly random occasions, for reasons they've never explained, the band turns up onstage in costumes — a cape, a Viking helmet, and even a rubber horse's head, which Gordie soon yanks off and tosses into the crowd.

The most emphatic place in a sentence is the end—the sentence's destination. So if you have something you especially want your readers to notice, try to put it at the end.

Do not end a sentence by trailing off into unnecessary detail:

23.2

✗ . . . the constitutional amendment that gave women the right to vote was ratified, and this was the 19th amendment to the U.S. Constitution.

✔ . . . when the 19th constitutional amendment was ratified.

If you succeed in starting your sentences strong and ending them stronger, sometimes you'll find that you've piled a lot of obstacles in the reader's way in the middle.

✗ Bob, everybody's favorite nursing home resident, not just because he's outgoing and friendly but also because he still practices, for us, the craft with which he earned his living for three-quarters of a century, was a professional magician.

Often, a problem like that results from trying to pack too many ideas into one sentence. Here the writer is trying to tell us both how Bob earned his living and why he is everybody's favorite resident. However, presenting the two ideas together, at the level of detail the writer has provided, overburdens the sentence.

✔ Bob, everybody's favorite nursing home resident, earned his living for three-quarters of a century as a professional magician. We love him not just because he's outgoing and friendly but also because he still practices his craft for us.

Now the first sentence ends with the interesting fact that Bob has long been a magician. The second sentence begins with *We love him*, referring back to *everybody's favorite resident* in the first sentence, and it ends with the information that Bob still practices magic.

23.3 Avoid Dangling Words and Phrases

Beware of words or phrases that attach incorrectly or awkwardly to the rest of the sentence. They are apt to confuse your readers.

23.3

Avoid Dangling Modifiers

The connections between the parts of a sentence can go wrong if a phrase is placed closer to something it could possibly be modifying than to what you intend it to modify. (This is the same principle that applies to limiting modifiers like *almost*, *merely*, *nearly*, *only*, and *simply*, which are discussed on p. 260, Sec. 23.2). Here *we*, the staff, seem to be sneaking those illicit treats:

✗ When sneaking illicit treats, we notice the residents look guilty.

This mistake goes by the name of **dangling modifier** or **dangler**. To correct a dangling modifier, you usually have two options. First, you can revise the main clause so that the modifier comes just before the subject:

✔ When sneaking illicit treats, the residents look guilty.

> Here, it's clear that the residents are the ones sneaking the illicit treats.

Second, you can revise the modifier so that it includes a subject and a verb of its own.

✔ We notice the residents look guilty when they are sneaking illicit treats.

> The modifier has been moved to the end of the sentence.

Writers often make a subtler version of this mistake by trying to connect a modifier to a possessive noun, like *Mary's* in this example:

✗ Born on August 18, 1920, Mary's life took many turns.

> This says that Mary's life was born in 1920 — not what the writer meant.

✔ Born on August 18, 1920, Mary lived a life that took many turns.

> The revision says clearly that Mary was born in 1920.

23.3   Avoid Dangling Prepositions

Little words like *at*, *for*, *in*, *on*, and *with* are often **prepositions**, which attach a noun, pronoun, phrase, or subordinate clause to the rest of the sentence. In a first draft, writers are liable to place these awkwardly at the end of the clause:

✘ Bob showed us the set of silk scarves that he once entertained the Queen of England with.

If you find prepositions at the ends of clauses in your writing, consider whether a different word order would be more graceful. You may also need to change *that* to *which* to accommodate the change:

✔ Bob showed us the set of silk scarves with which he once entertained the Queen of England.

In many cases, though, you'll find that the little word at the end actually belongs there. Sometimes there is no more graceful word order. Then, too, the same words that function as prepositions can also serve as **particles**, or bits of phrasal verbs (see p. 291, Sec. 25.1), and when this is their role, they must follow the main part of the verb.

He urged us, "Pick the scarves up — try them on. That's what they're here for."

> *That's for what they're here* would be much more awkward than the original wording. Besides, both sentences are in a quotation and should represent the speaker's words accurately.

23.4

Writer to Writer

Is "with which" or "with whom" always the best option?   Not necessarily.

When you're deciding whether to begin your relative clause with a preposition plus *which* or to put *that* at the beginning and a preposition at the end — as in the examples about Bob, above — consider the level of formality you're aiming for. In formal academic prose, the first of those alternatives (*with/for/to whom, at/from/in/with which*) is generally preferred. In more conversational contexts, though, that version can sound stuffy.

In conversation, most people would say "one resident that I've learned from" rather than "one resident from whom I've learned." So if you want to be informal, choose the *that* option. When *that* replaces another relative pronoun (here, it replaces *whom*), the preposition (*from*) joins the verb instead of remaining with the pronoun.

In phrases like our example, it's even okay to delete *that* in informal contexts as long as the phrase or sentence remains clear without it. Further, when the relative pronoun is referring to a person, some good writers consider *that* dehumanizing but think of *whom* as out of date, so they choose *who*: "one resident *who* I've learned from." This isn't strictly grammatical, but it is conversational.

23.4 Make a Clause Negative ⊕

To turn verbs negative, English generally uses the adverb *not*, and it has definite conventions about where the adverb should go.

For simple present or past forms of *be* (see p. 299, Sec. 25.2), add *not* after the verb:

Tom is not a member of the band.

For simple present forms of a verb other than *be*, add *do* or *does* plus *not* before the base form of the verb:

Tom does not want to be a member of the band.

For simple past forms of a verb other than *be*, add *did* plus *not* before the base form of the verb:

> Tom did not want to be a member of the band.

23.4

For verb phrases made up of one or more helping verbs and a present or past participle (*is listening, was playing, must have been studying*), add *not* after the first helping verb:

> Tom is not listening. Tom was not playing. Tom must not have been studying.

Many of these negative verb forms are often written with a contraction: *isn't listening, wasn't playing, mustn't have been studying*. But it is best to avoid contractions in formal academic writing. Note that *can't* is a special case: when it is expanded to its full form, it is written without a space: *cannot*.

Another word that can turn a verb negative is *never*.

> Tom never listens.

Alternatively, you may negate the subject of the clause:

> No one else is a member of the band.

> None of the band members have met Tom.

> Not everyone knows how to play a musical instrument.

Clauses can also be made negative by using the negative conjunction *nor*:

> Nor is everyone able to sing.

English only allows a single negative in a clause that expresses a negative idea:

> ✗ I can't get no satisfaction.

> ✔ I can't get any satisfaction.

People use "double negatives" like *can't get no* in colloquial contexts, but they are scarcely ever found in standard English, let alone academic prose.

23.5 Ask a Question ⊕

Questions are sentences that seek information. English has three types of questions: **yes/no questions**, **open questions**, and **tag questions**. There are **indirect questions** as well, which are statements about a question that has been asked.

➤ **Learn more about questions on pp. 338–339, Sec. 28.2.**

23.5

Ask Yes/No Questions

The term for these questions comes from the usual possible answers.

Most yes/no questions begin with an auxiliary or helping verb (see p. 299, Sec. 25.2). The subject comes next, the main verb after that, and the object of the verb or other information at the end.

> MAIN VERB
> Do you like dogs?

> MAIN VERB
> Did you have a dog as a child?

> MAIN VERB
> Have you ever adopted a dog?

> MAIN VERB
> Will you adopt a dog if you find one you like?

However, if your main verb is a form of *be* or if a form of *be* is the only verb in the sentence, put it first:

> Am I alone in liking bulldogs?

> Are bulldogs your favorite breed too?

> Were there any bulldogs in the animal shelter last week?

This exception with *be* does not apply to questions in tenses that always require auxiliary verbs:

> Will you be disappointed if you don't find a bulldog soon?

The simple future tense (see p. 297, Sec. 25.2) of *be* is *will be*, so the question starts with *will*, as it would for a future-tense question with another verb.

Will you choose a different dog if you don't find a bulldog?

To make a yes/no question negative, turn the auxiliary word or the form of *be* into a negative contraction: *don't, didn't, haven't, won't, aren't*. Or add *not* after the subject or placeholder:

Don't you like dogs?

Were there **not** any bulldogs?

Ask Open Questions

These are questions that have many more possible answers than yes or no. They are also called **wh- questions**, since most (but not all) start with the letters *wh*:

what	who
which	why
when	how (how many, how old, how often)
where	

Open questions take a form similar to yes/no questions. Often you can just add a question word or phrase to the beginning of a yes/no question to form an open question:

How much does the animal shelter charge for a dog?

Why do you like bulldogs?

With forms of *be* or when the question word or phrase is the subject, the question word or phrase comes first and is followed by the verb:

How old is that dog?

Where is the animal shelter?

Who owns that dog?

To make an open question negative, just add a form of *not*—
generally -*n't* as part of a contraction—to the sentence:

Why don't you adopt a dog?

When can't you visit the shelter?

Ask Tag Questions

Tag questions are usually intended to confirm information you
think is correct. They are tagged on to, or attached to the end of,
a statement.

You want a dog, don't you?

Use a negative tag with a positive statement, and a positive tag
with a negative statement:

You like bulldogs, don't you?

> If you do like bulldogs, the answer to this would be "Yes, I do."

You don't like Airedales, do you?

> If you don't like Airedales, the answer would be "No, I don't."

Use Indirect Questions

Use an indirect question when you are reporting a question that
someone else has asked, and don't end it with a question mark.

She is asking who owns that dog.

He wondered if you want a dog.

24. Choose Engaging Language

In spoken conversation, some people turn others off by being disrespectful, and some people strike others as boring. Using language that engages your readers in writing begins with a respectful approach to their needs, interests, values, and beliefs. It continues with the use of clear, concise, lively phrasing. Concise phrasing not only helps a writer be clear but also shows respect for readers' time. Lively phrasing gives pleasure to readers—and no doubt to the writer as well.

24.1

24.1 Choose Your Words Carefully

Once you've structured your sentences properly, you can focus on the words that are in them. Consider the tone of your genre and aim for words that strike that tone.

Choose the Right Level of Formality

In genres such as texts and emails to your friends, anything goes. In more formal writing, though, readers expect to be treated as colleagues, not pals. And they expect to see well-considered, grammatical sentences and well-chosen vocabulary.

Words that an up-to-date dictionary has tagged *slang*, *used in email*, or the like probably do not belong in writing intended for anyone except close friends. The same goes for words or uses of words that feel informal but aren't in any dictionary except perhaps urbandictionary.com.

✗ In a passionate blog post, the author argues that men must be *woke* to the way patriarchy oppresses women.

✔ In a passionate blog post, the author argues that men must *recognize* the way patriarchy oppresses women.

Words tagged *colloquial* or *informal* usually do not belong in academic papers or any other equally formal writing:

24.1

✘ According to Gates Foundation statistics, 77 percent of those who die of malaria are kids under the age of five.

✔ According to Gates Foundation statistics, 77 percent of those who die of malaria are children under the age of five.

However, informal language tends to enliven personal essays, journalism, and similar kinds of semiformal writing:

Even little kids like some tracks by Vogon Soup.

Avoid Unnecessarily Technical Language

Jargon lies at the other end of the language spectrum from colloquial words. Jargon is made up of terms—for instance, *pathogens* and *antimicrobial agents*—that are familiar to people in a particular field or who share a particular interest but that hardly ever come up in general conversation. It is fine to use the jargon of a field you're writing about if the term is more exact than any general-vocabulary term you know and if it seems to be widely used in that field.

Don't get carried away with jargon, though:

✘ The epidemiology of pathogenic resistance to antimicrobial agents warrants careful scrutiny.

Unless you're confident that your readers already understand the specialized terms you want to use, introduce them gradually or avoid them:

✔ Now that some disease-causing microbes can survive treatment with the drugs and other substances that were developed to kill or control them, it is important to study how and where the resistant microbes are spreading.

> *Microbes* and *resistant* are on the borderline of jargon, but the context helps clarify them.

General-purpose dictionaries aren't much help with jargon. They may give words that are jargon a tag like *medicine*, give no tag, or leave them out. If you need to use specialized terms and want to make sure you're using them accurately, check a special-purpose resource like a medical dictionary.

24.1

Avoid Bias and Stereotyping

No one with a well-developed sense of fairness enjoys insulting people or seeing them insulted. Instead, we tend to sympathize with whoever's been insulted and to dislike the person who's responsible. Insults can be direct, or they can take the form of assumptions—for instance, that a woman is less powerful than a man, that an old person must be forgetful, or that a member of a certain political group must be narrow-minded. Unless you are presenting definite evidence to the contrary, do not state or imply that any person or group is inferior or superior to others, and do not state or imply that specific members of a group have stereotypical traits.

Be especially sensitive in how you write about anything that touches on these human characteristics:

age	physical attributes and abilities
citizenship	political opinions
gender	race/ethnicity
health status	religion
intelligence	sexual orientation
mental health	socioeconomic status

When you're writing about groups of people or members of those groups, try to use the words they themselves prefer. Unfortunately, even among advocacy organizations there is no consensus on, for example, whether *people with autism*, *autistic people*, or *people with ASD* (autism spectrum disorder) is preferred. A little research on the web will help you find the terms to avoid and will explain the rationales for recommended terms.

Do not use *he* habitually to refer to a nonspecific individual. Even if doing so is convenient, it is sexist and outdated.

24.1

✗ A researcher who wants to do something about the malaria crisis will find that he needs to decide whether to work on vaccines, prevention, or treatment.

Sentences with this problem can be revised in any of several ways. You can change *he* to *he or she* (although this implies the existence of only two genders):

✔ A researcher investigating the malaria crisis will find that he or she needs to decide whether to work on vaccines, prevention, or treatment.

You can make the singular noun plural, so that the matching pronoun becomes the gender-neutral *they*:

✔ Researchers investigating the malaria crisis will find they need to decide whether to work on vaccines, prevention, or treatment.

You can get rid of the pronoun:

✔ A researcher investigating the malaria crisis needs to decide whether to work on vaccines, prevention, or treatment.

An option that was widely considered ungrammatical until recently but is gaining currency (see the Writer to Writer box on p. 274) is to use *they* and *them* with a singular antecedent.

A researcher . . . they . . . .

Also avoid using gender-specific words for nonspecified people. There's always a gender-neutral form that you can use instead.

businessman → businessperson

congressman → representative

mankind → humanity, humankind

policeman → police officer

waitress → server

Be careful to avoid gender bias when citing the work of other writers. Although citation styles vary (see Part 6), most styles call for the use of the source's last name only. Sticking to writers' last names also helps put the focus on their authority and position, rather than their (irrelevant) gender.

> ## Writer to Writer
>
> ***Can you use*** they ***in the singular? What about nongendered pronouns?*** Traditionally, the pronoun *he* or *she* or *him* or *her* would be used to match the gender of its antecedent. Because such pronouns can end up excluding people, the plural pronoun *they* is becoming more common when referring to one person. "Every camper should bring *their* sleeping bag on the field trip."
>
> Some people don't consider themselves either male or female. It is, of course, respectful and appropriate to refer to people by the names they've asked that others use. The same goes for a person's preferred pronoun, whether that's *he, she, hir, they, ze,* something else, or no pronoun at all but instead the person's name: "Kyle gets angry when *Kyle's* friends are unkind to each other."
>
> If you don't know and can't readily find out (online, for instance) what usage a given person prefers, *they* and *them* are acceptable.

Use the Standard Version of Words

English contains many pairs of similar words, one of which is considered to be standard and the other of which is less common. These include pairs such as *geographic* and *geographical*, and *preventive* and *preventative*, for example.

You're not expected to memorize which version is standard in every case. Look the word up in a dictionary. If the entry appears under, say, *geographic*, use that version in your document. If the word appears under the other variant but the dictionary says "geographic *or* geographical," use whichever variant it gives first.

24.2 Hone Your Phrasing

Say what you mean. There are renowned writers who are known for their rhetorical flourishes, but many more get straight to the point. Academic writing in particular values above all communicating clearly to the intended audience.

24.2

Avoid Exaggeration

In social conversation, it's normal to say things like, "Those were the most beautiful strawberries I've ever seen!" and "I could eat a truckload of them!" But in more formal contexts and when you're writing for readers who don't know you well, it's important to show that you're reliable. Readers have a sense of what the world is like. Exaggerations tend to affect them much the way insults do: they begin to mistrust the writer. Avoid stating opinions or conclusions that are more than the facts will bear out, and whenever possible, present the information that's the basis for your opinion or conclusion, so that readers can evaluate it for themselves.

✗ One of the biggest problems in the United States today is that unhealthy food is available everywhere and anyone can afford it. By contrast, healthy food is a nightmare to find, and it is priced out of almost everyone's reach. The devastating result is that everybody in the country makes pathetic eating choices every day.

The highlighted words are exaggerations.

✔ Unhealthy food is convenient to buy, and most people can easily afford it. By contrast, healthy food can be hard to find, and it is more expensive. The unfortunate result is that many people make poor eating choices regularly.

When the exaggerations are removed, it is easier to agree with the writer's point.

24.2

Writer to Writer

Should you emulate expert authors?   Yes, but not indiscriminately.

Reading widely is one of the best things you can do improve your writing. By paying close attention not just to the content of writing by authors you admire but also to their style, you can learn from them.

Do not assume, however, that their writing is perfect down to the last detail. No one is perfect — not prize-winning authors and journalists, not editors, no one. Newspapers and news websites, in particular, are prone to error because of the time pressure their staffs are under.

If you come across a detail that puzzles you in a good source — an unfamiliar spelling, for instance, or a punctuation mark in a place you wouldn't expect to find it — don't assume you should take that as your model from now on. Keep the detail in mind and look for evidence pro or con in comparable publications. You may be surprised by how many errors can be found in even the most professional publications and websites.

Favor Words You Know

As you polish your writing, you may want to use a thesaurus or dictionary to find exactly the words you need. However, not all the choices a reference source offers you will be equally good. If you used the word *terrible* but suspect that another word will make it clearer what kind of terrible you mean, don't choose, for example, *atrocious* or *egregious* or *vile* because you like the sound of it. Choose it when the word is already familiar to you and you know it has the shade of meaning you want. If you *love* the sound of an unfamiliar word, check a dictionary or learn about it by looking at some uses of it in a reliable source like the *Wall Street Journal*.

Using words that are new to you may even be necessary when you're writing in a discipline full of specialized terminology. Check your textbook or an online source such as Google Scholar to make sure you understand the new terms you use.

In general, when you have a choice between a simple word and a longer, fancier one that has the same shade of meaning, choose the simple word.

24.2

assist → help	initiate → start
employment → job	purchase → buy
expeditious → fast	reside → live
frequently → often	sufficient → enough
identical → same	terminate → end
individual → person	utilize → use

✗ The utilization of monosyllabic locutions is recommended as preferable.

✔ Aim for brevity. Words of one syllable are the best.

Writer to Writer

Between *or* among? Use *between* when you're discussing two things or two sets of things: *Between you and me, the genetic differences between golden retrievers and yellow Labradors.* Use *among* for three or more: *I can't choose a favorite writer among Jane Austen, Charles Dickens, and Leo Tolstoy.* An exception arises when you're discussing three or more things but only two at a time. Then use *between: voyages between America, Europe, and Asia.*

To Be Vivid, Be Specific

Writers may feel strongly about a topic, such as the urgency of climate change, and want to transmit that passion to their readers. Rather than beginning a paper with general statements about what climate change is or how it has occurred, the writer might begin by sketching a memorable scene:

The building I live in has been standing for more than 150 years, but its roof was no match for the three blizzards in a row that hit

24.2

us last winter. After the first blizzard, melted snow, tinted brown from the roof's insulation, began leaking into my apartment. The filthy-looking water trickled down the white walls and through the ceiling of my bedroom — onto the dresser, the TV, and eventually my bed. Where I set out buckets to catch the drips, the liquid hit the plastic with a bang. Bang! Bang! Bang! This went on at a rate of about once a second for sixteen days.

Last winter was the snowiest that my city has experienced in its recorded history, and living through it brought home to me how destructive and traumatic abnormal weather can be. The great majority of scientists who study the Earth's climate agree that climate change is occurring at an alarming rate.

Now readers, too, can see, vividly and specifically, what the writer sees. Detail can bring a scene to life or make an idea persuasive. Details that have little to do with the point the writer wants to make, however, are best omitted.

Give Every Word a Job to Do

As you revise, look for words and phrases that aren't carrying their weight, and cut or change them. When you see a bland phrase, consider how to make it livelier while still being clear. When you see a long-winded phrase, think about how you might convey your point more concisely. Cut unnecessary words or phrases. Using a thesaurus to look up words you've written but don't like can often provide inspiration — as long as you understand and feel comfortable with the replacement word (see p. 276).

✗ There has never been a winter when more snow fell in my city since people began keeping records of annual snowfalls.

✔ Last winter was the snowiest that my city has experienced in its recorded history.

24.2

✘ If you asked all the major researchers who study the climate of planet Earth, most of them would be in agreement that the climate of this planet is going through a change at a much faster rate than would normally be expected by scientists.

✔ The great majority of scientists who study the Earth's climate agree that climate change is occurring at an alarming rate.

Writer to Writer

While *or* although? *While* can mean *at the same time as*: *While the pyramids were being built in Egypt, woolly mammoths still inhabited Wrangel Island in the Arctic Ocean.* But it can also mean the same thing as *although*: *While the two candidates took similar positions on most issues, they diverged sharply on gun control.*

Using *while* for the *although* meaning is fine as long as the usage doesn't conflict with the time-related meaning—as it does in *While the seventeenth century brought new, labor-saving ways of producing goods, the nineteenth century was even more fertile technologically.* Change that and similar *whiles* to *though* or *although*.

Favor the Active Voice

In the **active voice**, the subject of the sentence is the actor:

Tuberculosis sickens many people.

In the **passive voice**, the subject of the sentence is acted upon:

Many people are sickened by tuberculosis.

Ordinarily, when you use the active voice, your writing will be more direct and forceful:

✘ Roughly 1.5 million people a year are killed by tuberculosis.

✔ Tuberculosis kills roughly 1.5 million people a year.

With *tuberculosis* as the subject, the verb can take the active form *kills* rather than the passive form *are killed by*.

To make a passive sentence active, you don't always need to turn it around the way we did in the previous examples. Sometimes you can simply change the verb:

24.2

✔ Roughly 1.5 million people a year die of tuberculosis.

> In this sentence, *people* remains the subject, but the verb *die* is active.

The passive voice is more common than the active in some disciplines, such as the sciences, to emphasize a result or outcome. It's also fine in situations in which you do not want to identify the actor or the actor is not important. Here, for example, it's beside the point to say who uses the antibiotics:

> Antibiotics are used to treat tuberculosis.

The passive voice serves a good purpose when it allows you to start or end a sentence in a way that flows smoothly from the previous sentence into the current one. For instance, compare these two passages:

> Tuberculosis poses a serious problem for public health. Bacteria cause tuberculosis, and infected people spread it when they cough, sneeze, laugh, spit, or speak. Killing the bacteria with antibiotics combats the disease.

> Tuberculosis poses a serious problem for public health. It is caused by bacteria and is spread when infected people cough, sneeze, laugh, spit, or speak. It is combatted by killing the bacteria with antibiotics.

Although all the verbs in the first passage are in the active voice, the train of thought seems disorganized, jumping from tuberculosis to the bacteria and back to tuberculosis, to infected people and back to tuberculosis, and to killing the bacteria and back to tuberculosis. In the second passage, tuberculosis is the subject of all three sentences, reinforcing the fact that the passage is about the disease.

Writer to Writer

Farther *or* further? *Farther* is preferred for physical distance: *The star Sirius is farther from Earth than Alpha Centauri. Further* is preferred for other kinds of distance, including distance in time and metaphorical distance: *going further back through the centuries, nothing could be further from the truth. Further* can also mean *additional*: *a further point to keep in mind.*

24.2

Look for Alternatives to Forms of *Be*

In this passage, notice how many verbs are *was* or another form of *be*:

✗ Harriet Tubman was a remarkable American. She was born a slave in the 1820s (the exact year is not known) in Maryland. In 1849 she was able to escape to Philadelphia, in the free state of Pennsylvania. She was not satisfied to live comfortably as a free woman, however, when there were so many others who were still slaves. There was a series of trips that she made back south, guiding her parents, several of her brothers and sisters, and about 60 other people to freedom. In the Civil War, she was at first a cook and a nurse for the Union Army, then an armed scout and spy. She was the first woman to lead an armed expedition in the war, and a raid she was in charge of liberated 700 slaves in South Carolina.

It's not easy to get rid of every instance of *be*, but often you can find another verb that will work harder for you:

✔ Harriet Tubman won renown as a remarkable American. She was born a slave in the 1820s (the exact year is not known) in Maryland. In 1849 she escaped to Philadelphia, in the free state of Pennsylvania. She refused to live comfortably as a free woman, however, when so many others remained slaves. She made a series

24.2

of trips back south, guiding her parents, several of her brothers and sisters, and about 60 other people to freedom. In the Civil War, she at first worked as a cook and a nurse for the Union Army, then as an armed scout and spy. She became the first woman to lead an armed expedition in the war, and a raid she led liberated 700 slaves in South Carolina.

> *Escaped* is a more direct way of saying *was able to escape*, and *refused* is stronger and more concise than *was not satisfied*.

Although the verb *be* in its various forms — *am, are, is, was, were* — is versatile, and sometimes even irreplaceable, it is often not the strongest choice.

Make Your Own Figures of Speech

Figures of speech are words and phrases not intended to be taken literally. Most familiar ones — like "a dime a dozen," "plenty of fish in the sea," "the icing on the cake" — have been used for so long that all connection to their literal sense has been lost. They don't bring a vivid image to mind. They're clichés. Avoid them.

If your goal is to make readers see something or understand something the way you saw or understood it, stop and think: How does it strike *you*? Was that filthy-looking water leaking through the ceiling "like a mudslide in miniature"? Did those sixteen days "feel like a practical joke gone horribly wrong"?

Don't force it. It's better to do without figures of speech than to write foolish ones.

✗ Tuberculosis makes a person as sick as a dog.

> Besides being a cliché, this phrase conveys almost nothing about what it feels like to have tuberculosis.

✗ Tuberculosis often makes a person feel exhausted, like a cell phone that hasn't been charged in a week.

> This is more original, but who's to say what a cell phone feels like?

✔ Tuberculosis often leaves people feeling exhausted and out of breath — as if they'd run for miles and still had miles to go.

> This conveys the feeling more vividly than *exhausted and out of breath* does alone.

Pay Attention to Relationships among Words

As readers encounter your words, sounds and images come into their minds. Writing conveys ideas, too, of course. As a writer, you should work to control the sounds, images, and ideas your words bring to mind.

Often such control involves deliberately repeating related words:

> Few climate scientists would attempt to predict the weather for specific places at specific times. Using temperature data, however, climate science can make confident predictions about global trends.

The word forms themselves help tie the ideas of *climate scientists* to *climate science* and *predict* to *predictions*.

✘ We react in one way to weather-related disasters that affect individuals on the other side of the world and in another to catastrophes that happen to people we know.

Here, is the writer trying to draw some distinction between *disasters* and *catastrophes*? Between *individuals* and *people*? It's unclear.

✔ We react in one way to weather-related disasters that affect people on the other side of the world and in another to disasters that happen to people we know.

Disasters and *people* now repeat, helping to establish clearly that the writer is presenting a difference between things that happen at a distance and similar things that happen closer to home.

Making words sound similar is important. It can even be required in some situations (see parallelism, p. 253, Sec. 23.1). But repetition must be used with care. It can work for you or against you. Avoid unintentional repeats or echoes, particularly ones that are close together:

24.2

✗ It's not odd that all prime numbers except 2 are odd; all other even numbers are multiples of 2.

Ideas, like sounds, can repeat in undesirable ways:

✗ Bob has recently been writing an autobiography of his life.

> An *autobiography* is the story of the writer's life; *of his life* is repetitive.

This blunder is called **redundancy**. So many turns of phrase can be redundant that it would be impossible to list them all. Some notorious redundancies, however, are these:

added bonus	HIV virus
advance notice	The *V* in *HIV* stands for virus.
advance reservation	mutual cooperation
armed shooter	overexaggerate
both . . . different	past history
both the same	PIN number
consensus of opinion	The *N* in *PIN* stands for number.
end result	reason is because, reason why
final outcome	return back, revert back
free gift	successful achievement
future plans	total extinction
general public	true fact

As for the images in readers' heads, beware of **mixed metaphors** — different figures of speech that call confused jumbles of images to mind:

✗ The water came pouring in like a freight train, soiling everything in its path.

> Do trains *pour in* or *soil* things? This sentence may be lively, but it's confused and confusing.

24.2

Similarly, avoid using words that have more than one meaning in a context that's likely to bring the wrong image or meaning to mind:

✗ Prison inmates are forbidden to have cell phones.

> Mobile phones? Phones in their cells?

Limit Your *-tion*, *-ing*, and *-ly* Endings

Be particularly suspicious of the ending -tion. It makes almost everything it touches abstract—and the more abstract an idea is, the less vivid it will be:

✗ The solution must include government reprioritization of climate research and subsidization of it.

An excess of -tion endings tends to result from trying to load too much of your meaning into nouns (*solution, reprioritization, subsidization*) and stringing them together with flabby verbs (*must include*). Solve the problem by changing some of the nouns to verbs or verb phrases (like *solving this problem, focus on*, and *fund*).

✔ Solving this problem will require the government to focus on and fund climate research.

The ending *-ing* isn't as bad, but a sentence full of *-ing*s that are not intended to be parallel (see p. 253, Sec. 23.1, for more on parallelism) will tend to sound sing-songy—as if you didn't notice how what you wrote would sound. What's more, the parallel forms suggest that the ideas the words convey have more in common than they do:

24.2

✗ Improving weather forecasting and revising the goals of urban planning may be helping.

For ideas that are not parallel, variety in word forms is best.

✔ Improvements in weather forecasting and revisions to the goals of urban planning may help.

Not all adverbs end in -ly, but most words that end in -ly are adverbs. Too many -ly endings, like too many -ings, will also give a sing-songy effect. Worse, they are a tip-off that you're stuffing your writing full of adverbs (see p. 324, Sec. 27.2):

✗ Unfortunately, the U.S. government currently spends billions of dollars annually simply to repair damage that natural disasters routinely cause.

You can often cut some -ly adverbs, and you may be able to replace others you feel you need with synonyms:

✔ The U.S. government now spends billions of dollars a year to repair damage that natural disasters cause.

State Things Affirmatively

Statements that negate the verb usually make your readers work harder than they should. They force readers to turn your ideas around to understand what you *are* saying when you are *not* saying something else. The extra work they put in is likely to rob your writing of force and directness. Look for affirmative ways to make your points:

✗ Climate change is not just a minor, distant problem.

✔ Climate change is a serious, immediate problem.

A sentence can include a negative word like *no* without being a negative statement:

✔ No one who has lived through a natural disaster wants to repeat the experience.

> The statement starts with a negative word, but the statement itself is affirmative.

If you make a habit of writing affirmative statements, an occasional negative statement will stand out and become forceful:

Much progress has been made in weather forecasting and in construction techniques to minimize damage from storms. It would inspire even more confidence if research into reversing climate change were making similar progress, but this is not the case.

25. Use Verbs Skillfully

Without verbs, English would be just a great big pile of stuff—a heap of nouns, noun phrases, and connecting parts unable to move, change, affect one another, or do anything else, because *doing* is the province of verbs. We may lose sight of that fact after reading one too many verbs like *incentivize* and *prioritize* and *signify*—verbs that merely suggest abstract concepts. The best verbs show some life. They conquer and comfort, praise and disparage, live and breathe.

25.1 Match the Number of a Verb and Its Subject

Number means singular or plural, one or more than one. Number is not generally an issue if you're writing in the first person (that is, if your subject is *I* or *we*) or second person (*you*), because the verbs use the simple **base form**, with no ending: *I throw. You catch. We play.*

Most of your writing, though, including nearly all the academic writing you do, will be in the third person, and here number does matter. The verb for a singular subject needs an *-s* or *-es* ending: *She throws. He catches.* The verb for a plural subject uses the base form, with no ending: *They play.*

An important exception to this pattern is the highly irregular verb *be: I am. You are. He/she is. We are. You are. They are.*

My father is self-reliant and hardworking, and so is my mother.

My parents are both thrifty. I am influenced by their values.

All of that information about verb forms and number seems simple until you start writing real sentences about real topics. Then number is liable to give you trouble in a variety of situations.

Watch Out for Words That Interrupt the Subject and Verb

Mistakes with number are especially common when something with a different number from the subject's pops up to throw the writer off track.

25.1

✗ The trouble they have taken to provide for members of their families in two countries inspire me.

✔ The trouble they have taken to provide for members of their families in two countries inspires me.

> The subject of the verb is *trouble*, not *countries* or *families* or *members*.

Treat Most Compound Subjects as Plural

A **compound subject** is made up of two or more things, which, taken together, call for a plural verb:

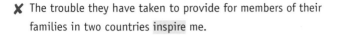

My mother and my older brother are champion networkers, so they have plenty of friends to fall back on.

If the two are really one, though, use a singular verb:

My best friend and roommate thinks my family is old-fashioned.

> *Thinks* is correct here only because the best friend is also the roommate.

Note that the parts of a compound subject are joined by *and*. Words that come after *along with, as well as, besides, in addition to, together with,* and similar words and phrases don't actually become part of the subject of a sentence. These additions are usually set off with commas, dashes, or parentheses.

My younger brother, along with my father, prefers to do things for himself.

> The subject is only *my younger brother*, so the verb needs to be singular.

Match the Number of the Verb to the Nearer or Nearest of Alternative Subjects

Alternative subjects are connected by *or* or *nor*:

25.1

A resident or her family member needs to make the plans.

Resident and *family member* are alternative subjects here.

When both subjects are singular, as they are in that example, or when both are plural, there's little cause for confusion. But sometimes the alternatives are different in number, and then the verb should match the subject that's closer to it in the sentence.

✔ Neither the head of staff nor the committee members have time to make the plans.

Because *members* is closer to the verb, the verb is plural.

✘ I don't know whether my brothers or my mother have more friends.

✔ I don't know whether my brothers or my mother has more friends.

Mother is closer to the verb, so the verb should be *has*.

If the corrected version seems awkward, you have the option of reordering the subjects.

I don't know whether my mother or my brothers have more friends.

Watch Out for Verbs That Come Before Their Subjects 🌐

Not all sentences put the subject before the verb. In fact, nearly all sentences whose main clauses begin with *there is* or *there are*, and some sentences that begin with *it is*, put the subject after the verb.

✘ In sum, there is many people who are on our side even without taking paid specialists into account.

✔ In sum, there are many people who are on our side . . .

> *There* isn't a subject. It's just a placeholder for the subject, *people*, which comes after the verb.

It's often better to turn *there is* and *there are* sentences around (see p. 237, Sec. 20.1):

In sum, many people are on our side . . .

> Now the subject is in its usual position before the verb and the sentence is more concise.

Other kinds of sentences, too—often ones whose verb is a form of *be*—put the subject after the verb.

✘ Especially deserving of appreciation is the night workers.

✔ Especially deserving of appreciation are the night workers.

> This sentence is equivalent to *The night workers are especially deserving of appreciation*, so the verb must be plural.

Among those who have helped us the most is our neighbor.

> This sentence is equivalent to *Our neighbor is among those who have helped us the most.*

Understand Phrasal Verbs ⊕

Phrasal verbs add an additional word or words to a verb to convey a meaning different from that of the verb alone. Some of them have objects, and in many cases the object can be placed between the parts of the verb: *Bring it on! Find this out.* Longer objects, among others, are more likely to be placed after both or all parts of the verb: *Find out the information. Bring back whatever you discover.*

If you read a familiar verb and don't understand it in context— for instance, the verb *drop* in *Drop by if you like*—look up the phrase (*drop by*) in your dictionary. If it's a common phrasal verb, the dictionary will give it an entry separate from the entry for the verb alone.

25.1

Common Phrasal Verbs

ask around/out	find out	lock up/out
break down/up	get around/along	look after/up/out
bring back/on/up	get back to/at	pick off/out/up
call in/off/(up)on	give in/up	put off/on/out
check in/out	go on/over	sign in/out/up
come across/ forward/up	grow apart/on/ out/up	think about/up
drop by/in/off/out	hand in/out	turn around/in/on/ off/up
fill in/out/up	hang on/out/up	work out

➤ Learn more about phrasal verbs in the box on p. 239 (Sec. 20.3).

Do Not Confuse a Noun Complement with Either an Object or the Subject

A **noun complement** is not an object of the verb—not something being acted upon. Nor is it the subject of the sentence. Rather, it's something being equated with the subject: *She is my best friend.* Only certain verbs—most commonly *be*—take complements, and the number of the subject and the number of the complement may differ. The number of the verb should match the number of the subject.

My parents' fallback, when no one in the family is able to help them, is friends.

The subject of the sentence is *fallback*, so the verb is singular.

✗ The only problem with strategies like theirs are unreliable friends.

✔ The only problem with strategies like theirs is unreliable friends.

The subject is not *strategies* or *friends* but *problem*.

Use Singular Verbs with Singular Indefinite Pronouns

Indefinite pronouns refer to nonspecific people or things. The following indefinite pronouns are all grammatically singular, even if some of them seem to have a plural meaning:

anybody	neither
anyone	nobody
anything	no one
each	nothing
either	others
everybody	somebody
everyone	someone
everything	something

Anyone who has relatives who immigrated from other countries knows what I am talking about.

✘ Each of my family members are that way — except me.

✔ Each of my family members is that way — except me.

That, at least, is the rule according to traditional grammar. However, constructions like *Anybody who thinks they must . . .* , in which the traditionally plural *they* refers to the singular indefinite pronoun *anybody*, are increasingly common. Avoid such uses in formal writing.

Bear in mind that *each*, when it follows a plural pronoun or noun, is not an indefinite pronoun but a modifier, and the verb that follows it should be plural.

They each have an independent streak.

The subject is the plural pronoun *they*, so it takes the plural verb *have*.

Neither is another word that may need special care.

✘ Neither of my parents like to ask strangers for help.

✔ Neither of my parents likes to ask strangers for help.

> Even though *parents* is plural, the subject is the singular pronoun *neither*, so it takes the singular verb *likes*.

But when *neither* is paired with *nor*—as in *Neither my mother nor my brothers ask for help*—these words are not indefinite pronouns but modifiers of alternative subjects (see p. 290). The number of the verb should match the number of the subject closer to the verb.

Use the Right Verb Forms with Collective Nouns

Collective nouns gather up multiple people or things and treat the group as a whole. Examples of collective nouns include *army, band, bunch, committee, family, group,* and *team,* but there are many more. Collective nouns are usually treated as singular:

My family eats dinner every night at six.

The band has five members.

Collective nouns are often followed by phrases that specify what the group consists of: *an army of ants, a band of brothers, a bunch of grapes.* When a noun phrase on this pattern—"a singular of plurals"—is a subject, the verb is still usually singular:

An army of ants swarms into the house if we leave food sitting out.

The exception is when the members of the group are acting as individuals rather than as a unit:

My band of brothers all volunteer at the homeless shelter.

Use the Right Verb Forms with Mass Nouns and Count Nouns ⊕

25.1

A **mass noun**, or **noncount noun**, names something that isn't being counted:

> They served iced tea, seltzer, and fruit at the reception.

A **count noun** names something that is being counted or could be:

> They offered a choice of three different teas and several different fruits.

One noun may function both ways, as in these examples. But most nouns function primarily one way or the other. Liquids (*milk, beer*), powders (*sand, rice*), and materials (*cloth, steel*) are likely to be mass nouns. All the same, there's no clear rule about which kinds of things are which kind of noun. *Luggage* is a mass noun, *suitcase* is a count noun, and the two can mean the same thing.

Count nouns are used with *each* or *many* (*each book, many projects*); the things they describe have distinct boundaries and can be made plural. Noncount nouns are used with *much* (*much money, much sleep*) and describe things with indistinct or no boundaries.

Mass nouns always take singular verbs:

✗ Fruit are my favorite kind of food.

✔ Fruit is my favorite kind of food.

The verbs for count nouns depend on whether one or more than one item is being referred to:

> A fruit I especially like is mangoes. Two fruits I like almost as well are watermelon and apples.

> Don't get tripped up by the plural *mangoes*. The subject of this sentence is *a fruit,* so it takes the singular verb *is.*

Watch Out for Nouns That Look Plural but Are Not

Not all nouns that end in -s are plural, and the singular ones take singular verbs.

25.2

Economics is my favorite subject.

Some nouns with -s endings are never plural. Others are sometimes singular and sometimes plural, depending on meaning.

Statistics makes me think.

> As a field of study, *statistics*, like *economics*, is singular.

The statistics make the point.

> Referring to facts or items of data, *statistics* is plural.

Nouns that end in -s and can be singular include:

acoustics	linguistics
biceps	mathematics
blues (music)	news
crossroads	physics
economics	politics
gymnastics	robotics
lens	statistics

If you're unsure about the number of a particular word in a particular context, check a dictionary.

25.2 Use Verb Tense to Indicate Time ⊕

Unless you give some indication to the contrary, readers will probably assume that you're narrating chronological events in time order, presenting causes before effects, explaining problems before solutions, and so on. In these cases, a simple past (or present or future) tense may be all you need. Sometimes, though, you'll want to start in the middle of a sequence. Then verb tenses can help you make clear what came before what, either logically or chronologically.

Consider this paragraph:

> My father responded to the world more openly before
> September 11, 2001. Since then, even though my family is
> Hindu, not Muslim, we have at times been targets of ethnic
> discrimination — people making hateful remarks or vandalizing
> our property. This has hit my father especially hard, because he
> had believed in America as a land of freedoms and opportunity for
> people like us. And in 2001 my brothers and I were very young.
> Our father didn't want us to grow up to be fearful or angry.

The paragraph starts by dividing the writer's father's world into pre- and post-9/11. It goes on to talk about things that have happened since 9/11 and their effect on her father, circles back to how her father felt before 9/11, points out something that was the case at the time of 9/11, and ends with an observation about what, at that time, her father wanted for the future. The writer's verb tenses help readers stay with her the whole way.

The tables that follow demonstrate the verb tenses you have at your disposal.

Simple Tenses for Regular Verbs

The *simple tenses* are generally used for facts (*The Earth revolves around the sun*), states of being (*I felt terrific*), and recurring actions (*I will walk to school every day*).

	Formula	Example
simple present	verb with no ending (first-, second-, and third-person plural); or verb + *-s* or *-es* (third-person singular)	*Today I/you/we/they <u>smile</u>.* *Today I/you/we/they <u>cook</u>.* *Today he/she <u>smiles</u>.* *Today he/she <u>cooks</u>.*
simple past	verb + *-d* or *-ed*	*Yesterday I <u>smiled</u>.* *Yesterday I <u>cooked</u>.*
simple future	*will* + verb	*Tomorrow I <u>will smile</u>.* *Tomorrow I <u>will cook</u>.*

Perfect Tenses for Regular Verbs

The *perfect tenses* are formed with a helping verb or verbs plus a past participle. For regular verbs, the past participle is the same as the simple past. The *present perfect* places the action in the past. The *past perfect* places the action earlier in the past, before another past time frame or point in time. And the *future perfect* places the action earlier in the future, before another future time frame or point in time.

25.2

	Formula	Example
present perfect	*have/has* + past participle	*I/you/we/they have cooked rice many times.* *She/he has cooked rice many times.*
past perfect	*had* + past participle	*I had cooked rice before my guests arrived.*
future perfect	*will have* + past participle	*I will have cooked rice before I go to the party.*

Progressive Tenses for Regular Verbs

The *progressive tenses* are formed with a helping verb or verbs plus a present participle. For regular verbs, the present participle is the *-ing* form of the verb. Progressive tenses are used for actions that continue over time.

	Formula	Example
present progressive	*am/are/is* + present participle	*I am cooking rice now.* *We/you/they are cooking rice now.* *She/he is cooking rice now.*
past progressive	*was/were* + present participle	*I/she/he was cooking rice last night.* *We/you/they were cooking rice last night.*
future progressive	*will be* + present participle	*I will be cooking rice when you arrive.*
present perfect progressive	*have/has been* + present participle	*I/we/you/they have been cooking rice almost every week.* *She/he has been cooking rice almost every week.*
past perfect progressive	*had been* + present participle	*I had been cooking rice for years before I tried not adding salt.*
future perfect progressive	*will have been* + present participle	*I will have been cooking rice regularly for five years next year.*

A helping verb can be a form of *have*, *do*, or *be*:

> have, has, had
>
> do, does, did
>
> be, am, is, are, was, were, being, been

Or it can be one of nine **modal auxiliaries**:

can	shall
could	should
may	will
might	would
must	

Can, may, shall, and *will* generally signal more definite possibilities than *could, might, should*, and *would*. For instance, *I can check the bus schedule* implies that the writer is likely to do so; *I could check the bus schedule* is more like an idle thought or an offer to check the schedule if requested. *I may go to the party* is a shade more definite than *I might go*.

Sometimes *could, might, should*, and *would* express a higher level of politeness than the other modals or verbs without modals: *Could you give me a ride?* is a shade more polite than *Can you give me a ride? I would like* is more polite than *I want*.

Could is also the past tense of *can*, so *I could check the bus schedule* might alternatively be in the past: *Yesterday I realized I could check the bus schedule.*

Don't Get Tripped Up by Irregular Verbs ⊕

If you give your verbs a workout with sequences that travel forward and back in time, you'll need to keep in mind that some verbs, including many of the most common ones, have irregular past tenses and past participles.

As noted in the verb charts on pages 297–298, the past and perfect tenses of regular verbs are easy to create:

25.2

Yesterday he cooked a delicious dinner.

Simple past tense

He has cooked dinner many times.

Past perfect tense

For irregular verbs, the simple past and past participle forms are less predictable.

Yesterday I wrote the final draft of my paper.

Irregular verb, simple past tense

I have written a new draft of the paper every day this week.

Unlike regular verbs, irregular verbs often have past participles that are different from the simple past tense.

✗ I seen the show on television.

✔ I saw the show on television.

✔ I have seen the show on television.

✔ It broke.

✗ It had broke.

✔ It had broken.

✗ It costed plenty.

✔ It cost plenty.

Some irregular verbs that give writers trouble are these:

Base form of verb	Past tense	Past participle
arise	arose	arisen
be	was, were	been
become	became	become
begin	began	begun
bend	bent	bent
bite	bit	bitten, bit
blow	blew	blown
break	broke	broken
bring	brought	brought
build	built	built
burst	burst	burst
catch	caught	caught
choose	chose	chosen
come	came	come
cost	cost	cost
dive	dived, dove	dived
do	did	done
draw	drew	drawn
drink	drank	drunk
drive	drove	driven
eat	ate	eaten
fall	fell	fallen
fight	fought	fought
fly	flew	flown

25.2

(*Continued*)

25.2

Base form of verb	Past tense	Past participle
forget	forgot	forgotten
freeze	froze	frozen
get	got	gotten, got
go	went	gone
grow	grew	grown
have	had	had
hear	heard	heard
hide	hid	hidden
hurt	hurt	hurt
keep	kept	kept
know	knew	known
lay (= place [something] on a surface)	laid	laid
lead	led	led
let	let	let
lie (= rest)	lay	lain
prove	proved	proven, proved
read	read	read
ride	rode	ridden
ring	rang	rung
rise	rose	risen
run	ran	run
see	saw	seen
send	sent	sent
set (= place [something] on a surface)	set	set

Base form of verb	Past tense	Past participle
shake	shook	shaken
shoot	shot	shot
shrink	shrank	shrunk
sing	sang	sung
sink	sank	sunk
sit (= take a seat)	sat	sat
slay	slew	slain
speak	spoke	spoken
spring	sprang	sprung
stand	stood	stood
steal	stole	stolen
sting	stung	stung
strike	struck	struck, stricken
swear	swore	sworn
swim	swam	swum
swing	swung	swung
take	took	taken
throw	threw	thrown
wake	woke, waked	waked, woken
wear	wore	worn
write	wrote	written

25.2

If you aren't sure of the past tense or past participle for a verb, check the base form of the verb in a dictionary. If no irregular forms are given in the entry, the verb is regular.

25.3 Use Special Moods in Special Cases ⊕

Statements, exclamations, and questions are all in the **indicative mood**. Here are indicative clauses of the three types:

Statement

My parents don't expect strangers to do anything for them.

Exclamation

They won't even ask for help!

Question

Would it cross my father's mind to ask a waiter for a napkin?

Usually, statements do the work, and exclamations and questions provide special effects. Make it a habit to phrase your thoughts as statements.

Use the Imperative for Commands

Commands, the **imperative mood**, are easy as long as you remember that the subject of a command is always *you*, and it's implied rather than actually appearing in the sentence. Here the writer is addressing a command at her parents:

Speak up for yourselves! That's what I want to say to them.

Use the Subjunctive for Hypotheticals

The tricky mood is the **subjunctive mood**, used for things that are not, or aren't necessarily, true, including wishes, most *as if* comparisons, and some *if* and *that* statements. In sentences of these kinds, use the past tense to describe the untrue condition or wish:

She wishes that she had a million dollars.

She is acting *as if* she had a million dollars.

If she had a million dollars, she would buy a new car.

> When the subjunctive (*had*) is used in an *if* clause, the subjunctive (*would*) is also used in the main clause.

Do not use the subjunctive mood in *as if* comparisons and *if* statements when they describe something you believe is true or is likely to come true:

> Her financial trouble is serious. She is acting *as if* she has barely enough money to live on.

> *If* she has enough money at the end of the week, she will buy new tires for her car.

25.3

The switch to the past tense of verbs in subjunctive clauses is simple with every verb except *be*, because all verbs except *be*, regular and irregular, use the same past-tense form for both singular and plural in the first, second, and third person:

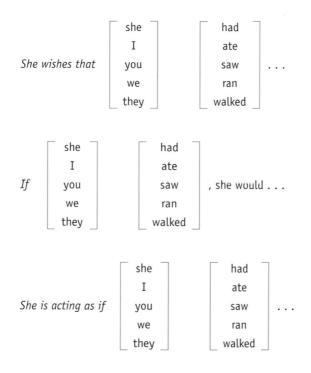

The past tense of *be*, however, has two forms: *was* and *were*. In the subjunctive mood, only *were* is used, even for singular subjects:

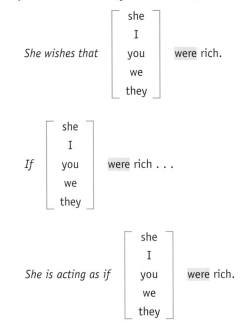

A present-tense version of the subjunctive mood, in which the verb appears in its base form, also exists. Use this for suggestions, requests, and orders:

I have suggested that my father speak up in public.

Because this is just a wish and not an assertion that the writer's father does speak up, the verb is the subjunctive *speak*, not the indicative *speaks*.

For the most part, the subjunctive uses the past tenses of verbs, so it is often no different from the past indicative. A difference arises when the verb is *be* and its subject is singular:

If Amal *were* to go to the party, he *might* dance.

In a subjunctive *if* clause, do not use the conditional form *would*:

✗ If Amal *would have* gone to the party, he *would have* danced.

✔ If Amal had gone to the party, he would have danced.

25.3

Writer to Writer

When should you use the subjunctive mood? You may not know that it's called the subjunctive, but you probably already use it.
Use the subjunctive mood of verbs mainly for hypotheticals.

If wishes were horses, beggars would ride.

Subjunctive (wishes aren't horses)

If I could, I would go to the party.

Subjunctive (the speaker cannot be at the party)

Use the indicative—the mood you use most of the time—for real possibilities:

If I can, I will go to the party.

Indicative (the speaker will try to go)

26. Use Pronouns to Be Clear

Pronouns stand in for nouns. Reading would be awkward and difficult without them:

✗ The band Vogon Soup has been together long enough that Vogon Soup knows Vogon Soup's strengths.

Once readers know what the topic is, pronouns become a shorthand way to refer to it. Reading a name, or any noun, again and again is distracting. And because most pronouns are shorter than the nouns they replace, they save readers—and writers—time.

✓ The band Vogon Soup has been together long enough that it knows its strengths.

Most pronouns cause little or no trouble. The situations in which pronouns are most likely to go wrong are discussed here.

26.1 Match Pronouns with Their Roles ⊕

These are *subject pronouns*, suitable for use as the subjects of clauses—the agents performing the actions:

I

you

he, she, it

we

you

they

These are *object pronouns*, suitable for use as objects—the agents being acted upon:

me

you

him, her, it

us

you

them

Both subject and object pronouns may be masculine (*he/him*), feminine (*she/her*), or neutral (*I/me, you/you, it/it, we/we, they/them*). In English, masculine pronouns are used for boys and men; male domestic animals, such as dogs, whose gender is known; and animals of other kinds that are obviously male, such as stallions and bulls. Feminine pronouns are used equivalently, and gender-neutral pronouns are used for everything else.

In academic prose people are generally referred to by their last names, so the issue of gender does not come up. When you want to refer to strangers by their first names, do not assume that a typically male name indicates a male or a typically female name indicates a female. If you can readily verify the gender of the person—say, online—it's best to do so. See also page 144.

Watch Out When Using Pronouns Together

Hardly anyone gets subject and object pronouns wrong in simple sentences:

> I often work the evening shift.

> The members of Vogon Soup went out to lunch with me a few weeks ago.

That people have no trouble writing sentences like those is evidence that they know what the right pronouns are, even without thinking about it. But many writers get thrown off when they introduce a complication, such as another pronoun or a person's name:

✗ Me and a nurse named Sally often work the evening shift.

✗ The members of Vogon Soup went out to lunch with she and I a few weeks ago.

When you're using a pronoun paired with a name or another pronoun, in your mind omit the other person to make sure the pronoun you've used is correct.

26.1

✘ Me often work the evening shift.

✔ I often work the evening shift.

✔ She and I often work the evening shift.

✘ The members of Vogon Soup went out to lunch with I a few weeks ago.

✔ The members of Vogon Soup went out to lunch with her a few weeks ago.

✔ The members of Vogon Soup went out to lunch with me a few weeks ago.

✔ The members of Vogon Soup went out to lunch with her and me a few weeks ago.

If any of the correct examples above startled you, practice making the mental omissions when you find paired pronouns in your writing. Soon you'll be writing all correct pronouns in your first drafts.

Use *Who* for Subjects and *Whom* for Objects

In questions and in relative clauses, *who* and *whoever* are used as subject pronouns, and *whom* and *whomever* are used as object pronouns. *Whom* and *whomever* are often thought of as formal or even stilted, but that doesn't disqualify them from use in formal academic writing, especially if the alternative flouts grammar.

The grammar of questions is easy. Just supply an answer with a pronoun in it.

✘ Whom deserves our respect?

> One answer is: *He/she deserves our respect.* It is obvious that a subject pronoun is needed, so the object pronoun *whom* is wrong.

✔ Who deserves our respect?

> *Who* is the subject of the verb *deserves*.

✘ Who does the public respect?

> Again, answer the question: *The public does respect him/her. Him* and *her* are object pronouns, so the object pronoun *whom* would be correct.

Using *who* where grammar calls for *whom* is, however, common in speech and increasingly common even in relatively formal writing.

To check the grammar of relative clauses, turn them into questions.

✘ She is a woman whom deserves our respect.

> *Who/whom* deserves our respect? *She* does. *She* is a subject pronoun, so the subject pronoun *who* is needed.

✔ She is a woman who deserves our respect.

✘ He is a man who the public respects.

> *Who/whom* does the public respect? The public respects *him*. *Him* is an object pronoun, so the object pronoun *whom* is needed here.

✔ He is a man whom the public respects.

If you dislike *whom*, see if the sentence reads well without either pronoun.

✔ He is a man the public respects.

Sometimes the object of the verb is actually a whole subordinate clause, in which case the pronoun is the subject of that clause. In such constructions, use a subject pronoun, *who* or *whoever*:

✘ Bob, the magician, performs for whomever is around.

✔ Bob, the magician, performs for whoever is around.

> *Whoever is around* is a subordinate clause, and *whoever* is its subject — so *whoever* is correct.

Use Reflexive Pronouns to Refer to the Subject of the Sentence or Clause

26.1

Myself, yourself, himself, herself, itself, ourselves, yourselves, and *themselves* are reflexive pronouns. Use them when you have an object that's the same as the subject or something else that comes before the pronoun in the clause.

Bob will sometimes perform for himself.

Himself makes clear that Bob is both performer and audience.

Do not use reflexive pronouns as subjects, and do not use them as objects when the subject is someone or something else.

✘ Bob and myself were in the common room.

✔ Bob and I were in the common room.

The reflexive pronoun *myself* cannot serve as a subject; it must be replaced with *I.*

✘ Bob performed for the nurses and myself.

✔ Bob performed for the nurses and me.

The reflexive pronoun *myself* can't serve as an object unless *I* is the subject or plays another major role in the clause.

Choose the Right Pronouns in Comparisons

Use a subject pronoun in a comparison when you're comparing the person or thing with a subject:

Horace is taller than Gordie.

✘ Horace is taller than him.

✔ Horace is taller than he.

Horace is the subject of the sentence, so someone being compared with Horace should be referred to with a subject pronoun.

If a sentence on that pattern seems artificial to you, try adding another word or two:

✔ Horace is taller than he is.

Object pronouns in *as* or *than* comparisons are not always wrong. Consider this sentence:

26.1

Horace likes Eliot even more than Gordie.

Does that mean that Horace likes Eliot even more than Gordie likes Eliot or that Horace likes Eliot even more than Horace likes Gordie? The sentence is unclear and needs revision. Here are two options:

Horace likes Eliot even more than Gordie does.

Horace likes Gordie, but he likes Eliot even more.

Use a Subject Pronoun for a Subject Complement

Subject complements are not objects of the verb—they're not being acted upon. They name something that is being equated with the subject in some way. So a pronoun that is used as a complement should be a subject pronoun. Noun complements usually follow a form of *be*.

✘ The most popular player in the band is him.

✔ The most popular player in the band is he.

> The subject is *player*, and the pronoun at the end is its complement. So *him* is wrong; the subject form is *he*.

✘ Is that her knocking on the door?

✔ Is that she knocking on the door?

> The subject is *that*, and the pronoun is its complement.

Often when complements are used correctly, they sound strange. In an everyday conversation, the speaker would probably use the ungrammatical pronouns above. In writing, where you have time to consider what you've written, there is no need to choose between sounding stilted and being ungrammatical. Find a revision that sounds natural to you and is also grammatical.

26.2

✔ He is the most popular player in the band.

✔ Is she knocking on the door?

26.2 Make Pronouns Agree with Their Antecedents ⊕

An **antecedent** is the noun (or other pronoun) that a pronoun refers to and stands in for.

Gordie is surprisingly short. He is five foot six. Dramatic costumes look good on him.

> *Gordie* is the antecedent for *he* and *him*.

Hardly anyone has trouble with antecedent/pronoun pairs like *Gordie/he, guitar/it,* and *drums/they.* Only a few kinds of antecedents are likely to trip writers up.

Watch Out for Indefinite Pronouns

Words like *anybody* and *everyone* are singular **indefinite pronouns.** (For a list of common singular indefinite pronouns, see p. 293, Sec. 25.1). These words can serve as antecedents for simpler pronouns like *him* and *her.* When they do so in formal writing, these simpler pronouns, too, should be singular (see p. 296 for exceptions):

✘ Everyone who wants to sit at the concert should bring their own chair.

✔ Everyone who wants to sit at the concert should bring his or her own chair.

> The *their* version is increasingly common, but traditional grammar considers it wrong. *Everyone* is singular, so the pronouns that refer to it ought to be singular.

If that sounds artificial to you, look for a natural-sounding, correct alternative. Consider whether you can get your idea across without using words that must agree with the subject:

> Everyone who wants to sit at the concert should bring a chair.

Or revise your sentence to make the subject plural:

> People who want to sit at the concert should bring their own chairs.

Watch Out for Collective Nouns

Collective nouns refer to multiple people or things as a whole (for more on collective nouns, see p. 294, Sec. 25.1). Collective nouns should generally be treated as singular, and therefore pronouns that refer to them should be singular as well.

✗ The band has been together for four years, and they have played at Hooper's six times.

✔ The band has been together for four years, and it has played at Hooper's six times.

You can make an exception to the rule when your meaning makes it illogical to treat the collective as a whole:

The band wrote their autographs on a poster for me.

The audience set their chairs on the floor.

Although the wording is not incorrect in the two examples above, you can often revise such sentences to avoid having to treat the collective noun as a plural.

All the band members autographed a poster for me.

People who brought chairs set them on the floor.

When a collective noun is treated as singular in one part of the sentence, it is wrong to treat it as plural elsewhere in the same sentence:

✗ The band, which has been together for four years, wrote their autographs on a poster for me.

> The singular verb *has* tells us that *band* is being treated as singular, so the pronoun should treat it that way too.

Such problems usually aren't hard to finesse once you recognize them:

✔ The band, which has been together for four years, autographed a poster for me.

Remember that writing, unlike speech, gives you a chance to correct yourself before anyone else reads your work. Your readers will expect you to get it right. If you don't, they will probably assume you don't know any better.

26.3 Avoid Vague Pronoun References

Pronouns refer to nouns or noun phrases—their antecedents. Readers generally expect to have read these nouns and phrases before they get to the pronoun:

The guitar is a special one. It was made entirely by hand in Spain.

> The antecedent for *it* is *guitar*.

Researchers are looking into the question of whether the use of bed nets to combat malaria is causing mosquitoes to hunt for food earlier in the day, before people are in bed. They are trying to answer it as soon as possible.

Watch Out for Pronouns That Refer to Whole Clauses or Sentences

26.3

✗ Although malaria primarily infects the populations of developing countries, it is a problem of global significance. This is apparent in statistics about the disease.

> Does *this* mean that statistics show both that malaria infects people in developing countries and that it's a global problem, or only the latter — or something else?

Where you find such sentences in your writing, look for a noun or phrase that will clarify what *this* means and put it after *this*, turning *this* into an adjective:

✔ Although malaria primarily infects the populations of developing countries, it is a problem of global significance. This latter fact is apparent in statistics about the disease.

Or replace *this* with something specific:

✔ . . . it is a problem of global significance. Its pervasiveness is apparent in statistics about the disease.

No doubt statistics do also bear out that malaria infects people in developing countries. But if the statistics the writer wants to introduce back up only the point about global significance, it's best to bring that point into sharp focus.

Let's say, though, that the writer does want to share statistics both about developing countries in particular and about the world as a whole. In this case, it would be better to present the two situations in coordinate clauses (see p. 245, Sec. 21.4), rather than in a subordinate and a main clause (see p. 242, Sec. 21.3), and to change the singular adjective *this* to the plural *these*:

✔ Malaria primarily infects the populations of developing countries, but it is a problem of global significance. These facts are apparent in statistics about the disease.

Occasionally pronouns precede what they refer to:

> This is a fact: malaria kills millions each year.

26.3

This word order reverses the sequence that readers expect, so it can be confusing, and annoying, too. Try not to make readers wait too long to find out what a pronoun they've already read refers to. Use pronouns before their antecedents only for special effects.

In the previous example, the antecedent for the pronoun *this* is not a noun but a whole clause. Some readers object on principle to all such uses of the pronouns *this, that, these, those,* and *which.* The bigger the idea that these pronouns are meant to sum up, the larger will be the proportion of readers who object to them.

Avoid Using the Same Pronoun When Referring to Different Things

Obviously, over the course of a long document, pronouns such as *it* and *they* will turn up all over the place and will carry many different meanings. This is fine. What isn't fine is using the same pronoun in two different senses within a sentence or short passage:

> ✗ Gordie and Horace were jamming, trying to figure out how the chorus to a new song should go. They could hardly be heard over their instruments, because they were so loud.

The first *they* refers to Gordie and Horace, and the second *they* refers to the instruments, but readers are likely to be briefly confused before they figure out that information for themselves. It's better to repeat a noun that refers to the same thing than to repeat a pronoun where its uses mean different things:

> ✔ . . . They could hardly be heard over their instruments, because the instruments were so loud.

Avoid Using a Pronoun When It Might Refer to More than One Thing

In this example, who are *they*?

> ✗ Gordie and Horace were jamming, trying to figure out how the chorus to a new song should go. Steve, Buzz, and Eliot joined in, and they finally got it to sound right.

26.3

Maybe the writer meant this:

> Steve, Buzz, and Eliot joined in, and Gordie and Horace finally got it to sound right.

Or maybe he meant this:

> Steve, Buzz, and Eliot joined in, and the three of them finally got it to sound right.

Or maybe this:

> Steve, Buzz, and Eliot joined in, and the five of them finally got it to sound right.

Any of those sentences is fine, as long as it's the one that says what the writer meant.

Use the Pronoun *You* Only When You Mean Your Readers

Do not use *you* in formal writing to mean people in general:

> ✗ Malaria is caused by a parasite, which is spread by mosquitoes. You can combat it by killing the parasite, the mosquitoes, or both.
>
> The writer is not expecting readers to go out and kill parasites or mosquitoes.

You in such contexts is considerably worse than using the passive voice (see p. 279, Sec. 24.2).

> ✔ Malaria is caused by a parasite, which is spread by mosquitoes. It can be combatted by killing the parasite, the mosquitoes, or both.

Use *They* Only to Refer to Particular People or Things

They needs an antecedent. If you haven't specified to whom or what the word refers, don't use it.

26.3

✗ They say that bed nets have saved countless lives and could save many more.

✔ Public health officials say that bed nets have saved countless lives and could save many more.

Use the Placeholder Pronoun *It* Sparingly

The pronoun it is unusual in that it doesn't always need an antecedent. The rules of English allow it to hold the place where the subject of a sentence would ordinarily be, so that the real subject can come at the end of the clause:

It complicates the problem that malaria poses its greatest threat in tropical regions.

The sentence above is grammatically equivalent to this one:

That malaria poses its greatest threat in tropical regions complicates the problem.

It does come in handy to be able to switch the parts of a sentence so that the subject comes at the end, but when you've written such a sentence, look at it critically. In those examples, the sentence that starts with the true subject is more direct and forceful, and the writer should use that version unless the ideas presented just before and after this sentence make the *It* sentence fit in more naturally.

Often, formulas that cause a sentence to start with it—*It is well known that*, *It is worth noting that*, and *It may surprise many to learn that*, for instance—do no real work and should be cut.

Do not use *it* without an antecedent like this:

✗ On the foundation's website, it shows a running tally of malaria deaths.

Usually with this pattern, the word or words that should be the subject of the sentence are nearby and you'll easily be able to replace *it* with them:

✔ The foundation's website shows a running tally of malaria deaths.

27. Use Adjectives, Adverbs, and Articles Expertly

Adjectives and adverbs add color and detail to the nouns and verbs that are the pillars of writing. There's a big difference between a *thin white* sandwich and a *greasy, overstuffed* one. (For a discussion of the comma use with those adjectives, see p. 330.) When a little boy cries, is he crying *softly, angrily,* or *uncontrollably*? Again there's a big difference.

Because nouns and verbs give writing its structure, try to build as much meaning into them as you can. For instance, the boy might well *whimper, howl,* or *wail*—and do it without the help of any adverbs. (For more about limiting your use of modifiers, see p. 263.) Still, you'll often need adjectives and adverbs. Just make sure they clarify rather than clutter your writing.

As for articles—*a, an,* and *the*—using them correctly, where they're required, helps demonstrate to readers that you have a good command of English.

27.1 Use Adjectives to Modify Nouns and Pronouns

Not only do adjectives enhance nouns and pronouns, but they provide extra information. They tend to answer the questions that naturally come up in relation to nouns: Which one? What kind? How many? How much?

Often, adjectives come before the nouns they modify:

The summer when I was six years old and ready to start school, we moved to a new town, Springfield.

Six modifies *years,* and *new* modifies *town.*

Adjectives can also come after the noun:

My family is Chinese American, and we looked different from most people in Springfield.

In these clauses, a **linking verb** connects the adjective to the noun: is (a form of *be*) connects the adjective *Chinese American* to the noun *family*, and *looked* connects the adjective *different* to the pronoun *we*. Linking verbs—for instance, *feel, seem, believe,* and *think*—express an attitude or a state of being. Note that a verb may function as a linking verb in some cases but not others.

We look different, but I feel as normal as everyone else.

In this sentence, the verbs *look* and *feel* are linking verbs, connecting the adjectives *different* and *normal* to the pronouns *we* and *I*.

We look at it differently, and I feel strongly about my point of view.

In this sentence, the verbs are not linking verbs. Rather than connecting nouns and adjectives, the verbs *look* and *feel* are being modified by the adverbs *differently* and *strongly*.

Groups of words can function together as adjectives:

Our new house had been on the market for months. Our next-door neighbor, who never once said a word to us, had a reputation for being unfriendly.

These phrases modify the nouns *house, neighbor,* and *reputation*.

Phrases, clauses, and words that look similar—or identical—to the ones in the examples above aren't always adjectives. Everything depends on how you are using the words in the sentence and what other words they are modifying.

27.2 Use Adverbs to Modify Verbs, Adjectives, and Adverbs

Adverbs help answer the questions that nouns and their modifiers cannot: How? When? Where? Why?

Adverbs can modify verbs:

> We quickly learned that his reputation was well deserved.

The adverb *quickly* modifies the verb *learned.*

Adverbs can modify adjectives:

> Starting on our very first day in Springfield, I was terribly uncomfortable there.

The adverb *very* modifies the adjective *first*, and the adverb *terribly* modifies the adjective *uncomfortable.*

Adverbs can modify other adverbs:

> I was so horribly uncomfortable living there!

The adverb *so* modifies the adverb *horribly.*

And groups of words can function together as adverbs:

> I was desperate to start first grade. As my mother packed my lunch on the first morning of school, she put in a bowl of my favorite comfort food, sesame noodles.

Here the first highlighted phrase modifies the adjective *desperate*, and the second modifies the verb *put.*

Writer to Writer

More than *or* over? Less than *or* fewer than *or* under?   For many years, handbooks and style guides included a rule that *over* and *under* should not be used with numbers (that is, you shouldn't write "*over* 20 tons" or "*under* 100 research subjects"). Today, it's fine to use *over* and *under* interchangeably with *more than*, *less than*, and *fewer than*.

Fewer than and *less than* continue to be used in different ways. *Fewer than* is for individual things: *fewer than the 932 breeding pairs recorded in 2010*, *fewer than 12 items*. *Less than* is for quantities or amounts — things you wouldn't count: *less than 10 gallons*, *less than four hours*. Anything that you put a number to, you can count. The question is how you're thinking of it. For example, "*Fewer than* $1 million" is peculiar, and in almost all contexts wrong, because surely you're thinking of that million dollars as an amount, not as individual dollars to be counted.

Rule or not, consider using *over* and *under* for numbers or amounts you're thinking of as *levels*: *over* 500,000 people attended the protest. This is the way many journalists think of the words, and it jibes with common words and phrases like *an overcapacity crowd* and *underweight*.

27.3

27.3 Know When to Use *Good, Well, Bad,* and *Badly*

Many people have pairs of these words mixed up in their minds, in part because they've heard *good* and *bad* said informally in situations where more formal language would call for *well* and *badly*. When you're reaching for one of these words to use as an adverb, always use *well* or *badly*.

✗ My mother cooked really good.

✔ My mother cooked really well.

> The modifier answers the question *How?* Because the word is modifying a verb, the adverb *well* is needed.

✘ I wanted that bowl of noodles bad.

✔ I wanted that bowl of noodles badly.

> The word is modifying the verb *wanted* — not *I* and not *that bowl of noodles* — so the adverb *badly* is needed.

The result may be clearer if the adverb is placed next to the verb it modifies:

I badly wanted that bowl of noodles.

(For more about the placement of modifiers, see p. 263.)

When you want an adjective, *bad* is always right—unless, of course, you mean *good* or *well*. *Well* can be either an adjective or an adverb, which adds to the confusion between *good* and *well*.

I feel good is correct if you're describing a positive general state of mind. *Feel* is being used as a linking verb to connect the subject with a *good* feeling. *I feel well* means that the writer feels healthy; here *well* is also an adjective.

27.4 Compare with Care

Superlative adjectives—such as *biggest, smallest, hungriest, most peculiar, least desirable*—announce that you're ranking something at the top or bottom among at least three things. **Comparative** adjectives—such as *bigger, smaller, hungrier, more peculiar, less desirable*—do the job when you're ranking only two things.

✘ Do you like noodles or sandwiches best?

✔ Do you like noodles or sandwiches better?

> Only two choices are offered, so *better* is correct.

✘ I was the more eager of all the kids when lunchtime started.

✔ I was the most eager of all the kids when lunchtime started.

> The writer is comparing herself with all the other kids, so *most* is correct.

This rule doesn't apply to comparisons with *than*:

✗ *I* was the most eager than all the other kids when lunchtime started.

✔ I was more eager than all the other kids when lunchtime started.

> The word *than* turns any ranking into a comparison between the person or thing being discussed and everyone or everything else described.

As for whether to give an adjective an *-er* or *-est* ending (as in *gladder, gladdest*) or to use *more* or *most* or *less* or *least* with the adjective (as in *more delighted, most delighted*), use the ending if you know the adjective has one. Most one-syllable and many two-syllable adjectives do. If you're not sure, check a dictionary. If it doesn't show *-er* and *-est* endings for the adjective, use the additional word.

To spell the comparative and superlative forms of adjectives that end in -y correctly, change the -y to -ie-: *hungry, hungrier, hungriest; tasty, tastier, tastiest*.

Writer to Writer

How should *literally* be used? The word indicates that what you're saying is exactly what you mean and is not a metaphor or an exaggeration. "She was *literally* climbing the walls" might be said of a gecko but not of a person. "He *literally* swept me off my feet" describes a wrestling move or acrobatics rather than a typical romance.

27.5 Use Articles Artfully ⊕

The words *a*, *an*, and *the* are **articles**. (The term comes from the Latin *articulus*, meaning "part," or in this case, specifically a "small connecting part.") *A* and *an* are called **indefinite articles**, because they are used with nouns that aren't "definite," or specific, creatures or things of that type:

> I want a dog.

27.5

> I want an Afghan hound.

> The speaker isn't specifying any particular dog or Afghan hound.

Indefinite articles are used only with singular nouns, and they mostly appear with nouns that bring something new into the discussion:

> I liked a dog at the animal shelter. It was an Airedale.

A is used before nouns that begin with a consonant sound, as in *a cat* and *a mouse*, while *an* is used before nouns that begin with a vowel sound, as in *an ant* and *an elephant*. Note, though, that a noun may begin with a vowel (most often *u*) that is pronounced as a consonant (most often *y*), and in this case the correct article is *a*, as in *a unicorn*.

The is called a **definite article** because it's used when a definite, or specific, creature or thing is being discussed:

> The Airedale was deaf.

The definite article is used with both singular and plural nouns. Generally, things referred to with a definite article will have already been mentioned, or the writer is assuming readers already know about them, or they are being described in a way that make them specific:

> I wondered whether the Airedale's deafness would be a problem if I adopted him.

> Both the Airedale and its deafness have already been mentioned.

> Most of the other dogs in the shelter barked a lot.

> The shelter has already been mentioned, and readers can infer that the animal shelter houses other dogs too.

The other animal I was tempted to adopt was a rabbit.

The writer is specifying which animal he liked in addition to the Airedale.

27.5

Articles can be used in front of nouns that are typically considered noncount if the noun is acting like or taking the place of a count noun: *Would you like a [bottle of] water?* (For more on using count and noncount nouns, see p. 295, Sec. 25.1.)

The comes up in some geographic references but not in others. Use *the* before countries whose names are plural in form: *the Netherlands, the United States*; names for points on the globe or geographical areas: *the North Pole, the Middle East*; mountain ranges: *the Rockies, the Himalayas*; deserts: *the Sahara Desert, the Gobi Desert*; peninsulas and similar geographic features: *the Arabian Peninsula, the Florida Panhandle*; island chains: *the Pacific Islands*; bodies of water: *the Caspian Sea, the Mississippi River*; and groups of lakes: *the Great Lakes*.

Do not use *the* before the names of continents, states, cities and towns, streets, individual mountains, individual islands, or individual lakes.

The rules given above have a few exceptions, such as *The Gambia, The Hague*, and *The Bronx*.

Articles and pronouns can be used interchangeably but never together in front of common nouns. Use a pronoun before a common noun to highlight possession: *Why are you eating my food?* carries a different shade of meaning than *Why are you eating the food?*

28. Use Punctuation to Help Readers

You can "hear" punctuation in a spoken conversation: a sentence that rises at the end, for example, usually takes a question mark. But it really works the other way around: punctuation helps us simulate speech, indicating puzzlement, enthusiasm, detours, and so on.

The punctuation mark that is hardest to intuit is the comma. Although commas sometimes indicate pauses, they can also signal things about sentence structure that are helpful to know and that aren't apparent in speech.

The punctuation rules given in this chapter describe American usage. Other countries, including other English-speaking ones, follow somewhat different rules.

28.1 Use Commas to Keep Your Sentences Organized

Commas separate parts of a sentence. Sometimes they help make clear the structure of the sentence, and sometimes they give other clues about what you mean. A joke that turns up on T-shirts and coffee mugs illustrates this point. It goes like this:

> Let's eat Grandma.
>
> Let's eat, Grandma.
>
> *Commas save lives!*

Use a Comma and a Coordinating Conjunction to Separate Two Main Clauses

When you join two clauses each of which could stand on its own as a sentence (see p. 251), put a comma, together with one of the conjunctions *and*, *but*, *for*, *nor*, *or*, *so*, and *yet*, between them:

> ┌─────── MAIN CLAUSE ───────┐
> Forensic linguistics is a developing science, so
>
> ┌─────────── MAIN CLAUSE ───────────┐
> many police departments are not yet familiar with it.

Note that a conjunction doesn't always signal the start of a new clause and therefore doesn't always need to be preceded by a comma. Do not habitually put a comma in front of a conjunction that's just introducing another part of the same clause:

28.1

> The history of DNA evidence suggests a parallel and may be useful to this discussion.
>
> Here, the conjunction *and* joins the verbs *suggests* and *may be*, but the two verbs do not mean two main clauses. The subject of both is *history*.

Not . . . but sentences, in particular, tempt writers to put commas where they don't belong:

✗ DNA evidence is not an end in itself, but a tool.

✔ DNA evidence is not an end in itself but a tool.

> This sentence has one subject and one verb, so it's incorrect to use commas to set the word *tool* off from the rest of the clause.

For more on this subject, see compound sentences (p. 240, Sec. 21.2) and run-ons and comma splices (p. 250, Sec. 22.2).

Use Commas to Set Off Introductory Elements

When a sentence begins with a subordinate clause (see p. 242, Sec. 21.3), a comma is usually needed to separate it from the main clause:

┌──────── SUBORDINATE CLAUSE ────────┐
If a person is wrongfully accused of a crime,

┌──────────── MAIN CLAUSE ────────────┐
forensic linguistics may help establish the person's innocence.

> *If* indicates that the first clause is subordinate.

Confusion can arise when the comma is left out:

✗ Even when DNA evidence was new police labs used it not just to convict but also to exonerate.

28.1

✔ Even when DNA evidence was new, police labs used it not just to convict but also to exonerate.

> The comma not only helps readers find the main part of the sentence but also prevents them from reading "new police labs" as a connected phrase.

In some cases, such as short and simple introductory elements that can't connect to the next word or words in a misleading way, the use of a comma is a judgment call. In general, however, using a comma will help readers find the beginning of the main part of the sentence.

In England in the 1980s, DNA evidence proved that a man who had confessed to killing a teenager was innocent and that another man was guilty.

Similarly, principles behind forensic linguistics led a U.S. appeals court to overturn the 1963 conviction of Ernesto Miranda.

Sometimes long introductory elements contain two clauses after a subordinating conjunction:

✔ Even when DNA evidence was new and most people had yet to hear about it, police labs used it not just to convict but also to exonerate.

If the conjunction applies to each clause (*Even when . . . most people had yet to hear about it*), do not put a comma between the two unless you have a particular reason for doing so.

Use Commas to Set Off Detours

Once you've gotten a sentence started, use commas (or dashes, p. 349 or parentheses, p. 350, both in Sec. 28.5, in special situations) to set off information that detours from the main point, such as background information or asides. Use commas before and after such elements when they're in the middle of a sentence. Use a single comma (or one dash or a pair of parentheses) when the element comes at the end.

Police officers, furthermore, have read suspects their "Miranda rights" ever since.

> *Furthermore*, a transition word, connects the information in this sentence to what came just before and is thus a detour between the subject and verb.

The FBI, which put a great deal of money and effort into trying to catch the Unabomber, had no success for years.

> The FBI's lack of success is the main point of this sentence. What the FBI did to try to catch the Unabomber is a detour.

This principle doesn't mean that the information or ideas you set off with commas is inessential to your *overall* point. But any given sentence or main clause has, or should have, a point of its own. Material that detours from that point should be set off. (See also p. 349, Sec. 28.5.)

Many good writers make a distinction between *that*, with no comma, and *which*, preceded by a comma, to give their readers one more clue about whether they consider an element essential to the point of the sentence. In the example below, the writer considers the subordinate clause beginning with "that explained" essential:

The Unabomber threatened to kill more people unless major newspapers published a 35,000-word manifesto that explained his ideas about society.

> The writer doesn't expect readers to know what the manifesto was unless he tells them a bit about it, so this characterization is necessary.

In the next example, the clause beginning with "which are" is inessential:

The *New York Times* and the *Washington Post*, which are two of the country's most widely read newspapers, published it in 1995.

> The main point of the sentence is that the *Times* and *Post* published the manifesto. The highlighted characterization of the two papers is an aside.

Who, when, and *where* can be used either like *that,* without a comma, if they're necessary to the main point of the sentence, or like *which,* after a comma, if they're not.

28.1

A man who was the brother of Ted Kaczynski, who ultimately pleaded guilty to the bombings, tipped off the FBI that the person they were looking for was Ted.

> The first *who* clause is essential because it identifies the man as Kaczynski's brother. The second *who* clause contains valuable information, but it's not essential to the main point of the sentence.

Bear in mind that readers can find it frustrating to be sent on too many detours, even if these are correctly signaled with commas:

✗ A man who was the brother of Ted Kaczynski, who ultimately pleaded guilty to the bombings, and the brother's wife, having recognized the writing style and ideas, tipped off the FBI that the person they were looking for was Ted.

One more decision about detour-related commas comes up with proper names. Do not set off names that are essential to the sentence and the point it is making:

FBI Supervising Special Agent Joel Moss conducted linguistic analysis on writing related to the Unabomber case.

Do set off names when the meaning would be clear and the sentence structure smooth without them:

The brother's wife, Linda Kaczynski, helped her husband get through the ordeal of turning Ted in.

> The wife's name is not essential to the sentence, so it is set off with commas.

Use Commas in Series

Commas separate the elements of series of three or more:

Ransom notes, spoken or written threats, emergency calls, online scams, and police interrogations all provide forensic evidence.

When you've written a series, look it over to make sure its elements are parallel (p. 253).

Some writers put what's called a **serial comma** or **Oxford comma** before the conjunction and the final element of a series, as we do in this guidebook; others do not. See the Writer to Writer box on page 337.

28.1

As with nouns presented in a series, two or more adjectives or adjectival phrases require commas between them if they modify the noun separately:

> Detectives are only beginning to make sophisticated, effective use of language to clear the innocent and catch the guilty.

You can test whether adjectives are separate by mentally replacing the comma with *and* or *but*:

> Detectives are only beginning to make sophisticated and effective use of language to clear the innocent and catch the guilty.

If one of these replacements has minimal effect on the meaning, use a comma. If, however, the second adjective is part of what the first one modifies, leave the comma out.

> Scientific forensic linguistics has tremendous untapped potential.

Here it's forensic linguistics that's being called scientific, and the untapped potential that's being called tremendous. (You wouldn't say *scientific and forensic linguistics* or *tremendous and untapped potential*.)

Use Commas to Set Off Most Quotations

Use a comma, or sometimes a colon (see p. 345, Sec. 28.5), to set off a direct quotation that is complete in itself:

> The Unabomber's manifesto begins, "The Industrial Revolution and its consequences have been a disaster for the human race," and goes on to condemn modern society.

But don't use a comma before a quotation that's part of the flow of your sentence:

28.1

✗ Kaczynski goes on at length about the, "industrial-technological system" and what's wrong with it.

✔ Kaczynski goes on at length about the "industrial-technological system" and what's wrong with it.

For more information on punctuating quotations, see pages 142–146, Sec. 9.2.

Use Commas in Other Places Where Readers Expect Them ⊕

In place names and addresses:

The mailing address for FBI Headquarters is 935 Pennsylvania Avenue NW, Washington, DC 20535-0001.

In dates:

On September 10, 1995, newspapers published the Unabomber's manifesto.

> Other countries, including many in Europe, South America, and Africa, put the day of the month first, the month second, and the year third, and do not use commas in dates.

In numbers, except years, of four or more digits:

DNA testing is usually conducted on only small sections of the human genome, which is about 3,200,000,000 base pairs long and contains 20,000–25,000 genes.

> Other countries, especially in Europe, use periods instead of commas in numbers and commas instead of decimal points.

Between words that one would otherwise misread:

He changed his mind completely because of the evidence presented.

> Did he change his mind completely? Or was it completely because of the evidence that he changed his mind?

His brother visited him once on Tuesday.

> This means that on Tuesday his brother visited him once. What about the rest of the week?

When directly addressing someone:
Let's eat, Grandma!

With *yes* or *no* unless that word is modifying another word:
Yes, please, let's stop discussing commas. No, thanks, I don't
want to read any more about them. No thanks to me, this
discussion may have gone on too long.

Writer to Writer

Should you put a comma before* and *or* or *in a series?   Commas
that come before the conjunction and the final element of a series
are called *serial commas* or *Oxford commas*. Some writers use them,
and some don't.

If you find it more natural to leave serial commas out, that's fine.
Most newspapers and news websites do without serial commas.
Their intention is to speed their readers on their way rather than
encouraging them to pause as they approach the end of every
series.

Leaving serial commas out, however, occasionally leads to
confusion:

✗ I interviewed Jack Hitt, a forensic linguist and a convicted
felon.

Does this say that Jack Hitt is a forensic linguist and a felon, or
did the writer interview three people? If you choose to use serial
commas and make a habit of it (as this book does), you — and your
readers — won't need to think about such issues whenever you write
a series. In this case, Jack Hitt is a writer, not either of the two other
things.

28.2 Use Periods, Question Marks, and Exclamation Points to Reinforce Meaning

The period, the question mark, and the exclamation point are the three end punctuation marks, though periods have other uses as well.

End Most Sentences with Periods ⊕

A sentence *can* end with a question mark or an exclamation point, but those are special cases for special effects. The great majority of the sentences you write should end with periods.

Cap-and-lowercase abbreviations (like *Dr.* and *Jr.*) also end with periods, but most all-cap abbreviations are written without them (see p. 358, Sec. 29.3, for more on abbreviations). If an abbreviation that ends with a period also ends the sentence, use only one period:

> I once met Henry Louis Gates Jr.

But if such an abbreviation concludes a sentence that ends with another punctuation mark, use both the period and the other mark:

> Have you ever met Henry Louis Gates Jr.?

Periods are also used in numbers, as decimal points (2.0) in American English, and in URLs, or web addresses (*www .macmillanlearning.com*).

Reserve Question Marks for Actual Questions

Use question marks for questions, of course:

> Will my mother ever change?

Put the question mark at the end of the question, not necessarily at the end of the sentence:

> ✗ Will my mother ever change, I ask myself?
>
> > The question here is not *I ask myself* but *Will my mother ever change.*
>
> ✔ Will my mother ever change? I ask myself.

Do not use question marks for statements of doubt:

> ✗ I wonder if my mother will ever change?
>
> > This is a statement: the writer is stating that she wonders about something.

> ✔ I wonder if my mother will ever change.

Do not use a question mark for a sentence that has the form of a question if it is actually a request or is otherwise not intended to elicit an answer:

> She, on the other hand, wonders if I will ever learn to hold my tongue. "Would you please avoid embarrassing me," she will say.
>
> > The mother is not expecting to be told yes or no; she is making a request.

Use Exclamation Points Sparingly

Social email, texts, and ads use lots of exclamation points to show warmth and enthusiasm. But this convention does not carry over to more formal writing. Hardly ever are exclamation points found in academic or business writing.

> ✗ But then a salesperson will be rude, or someone we know will share an opinion that I find offensive, and I'll find myself speaking up before I even realize what I'm doing!

28.3 Use Quotation Marks When You Borrow Words

Quotation marks are essential in any document that draws passages directly from sources (see p. 142, Sec. 9.2, to learn more about bringing quotations into your writing). But they have several other uses as well, including setting off terms that will be new to your readers, signaling that you are referring to a word itself instead of using it in a normal sense, and identifying a source by title.

Put Quotation Marks around Direct Quotations

28.3

Put an open double quotation mark where you begin to borrow another person's exact words, and put a close double quotation mark where you stop borrowing, whether the quote is a complete sentence or only part of one:

> The passage that contains Hillel's question "If I am not for myself, who is for me?" continues by posing two more. The second question helps to explain the first, I think. It begins, "But if I am only for myself," suggesting that it's not a virtue to be concerned only with ourselves, and it continues, "what am I?"

> In the first sentence, there is no comma after the word *question* because the quotation is part of the flow of the sentence.

For a fuller discussion of attributing and punctuating quotations, see pages 142–146, Sec. 9.2.

Use single quotation marks only to set off a quotation within a quotation.

> One blogger wrote, "To me, 'If not now, when?' is the essential question."

Put Quotation Marks around New Terms and Words Used as Words

Use quotation marks to set off new terms that you're introducing:

> Hillel's followers, the "House of Hillel," have an important place in the history of religion.

> In a sentence like this one, quotation marks are a substitute for wording such as *called* or *who are known as*. It is unnecessary to use both such wording and quotation marks.

After you've introduced a new term, it is no longer new to the reader — so if you use it again, you should not put quotation marks around it.

When you use a word *as* a word—rather than using it in the usual way, to refer to something else—you can put quotation marks around it:

> The use of "for" in Hillel's questions is unusual, but that's the word that appears in every translation I've seen.

28.3

Another correct option is to put words as words in italics, as this book does:

> The use of *for* in Hillel's questions is unusual.

Whichever format you choose, follow it consistently throughout your document.

Do not use quotation marks for common expressions or to call attention to ordinary, if perhaps uncommon, words:

> ✗ You might consider these questions "unusual," but they are "part and parcel" of my heritage.

Put Quotation Marks around the Titles of Short Works

Use quotation marks to set off the titles of articles, songs, short stories, poems except book-length ones, episodes of television series, and other short works. (See Part 6 for a fuller discussion of how various documentation styles set titles of short works.)

> "Words on Trial," by Jack Hitt, in the July 23, 2012, issue of *The New Yorker*, discusses forensic linguistics.

> My favorite song by Vogon Soup is "Paula Nancy Millstone Jennings."

For the titles of longer works, use italics (see p. 356, Sec. 29.2) instead of quotation marks.

Place Quotation Marks Correctly with Other Punctuation

When you use quotation marks, put periods and commas inside the close quotation mark.

> Hillel's first two questions contain an unusual use of "for."

Make an exception to this rule when you are citing the quotation:

> According to the *New Yorker* article, an FBI forensic linguist
> cracked the Unabomber case "by analyzing syntax, word choice,
> and other linguistic patterns" (25).

For more on citing sources, see Part 6.

Put question marks and exclamation points inside the quotation marks if they're part of the quote, but not otherwise.

> Hillel's third question is "If not now, when?"

> Are you surprised that the Unabomber's manifesto includes the
> words "chimerical" and "anomic"?

28.4 Use Apostrophes in Contractions and Possessive Nouns

Although the same key is used to type an apostrophe and a single quotation mark, the two have different uses.

Use Apostrophes in Contractions

Some readers of formal academic writing object to **contractions**— shortened forms that leave out some of the characters of the original (for example, *you're* is a contraction of *you are*, and *don't* is a contraction of *do not*). If you think your readers won't mind contractions and you do include them in your writing, use an apostrophe to show where letters (or numbers) are missing:

> I can't help thinking that my parents were naïve in the '90s, but
> I'll never get them to agree with that.

Note that when the apostrophe comes at the beginning of a word or number, your word-processing software will probably render it as an open single quotation mark, which faces the wrong way. To get it right, add a second apostrophe, which the software will turn into a close single quotation mark, and then delete the first one.

Writer to Writer

Is it okay to use contractions?   It isn't in the most formal kinds of writing or if your instructor has asked you not to. Otherwise, if the contracted form is the way you'd say it, it's probably fine. Just don't get carried away with elaborate constructions like *He wouldn't've.* And bear in mind that *'d* can mean either "had" or "would," and *'s* can mean either "is" or "has." So if those contracted forms seem likely to give your readers pause in context — as in *He's no money* — spell the word out.

28.4

Use Apostrophes to Show Possession

Possessives are a grammatical form that may or may not have to do with possession, or ownership:

> my parents' house
>
> my mother's mother

Use an apostrophe plus s to form the possessive of a singular noun or a plural noun that does not end in s.

> Hillel's questions
>
> children's memories

Some but not all writers add an apostrophe s to form the possessive of a singular noun ending in s (see the Writer to Writer box on p. 344).

Use an apostrophe alone to form the possessive of a plural noun that ends in s:

> bloggers' points of view
>
> Americans' attitudes

28.4

Writer to Writer

How should you write the possessive of a singular noun that ends in s or z? In other words, *Pope Francis's speech* or *Pope Francis' speech*? The *Modern Language Association Handbook* and the *Chicago Manual of Style*, each of which is widely consulted on questions like this one, give different answers. And they—along with the style guides of other groups such as the American Psychological Association and the Associated Press—make different exceptions to their own rules.

If you've been instructed to follow a particular style, learn and use those rules. If not, do whatever makes sense to you, but do it consistently.

One possible rule is to add an *s* only when you pronounce one when saying the possessive out loud: *Albert Camus' writings* (the *s* in *Camus* is silent) but *Moses's tablets* and *Pope Francis's speech*.

Another rule that's even easier to follow is to always use only an apostrophe with singular nouns and names that end in an *s* or *z* sound: *the United States' recent history, Pope Francis' popularity*.

This book follows the latter rule.

Distinguish among Words Used as Adjectives

Adjectives and **attributive nouns**—nouns that are being used as adjectives—do not use apostrophes, so it's important to recognize that these forms are different from possessives.

an American's rights under the law = singular possessive

Americans' rights = plural possessive

the American legal system = adjective

the United States legal system = attributive noun

Watch Out for Possessive Adjectives and Pronouns. Confusingly, **possessive adjectives and pronouns** differ from possessive nouns in not using apostrophes.

my, mine, your, yours, her, hers, his, its, our, ours, their, theirs

This difference is doubtless one reason so many people have trouble distinguishing between its, possessive, and it's, contraction. You wouldn't add an apostrophe to *my* or *mine* or *his* or *her* or *hers* — so anywhere you could substitute one of these other possessives (not for meaning but to test whether the structure seems all right), use its. Anywhere you could substitute it is, use it's.

> It's a great country, and its legal system, though hardly perfect, is widely admired.
>
> > *It's* is a contraction that could be replaced with *It is*, so it has an apostrophe. The second *its* is possessive (equivalent to *the country's*), and it cannot be replaced with *it is*, so it should not contain an apostrophe.

The difference between its and it's may seem trivial. But many people who are accustomed to making the distinction see this the other way around: once a person understands the principles of using apostrophes, the effort it takes to get them right is trivial.

28.5 Use Other Punctuation Marks Appropriately

Several other forms of punctuation can help convey your ideas to your readers. These include the colon (:), the semicolon (;), the hyphen (-), dashes (— and –), parentheses ( ), brackets ([]), ellipsis marks (. . .), and the slash (/).

Use Colons to Point at What Comes Next

Text followed by a colon is often used to lead in to examples or a list of bullet points or some other series that does not look like ordinary paragraphed writing:

> Hillel's three questions are these:
>
> > If I am not for myself, who will be for me?
> >
> > If I am only for myself, what am I?
> >
> > If not now, when?

Colons can also be used in a similar way within paragraphs and sentences. The text before or after the colon can be, but does not need to be, a complete sentence.

> This is worth remembering: patience is a virtue.

Do not use a colon where the words alone make the meaning clear:

> ✗ The members of the class include: Drina, Gabriela, Phil, Roger, and Sandra.

After the likes of "So-and-so said," a colon is generally better than a comma if the quotation runs to more than a full sentence:

> Hillel also said: "What is hateful to you do not do to your neighbor. That is the whole Torah. The rest is commentary."

Use Semicolons between Equivalent Elements

You may use a semicolon instead of a comma and a conjunction between the clauses of a compound sentence (see p. 251, Sec. 22.2):

> My father's father talks to strangers; my mother's mother does, too.

Do not, however, use semicolons between clauses just because you can. If the sentence seems equally good to you with a conjunction, use a comma and the conjunction. If the sentence is very long, consider making the two clauses into separate sentences.

Also use semicolons to impose order on unruly series. If one or more of the elements in a series contains a comma, use semicolons to separate the elements:

> My father grew up in Mumbai, India; my mother grew up in Delhi; and my brothers and I grew up in Alameda, California.

Use Hyphens Mainly to Help Readers Understand Relationships

English often combines two or more words, or joins a word and a combining form, to make a compound word—but it doesn't do it in a consistent way.

28.5

Some compounds are closed:

> bookstore, coworker, daylight, fireball, motherland, nationwide, nonsmoking, steelworker

Some compounds are open:

> book club, day labor, fire fighter, mass media, mother ship, non sequitur, steel wool

And some compounds use hyphens:

> co-owner, fire-eater, mass-produce, mother-of-pearl, nation-state, non-self-governing

To make things worse, words that are not hyphenated compounds may need to be hyphenated when you use them together as an adjective that comes before a noun.

> fire-eating juggler, steel-wool scrubber, works-cited list

Check a dictionary. Dictionaries give entries for closed, open, and hyphenated compound words. So when you don't know whether a combination is written with a space, a hyphen, or neither, look it up. If you don't find an entry for the combination, check the entries for the parts.

Use hyphens to make compound adjectives. In addition to hyphens in compounds that you find in the dictionary, you'll need to use hyphens between words that function together as an adjective before a noun.

> a massive-scale search

> a 17-year-long campaign of terror

When such a combination comes after the noun, do not hyphenate it unless it is likely to be misread otherwise:

> a search on a massive scale

28.5

Avoid assembling long strings of words that need hyphens to be readily understandable:

> ✗ a federal-government-funded crime-control initiative

> ✔ a crime-control initiative funded by the federal government

Do not put a hyphen between an adverb that ends in -ly and an adjective. Most words that end in -ly are adverbs:

> a federally funded initiative to control crime

> a completely new problem set

Do not add hyphens to internet addresses. When you need to divide a URL or email address between two lines, do not add a hyphen. Break it before a period or after a slash.

> www.macmillanlearning
> .com/Catalog/page/ourimprints

Hyphenate between syllables at the end of a line. Any word that's more than a few letters long may need to be hyphenated for the sake of a line break—if, that is, the layout of your document requires the word to begin on one line and end on the next.

When you need a line break, always make it between syllables. If you're not sure where a word's syllables begin and end, check a dictionary. Most dictionaries use dots to show where the syllable breaks are.

Wherever possible, avoid adding an end-of-line hyphen to a compound that already contains a hyphen:

> ✗   a govern-
>   ment-funded initiative

If you don't see an easier way to correct a clumsy line break like that one, consider revising the sentence:

✔   an initiative

funded by the government

Use Dashes for Major Breaks in Thought

To add a long or notably important aside or comment on the material in the main part of a sentence, set it apart with dashes. Put the aside after one dash at the end of the sentence or between a pair of them in the middle. Dashes tend to make what comes after or between them feel emphatic.

> The Unabomber case was one of the FBI's most expensive investigations — which is saying a lot.
>
> > The writer is stepping outside his role of reporting on the Unabomber case to inject an opinion, so a dash works well here.

Use no more than two dashes in any sentence. A sentence littered with dashes can leave readers struggling to keep straight which phrases are the main part of the sentence and which are detours.

> ✗ Other targets of major FBI investigations over the years have included the Ku Klux Klan, Nazi agents — during World War II — Communist agents — during the Cold War — and, outrageously enough, Dr. Martin Luther King, Jr.
>
> > These two pairs of dashes are liable to leave the reader confused. The material between them is not crucially important, so two pairs of parentheses would work better.

Writer to Writer

Aren't there actually two kinds of dashes?   Yes, there are: *em* dashes and *en* dashes.

The term *dash* by itself generally refers to an em dash. To make an em dash in Word, type two hyphens closed up with the words on either side. The dash probably won't appear until you've added a space at the end of the second word.

You may be following a style, such as MLA, that specifies how em dashes should be styled. If not, it's your choice whether or not to add spaces before and after them. If you decide to use spaces, do it consistently.

En dashes are shorter than em dashes and longer than hyphens. Use them:

- between numbers (*2016–2020*)

- between place names (*the New York–Boston route*)

- where the meaning is *versus* (*a Patriots–Seahawks game*)

- between a hyphenated or open compound and a prefix, suffix, or word you've added to the beginning or end of the compound (*a Coca-Cola–flavored cake*).

However, use a word, not an en dash, after *from* or *between*. (*She worked full time* from *2014 to 2016. She'll be full time again* between *May* and *September.*)

Microsoft Word will make an en dash for you if you type "space hyphen hyphen space" and then the number or word that comes next (plus a space after that word). When the program's designers decided that en dashes should be created this way, they made a curious choice, because hardly ever should an en dash in finished work have spaces around it. So after the en dash appears, go back and delete the spaces.

Use Parentheses for Explanatory and Other Minor Asides

Parentheses are almost always used in pairs. They tend to de-emphasize the material between them and suggest that that material is not necessary for understanding the overall point of your sentence.

The Unabomber case went to trial (Kaczynski's brother and mother sat in the front row), but Kaczynski soon pleaded guilty to all charges.

> The detail about Kaczynski's brother and mother is irrelevant to the writer's larger point: the outcome of the trial.

28.5

Avoid putting essential information or ideas in parentheses:

✗ In his manifesto, Kaczynski writes about the "industrial-technological system" (and how harmful it is).

> Kaczynski's main focus was the harmfulness of the industrial-technological system, so this idea is essential and should not be in parentheses.

You can enclose whole sentences in parentheses. When you do, to get the rest of the punctuation and the capitalization correct, you'll need to decide whether the contents are parenthetical to the sentence or to the larger idea you're exploring in the paragraph.

Principles behind forensic linguistics led a U.S. appeals court to overturn the 1963 conviction of Ernesto Miranda. (Police officers have read suspects their "Miranda rights" ever since.) But the same principles have also led to many convictions (see page 6 of this report).

> The information in the first pair of parentheses digresses from the writer's larger point. It can stand as a sentence on its own. The remark in the second pair of parentheses is not an independent thought, so the writer has placed it inside the related sentence.

Use parentheses around acronyms that you are introducing (see p. 358, Sec. 29.3):

Information technology (IT) can be used to exactly record and analyze language.

Also use parentheses around the numbers in enumerations, unless you're following a style that recommends treating them otherwise:

> Hillel's three questions are (1) If I am not for myself, who will be for me?, (2) If I am only for myself, what am I?, and (3) If not now, when?

Use Brackets inside Parentheses and Quotations

You can use brackets as parentheses within parentheses (a pair of parentheses inside another pair of parentheses is confusing and incorrect):

> The name Unabomber comes from the designation that the FBI used for the case ("UNABOM" [an acronym for "UNiversity and Airline BOMber"]) before it was solved.

Also use brackets to add information within a quotation or to clarify something that might be confusing or ungrammatical now that you have taken the quotation out of its original context:

> According to the report, "Analysis of the data demonstrated that each [subject in the experiment] exhibited a unique word-use pattern."

> In the report itself, *each* alone was clear, because the previous sentences had been discussing the experimental subjects. Here the word is mysterious unless what it refers to is specified.

> The researcher reported that they "compare[d] word-use patterns using software that [they] developed."

> The researcher's original wording was *we compare* and *we developed*, and the minor changes are needed to make the wording fit the current writer's sentence.

For more information on using brackets when modifying quotations, see page 144, Sec. 9.2.

Use Ellipsis Marks to Indicate Omissions

Use ellipsis marks in quotations to indicate where you have omitted words or whole sentences. For omissions within a sentence, replace the omitted words with a three-point ellipsis (. . .):

28.5

> "When in the Course of human events, it becomes necessary for one people to dissolve the political bands which have connected them with another, . . . a decent respect to the opinions of mankind requires that they should declare the causes which impel them to the separation."

> If a comma comes right before the material you omit, leave it in if you think it will help the reader follow the sentence.

For omissions of whole sentences, add the period or other end punctuation mark before the ellipsis marks to indicate the omission (. . . .):

> "We hold these truths to be self-evident, that all men are created equal . . . . The history of the present King of Great Britain is a history of repeated injuries and usurpations, all having in direct object the establishment of an absolute Tyranny over these States."

See page 145, Sec. 9.2, for more detailed information about using ellipses.

In social email, people often use ellipsis marks to trail off or to show uncertainty or shyness. Do not do that in more formal writing.

Use a Slash for Poetry or Song Lyrics, and Use It, Sparingly, for Alternatives

Use slashes with spaces on both sides to indicate the ends of lines in the original when you quote poetry, song lyrics, or the like:

> The song begins like this: "Paula Nancy Millstone Jennings / At her table poetry penning / Loved to tell of dying swans. / Now her poetry's gone, all gone."

Alternatives like *Mr./Ms.* and *and/or* are graceless and should be avoided where possible. Where they're unavoidable, use a slash in them.

29. Use Sentence Mechanics to Orient Readers

Sentence mechanics — capitalization, italics, abbreviations, acronyms, and spelling — help readers make sense of the information you are sharing with them. Understanding some basic guidelines about sentence mechanics will enhance your ability to convey information clearly and concisely. The guidelines given here are commonly followed, though particular citation styles and publications' "house" styles may make exceptions.

29.1 Use Capital Letters to Mark Beginnings

The capital letter that starts a sentence, together with the punctuation mark that ended the previous sentence, signals to the reader that a new thought is under way. Similarly, capitals in the middle of a sentence mark the beginnings of proper names, of the words in a title, or of some other special uses of language.

Capitalize Proper Nouns

People, places, organizations, branded products, landmarks, months, days of the week, and creative works like articles, books, movies, and songs all have names, and (unless they or the creators of a product have a well-known preference to the contrary) you should begin these names with capital letters.

> Last year my brother Steven visited our grandparents in Mumbai, India, and brought them an Apple tablet — an iPad — as a gift from our parents.

Capitalize Titles That Immediately Precede a Person's Name

> Steven told them that Queen Elizabeth has been photographed using the same kind of tablet.

This rule does not apply if there is so much as a comma between the title and the name:

> Steven told them that the United Kingdom's queen, Elizabeth II, has been photographed using the same kind of tablet.

(See p. 334, Sec. 28.1, for information about when to set off names with commas.)

The rule also does not apply to descriptions that aren't really titles:

> The Vogon Soup guitarist Gordie Jones has an Apple tablet too.

Capitalize Most Adjectives Derived from Proper Names

> The Indian way of life is different from the American way.

Capitalize Most Words in the Titles of Works

The major words in the titles of short works that you enclose in quotation marks and in the titles of substantial works that you italicize should generally be capitalized. (See Part 6 for more examples.)

Do not capitalize articles (*a, an, the*), conjunctions (for example, *and, but, so*), or prepositions (*in, on, over*) unless they are the first or last word of the title or subtitle.

Do capitalize *is* and *are*. Although they're as short as the words that are not capitalized, they are verbs.

> I gave Steven the phrase book *Say It in Hindi* to take with him.

> He played "While My Guitar Gently Weeps," "I Me Mine," and "All You Need Is Love" for our grandparents.

Follow the Specialized Capitalization of Organizations and Brands

The person, company, or organization whose name it is gets to decide, within limits, how the name should be written:

> My parents bought the iPad on eBay.

29.1

However, when you begin a sentence with a name that starts with a lowercase letter, the rule above will come into conflict with the rule that sentences start with capital letters.

29.2

> eBay sells all kinds of things.

In such cases, use the name in the form its owner prefers (except when that form is all caps—see below) but see if you can revise the sentence so that it begins with some other word.

> People buy all kinds of things on eBay.

When you come across an organization or product that gives its name in all caps—or in all lowercase letters—do not follow that style unless you are being paid as an advertiser.

> ✗ My VISA card was declined, so I ended up spending the evening at home alone, on reddit.

Capitalize just the initial letter.

> ✔ My Visa card was declined, so I ended up spending the evening at home alone, on Reddit.

29.2 Use Italics in Specific Cases

Italicize the Titles or Names of Substantial Works

Use italics for the names of books, journals, magazines, newspapers, plays, movies, radio and television programs, symphonies, ballets, albums, paintings, and sculptures.

> The *International Journal of Speech, Language, and the Law* presents research in and analysis of forensic linguistics.

> The author was interviewed in *Newsweek* and on NPR's *Fresh Air*.

Italicize Foreign Words

English has adopted words from many other languages and made them ours. *Bagel, curry, espresso,* and *salsa* all come from other languages and cultures, but the words are included in English dictionaries, so there is no need to italicize them. Italicize foreign words that do not appear in the dictionary.

> *Daadi* and *Dada* — that's Hindi for "Grandma" and
> "Grandpa" — loved their gift and asked Steven to use
> it to take a photograph of them to send to my family.

29.2

Use Italics for Emphasis

> "We *must* get some of the parrots that feed in your garden into
> the picture!" he told them.

When your emphasis is likely to be obvious to the reader or when you've already changed or added a word for emphasis, do not italicize. The word *do* in sentences like this one, for example, is inherently emphatic:

> ✗ I *do* hope my grandparents will enjoy using the iPad.

> Because *do* conveys emphasis, italics are unnecessary.

To decide whether italics are useful or overkill, take them out, read the sentence aloud or in your mind, and see whether the natural emphasis is the same as (or better than) the emphasis with the italics.

If for design reasons you choose to italicize elements other than the ones presented above, and then at some point within those elements you find that the rules for italicizing apply, remove the italics from the words that you would ordinarily italicize:

> *The author is a frequent contributor to the* Central University
> Sentinel.

> This note about the author is italicized. The *Sentinel* is a publication, so its name would ordinarily appear in italics. To make the same distinction in italicized text, un-italicize the name.

29.3 Use Abbreviations and Acronyms to Help, Not Frustrate, Readers

Use Only Standard Abbreviations

29.3

Abbreviations of titles like *Mr., Ms., Dr., Rev.,* and *Prof.* before names are in fairly standard use in running text, as are abbreviations like *Jr., MD, DDS,* and *PhD* after names. Whether or not to use periods in academic degrees may be specified by a style or else is a matter of choice.

The abbreviations *a.m.* and *p.m.* (meaning morning and afternoon), *BC* and *AD* (for "before Christ" and "anno Domini") or *BCE* and *CE* ("before the common era" and "common era"), and °F and °C ("degrees Fahrenheit" and "degrees Celsius") are in standard use in references to specific times, years or periods, and temperatures:

> 10:00 a.m.
>
> the sixth century BC (or BCE)
>
> AD 78 (or 78 CE)
>
> 70°F is 21°C

Few other abbreviations, apart from acronyms, belong in text. However, abbreviations like *Mon.* and *Tues., Jan.* and *Feb., St.* and *Rd.,* and *m.p.h.* are fine in tables and other places where space is tightly limited.

Use the postal abbreviations for states (*AL, AR,* and so on) in mailing addresses, but spell out state names elsewhere. Anywhere you use abbreviations, use them consistently.

Do not use texting abbreviations like *btw* and *LOL* in formal writing.

Use Acronyms to Simplify

Acronyms are abbreviations made up of the initial letters of words. Most of them are written in all caps without periods: *AAA, HMO, ISP, USPS.* A few exceptions, like *U.S.* and *U.N.,* are often written with internal periods as well as final ones, largely to keep readers from being tempted to read them as words.

Writer to Writer

What format should you use when referring to decades? That is, did the Beatles perform in "the 1960s," "the '60s," "the Sixties," or "the sixties"? You won't go wrong with "1960s," but if you want to write it the way most people say it, you'll need to choose a different option. The *Chicago Manual of Style* likes either "the '60s" or "the sixties"; MLA prefers "the sixties" but accepts "the '60s"; the Associated Press likes "the '60s"; and so on. Choose the format prescribed by the style you're using or the one that makes the best sense to you in context.

The numeral version is a clipped, or shortened form — like "'em" in "Go get 'em!" Therefore, the punctuation at the beginning is an apostrophe, not an open single quotation mark. Word-processing programs are likely to supply the single quotation mark. To replace it with an apostrophe, you'll need to type the mark again and then delete the single quotation mark.

A decade isn't the proper name of anything, so if you spell it out, there's no reason to capitalize it. Follow consistently whatever style you use. And note that none of this applies to any century's first decade. "The 2000s" is not a decade. Refer to, for example, 2000–2009 as "the first decade of the twenty-first century" or the like.

29.3

Check a dictionary or an organization's website if you have doubts about how to write an abbreviation.

Note that when giving the words the acronym stands for, you need not capitalize them simply because they are capitalized in the acronym:

the Association of Southeast Asian Nations (ASEAN)

> This is the proper name of an organization, so the capital letters in the text are correct.

an application programming interface (API)

> This is a generic term, so the words should not be capitalized.

The convention of introducing acronyms in parentheses is intended to alert readers that you will be using the acronym instead of the name from then on. Include the acronym only if you refer to the organization or thing again in your document.

If you end up referring to it just once or twice more, consider whether your writing might be more readable without the acronym. You might choose to repeat the full name or use the part of the acronym that has a generic meaning, like "the association" or "the interface."

If you believe that a particular acronym will be familiar to readers and feel that it needs no introduction — for instance, *DNA, the FBI,* and *NASA* — you may use the acronym instead of the full name the first time you refer to the thing or organization.

Writer to Writer

How should acronyms be introduced?   Different stylebooks recommend different procedures, but a common and practical one for introducing an acronym, in order to use it repeatedly in place of a longish proper name or specialists' term, is to spell out the name or term the first time you use it and follow it with the acronym in parentheses: *the Affordable Care Act (ACA), a patient-centered medical home (PCMH).*

Once you've introduced an acronym, stick with it and do not repeat the *Affordable Care Act (ACA)* formula. Use acronyms to reduce clutter, not add to it. An exception might be if you introduced an acronym several pages prior without having reused it; readers may have forgotten what it stands for. In such cases, consider waiting to introduce the acronym until you begin using it repeatedly.

29.4 Spell Well ⊕

English spelling is notoriously confusing. Not only has English incorporated or adapted words from other languages that have different spelling conventions, but it is not written phonetically.

If it were, *cough, dough, enough, thorough*, and *through* would rhyme, and *through* and *threw* would be spelled the same.

Spelling everything right won't necessarily help orient your readers, the way most aspects of sentence mechanics will. But misspelling words can definitely disorient readers. Here are a few common spelling situations that trip people up.

29.4

If a word has a single syllable, a single vowel, and a single-consonant ending that is not *w, x,* or *y*, make other forms of it (except the plural of a noun) by doubling the consonant: *big, bigger, biggest; shop, shopped, shopping, shopper*. But it's *cough, coughed, coughing*, because the base word has two vowels and also a double-consonant ending; and it's *show, showed, showing*, because the word ends in *w*.

Also double the consonant for similar multisyllable words in which the last syllable is stressed: *occur, occurred, occurring, occurrence*. But it's *repeat, repeated, repeating*, because the second syllable has two vowels, and *listen, listened*, because the second syllable is not stressed.

To make an *-ing* form from a verb that ends in *-e*, drop the *-e*: *bike, biking; dance, dancing; huddle, huddling*.

To pluralize most nouns ending in *-y*, change the *-y* to *-ie-*: *baby, babies; body, bodies; company, companies; flurry, flurries*.

To make most other forms of verbs and adjectives ending in at least one consonant followed by *-y*, change the *y* to *i* before adding the suffix, except when the suffix begins with *i*: *carry, carries, carried, carrying; happy, happier, happiest*.

In nouns and verbs that end with *-y* after a vowel, add just *-s* to make the noun plural or the appropriate suffix to make other forms of the verb: *key, keys; play, plays, played, playing*.

To pluralize nouns ending in *-s, -ss, -ch, -sh, -x,* and *-z*, add *-es*: *lens, lenses; pass, passes; bench, benches; fox, foxes; waltz, waltzes*. But note that it's *quiz, quizzes*: the singular noun has a single syllable, a single vowel, and a single-consonant ending that is not *w, x,* or *y*, and the doubling-the-consonant rule takes precedence.

Do not add an apostrophe when making a noun plural, regardless of how it ends: *bananas, coffees, Fridays, tattoos*.

Part 6

Document Sources

MLA   **APA**   *Chicago*   **CSE**

Part 6: Document Sources

Documenting sources not only shows respect for the writers whose work has shaped your thinking about an issue but also helps your readers locate sources they may want to consult.

30. Use MLA Style

31. Use APA Style

32. Use *Chicago* Style

33. Use CSE Style

For information about technological tools that can help you prepare a bibliography or list of works cited, see page 138.

30. Use MLA Style

Modern Language Association (MLA) style, used primarily in the humanities, emphasizes the authors of a source and the pages on which information is located in the source. Writers who use the MLA documentation system cite, or formally acknowledge, source information within their text using parentheses, and they provide a list of sources in a works-cited list at the end of their document.

For more information about MLA style, consult the *MLA Handbook*, Eighth Edition. Information about the *MLA Handbook* can also be found at **mla.org**.

For an essay formatted in MLA style, turn to p. 394.

Directory of MLA Style

(continued)

MLA 30.0

30.1 Cite Sources in the Text of a Document

MLA style uses parentheses for in-text citations to acknowledge the use of another author's words, facts, and ideas. When you refer to a source within your text, place the author's last name and specific page number(s)—if the source is paginated—within parentheses. Your reader then can go to the works cited list at the end of your document and find the full citation there.

MLA 30.1

1. Basic Format for Direct Quotation Often you will want to name the author of a source within your sentence rather than in a parenthetical citation. By doing so, you create a context for the material that you are including and indicate where the information from the author begins. When you are using a direct quotation from a source and have named the author in your sentence, place only the page number in parentheses after the quotation. The period follows the parentheses.

> Vargas reports that "each year, unintentional drownings kill more than 830 children younger than 14 and cause, on average, 3,600 injuries" (B1).

Vargas' article appears in the *Washington Post*, a newspaper. The page number is preceded by a section letter, in this case "B."

When you have not mentioned the author in your sentence, you must place the author's name and the page number in parentheses after the quotation. Again, the period follows the parentheses.

> After car accidents, "drowning is the second-leading cause of unintentional deaths" among toddlers (Vargas B1).

When you are using a block (or extended) quotation, the parenthetical citation comes after the final punctuation and a single space.

If you continue to refer to a single source for several sentences in a row within one paragraph—and without intervening references to another source—you may reserve your reference until the end of the paragraph. However, be sure to include all of the relevant page numbers.

2. Basic Format for a Summary or Paraphrase When you are summarizing or paraphrasing information from a source, you are still required to cite the source. If you name the author in your sentence, place only the page number in parentheses after the paraphrase or summary. Punctuation marks follow the parentheses. When you have not mentioned the author in your sentence, you must place the author's name and the page number in parentheses after the quotation.

> Vargas points out that drowning doesn't happen in the manner you might expect; children slip underwater quietly, making very little noise to alert unsuspecting parents or guardians (B1).

3. Entire Source If you are referring to an entire source rather than to a specific page or pages, you will not need a parenthetical citation.

> The explorations of race in ZZ Packer's *Drinking Coffee Elsewhere* can be linked thematically to the treatment of immigrants in Jhumpa Lahiri's work.

4. Corporate, Group, or Government Author Cite the corporation, group, or government agency as you would an individual author. You may use abbreviations for the source in subsequent references if you add the abbreviation in parentheses at the first mention of the name.

> The Brown University Office of Financial Aid (BUOFA) has adopted a policy that first-year students will not be expected to work as part of their financial aid package (12). BUOFA will award these students a one-time grant to help compensate for the income lost by not working (14).

5. Unknown Author If you are citing a source that has no known author, such as the book *Through Palestine with the 20th Machine Gun Squadron*, use a brief version of the title in the parenthetical citation.

> The members of the squadron rode horses while the cooks were issued bicycles, requiring the cooks to exert quite a lot of effort pedaling through the desert sand (*Through Palestine* 17).

6. Two or More Works by the Same Author For references to authors with more than one work in your works cited list, insert a short version of the title between author and page number, separating the author and the title with a comma.

MLA
30.1

(Ishiguro, *Unconsoled* 146)

(Ishiguro, *Remains* 77)

7. Two or More Authors with the Same Last Name Include the first initial and last name in the parenthetical citations.

(G. Martin 354)

(F. Martin 169)

8. Two Authors Include the last name of each author in your citation.

As Gostin and Gostin explain, "Interventions that do not pose a truly significant burden on individual liberty are justified if they go a long way towards safeguarding the health and well-being of the populace" (214).

9. Three or More Authors Use only the last name of the first author and the abbreviation "et al." (Latin for "and others"). Note that there is no comma between the author's name and "et al."

(Barnes et al. 44)

10. Literary Work Along with the page number(s), give other identifying information, such as a chapter, scene, or line number, that will help readers find the passage.

The sense of social claustrophobia is never as palpable in *The Age of Innocence* as when Newland realizes that all of New York society has conspired to cover up what it believes to be an affair between him and Madame Olenska (Wharton 339; ch. 33).

**MLA
30.1**

11. Work in an Edited Collection or Anthology Cite the author of the work, not the editor of the anthology.

> In "Beneath the Deep, Slow Motion," Leo says, "The Chinese call anger a weary bird with no place to roost" (Barkley 163).

12. Sacred Text Give the name of the edition you are using along with the chapter and verse (or their equivalent).

> He should consider that "Where no counsel is, the people fall: but in the multitude of counselors there is safety" (*King James Bible*, Prov. 11.14).

> In the Qu'ran, sinners are said to be blind to their sins ("The Cow" 2.7).

13. Two or More Works Cited Together Use a semicolon to separate entries. Entries do not need to be alphabetized.

> Forethought is key in survival, whether it involves remembering extra water on a safari trail or gathering food for a long winter in ancient times (Wither and Hosking 4; Estes and Otte 2).

14. Source Quoted in Another Source Ideally, you will be able to find the primary, or original, source for material used in your research project document. If you quote or paraphrase a secondary source—a source that contains information about a primary source—use the abbreviation "qtd. in" (for "quoted in") when you cite the source.

> MIT professor Richard Lundgren has stated, "Global warming is small and magnified by the alarmists with deeply compromised political pressure, data fudging, and out and out guesswork" (qtd. in de Garmo A13).

15. Source without Page Numbers Give a section, paragraph, or screen number, if used, in the parenthetical citation. Note the comma before the paragraph reference, which is not used before page numbers.

> Teters believes the mascots dehumanize Native Americans, allowing spectators to dismiss the Native Americans' true culture as well as their hardships (Saraceno, par. 20).

If no page numbers are provided, list only the author's name in parentheses.

> Although his work has been influenced by many graphic artists, it remains essentially text based (Fitzgerald).

30.2 Prepare the List of Works Cited

MLA-style research documents include a reference list titled "Works Cited," which begins on a new page at the end of the document. If you wish to acknowledge sources that you read but did not cite in your text, you may include them in a second list titled "Works Consulted." In longer documents, a list of works cited may be given at the end of each chapter or section. In digital documents that use links, such as websites, the list of works cited is often a separate page to which other pages are linked. To see a works cited list in MLA style, see page 400.

The list is alphabetized by author. If the author's name is not given, alphabetize the entry using the title of the source. To cite more than one work by the same author, alphabetize the group under the author's last name, with each entry listed alphabetically by title (see item 21 on p. 373).

All entries in the list are double-spaced, with no extra space between entries. Entries are formatted with a hanging indent: The first line of an entry is flush with the left margin, and subsequent lines are indented one half inch. Unless otherwise noted, use commas to separate items within each entry. Titles of longer works, such as books, journals, or websites, are italicized. Titles of short works, such as articles or chapters, are enclosed in quotation marks. MLA generally indicates the "container" of the source—the larger object, if any, in which the source can be found. Some sources may have multiple levels of containers, such as a periodical article that is accessed via a database. Occasionally, sources may be identified by a descriptive label (editorial, map, letter, photograph, and so on).

Since sources today can often be found in both print and digital form—for instance, you can easily access a *New Yorker* article in the print magazine or on its website—the source types that follow include model citations for both media. The section on digital sources (see p. 389) features source types that are native to digital formats, such as blogs or social media platforms.

Books, Conference Proceedings, and Dissertations

16. One Author List the author's last name first, followed by a comma and the first name. Italicize the book title and subtitle, if any. List the publisher (abbreviating "University Press" as "UP"), and then insert a comma and the publication year. End with a period.

> Page, Scott E. *The Model Thinker: What You Need to Know to Make Data Work for You.* Basic Books, 2018.

Cite an online book as you would a print book, providing the website and DOI (digital object identifier, a unique number assigned to specific content). If a DOI is not available, provide a stable URL.

> Swinnen, Johan F. M. *The Economics of Beer.* Oxford UP, 2011. *Oxford Scholarship Online,* doi:10.1093/acprof:oso/9780199692801.001.0001.

> Piketty, Thomas. *Capital in the Twenty-First Century.* Translated by Arthur Goldhammer, Harvard UP, 2014. *Google Books,* books.google.com/books?isbn=0674369556.

Cite an e-book as you would a print book, and then provide the name of the e-reader.

> Doerr, Anthony. *All the Light We Cannot See.* Nook ed., Charles Scribner and Sons, 2014.

17. Two Authors List the authors in the same order as on the title page, last name first for only the first author listed. Use commas to separate the authors' names.

> Brynjolfsson, Erik, and Andrew McAfee. *The Second Machine Age: Work, Progress, and Prosperity in a Time of Brilliant Technologies.* W. W. Norton, 2014.

18. Three or More Authors Provide the first author's name (last name first) followed by a comma, and then the abbreviation "et al." (Latin for "and others").

> Cunningham, Stuart, et al. *Media Economics*. Palgrave Macmillan,
>
> 2015.

19. Corporate or Group Author Write out the full name of the corporation or group, and cite the name as you would an author. If this name is also the name of the publisher, you may omit it in the author position.

> Human Rights Watch. *World Report of 2015: Events of 2014*. Seven Stories
>
> Press, 2015.

20. Unknown Author When no author is listed on the title or copyright page, begin the entry with the title of the work. Alphabetize the entry by the first word of the title other than "A," "An," or "The."

> *The Book of Nature*. Kunth Verlag, 2010.

21. Two or More Books by the Same Author Use the author's name in the first entry. Thereafter, use three hyphens followed by a period in place of the author's name. List the entries alphabetically by title.

> Pollan, Michael. *How to Change Your Mind*. Penguin Books,
>
> 2018.
>
> ---. *Cooked: A Natural History of Transformation*. Penguin Books,
>
> 2013.

22. Editor(s) Cite the name of the editor(s) as you would an author, followed by "editor" or "editors."

> Horner, Avril, and Anne Rowe, editors. *Living on Paper: Letters from Iris*
>
> *Murdoch*. Princeton UP, 2016.

How do I cite books using MLA style?

MLA 30.2

But What If We're Wrong?

Thinking About the Present As If It Were the Past

Chuck Klosterman

BLUE RIDER PRESS | *New York*

---

blue
rider
press

An imprint of Penguin Random House LLC
375 Hudson Street
New York, New York 10014

Copyright © 2016 by Chuck Klosterman
Penguin supports copyright. Copyright fuels creativity, encourages diverse voices, promotes free speech, and creates a vibrant culture. Thank you for buying an authorized edition of this book and for complying with copyright laws by not reproducing, scanning, or distributing any part of it in any form without permission. You are supporting writers and allowing Penguin to continue to publish books for every reader.

Blue Rider Press is a registered trademark and its colophon is a trademark of Penguin Random House LLC

ISBN 9780399184123

Printed in the United States of America
20 19 18 17 16 15 14 13 12 11

BOOK DESIGN BY NICOLE LAROCHE

When citing a book, use the information from the title page and the copyright page (on the reverse of the title page), not from the book's cover or a library catalog.

➡ **See pages 372–378 for complete models for citing books.**

⌐A¬ **⌐————B————¬**
Klosterman, Chuck. *But What If We're Wrong? Thinking about the Present As If*

⌐——B——¬ **⌐——C——¬** **⌐D¬**
It Were the Past. Blue Rider Press, 2016.

A **The author.** Give the last name first, followed by a comma, the first name, and the middle initial (if given). End with a period.

B **The title.** Italicize the title and subtitle, separated by a colon (unless the title ends in a question mark or exclamation point, as above). Capitalize all major words, and end with a period.

C **The publisher.** Provide the publisher's name as listed on the book's title page. Abbreviate "University Press" as "UP." Do not include terms such as "Publisher" or "Inc." Follow with a comma.

D **The year of publication.** Use the most recent copyright date and end with a period.

23. Author(s) with an Editor or Translator List the author(s) first and then the title. Include the label "Edited by" or "Translated by" and the name of the editor or translator, first name first.

> Ferrante, Elena. *The Story of the Lost Child.* Translated by Ann Goldstein,
>
> Europa Editions, 2015.

**MLA
30.2**

24. Book in a Language Other than English You may give a translation of the book's title in brackets.

> Márquez, Gabriel García. *Del amor y otros demonios* [*Of Love and Other*
>
> *Demons*]. Vintage Books, 2010.

25. Edition Other than the First Include the number of the edition and the abbreviation "ed." (meaning "edition") after the title.

> Lavenda, Robert, et al. *Core Concepts in Cultural Anthropology.* 6th ed.,
>
> Oxford UP, 2016.

26. Multivolume Work Include the total number of volumes and the abbreviation "vols." after the date.

> Chapman, Roger, and James Ciment, editors. *Culture Wars in America: An*
>
> *Encyclopedia of Issues, Viewpoints, and Voices.* 2nd ed., M. E. Sharpe,
>
> 2014. 3 vols.

If you have used only one of the volumes in your document, include the volume number after the title.

27. Book in a Series If a series name and/or number appears on the title page, include it at the end of the citation, after the date.

> Trindade, Luís, editor. *Narratives in Motion: Journalism and Modernist*
>
> *Events in 1920s Portugal.* Berghahn, 2016. Remapping Cultural
>
> History 15.

28. Republished Book Indicate the original date of publication after the title.

> Melville, Herman. *Bartleby, the Scrivener: A Story of Wall-Street*. 1853. Book
>
> Jungle, 2010.

29. Book with a Title within the Title Do not use italics for the title within the title.

> Stuckey, Sterling. *African Culture and Melville's Art: The Creative Process in*
>
> Benito Cereno *and* Moby-Dick. Oxford UP, 2009.

30. Work in an Edited Collection or Anthology Give the author and then the title in quotation marks. Follow with the title of the collection in italics, the label "edited by," and the names of the editor(s) (first name first), the publication information, and the inclusive page numbers for the selection or chapter.

> Sayrafiezadeh, Saïd. "Paranoia." *New American Stories*, edited by
>
> Ben Marcus, Vintage Books, 2015, pp. 3–29.

If you are using multiple selections from the same anthology, include the anthology itself in your list of works cited and cross-reference it in the citations for individual works.

> Eisenberg, Deborah. "Some Other, Better Otto." Marcus, pp. 94–136.

> Marcus, Ben, editor. *New American Stories*. Vintage Books, 2015.

> Sayrafiezadeh, Saïd. "Paranoia." Marcus, pp. 3–29.

31. Foreword, Introduction, Preface, or Afterword Begin with the author of the part you are citing and the name of that part. Add the title of the work, "by" or "edited by" and the work's author or editor (first name first), and publication information. Then give the inclusive page numbers for the part.

> Dunham, Lena. Foreword. *The Liars' Club*, by Mary Karr, Penguin Classics,
>
> 2015, pp. xi–xiii.

If the author of the foreword or other part is also the author of the work, use only the last name after "by."

> Olson, Gregory Allen. Introduction. *Landmark Speeches on the Vietnam War*,
>   by Olson, Texas A&M UP, 2010, pp. 1–12.

MLA 30.2

If the foreword or other part has a title, include the title in quotation marks between the author and the name of the part.

> Walker, Alice. "Learning to Dance." Preface. *Hard Times Require Furious Dancing*, by Walker, New World Library, 2010, pp. xv–xvi.

32. Published Proceedings of a Conference Provide information as you would for a book, adding information about the sponsors, date, and location of the conference after the title.

> Kumar, Srijan, et al. *Community Interaction and Conflict on the Web*.
>   Proceedings of the 2018 World Wide Web Conference, 23–27 Apr.
>   2018, Lyon, France. International World Wide Web Conferences
>   Steering Committee, 2018.

33. Screenplay Provide information as you would for a book.

> Cholodenko, Lisa, and Stuart Blumberg. *The Kids Are All Right: The Shooting Script*. Newmarket Press, 2011.

34. Sacred Text Include the title of the version as it appears on the title page. If the title does not identify the version, place that information before the publisher.

> *The Oxford Annotated Bible with the Apocrypha*. Edited by
>   Herbert G. May and Bruce M. Metzger, Revised Standard Version,
>   Oxford UP, 1965.

> *The Qur'an: Translation*. Translated by Abdullah Yusuf Ali, Tahrike Tarsile
>   Qur'an, 2001.

35. Graphic Narrative or Illustrated Work List the primary author/illustrator in the first position. If the author is also the illustrator, simply list him or her in the first position.

**MLA
30.2**

Ellis, Adam. *Super Chill: A Year of Living Anxiously*. Andrews McMeel
Publishing, 2018.

Kerascoët, illustrator. *Beautiful Darkness*. By Fabien Vehlmann, Drawn and
Quarterly, 2014.

Smith, Lane. *Abe Lincoln's Dream*. Roaring Brook Press, 2012.

36. Dissertation or Thesis Cite as you would a book, with the title in italics, followed by the year the dissertation was accepted and the school. End with an appropriate label such as "Dissertation" or "Thesis."

Hitotsubashi, N. S. *The Life and Times of Beowulf: Monsters and Heroes in
the Named Lands of the North*. 2013. Wheaton College. Dissertation.

Sources in Journals, Magazines, and Newspapers

37. Article in a Journal Enclose the article title in quotation marks. Italicize the journal title, and then list the volume number, issue number, season and year of publication, and inclusive page numbers.

Matchie, Thomas. "Law versus Love in *The Round House*." *Midwest Quarterly*,
vol. 56, no. 4, Summer 2015, pp. 353–64.

For an article in an electronic journal, provide the print information, if given, and end with the DOI or URL.

MacDuffie, Allen. "Charles Darwin and the Victorian Pre-History of Climate
Denial." *Victorian Studies*, vol. 60, no. 4, Summer 2018, pp. 543–64,
www.jstor.org/stable/10.2979/victorianstudies.60.4.02.

For an article from a database, cite the database name before the DOI or URL.

Coles, Kimberly Anne. "The Matter of Belief in John Donne's Holy Sonnets."
Renaissance Quarterly, vol. 68, no. 3, Fall 2015, pp. 899–931. *JSTOR*,
doi:10.1086/683855.

How do I cite articles from periodicals using MLA style?

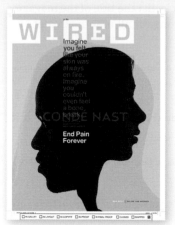

Periodicals include journals, magazines, and newspapers. This tutorial gives the citation for a print magazine article.

MLA 30.2

Models for citing articles from journals and newspapers, both in print and accessed electronically, are on pages 378–383.

CAITLIN OPPERMAN, *Wired*, May 2017, © Condé Nast Publications, Inc.

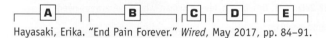

Hayasaki, Erika. "End Pain Forever." *Wired*, May 2017, pp. 84–91.

A **The author.** Give the last name first, followed by a comma, the first name, and the middle initial (if given). End with a period.

B **The article title.** Give the article title and subtitle (if any), separated by a colon. Enclose them in quotation marks, and capitalize all major words. End with a period.

C **The periodical title.** Italicize the periodical title. Capitalize all major words, and end with a comma.

D **The date of publication.** For journals, give the volume number ("vol."), issue number ("no."), and the season and year of publication. For magazines and newspapers, give the day (if listed), month, and year. Follow each element with a comma. Abbreviate the names of all months except May, June, and July.

E **Inclusive page numbers.** Use the abbreviation "p." or "pp." For numbers 100 and above, give only the last two digits and any other preceding digits if different from the first number (322–28, 592–603). Include section letters for newspapers, if given. End with a period.

38. Article in a Monthly or Bimonthly Magazine After the author's name and title of the article, list the title of the magazine in italics, the date (use abbreviations for all months except May, June, and July), and inclusive pages.

> McArdle, Megan. "The Freeloaders: How a Generation of File-Sharers Is Ruining
>
> the Future of Entertainment." *The Atlantic*, May 2010, pp. 34–35.

39. Article in a Weekly or Biweekly Magazine Give the exact date of publication, in day/month/year order.

> Greider, William. "Why the Federal Reserve Needs an Overhaul." *The Nation*,
>
> 3 Mar. 2014, pp. 12–19.

Cite online articles the same as you would a print article, and then give the URL.

> Grossman, Lev. "Why We've Always Needed Fantastic Maps." *Literary Hub*,
>
> 22 Oct. 2018, lithub.com/lev-grossman-why-weve-always-needed-
>
> fantastic-maps/.

40. Article in a Newspaper If the paper is not a national newspaper (such as *The Wall Street Journal*) or the city of publication is not part of its title, give the city in square brackets [Claremont, N.H.] after the title. List the date in day/month/year order followed by the page numbers (use the newspaper section letter before the page number, if given). If the article does not appear on consecutive pages, write only the first page number and a plus sign (+), with no space between.

> Valencia, Milton J. "Plan B Fueled Push to Restore Gas Service." *The Boston*
>
> *Globe*, 4 Dec. 2018, pp. A1+.

For newspaper articles found online, cite as you would a print article and give the URL.

> Butler, Michael. "Providing Leadership for Our National Treasures." *Knoxville*
>
> *News Sentinel*, 8 May 2017, www.knoxnews.com/story/opinion/columnists/
>
> 2017/05/08/providing-leadership-our-natural-treasures/101338844/.

How do I cite articles from databases using MLA style?

Libraries subscribe to services such as LexisNexis, ProQuest, InfoTrac, and EBSCOhost, which provide access to databases of digital texts. The databases list publication information, abstracts, and, sometimes, the complete text of documents in a specific subject area, discipline, or profession.

MLA 30.2

See Chapter 6 for more on searching with databases.

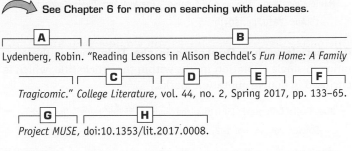

Lydenberg, Robin. "Reading Lessons in Alison Bechdel's *Fun Home: A Family Tragicomic*." *College Literature*, vol. 44, no. 2, Spring 2017, pp. 133–65. *Project MUSE*, doi:10.1353/lit.2017.0008.

A   **The author.** Give the last name first, followed by a comma, the first name, and the middle initial (if given). End with a period.

B   **The article title.** Give the article title and subtitle (if any), separated by a colon. Enclose the title and subtitle in quotation marks, capitalizing all major words. Place a period inside the close quotation mark.

C   **The periodical title.** Italicize the periodical title, including the article "The." Capitalize all major words, and end with a comma.

D   **The volume and issue number, if given.** Use the abbreviations "vol." and "no." and follow the volume number and issue number with commas.

E   **The date of publication.** For journals, give the month or season (if applicable) followed by the year of publication. For magazines and newspapers, give the day (if applicable), month, and year, in that order. Abbreviate the names of all months except May, June, and July. Follow the year with a comma.

F   **Inclusive page numbers.** Use the abbreviation "p." or "pp." For numbers 100 and above, give only the last two digits and any other preceding digits if different from the first number (322–28, 592–603). Include section letters for newspapers, if given. End with a period.

G   **The name of the database.** Italicize the name of the database, and follow with a comma.

H   **The DOI or URL.** Many sources from databases include a stable identifier called a permalink or a DOI (digital object identifier). If no DOI is available, include a URL for the database.

**MLA
30.2**

41. Unsigned Article in a Newspaper or Magazine Begin with the title of the article. Alphabetize by the first word other than "A," "An," or "The."

"I Am Part of the Resistance Inside the Trump Administration." *New York
Times*, 5 Sept. 2018, www.nytimes.com/2018/09/05/opinion/
trump-white-house-anonymous-resistance.html.

42. Article That Skips Pages Give only the first page number and a plus sign (+), with no space between.

Mahler, Jonathan. "The Second Coming." *The New York Times Magazine*,
15 Aug. 2010, pp. 30+.

43. Article with a Quotation in the Title Enclose the quotation in single quotation marks within the article title, which is enclosed in double quotation marks.

Díaz, Isabel González. "Enriching the 'Rags-to-Riches' Myth." *The Black
Scholar*, vol. 43, no. 1–2, Spring 2013, pp. 43–51.

44. Editorial in a Newspaper Include the word "Editorial" after the URL or page number(s).

"Mars Beckons." *The New York Times*, 27 Nov. 2018, www.nytimes
.com/2018/11/27/opinion/mars-exploration-nasa-insight-space.html.
Editorial.

45. Letter to the Editor Include the word "Letter" after the URL or page number(s).

Hasl, Rudy. "Jefferson's Mammoth." *Smithsonian*, June 2010, p. 6. Letter.

46. Review Start with the author and title of the review and then add the words "Review of" followed by the title of the work under review. Insert a comma and the word "by" or "edited by" (for an edited work) or "directed by" (for a play or film) and the name of the author or director. Continue with publication information for the review. Use this citation format for all reviews, including those for books, films, and video games.

> Walton, James. "Noble, Embattled Souls." Review of *The Bone Clocks* and
> *Slade House*, by David Mitchell. *The New York Review of Books*, 3 Dec.
> 2015, pp. 55–58.

Cite an online review as you would a print review, and then give the URL.

> Savage, Phil. "*Fallout 4* Review." Review of *Fallout 4*, by Bethesda Game
> Studios. *PC Gamer*, Future Publishing, 8 Nov. 2015, www.pcgamer.com/
> fallout-4-review/.

47. Published Interview Begin with the person interviewed.
If the published interview has a title, give it in quotation marks.
Next, write the words "Interview by," followed by the name of the
interviewer. Then supply the publication information.

> Musk, Elon. "Interviewing Elon Musk." Interview by David Gelles. *The
> New York Times*, 19 Aug. 2018, p. A2.

Cite an online interview as you would a print interview, and then
give the URL.

> Jaffrey, Madhur. "Madhur Jaffrey on How Indian Cuisine Won Western Taste
> Buds." Interview by Shadrach Kabango. *Q*, CBC Radio, 29 Oct. 2015,
> www.cbc.ca/1.3292918.

48. Article in a Special Issue After the author and the title
of the article (in quotation marks) include the title of the special issue (in italics), and then write the words "special issue of"
before the regular title of the periodical.

> Redd, Steven B., and Alex Mitz. "Policy Perspectives on National Security
> and Foreign Policy Decision Making." *2013 Public Policy Yearbook*,
> special issue of *Policy Studies Journal*, vol. 41, no. S1, Apr. 2013,
> pp. S11–S37.

MLA
30.2

Reference Works

49. Encyclopedia, Dictionary, Thesaurus, Handbook, or Almanac Cite as you would a book (p. 372).

50. Entry in an Encyclopedia, Dictionary, Thesaurus, Handbook, or Almanac (including a Wiki) Unless the entry is signed, begin your citation with the title of the entry in quotation marks, followed by a period. Give the title of the reference work, italicized, and the edition (if available) and year of publication. If a reference work is not well known (perhaps because it includes highly specialized information), provide the editor's name as well as all of the bibliographic information. If there is no date of publication, include your date of access.

> "The Ball's in Your Court." *The American Heritage Dictionary of Idioms*.
>> 2nd ed., Houghton Mifflin Harcourt, 2013.

Cite an online entry as you would a print entry, and then give the URL.

> "House Music." *Wikipedia*, 12 May 2019, en.wikipedia.org/wiki/House_music.

51. Map or Chart Treat as you would a book without authors, listing its title (italicized) and publication information. For a map in an atlas or other volume, give the map title in quotation marks followed by publication information for the atlas and page numbers for the map.

> "Greenland." *Atlas of the World*. 19th ed., Oxford UP, 2012, p. 154.

For a map or chart found online, cite as you would a print source, and then give the URL.

> "Map of Sudan." *Global Citizen*, Citizens for Global Solutions, 2011,
>> globalsolutions.org/blog/bashir#.VthzNMfi_FI.

52. Government Publications In most cases, cite the government agency as the author. If there is a named author, editor, or compiler, provide that name after the title. Do not abbreviate "Congress," "Senate," "House," "Resolution," or "Report."

> Canada, Minister of Aboriginal Affairs and Northern Development. *2015–16 Report on Plans and Priorities*. Minister of Public Works and Government Services Canada, 2015.

> United States, Department of Agriculture. *Hot Foods Purchases Approved for SNAP Recipients in 23 Georgia Counties*. Food and Nutrition Service, Oct. 2018, fns-prod.azureedge.net/pressrelease/2018/022718.

When documenting a bill, report, or resolution of the United States Congress, include the number and session of Congress from which it emerged.

53. Brochure or Pamphlet Format the entry as you would for a book (see item 16, p. 372).

> *The Legendary Sleepy Hollow Cemetery*. Friends of Sleepy Hollow Cemetery, 2008.

Field Sources

54. Personal Interview Start with the name of the person interviewed, an indication of how the interview was conducted ("Personal interview," "Telephone interview," or "E-mail inter-view"), and the date. (Note that MLA style is to hyphenate "e-mail.")

> Parlon, Charisse. Personal interview. 4 Feb. 2019.

55. Unpublished Letter If written to you, give the writer's name, the words "Letter to the author" (no quotation marks or italics), and the date the letter was written.

> Boyd, Edward. Letter to the author. 11 Aug. 2019.

If the letter was written to someone else, give that person's name.

56. Lecture or Public Address Give the speaker's name and the title of the lecture (if there is one). If the lecture was part of a meeting or convention, identify that event. Conclude with the event information, including venue, city, and date. End with the appropriate label ("Lecture," "Address," "Panel discussion," "Reading").

> Joseph, Branden. "1962." Dept. of Art History, U of Chicago, Cochrane Art
>   Center, Chicago, 11 Mar. 2010. Lecture.

> Smith, Anna Deavere. "On the Road: A Search for American Character."
>   National Endowment for the Humanities, John F. Kennedy Center for the
>   Performing Arts, Washington, D.C., 6 Apr. 2015. Address.

For lectures and public addresses found on the web, provide the URL after the date. End with the appropriate label.

> Khosla, Raj. "Precision Agriculture and Global Food Security." *US Department of
>   State*, 26 Mar. 2013, www.state.gov/e/stas/series/212172.htm. Address.

Media Sources

57. Film or Video Generally begin with the title of the film (italicized). Always supply the name of the director, the distributor, and the year of original release. You may also insert other relevant information, such as the names of performers or screenplay writers, before the distributor.

> *Black Panther*. Directed by Ryan Coogler, written by Ryan Coogler and
>   Joe Robert Cole, Walt Disney Studios Motion Pictures, 2018.

If you wish to emphasize an individual's role in the film or movie, such as the director or screenplay writer, you may list that name first.

> Olivier, Laurence, director and performer. *Hamlet*. Paramount, 1948.

For media other than film (such as videotape and DVD), cite it as for a film, unless you are discussing supplementary material found on the DVD, in which case your entry should refer to the DVD.

> "Sweeney's London." Produced by Eric Young. *Sweeney Todd: The Demon
>   Barber of Fleet Street*, directed by Tim Burton, DreamWorks, 2007, disc 2.

For videos found on the web, give the URL after the publication information.

> "Watch a Lion Fall from a Tree during Rescue from a Wire Snare Injury."
> *National Geographic,* accessed 3 June 2018, video.nationalgeographic.
> com/video/news/00000167-604d-d8d3-a5e7-e64fb3560000?source=
> featuredvideo.

MLA 30.2

58. Television or Radio Program If the program has named episodes or segments, list those in quotation marks. Then give the title of the program or series (italicized), the producer, and the date that the program first aired. Include the names of an author, a director, a host, a narrator, or an actor after the title of the program or series. If the material you're citing is an interview, include the word "Interview" and, if relevant, the name of the interviewer.

> "Federal Role in Support of Autism." *Washington Journal,* narrated by Robb
> Harleston, C-SPAN, 1 Dec. 2012.

> Walker, Scott. Interview by Margaret Hoover. *Firing Line,* PBS, 15 Feb. 2019.

If you accessed the program on the web, include the URL after the date of publication.

> "Hoaxing Yourself." *This American Life,* hosted and produced by Ira Glass,
> 2 Nov. 2018, www.thisamericanlife.org/660/hoaxing-yourself.

59. Sound Recording, Audio Clip, or Podcast Begin with the name of the person whose work you want to highlight: the composer, the conductor, the performer, or the host. Next list the title, followed by names of other artists (composer, conductor, performers), with an indication of their roles. The recording information includes the manufacturer and the date.

> Bizet, Georges. *Carmen.* Performances by Jennifer Larmore, Thomas Moser,
> Angela Gheorghiu, and Samuel Ramey, Bavarian State Orchestra and
> Chorus, conducted by Giuseppe Sinopoli, Warner, 1996.

If you wish to cite a particular track on the recording, give its performer and title (in quotation marks) and then proceed with the information about the recording. For live recordings, include the date of the performance between the title and the recording information. For recordings found online, include the URL after the publication date.

> Adele. "Hello," *25*. XL, 2015.

For audio clips accessed on the web, add the URL after the publication information.

> Goldbarth, Albert. "Fourteen Pages." *The Poetry Foundation*, 15 Apr. 2016,
>   www.poetryfoundation.org/features/audio/detail/89129.

60. Musical Score Give the composer, title, and date. Italicize the title unless it identifies the composition by form ("symphony," "suite"), number ("op. 39," "K. 231"), or key ("E-flat").

> Beethoven, Ludwig van. Symphony no. 5 in C Minor, op. 67. 1807.

If you are referring to a published score, provide publication data as you would for a book. Insert the date of composition between the title and the publication information.

> Minchin, Tim. *Roald Dahl's Matilda — the Musical*. 2012. Wise-Music
>   Sales, 2013.

61. Work of Art, Photograph, or Other Image Give the name of the artist, the title of the work (italicized), and the date of composition; the name of the collection, museum, or owner; and the city. If you are citing artwork reproduced in a book, add the publication information for the book at the end.

> Bradford, Mark. *Let's Walk to the Middle of the Ocean*. 2015, Museum of
>   Modern Art, New York.

> Feinstein, Harold. *Hangin' Out, Sharing a Public Bench, NYC*. 1948, Panopticon
>   Gallery, Boston. Photograph.

For online visuals, including charts or graphs, include the website (italicized), and the URL.

Hura, Sohrab. *Old Man Lighting a Fire*. 2015. *Magnum Photos*,

www.magnumphotos.com/C.aspx?VP3=SearchResult&ALID=2K1HRG681B.

"TV's Golden Age Is Real: TV Dramas Shown in America." *The Economist*,

24 Nov. 2018, www.economist.com/graphic-detail/2018/11/24/

tvs-golden-age-is-real.

**MLA
30.2**

62. Advertisement Provide the name of the product, service, or organization being advertised, followed by the title of the publication in which the ad appeared. Include the word "Advertisement" after the publication information. For advertisements found online, include the URL before "Advertisement."

AT&T. *National Geographic*, Dec. 2015, p. 14. Advertisement.

Toyota. *The Root*. Slate Group, 28 Mar. 2018, www.theroot.com.

Advertisement.

63. Cartoon Treat a cartoon like an article in a newspaper or magazine. Give the cartoonist's name, the title of the cartoon if there is one (in quotation marks), the publication information for the source, and the word "Cartoon."

Zyglis, Adam. "City of Light." *Buffalo News*, 8 Nov. 2015, adamzyglis

.buffalonews.com/2015/11/08/city-of-light/. Cartoon.

64. Live Performance Generally, begin with the title of the performance (italicized). Then give the author and director; the major performers; and theater, city, and date.

The Draft. By Peter Snoad, directed by Diego Arciniegas, Hibernian Hall,

Boston, 10 Sept. 2015.

Other Digital Sources

65. Entire Website For a website with no author, provide the name of the site in italics, followed by the sponsor or publisher, the copyright date or the most recent update date (in day/month/

year order), and the URL. A date of access is not required for web
sources if a copyright or recent update date is provided.

> *The Newton Project.* U of Sussex, 2016, www.newtonproject.sussex.ac.uk/
> prism.php?id=1.

**MLA
30.2**

66. Academic Course or Department Home Page For a
course page, give the name of the instructor, the course title in
italics, the department, the institution, the year, and the URL. For
a department page, give the department name, a description
such as "Department home page," the institution, the copyright
date or the most recent update date, and the URL.

> Doe, Sue. *CO150: College Composition.* Department of English, Colorado State
> University, 2019, English.colostate.edu/courses/sdoe/co150-19.

> Film Studies. Department home page. *Wayne State University, College of
> Liberal Arts and Sciences,* 2019, clas.wayne.edu/FilmStudies/.

67. Short Work from a Website Provide the name of the
author; the title of the work in quotation marks; the title of the
website, italicized; the date of publication, in day/month/year
order; and the URL.

> Enzinna, Wes. "Syria's Unknown Revolution." *Pulitzer Center on
> Crisis Reporting,* 24 Nov. 2015, pulitzercenter.org/projects/
> middle-east-syria-enzinna-war-rojava.

If no author is given, begin with the title of the work and proceed
with the rest of the publication information. If the title of the
website does not indicate the sponsoring organization, list the
sponsor before the URL. If there is no date of publication, give
the date of access after the URL.

> "Social and Historical Context: Vitality." *Arapesh Grammar and Digital
> Language Archive Project,* Institute for Advanced Technology in the
> Humanities, www.arapesh.org/socio_historical_context_vitality.php.
> Accessed 22 Jan. 2017.

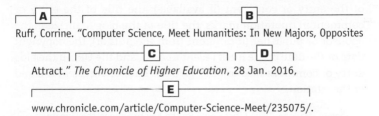

THE CHRONICLE OF HIGHER EDUCATION

TECHNOLOGY

Computer Science, Meet Humanities: in New Majors, Opposites Attract

By Corinne Ruff | JANUARY 28, 2016

Hannah Pho grew up playing the piano and went to a magnet high school for technology. When she applied to colleges and looked for programs that blended her seemingly disparate interests, she didn't find many options.

She chose Stanford University, where she became one of the first students in a new major there called CS+Music, part of a pilot program informally known as CS+X.

Its goal is to put students in a middle ground, between computer science and any of 14 disciplines in the humanities, including history, art, and classics. And it reduces the number of required hours that students would

Scan the website to find as much of the citation information as you can. If you cannot find a publication date, provide the date you accessed the website. Remember that the citation information you provide should allow readers to retrace your steps to locate the sources.

MLA 30.2

See pages 389–393 for complete models for citing sources from the web.

```
  ┌─A─┐ ┌──────────────────B──────────────────┐
Ruff, Corrine. "Computer Science, Meet Humanities: In New Majors, Opposites

     ┌──────────C──────────┐ ┌───D───┐
Attract." The Chronicle of Higher Education, 28 Jan. 2016,

┌────────────────────E────────────────────┐
www.chronicle.com/article/Computer-Science-Meet/235075/.
```

A **The author of the work.** Give the last name first, followed by a comma, and then the first name and the middle initial (if given). Insert a period. If no author is listed, begin with the title.

B **The title of the work.** Give the article title and subtitle (if any), separated by a colon. Enclose the title and subtitle in quotation marks, and capitalize all major words. Place a period inside the close quotation mark.

C **The title of the website.** Give the title of the entire site, italicized. If there is no clear title and it is a personal home page, use "Home page" without italics. If the sponsoring organization name is different than the title of the website, list that information next. Follow with a comma.

D **The date of publication or most recent update.** Insert the day, month, and year, in that order. Abbreviate the names of all months except May, June, and July. Follow the year with a comma. (If no publication date is given, provide the date of access at the end of the entry. After the URL, insert the word "Accessed" and the date you accessed the work.)

E **The URL.** List the URL for the article, and end with a period.

68. Message Posted to a Newsgroup, Electronic Mailing List, or Online Discussion Forum Cite the name of the person who posted the message; the title (from the subject line, in quotation marks); if the posting has no title, add the phrase "Online posting." Then add the name of the website (italicized), the sponsor or publisher, the date of the message, and the URL.

> Robin, Griffith. "Write for the Reading Teacher." *Developing Digital Literacies*,
>
>   NCTE, 23 Oct. 2015, ncte.connectedcommunity.org/communities/
>
>   community-home/digestviewer/viewthread?GroupId=1693&MID
>
>   =24520&tab=digestviewer&CommunityKey=628d2ad6-8277-4042
>
>   -a376-2b370ddceabf.

69. Blog To cite an entry or a comment on a blog, give the author of the entry or comment (if available), the title of the entry or comment in quotation marks, the title of the blog (italicized), the sponsor or publisher (if different from the author), the copyright date or the date of the most recent update, and the URL. If the blog entry or comment has no date, give the date of access at the end of the citation.

> Cimons, Marlene. "Why Cities Could Be the Key to Solving the Climate
>
>   Crisis." *Thinkprogress.org*, Center for American Progress Action Fund,
>
>   10 Dec. 2015, thinkprogress.org/climate/2015/12/10/3730938/
>
>   cities-key-to-climate-crisis/.

70. Email message Start with the sender of the message. Then give the subject line, in quotation marks, followed by a period. Identify the recipient of the message and provide the date of the message.

> Martin, Adrianna. "Re: Questions about the District Budget." Received by
>
>   the author, 19 Jan. 2017.

> Pabon, Xavier. "Brainstorming for Essay." Received by Brayden Perry,
>
>   24 Apr. 2019.

71. Facebook or Instagram Post or Comment Follow the general format for citing a short work on a website.

> Bedford English. "Stacey Cochran Explores Reflective Writing in the
> Classroom and as a Writer." *Facebook*, 15 Feb. 2016, www.facebook.com/
> BedfordEnglish/posts/10153415001259607.

> National Geographic. Photo of the Vatnajökull of Iceland, Europe's largest
> icecap. *Instagram*, photographed by Renan Ozturk, 26 Nov. 2018,
> www.instagram.com/p/BqnzWQ6AY-x/.

MLA 30.2

72. Twitter Post (Tweet) Provide the entire tweet in place of the title, and include the time after the date.

> Curiosity Rover. "Can you see me waving? How to spot #Mars in the night
> sky." *Twitter*, 5 Nov. 2015, 11:00 a.m., twitter.com/marscuriosity/
> status/672859022911889408.

73. Computer Software, App, or Video Game Cite computer software as you would a book.

> *Words with Friends*. Version 5.84, Zynga, 2013.

> Firaxis Games. *Sid Meier's Civilization Revolution*. Take-Two Interactive, 2008.

74. Other Sources For other digital sources, adapt the guidelines to the medium. The examples below are for a podcast of a radio program and a historical document available in an online archive.

> McDougall, Christopher. "How Did Endurance Help Early Humans Survive?"
> *TED Radio Hour*, National Public Radio, 20 Nov. 2015, www.npr.org/2015/
> 11/20/455904655/how-did-endurance-help-early-humans-survive.

> Constitution of the United States. 1787. *The Charters of Freedom*, US
> National Archives and Records Administration, www.archives.gov/
> exhibits/charters/.

MLA-Style Essay

> Information about the
> writer, class, and submission
> date is formatted according
> to MLA guidelines.

San Agustin 1

Lauren San Agustin

Professor Alexis Nulsen

CO-150

16 November 2018

> The title is
> centered.

Saving the Oceans and Building Consumer Trust

Across the globe, our oceans are suffering from pollution, most notably plastic pollution. From plastic straws
sipped in restaurants and fast-food chains to plastic bags
used to carry groceries, plastic is being used by everyone
in everyday life, and it is ending up in our oceans. Because
of plastic's potential for widespread harm to the environment, to marine life, and to human life, it is essential that
food industry corporations reduce their plastic usage. Chain
restaurants and fast-food companies who want to build
consumer trust should recognize that Earth's ecosystems
are incredibly important to our planet's sustainability and
respond by diminishing their use of plastic.

> The writer
> begins
> with a brief
> overview of
> the problem
> of ocean
> pollution
> caused by
> plastic.

The magnitude of the pollution crisis is immense.
Over the last seventy years, 18.2 trillion tons of plastic have
been produced, and only nine percent of plastic ends up
being recycled (Rice). This crisis is having real effects on our
oceans. In a single year alone, the amount of plastic that
ends up in the ocean is staggering.

San Agustin 2

A recent scientific study estimated that 4.8 to 12.7 million metric tons of plastic ended up in the ocean in 2010 (Jambeck et al. 770). Furthermore, those plastics are not going anywhere. Study author Jenna Jambeck explains: "Most plastics don't biodegrade in any meaningful sense, so the plastic waste humans have generated could be with us for hundreds or even thousands of years" (qtd. in Rice). During this process plastic breaks up into miniscule pieces called microplastics, which pose serious dangers for marine life. When microplastics end up in the ocean, fish, turtles, seals, and other sea creatures ingest them, either through "active foraging (i.e., mistaking plastic fragments and fibers for food) or from more incidental uptake from contaminated foods, sediments, or waters" (Santillo et al. 517).

> Three or more authors are cited using the first author's name, followed by "et al."

> Information cited in a source is identified using the abbreviation "qtd. in."

As just one example, in 2016, a killer whale known to scientists and researchers as "Lulu" washed up onto a Scottish shore, killed by plastic entanglement. The analysis of her necropsy revealed that she had very large amounts of plastic debris in her body, which caused a weakened immune system and an inability to reproduce, among other health problems (Bacon). Unfortunately, this type of case is not a rare occurrence in our oceans and is not limited to one species or one location.

In addition to damage to marine ecosystems, plastic pollution also poses potential harm to humans via the food chain. As Santillo and others explain, "[I]t is inevitable that

San Agustin 3

humans eating seafoods will ingest at least some microplastics, particularly in the case of species in which the entire soft flesh is consumed, such as mussels, oysters, and small fish" (519). The effects of humans ingesting plastic are unknown, but scientists have reason for concern about the toxic chemicals within microplastics:

> The presence of these compounds further increases the risks associated with ingestion of plastic debris by wildlife, and additionally, many of these compounds can undergo significant biomagnification and may potentially pose a direct risk to human health. These toxic agents have been linked to and are associated with many health problems, including developmental impairment (neurological impairment, growth abnormalities and hormonal imbalances), cancer, endocrine disruption, neurobehavioral changes, arthritis, breast cancer, diabetes and DNA hypomethylation. (Webb et al. 2)

A block quotation is indented. Page numbers are not provided for an online source.

For fast-food companies that serve fish or seafood products, the potential harm to humans is yet another reason why corporations must reduce usage of plastic.

Regardless of one's diet, plastic pollution has several detrimental impacts. Many coastal countries in the Middle East, Europe, and Asia rely on the ocean to provide food and to sustain their economy by way of exports. In countries such

San Agustin 4

as Indonesia, fishing is the primary source of income for many residents (Mathew). With fish and other marine animals being killed by pollution, both individual livelihoods and the economic well-being of developing countries are at risk. Eventually, the depletion of seafood resources will hit developed countries, too.

More consumers and corporations alike are wondering if it is ethical to continue using plastic and putting our planet at risk. Plastic straws pose a particular problem, as they are commonly used but difficult to recycle (Caron). In 2018, the backlash against plastic straws gained momentum in the United States, and Starbucks took action. With millions of customers visiting Starbucks daily for quick caffeine refuels, the company is a major contributor to the plastic straw usage in the United States — where 500 million plastic straws are used every day (Caron). Starbucks vowed that it will stop using plastic straws by 2020, opting instead for lids that can be recycled and straws that are compostable (Caron). In fact, following the lead of companies like Starbucks, more restaurants are not serving plastic straws with drinks unless they are requested. Other fast-food chains and food corporations should likewise begin to incorporate sustainability habits into the sales of their products. Doing so would help preserve our oceans and build trust and support among consumers.

Phasing out plastic straw usage is one small way to fight plastic pollution, but what about all the other items

San Agustin 5

made of plastic? In the United States, more than a third of plastic consumption comes from packaging products (American Chemistry Council). Fortunately, there are plenty of non-plastic alternatives for everyday items. For carrying groceries, for example, paper bags are available and are in fact even cheaper than plastic. Additionally, many grocers offer reusable bags for a low price, typically made out of reused fabric. Cutlery, unlike straws, would be harder to get rid of, but there are many sustainable options of eco-friendly cutlery made from coconut fibers, coconut shells, banana fibers, or Sal leaves, which come from trees that are abundant in India and Nepal (Gautam and Caetano 508). These alternatives offer both environmental and economic benefits. First, they make use of natural remnants and mature leaves, doing no harm to trees. Second, these natural alternatives are cheap to produce. The cost for businesses to incorporate these alternatives comes in production and shipping, but they are similar to the costs of making plastic (Gautam and Caetano 508). Eco-friendly products like these are superior to plastic because the functionality is the same, but they decompose naturally. Companies that incorporate these economical alternatives will gain the respect of customers who care about sustainability.

The argument that plastic is simply too abundant to get rid of completely is a valid claim. Reducing plastic usage will

San Agustin 6

not be quick. However, major corporations should still take small steps, like Starbucks promises to do with plastic straws. Then they can switch to alternative materials in the future and make those the norm. To many fast-food corporations, the financial gain of incorporating sustainable products may seem minimal, but the benefit of increased consumer trust and loyalty could be worth far more.

With plastic being dumped into the ocean every day, human beings need to ramp up preservation efforts now more than ever. These efforts should start with the corporations since they are major contributors to plastic usage. Given the severity of the environmental situation, and the viable and cheap alternatives to plastic, there is no obstacle to companies enacting conservation practices and at the same time improving their relations with customers. For the sake of its customers and the environment, fast-food companies must reduce their plastic usage immediately.

> Following MLA guidelines, the Works Cited heading is centered.

Works Cited

American Chemistry Council. "2017 Resin Sales and
Captive Use by Major Market." *American Chemistry,*
2018, plastics.americanchemistry.com/Plastics-
Statistics/ACC-PIPS-2017-Major-Market-Pie-Chart.pdf.

> Entries are listed alphabetically by author and formatted with hanging indents.

Bacon, John. "Killer Whale Lulu Contaminated with PCBs."
USA Today, 5 May 2017, p. 2A.

Caron, Christina. "Starbucks to Stop Using Disposable
Plastic Straws by 2020." *The New York Times*, 9 July
2018, www.nytimes.com/2018/07/09/business/
starbucks-plastic-straws.html.

Gautam, Anirudh Muralidharan, and Nídia Caetano. "Study,
Design and Analysis of Sustainable Alternatives to
Plastic Takeaway Cutlery and Crockery." *Energy Procedia*,
vol. 136, Oct. 2017, pp. 507–12. *ScienceDirect*,
doi:10.1016/j.egypro.2017.10.273.

> A source with more than three authors is listed by the first author's name, followed by "et al."

Jambeck, Jenna R., et al. "Plastic Waste Inputs from
Land into the Ocean." *Science*, vol. 347, no. 6223,
13 Feb. 2015, pp. 768–71. *Academic Search Premier*,
doi:10.1126/science.1260352.

Mathew, Sebastian. "Fishery-Dependent Information and
the Ecosystem Approach: What Role Can Fishers and
Their Knowledge Play in Developing Countries?" *ICES
Journal of Marine Science*, vol. 68, no. 8, 1 Sept. 2011,
pp. 1805–08. *Academic Search Premier*, doi:10.1093/
icesjms/fsr113.

San Agustin 8

Rice, Doyle. "Humans Have Produced 18.2 Trillion Pounds
of Plastic." *USA Today*, 19 July 2017, www.usatoday.
com/story/tech/science/2017/07/19/humans-have-
produced-18-2-trillion-pounds-plastic-thats-equal-
size-1-billion-elephants/491529001/.

Santillo, David, et al. "Microplastics as Contaminants
in Commercially Important Seafood Species." *Integrated
Environmental Assessment and Management*, vol. 13,
no. 3, May 2017, pp. 516–21. doi:10.1002/ieam.1909.

Webb, Hayden K., et al. "Plastic Degradation and Its
Environmental Implications with Special Reference to
Poly(ethylene Terephthalate)." *Polymers*, vol. 5, no. 1,
2013, pp. 1–18. *Academic Search Premier*, doi:10.3390/
polym5010001.

> Entries
> for online
> sources
> include URLs.

31. Use APA Style

American Psychological Association (APA) style, used primarily in the social sciences and in some of the natural sciences, emphasizes the author(s) and publication date of a source. Writers who use the APA documentation system cite, or formally acknowledge, information within their text using parentheses and provide a list of sources, called a reference list, at the end of their document. For more information about APA style, consult the *Publication Manual of the American Psychological Association*, Sixth Edition, and the *APA Style Guide to Electronic References*. Information about these publications can be found on the APA website at **apa.org**.

For an essay formatted in APA style, see page 429.

Directory of APA Style

APA 31.0

31.1 Cite Sources in the Text of a Document

APA uses an author-date form of in-text citation to acknowledge the use of another writer's words, facts, or ideas. When you refer to a source, insert a parenthetical note that gives the author's last name and the year of the publication, separated by a comma. Even when your reference list includes the day or month of publication, the in-text citation should include only the year. For a quotation, the citation in parentheses also includes the page(s) on which the quotation can be found, if the source has page numbers. (For sources that do not have pages, you may provide paragraph numbers.) Note that APA style requires using the past tense or present perfect tense to introduce the material you are citing: *Renfrew argued* or *Renfrew has argued*.

1. Basic Format for Direct Quotation When you are using a direct quotation from a source and have named the author in your sentence, place the publication date in parentheses directly after the author's last name. Include the page number(s) (with "p." for *page* or "pp." for *pages*) in parentheses after the quotation.

> Yousafzai (2013) wrote that the door to her all-girls school in Swat "was like a magical entrance to our own special world" (p. 2).

If you are using a direct quotation and have not mentioned the author's name in your sentence, place the author's last name, the publication date, and the page number in parentheses.

> (Yousafzai, 2013, p. 2).

2. Basic Format for Summary or Paraphrase When you are summarizing or paraphrasing, place the author's last name and date either in the sentence or in parentheses at the end of the sentence. Include a page or chapter reference if it would help readers find the original material in a longer work.

> Reid (2019) questioned how advances in artificial intelligence might undermine the value of human intelligence and knowledge in some realms (p. 15).

As the Watson experiment demonstrated, even the physical appearance of artificial intelligence devices is shaped by human preconceptions — and fears — of technology (Reid, 2019, p. 112).

3. Two Authors List the last names of both authors in every mention in the text. If you mention the authors' names in a sentence, use the word *and* to separate the last names, as shown in the first example. If you place the authors' names in the parenthetical citation, use an ampersand (&) to separate the last names, as shown in the second example.

Drlica and Perlin (2011) wrote that "although many infections tend to occur in persons having weakened immune systems, MRSA can infect anyone" (p. 3).

Everyone is susceptible to MRSA, not just those who are already weak or ill (Drlica & Perlin, 2011, p. 3).

4. Three, Four, or Five Authors In parentheses, name all the authors the first time you cite the source, using an ampersand (&) before the last author's name. In subsequent references to the source, use the last name of the first author followed by the abbreviation "et al." (Latin for "and others").

Individuals with body dysmorphic disorder (BDD) suffer from an "obsessive-compulsive spectrum disorder involving preoccupation with perceived defects in appearance" (Schneider, Mond, Turner, & Hudson, 2017, p. 125). This preoccupation can have numerous negative effects, including depression (Schneider et al., 2017).

5. Six or More Authors In all references to the source, give the first author's last name followed by "et al."

Finken et al. (2018) studied the causes and consequences of children born with small size for their gestational age.

6. Corporate or Group Author In general, cite the full name of the corporation or group the first time it is mentioned in your text. If you add an abbreviation for the group in square brackets the first time you cite the source, you can use the abbreviation in subsequent citations.

APA
31.1

> An international treaty signed to help combat the illicit trade of tobacco products is now in effect (World Health Organization [WHO], 2018). This protocol not only establishes a global tracing system to reduce and eliminate illicit tobacco trade but also will play an important role in protecting people around the world from a serious health risk (WHO, 2018).

7. Unknown Author Sources with unknown authors are listed by title in the list of references. In your in-text citation, shorten the title as much as possible without introducing confusion. Add quotation marks to article titles, and italicize book titles.

> Stress can cause physical symptoms such as loss of appetite, headaches, and back pains. ("Stress," 2018).

If a source identifies its author as "Anonymous," use that word to cite the author of the source.

> The rise in coastal water levels has been referred to as a national crisis (Anonymous, 2019).

8. Two or More Works Cited Together List the sources in alphabetical order and separate them with semicolons. If you are referring to two or more sources by the same author, order those sources chronologically.

> Rather than encourage exploration into more difficult and inaccessible energy stores, our new awareness of the finite nature of the earth's resources should incite a change in lifestyle that no longer strains the limits of our environment (Dietz & O'Neill, 2017; Klare, 2016).

9. Source Quoted in Another Source Ideally, you will be able to find the primary, or original, source for material used in your document. If you quote or paraphrase a secondary source—a source that contains information about a primary source—mention the primary source and indicate that it was cited in the secondary source. Include the secondary source in your reference list.

> Slater posited that the rise in online dating services has led to a decrease in commitment, as this technology fosters the notion that one can always find a more compatible mate (as cited in Weissmann, 2018).

10. Source with No Page Numbers Many web sources lack stable page numbers. If the source has numbered paragraphs, include the paragraph number using the abbreviation "para." If the paragraphs are not numbered, include the section heading and indicate which paragraph in that section you are referring to.

> Zerfas (2018) examined the rise in tactical urbanism, a kind of city planning that employs "small-scale, often temporary projects" to repurpose small bits of unusable public space as parks, gardens, and other areas designed for public use ("What is tactical urbanism?").

11. Two or More Authors with the Same Last Name Use the authors' initials in each citation.

> While C. Smith (2017) has noted an increase in early childhood psychiatric disorders, L. W. Smith (2018) suggested that many of these diagnoses in very young children might be inaccurate.

12. Email and Other Personal Communication Give the first initial(s) and last name of the person with whom you corresponded, the words "personal communication," and the date. Don't include personal communication in your reference list.

(A. L. Chan, personal communication, July 9, 2019)

13. Document from a Website To cite a quotation from a website, give the page number or paragraph number, if indicated, and include the source in your reference list.

Research by Evans, Marshall, Mercado-Crespo, and Smokowski (2018) showed that youth who help their bullied peers are more likely to have depression or anxiety, suggesting that they are "worried about being bullied next" (para. 3).

For an entire website, give the URL in parentheses in your text, and don't include it in your references list.

31.2 Prepare the List of References

The reference list contains publication information for all sources that you have cited within your document, with one main exception. Personal communications — such as correspondence, email messages, and interviews — are cited only in the text of the document.

Begin the list on a new page at the end of the document and center the title "References" at the top. Organize the list alphabetically by author; if the source is an organization, alphabetize the source by the name of the organization. All of the entries should be double-spaced with no extra space between entries. Entries are formatted with a hanging indent: The first line of an entry is flush with the left margin, and subsequent lines are indented one-half inch or five spaces. In longer documents, a reference list could be given at the end of each chapter or section. In digital documents that use links, such as websites, the reference list is often a separate page to which other pages are linked. For an example of a reference list in APA style, see pages 439–440.

Books, Conference Proceedings, and Dissertations

14. One Author List the author's last name followed by a comma and the first initial. Insert the date in parentheses and italicize the title, capitalizing only the first word, proper nouns, and the first word following a colon. Follow with the place of publication and the publisher, separated by a colon.

> Orenstein, P. (2016). *Girls and sex: Navigating the complicated new landscape.* New York, NY: HarperCollins.

APA recommends citing an e-book only if the print version is difficult or impossible to find. Cite an e-book as you would a print book, but identify the file format or e-reader type for the book in brackets following the title. If the book was found on the web and has a DOI (digital object identifier, a unique number assigned to specific content), provide the DOI at the end of the citation and precede it by "https://doi.org/." Otherwise, provide the URL preceded by "Retrieved from." Do not end the DOI or URL with a period.

> Clark, G. (2015). *The making of a world city: London 1991 to 2021.* https://doi.org/10.1002/9781118609705

> Emerson, L. (2016). *The forgotten tribe: Scientists as writers* [ePub]. Fort Collins, CO: The WAC Clearinghouse. Retrieved from https://wac .colostate.edu/books/perspectives/emerson/

How do I cite books using APA style?

APA 31.2

MAGIC

AND

LOSS

THE INTERNET AS ART

VIRGINIA HEFFERNAN

SIMON & SCHUSTER

NEW YORK LONDON TORONTO SYDNEY NEW DELHI

When citing a book, use the information from the title page and the copyright page (on the reverse of the title page), not from the book's cover or a library catalog.

See pages 409–415 for additional models for citing books.

A — B — C — D

Heffernan, V. (2016). *Magic and loss: The internet as art*. New York, NY:

E

Simon & Schuster.

A **The author.** Give the last name first, followed by a comma and initials for the first and, if any, middle names. Separate the initials with a space. Separate the names of multiple authors with commas; use an ampersand (&) before the final author's name.

B **The year of publication.** Put the most recent copyright year in parentheses, and insert a period afterward.

C **The title and subtitle, if any.** Use the full title and subtitle, italicizing both and separating them with a colon. Capitalize only the first word of the title, the first word of the subtitle, and any proper nouns or proper adjectives. End with a period.

D **The place of publication.** List only the first city given. Use an abbreviation for U.S. states and territories; spell out city and country names for locations outside the United States (Cambridge, England). For Canadian cities, also include the province. Insert a colon.

E **The publisher.** Give the publisher's name, omitting words such as "Inc." and "Co." Include and do not abbreviate such terms as "University," "Press," and "Books." End with a period.

15. Two or More Authors List the authors in the same order as the title page does, each with last name first. Separate authors with commas and use an ampersand (&) before the final author's name. List every author up to and including seven; for eight or more authors, give the first six names followed by a comma, three ellipsis marks, and the final author's name. (Do not use an ampersand.)

Watkins, D., & Brook, Y. (2016). *Equal is unfair: America's misguided fight
against income inequality*. New York, NY: St. Martin's Press.

16. Corporate or Group Author Write out the full name of a corporate or group author. If the corporation is also the publisher, use "Author" for the publisher's name.

Linguistic Society of America. (2016). *Annual report: The state of linguistics
in higher education*. Washington, DC: Author.

17. Unknown Author When there is no author listed on the title or copyright page, begin the entry with the title of the work. Alphabetize the entry by the first significant word of the title (not including "A," "An," or "The").

Going within to get out. (2013). Bloomington, IN: Balboa.

18. Two or More Works by the Same Author(s) Give the author's name in each entry and list the works in chronological order.

Sanders, B. (2016). *Our revolution: A future to believe in*. New York, NY:
Thomas Dunne Books.

Sanders, B. (2018). *Where we go from here: Two years in the resistance*.
New York, NY: Thomas Dunne Books.

19. Translated Book List the author first followed by the year of publication, the title, and the translator (in parentheses, identified by the abbreviation "Trans."). Place the original date of the work's publication at the end of the entry.

**APA
31.2**

> Sartre, J. P. (2019). *Being and nothingness* (S. Richmond, Trans.). New York, NY: Washington Square Press. (Original work published 1943)

20. Book in a Series Provide the name of the series, capitalizing all important words, a colon and volume number (if any), a period, and the title.

> Fidell, E. R. (2016). *Very Short Introductions. Military justice.* Oxford, England: Oxford University Press.

21. Republication Provide the most recent date of publication. Identify the original publication date in parentheses following the publisher information.

> Freud, S. (2010). *The interpretation of dreams* (J. Strachey, Ed. & Trans.). New York, NY: Basic Books. (Original work published 1955)

22. Book in an Edition Other than the First Note the edition ("2nd ed.," "Rev. ed.") after the title.

> Palmquist, M. (2017). *The Bedford researcher* (6th ed.). Boston, MA: Bedford/St. Martin's.

23. Multivolume Work Include the number of volumes in parentheses after the title.

> Delbanco, N., & Cheuse, A. (Eds.). (2010). *Literature: Craft and voice* (Vols. 1–3). Boston, MA: McGraw-Hill.

If you have used only one volume in a multivolume work, identify that volume by number and by title.

> Delbanco, N., & Cheuse, A. (Eds.). (2010). *Literature: Craft and voice: Vol. 1. Fiction.* Boston, MA: McGraw-Hill.

24. Edited Book Include "Ed." or "Eds." in parentheses.

Blair, K. L., & Nickoson, L. (Eds.). (2018). *Composing feminist interventions: Activism, engagement, praxis*. Fort Collins, CO: The WAC Clearinghouse. Retrieved from https://wac.colostate.edu/books/perspectives/feminist/

25. Authored Book with an Editor Include the editor's name and the abbreviation "Ed." in parentheses after the title.

Larkin, P. (2018). *Philip Larkin: Letters home, 1936–1977* (James Booth, Ed.). London, UK: Faber & Faber.

26. Selection in an Anthology or Edited Book Begin with the author of the chapter or selection, the publication date, and the title of the selection (not italicized). Follow this with the names of the editors (initials first) and the abbreviation "Ed." or "Eds." in parentheses, the title of the anthology (italicized), inclusive page numbers for the selection (in parentheses, with abbreviation "pp."), and place and publisher.

Sargeant, S. (2016). Psychology and models of health. In A. Tom & P. Greasley (Eds.), *Psychology for nursing* (pp. 21–34). London, England: Polity Press.

27. Foreword, Introduction, Preface, or Afterword Treat as you would a chapter in a book.

Joli, F. (2016). Foreword. In J. Arena, *Legends of disco: Forty stars discuss their careers* (pp. 1–2). Jefferson, NC: McFarland.

28. Published Proceedings of a Conference Cite information as you would for a book (p. 410).

Mayor, J., & Gomez, P. (Eds.). (2014). *Computational models of cognitive processes: Proceedings of the 13th neural computation and psychology workshop*. Singapore: World Scientific Publishing.

29. Paper Published in the Proceedings of a Conference
Treat a conference paper as you would a selection from an edited
collection.

Jacobs, G. M., & Toh-Heng, H. L. (2013). Small steps towards student-
    centered learning. In P. Mandal (Ed.), *Proceedings of the international
    conference on managing the Asian century* (pp. 55–64). Singapore:
    Springer.

30. Sacred Text Reference list entries are not required for clas-
sical works (generally considered as works that are more than
a thousand years old). For other religious sources, treat as you
would a book (see p. 410).

Smith, J., & Reorganized Church of Jesus Christ of Latter Day Saints.
    (1948). *The book of Mormon*. Independence, MO: Board of
    Publication of the Reorganized Church of Jesus Christ of Latter
    Day Saints.

31. Published Dissertation or Thesis If a published dissertation or thesis is available through a commercial database, give
the author, date, title, and a description in parentheses ("Doctoral
dissertation" or "Master's thesis"). Then give the database name,
followed by any UMI or order number in parentheses.

Selberg, S. (2013). *Seeing the person within: Visual culture and Alzheimer's
    disease* (Doctoral dissertation). Available from ProQuest Dissertations
    and Theses database. (UMI No. 3553975)

If the material is accessed from an institutional database or
other website, provide the URL.

Kim, J. (2012). *Promoting sustainable communities through
    Infill: The effect of Infill housing on neighborhood income
    diversity* (Doctoral dissertation). Retrieved from http://ufdc.ufl
    .edu/UFE0044904/00001

APA
31.2

32. Unpublished Dissertation or Thesis Format as you would a book, replacing the publisher information with a phrase such as "Unpublished doctoral dissertation" or "Unpublished master's thesis," followed by the name of the college or university.

> McQueen, J. Y. (2013). *On the road of phonological treatment: Paths of learning* (Unpublished honors thesis). Indiana University, Bloomington.

Sources in Journals, Magazines, and Newspapers

33. Article in a Journal Paginated by Volume Most journals continue page numbers throughout an entire annual volume, beginning again at page 1 only in the first volume of the next year. After the author and publication year, provide the article title, the journal title, the volume number (italicized), and the inclusive page numbers.

> Thonus, T. (2016). Time to say goodbye: Writing center consultation closings. *Linguistics and Education, 33*, 40–55.

If a DOI is available, include it at the end of the citation and precede it by "https://doi.org/." Do not end the DOI with a period. You do not need a retrieval date or database name.

> Logan, J. R. (2016, March 29). As long as there are neighborhoods. *City & Community, 159*, 23–28. https://doi.org/10.1111/cico .12149

If the article is obtained online but no DOI is provided, give the URL for the home page of the journal, preceded by "Retrieved from." Do not end the URL with a period.

> Hamlin, D., & Peterson, P. E. (2018). Have states maintained high expectations for student performance? *Education Next, 18*(4). Retrieved from http://educationnext.org/

34. Article in a Journal Paginated by Issue If every issue of
the journal begins at page 1, include the issue number in parentheses, not italicized, after the volume number.

**APA
31.2**

> Garicano, L., & Rayo, L. (2016). Why organizations fail: Models and cases.
> *Journal of Economic Literature, 54*(1), 137–192.

If the article is obtained online or through a database, publication
information is followed by the DOI or URL. Since the article was
published online, it may not have page numbers.

> Carillo, E. C. (2016). Engaging sources through reading-writing
> connections across the disciplines. *Across the Disciplines, 13*(1).
> Retrieved from https://wac.colostate.edu/docs/atd/

35. Article in a Magazine Give the publication date as year
and month for monthly magazines; year, month, and day for
weekly or biweekly magazines. Place the issue number, if any, in
parentheses directly after the volume number. Include all page
numbers. For articles accessed on the web, end with the URL of
the magazine's home page.

> Ball, M. (2018, November 19). Nation divided: The midterms delivered
> a split decision that primes both parties for battle. *Time, 192*(21),
> 28–36.

> Chodosh, S. (2018, November 28). Siberian unicorns lived
> alongside humans, and they were so much cooler than the
> mythical version. *Popular Science*. Retrieved from http://
> www.popsci.com/

How do I cite articles from print periodicals using APA style?

Periodicals include journals, magazines, and newspapers. This tutorial gives the citation for a print journal article. Complete models for citing articles from journals and newspapers are on pages 422–424.

APA 31.2

For a tutorial in citing digital periodical articles, see page 418.

A ————————————————— **B**

Harari, D., Swider, B. W., Steed, L. B., & Breidenthal, A. P. (2018).

C

Is perfect good? A meta-analysis of perfectionism in the workplace.

D — **E** — **F**

Journal of Applied Psychology, 103(10), 1121–1144.

A **The author.** Give the last name first, followed by a comma and initials for first and middle names. Separate the names of multiple authors with commas; use an ampersand (&) before the final author's name. End with a period.

B **The year of publication.** Give the year in parentheses, and then insert a period. For magazines and newspapers, include the month and, if relevant, the day (2010, April 13).

C **The article title.** Give the full title and subtitle (if any), separated by a colon. Do not underline, italicize, or insert the title in quotation marks. Capitalize only the first word of the title, the first word of the subtitle, and any proper nouns or proper adjectives. End with a period.

D **The periodical title.** Italicize the periodical title, and capitalize all major words. Insert a comma.

E **The volume number and issue number.** For journals, include the volume number, italicized. If each issue starts with page 1, include the issue number in parentheses, not italicized. Insert a comma.

F **Inclusive page numbers.** Give all numbers in full (317–327, not 317–27). For newspapers, include the abbreviation "p." for page number and section letter, if relevant (p. B12). End with a period.

How do I cite digital periodical articles using APA style?

Many periodicals can be accessed online, either through the magazine or journal's website or through a database (see Chapter 6). To cite a periodical article accessed digitally, give the print periodical information and then the web information.

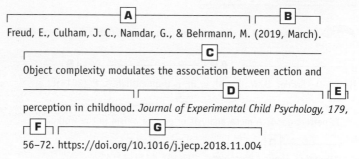

Freud, E., Culham, J. C., Namdar, G., & Behrmann, M. (2019, March).

A — Object complexity modulates the association between action and

perception in childhood. *Journal of Experimental Child Psychology, 179,*

56–72. https://doi.org/10.1016/j.jecp.2018.11.004

A **The author.** Give the last name first, followed by a comma and initials for first and middle names. Separate the names of multiple authors with commas; use an ampersand (&) before the final author's name. End with a period.

B **The date of publication.** Give the year in parentheses, and then insert a period. For magazines and newspapers, include the month and, if relevant, the day (2010, April 13).

C **The article title.** Separate the title and subtitle with a colon. Do not underline, italicize, or place quotation marks around the title. Capitalize only the first word of the title, the first word of the subtitle, and any proper nouns or proper adjectives. End with a period.

D **The periodical title.** Italicize the periodical title, and capitalize all major words. Insert a comma.

E **The volume number and issue number.** For journals, include the volume number, italicized. If each issue starts with page 1, include the issue number in parentheses, not italicized. Insert a comma.

F **Inclusive page numbers.** Give all numbers in full (317–327, not 317–27). For newspapers, include the abbreviation "p." for page number and section letter, if relevant (p. B12). End with a period.

G **The DOI or URL.** If the article has a DOI (digital object identifier), provide it, preceded by "https://doi.org/". If there is no DOI, include the words "Retrieved from" and the URL. Do not end the DOI or URL with a period.

36. Article in a Newspaper List the author's name and the complete date (year first). Next give the article title followed by the name of the newspaper (italicized). Include all page numbers, preceded by "p." or "pp."

APA
31.2

> Levenson, M. (2016, April 11). School closings bring pain, and not always
>
> savings. *The Boston Globe,* p. A1.

37. Unsigned Article Begin with the article title, and alphabetize in the reference list by the first word in the title other than "A," "An," or "The." Use "p." or "pp." before page numbers.

> RNA-only genes: The origin of species? (2012, April 28). *The*
>
> *Economist,* p. 40.

38. Letter to the Editor Include the words "Letter to the editor" in square brackets after the title of the letter, if any.

> Hernández, L. (2018, November 27). Venezuela is not a sponsor of terrorism
>
> [Letter to the editor]. *The Washington Post.* Retrieved from https://www
>
> .washingtonpost.com/

39. Editorial Include the word "Editorial" in square brackets after the title.

> O come all ye judges: The GOP Senate should confirm more nominees in
>
> December. [Editorial]. (2018, November 25). *The Wall Street Journal.*
>
> Retrieved from https://www.wsj.com/

40. Review After the title of the review, include the words "Review of the book . . ." or "Review of the motion picture . . ." and so on in brackets, followed by the title of the work reviewed and its author (for a book), the director (for a motion picture), or the artist (for a work of art or an art exhibition). Follow with publication information for the newspaper, magazine, journal, blog, or website in which the review appears.

> Chiasson, D. (2018, November 5). Sylvia Plath's last letters [Review of
> the book *The Letters of Sylvia Plath*, Sylvia Plath]. *The New Yorker,*
> 62–67. Retrieved from https://www.newyorker.com/

If the review is untitled, give the bracketed information in place of the title.

> Turan, K. (2010, November 26). [Review of the motion picture *The King's
> Speech*, 2010]. *The Los Angeles Times*, p. D1.

41. Published Interview Cite as you would a periodical article (see item 35 on p. 416).

> Massondo, A. (2010, July). Yellow-card journalism [Interview by C. Barron].
> *Harper's, 321*(1921), 17–18.

42. Two or More Works by the Same Author in the Same Year List the works alphabetically and include lowercase letters (*a, b,* etc.) after the dates.

> Iglehart, J. K. (2010a). The ACA's new weapons against health care fraud.
> *The New England Journal of Medicine, 363*, 1589–1591.

> Iglehart, J. K. (2010b). Health reform, primary care, and graduate
> medical education. *The New England Journal of Medicine, 363*,
> 584–590.

Reference Works

43. Encyclopedia, Dictionary, Thesaurus, Handbook, or Almanac Cite a reference work, such as an encyclopedia or a dictionary, as you would a book (see item 14 on p. 409).

> Priest, S. H. (Ed.). (2010). *Encyclopedia of science and technology
> communication* (Vols. 1–2). Thousand Oaks, CA: Sage.

44. Entry in an Encyclopedia, Dictionary, Thesaurus, Handbook, or Almanac Begin your citation with the name of the author or, if the entry is unsigned, the title of the entry. Proceed with the date, the entry title (if not already given), the title of the reference work, the edition number, and the pages.

> Ray, S., & Schwarz, H. (2016). Globalization. In *Encyclopedia of post-colonial studies*. Malden, MA: Wiley-Blackwell.

If the entry came from an online source, give the URL for the home page or index page.

> Cultural anthropology. (2017). In *Encyclopaedia britannica*. Retrieved from http://www.britannica.com

45. Government Publication Give the name of the department, office, agency, or committee that issued the report as the author. If the document has a report or special file number, place that in parentheses after the title. If the publication was found online, provide the DOI or the URL.

> Congressional Budget Office. (2018). *Public spending on transportation and water infrastructure, 1956 to 2017*. Retrieved from https://www.cbo.gov/

46. Brochure or Pamphlet Format the entry as you would a book (see item 14 on p. 409); insert "n.d." if there is no publication date.

> UNESCO. (n.d.). *The world heritage brochure*. Paris, France: UNESCO World Heritage Center. Retrieved from https://whc.unesco.org/en/documents/124632

Field Sources

47. Personal Interview Treat unpublished interviews as personal communications and include them in your text only (see item 12 on p. 407). Do not cite personal interviews in your reference list.

**APA
31.2**

48. Unpublished Letter Cite a personal letter only in the text (see item 12 on p. 407), not in the reference list.

49. Lecture or Public Address Cite a lecture or public address the same way you would cite an unpublished paper presented at a conference.

> Wolin, P. (2016, May 3). Descendants of light: American photographers of
>
>   Jewish ancestry. 92nd Street Y, New York, NY.

Media Sources

50. Film or Video List the director or relevant contributor, the date of release, the title, the medium in square brackets ("Motion picture," "DVD," or "Blu-ray disc"), the country where the film was made, and the studio or distributor.

> Gerwig, G. (Director). (2018). *Lady bird* [Motion picture].
>
>   United States: A24.

For videos found on the web, include the words "Video file" in square brackets after the title and give the URL after the publication information. If there is no author's name, list the screen name provided.

> Fateh, A. (2018, November 9). *WATCH: Video shows camp fire burning*
>
>   *through Paradise, California* [Video file]. Retrieved from https://www
>
>   .youtube.com/watch?v=WPVVG9rZ7OM

51. Television or Radio Program Cite as you would a chapter in a book. For a television program, list the director (if available), the broadcast date, and the title followed by "Television broadcast" or "Television series episode" in square brackets. Then add information on the series, location, and station.

> Jennings, T. (Writer, Producer, and Director), & Bomse, S. (Writer). (2010,
>
>   August 25). Law and disorder [Television series episode]. In D. Fanning
>
>   (Executive producer), *Frontline*. Boston, MA: WGBH.

For a radio program, the title should be followed by "Radio broadcast" or "Radio series episode" in square brackets.

Martin, M. (Host), Ali, B. K. (Host), Sedgwick, N. (Host), & Ali, S. (Host). (2018, November 8) 22. Confidence [Radio series episode]. In A. Riddell (Producer), *GrownUpLand*. London, UK: BBC Radio 4.

**APA
31.2**

If you accessed the program on the web, include the URL.

Glass, Ira. (Host and Executive Producer). (2018, November 2). Hoaxing yourself [Radio series episode]. In *This American Life*. Retrieved from https://www.thisamericanlife.org/660/hoaxing-yourself

52. Sound Recording, Audio Clip, or Podcast Name the author of the song, the date, the song title followed by "On" and the recording title in italics, the medium (in square brackets), and the production data.

Yorke, T. (2018). Unmade. On *Suspiria (Music for the Luca Guadagnino Film)* [CD]. London, England: XL Recordings.

For audio clips or podcasts accessed on the web, add the URL after the publication information.

Mahnke, A. (Host). (2018, November 26). Episode 102: Devil in the details. *Lore* [Audio podcast]. Retrieved from https://www.lorepodcast.com/episodes/102

53. Work of Art, Photograph, or Other Image Cite as you would a recording. Include the artist and publication date, if known. If the artist is unknown, begin with the title of the work. If the date is unknown, use "n.d." for "no date." Indicate the medium in square brackets. Identify the city and gallery or publisher.

> Vermeer, J. (1665). *Girl with a pearl earring* [Oil painting]. The Hague,
>   Netherlands: Mauritshuis.

If the source is found online, include the URL.

> Jet Propulsion Laboratory. (2014). Opportunity's *southward view of*
>   *"McClure-Beverlin Escarpment" on Mars* [Photograph]. Retrieved from
>   http://photojournal.jpl.nasa.gov/jpeg/PIA17943.jpg

Other Digital Sources

54. Nonperiodical Web Document Cite as much of the following information as possible: author, publication date, document title, and URL. If the format is noteworthy, include a description of the material in brackets after the title. Use "n.d." and include a retrieval date before the URL only when the original publication date is unknown. Include the publisher in the retrieval statement if it is not listed as the author.

> USA.gov. (2019, February 13). *Saving and investment options*. Retrieved from
>   https://www.usa.gov/saving-investing

For a chapter or section within a web document, give the section title as well as the main document.

> Mayo Clinic. (2018, March 16). Dental care. In *Adult Health*. Retrieved from
>   https://www.mayoclinic.org/healthy-lifestyle/adult-health/basics/
>   dental-care/hlv-20049421

Scan the website to find as much of the citation information as you can. The information you provide should allow readers to retrace your steps to locate the sources.

For additional models for citing sources from the web, see pages 424–428.

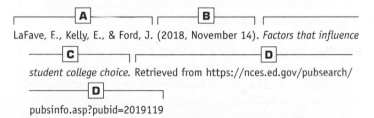

LaFave, E., Kelly, E., & Ford, J. (2018, November 14). *Factors that influence student college choice*. Retrieved from https://nces.ed.gov/pubsearch/pubsinfo.asp?pubid=2019119

A **The author of the work.** Give the last name first, followed by a comma and initials for first and middle names (if any). Separate the names of multiple authors with commas; use an ampersand (&) before the final author's name. If no author is listed, start with the title and follow it with the date.

B **The date of publication.** Give the year in parentheses and include the month and day, if available. If there is no date, use "n.d." in parentheses. End with a period.

C **The title of the work.** Give the article title and subtitle (if any), separated by a colon. Capitalize only the first word of the title, the first word of the subtitle, and any proper nouns or proper adjectives. Italicize the title of reports; if the work is an article, do not italicize the title or enclose it in quotation marks.

D **Retrieval information.** Insert "Retrieved from" and the URL for the work. Include a retrieval date if the material is likely to be changed or updated, or if it lacks a set publication date.

APA
31.2

55. Email Message or Real-Time Communication Because email messages are difficult or impossible for your readers to retrieve, APA does not recommend including them in your reference list. You should treat them as personal communications and cite them parenthetically in your text (see item 12 on p. 407).

56. Article Posted on a Wiki Include a retrieval date only if the material does not include a specific publication date.

> Sensory deprivation. (2019, February 25). Retrieved from https://
> en.wikipedia.org/wiki/Sensory_deprivation

57. Message Posted to a Newsgroup, Email List, or Online Discussion Forum List the author, posting date, message title, and a description of the message in brackets. Then add the retrieval information, including the name of the list or forum.

> Nelms, J. (2016, January 14). Re: Evaluating writing faculty [Online
> discussion list post]. Retrieved from https://lists.asu.edu/cgi-bin/
> wa?A1=ind1601&L=WPA-L#50

58. Blog To cite an entry on a blog, give the author (or screen name), the date the material was posted, the title of the entry, a description of the entry in brackets ("Blog post" or "Blog comment"), and the URL.

> Stewart, E. (2018, November 29). Gender reveals sparking controversy
> [Blog post]. Retrieved from https://thesocietypages.org/
> socimages/2018/11/29/gender-reveals-sparking-controversy/

59. Twitter Post (Tweet) Give the author's real name, if known, followed by the screen name in brackets. If the real name is not known, provide only the screen name without brackets. Provide the date, the complete text of the tweet followed by "Tweet" in brackets, and the retrieval URL.

> Shapiro, A. [arishapiro]. (2019, April 4). More than a million Venezuelans
> have already moved to Colombia, and 5,000 more arrive every day. No

one knows how much longer the country can sustain this.
#LeavingVenezuela [Tweet]. Retrieved from https://twitter.com/
arishapiro/status/1113844596549799942

60. Facebook Page, Post, or Status Update Start with the author or organization name followed by the date and text of the post. Then include the description of the entry in brackets ("Facebook page," "Facebook post," or "Facebook status update") and the retrieval URL.

Macmillan Learning. (2018, November 30). Human perception is both
a "bottom-up" and "top-down" process. https://buff.ly/2r55UDR #psych
#teaching #learning [Facebook post]. Retrieved from https://www
.facebook.com/MacmillanLearn/

61. Instagram Post Give the account holder's last name and first name, separated by a comma, followed by the username in brackets. If names are not available, begin with the username, without brackets. If the post has no date, use "n.d." in parentheses. Include the title or caption (up to forty words). If the post does not have a title, use a description of the post in square brackets. End with the URL.

National Geographic [@NatGeo]. (2018, September 8). [Photograph of
the 30th annual Phagwa/Holi celebration in Richmond Hill, Queens,
New York]. Retrieved from https://www.instagram.com/p/Bneu54sD_LL/

62. File Obtained Online Cite as you would a nonperiodical web document (see item 54 on p. 424). Identify the medium in square brackets after the title.

Jessedee. (n.d.). 5 presentation lessons from *The King's Speech*
[PowerPoint slides]. Retrieved October 9, 2016, from https://
www.slideshare.net/jessedee/presentation-lessons-from-the-
kings-speech-6551851

**APA
31.2**

63. Computer Software If a person is named as having rights to the program, software, or language, list that person as the author. Otherwise, begin the entry with the name of the program and "Computer software" in square brackets.

Microsoft Office 365 [Computer software]. Redmond, WA: Microsoft.

64. General Advice about Other Sources For all other sources, APA suggests that you use as a guide a source type listed in their manual that closely resembles the source type you want to cite.

APA-Style Essay

> APA notes that requirements for title pages on student essays vary. Check with your instructor first.

Running head: SCHOOL CRIMES BRING POLICE PRESENCE   1

School Crimes Bring Police Presence on School Grounds:

A Literature Review

Jessica Adler

Binghamton University

> Information about the writer and institution is provided on the cover page.

SCHOOL CRIMES BRING POLICE PRESENCE   2

Abstract

The first line of the abstract is not indented.

The heading "Abstract" is centered.

In response to an increase in school crimes in recent years, this paper looks at the research surrounding elevated crime rates in schools located in areas of lower socioeconomic status and with higher concentrations of people of color. It examines the literature on why students in these schools are more likely to commit crimes and acts of violence, while also addressing racial and ethnic biases that affect increased rates of discipline. In addition, it assesses the expanded police presence at schools, noting how it has created a prison-like atmosphere and contributed to the school-to-prison pipeline. In order to counteract this system, school administrators must focus on creating a welcoming and safe environment that fosters student learning.

Keywords: school, crime, socioeconomic status, people of color, school-to-prison pipeline

Keywords list the main topics addressed in the paper.

School Crimes Bring Police Presence on School Grounds:

A Literature Review

The concept of school violence has only been part of social science literature since 2002, even though school crimes and violence have been documented since at least the 1980s (Benbenishty & Astor, 2005). After a decline between the years of 1992 and 2011, school crimes have increased (Robers, Kemp, Rathbun, & Morgan, 2014). School violence and crime have been closely researched with regards to the school and students' demographics, such as race, gender, age, and class. Furthermore, such research often associates school crime with the community and background surrounding the school and students (Fergusson, Campbell, & Horwood, 2004).

With increased school crime rates, disciplinary actions have become more common on school grounds. The "school-to-prison pipeline" is a metaphor used to show the many ways that schools have become channels to the criminal justice system. This idea encompasses the many disciplinary policies that have been implemented in our education system as well as an atmosphere that has increased the likelihood of partic-ipating in violent and criminal acts (Crawley & Hirschfield, 2018). This essay explores the elevated crime rates in schools in lower socioeconomic areas with high proportions of students of color. In addition, it assesses the expanded police presence that has created a prison-like atmosphere, to the point where students begin to feel that they truly are criminals.

The essay's title is repeated and centered.

The writer frames the issue with a historical overview.

For a source with three authors, an ampersand is inserted before the final author's name.

The writer's thesis statement

SCHOOL CRIMES BRING POLICE PRESENCE   4

Background and Context for School Crime

Community is a major factor associated with violence and crime rates in schools. Schools in poorer areas tend to have higher crime rates in part because they have fewer financial resources, which means fewer guidance counselors, outdated classroom technology, or minimal support services (Chen, 2008; Deming, 2011). Suspensions for violent acts tend to decrease as economic status, family stability, housing quality, and community stability increase. Living conditions are a significant factor, as it has been found that students whose homes are overcrowded or of poor conditions are suspended at higher rates (Hellman & Beaton, 1986). However, Black students, both male and female, have been reported to commit fewer crimes than their White peers, yet they still experience higher rates of suspension, suggesting that racial and ethnic biases by police and other authorities may be at work (Welsh, Greene, & Jenkins, 1999).

"Good" and "Bad" Neighborhoods

Spring (2016) discussed the stereotypes of "good" and "bad" neighborhoods and the expectations that the "good" neighborhoods have better resources and schools compared to the "bad" neighborhoods. Additionally, the "good" neighborhoods are usually considered to be the communities with more affluent and White people, compared to the "bad"

Citation information is provided in parentheses.

When the author's name is mentioned in the sentence, only the year of publication is provided in parentheses.

neighborhoods, which have higher populations of working class and poor families and minorities. When researching this idea, I saw how the segregation of White and Black neighborhoods tends to be correlated with the institutional resources and the cognitive and learning outcomes of the specific schools. Bennett (2011) has even shown that Black students in segregated neighborhoods have lower standardized test scores than Black students in integrated neighborhoods, suggesting that racial segregation is a further negative influence upon students' academic performance (Discussions and Conclusions, para. 3).

    The topic of school violence is important because of its increasing occurrence throughout the United States. Many of these acts have been performed by White individuals, and yet the stereotype persists that "bad" neighborhoods are those with lower socioeconomic income and higher concentration of people of color. This paper helps to begin the conversation we need to have about schools in lower socioeconomic areas and minority neighborhoods.

The Importance of Education and a Quality Learning Environment

    Spring (2016) mentioned that educational reformist Horace Mann dreamed of ending crime through the public education system. Studies have shown a relationship between the level

APA 31.2

> The section name and paragraph number are provided for a web source without page numbers.

> The writer uses headings to signal sections of the essay.

APA
31.2

SCHOOL CRIMES BRING POLICE PRESENCE   6

of educational attainment and criminal convictions, meaning the higher a person's educational attainment, the less likely that person is to participate in criminal actions. Additionally, Spring pointed out that educational attainment has much to do with neighborhood conditions, peer groups, and family wealth. As I have seen throughout my research, higher quality schools tend to have lower rates of crime, suggesting that school quality raises student productivity. Analyzing school district data, Deming (2011) observed that minority students who won a lottery to attend a higher-performing school committed less crime:

> African American males and youth who are at highest risk for criminal involvement . . . are also more likely to remain enrolled and "on-track" in school, and they show modest improvements on school-based behavioral outcomes such as absences and suspensions. (p. 2065)

These schools have better financial and educational resources, smaller class sizes, and often more experienced teachers and administrators. In addition, students are surrounded by peers who have strong work ethics, which creates a conducive environment for all students to succeed (Deming, 2011). Given all of these factors, a quality

Following APA style, a longer quotation is set off as a block quotation.

Ellipsis marks indicate that words have been removed from the quotation.

The page number where the quotation can be found is provided.

education can help students avoid committing acts of crime or violence.

Police on School Grounds

Schools are supposed to be a place where children can go to learn and feel safe around their friends and the school faculty. Within the past two decades, however, schools have increased their police presence on school grounds. While some benefits are associated with increased police presence on school grounds, it is important to consider how police presence affects people of color in general and students of color in particular. Research has found that security measures such as metal detectors actually increased the amount of violent acts committed in school (Chen, 2008, School Crime and School Safety Programs, para. 9). Here the school-to-prison pipeline metaphor can be seen to describe many of the disciplinary policies that have been put in place. The implementation of police presence on campus has only decreased the probability of school success for students, since expulsion and suspension from school have been shown to leave students at risk for other negative outcomes inside and outside of school (Skiba, Arredondo, & Williams, 2014).

SCHOOL CRIMES BRING POLICE PRESENCE   8

In addition, school disciplinary measures may be subject to racial disparities, with higher rates of suspension and expulsion for Black students. Specifically, Black females have encountered higher rates of suspension and expulsion, with Black males following closely after. Because of the strong police presence, Black and Hispanic students may feel less safe compared to White and Asian students. The combined threat of disciplinary measures and these "unsafe" feelings may lead Black and Hispanic students to stay at home instead of attending school or to increased rates of violence inside and outside of school (Lacoe, 2014). Students may begin to fear coming to school because of frequent crackdowns by police and school personnel. Furthermore, the zero-tolerance approaches implemented by many schools may make it difficult for troubled students to find the proper support. When students have no trust in the school administration, the result is often elevated acts of crime and violence (Hirschfield, 2018).

Saltman (2018) pointed out that working-class and poor minority students experience many instances of control in school. In the way they speak and how they watch the students, the police presence in such schools may begin to treat students as racialized and disciplined subjects. "Working-class students are subject to pedagogies of control and repression oriented around . . . warehousing them for a future of social and economic marginalization and disposability — the school-to-prison pipeline exemplifying this path" (Saltman, 2018, p. 21). Saltman further discussed the idea that schools should be a place where students learn and grow in knowledge, but instead students of minority working class and poor families may come to see themselves "through the lens and assumption of criminality" as a result of such disciplinary practices (2018, p. 49).

Conclusion

It is clear that there are major economic and racial factors associated with elevated acts of crime and violence occurring in specific schools. Many disciplinary actions have been put in place to counteract these acts, and while some have worked, others have only given way to more violence. Specifically, police presence on school grounds has led many poor and minority students to feel that they are not entirely safe in school. It is unfortunate that this has become the case, as school is supposed to be a place where students are excited to attend and learn.

Increasing numbers of police officers on school campuses in some cases has strengthened the school-to-prison pipeline because their presence has created an atmosphere that criminalizes students for both significant and

SCHOOL CRIMES BRING POLICE PRESENCE   10

insignificant acts. Additionally, suspension and expulsion
rates appear to be subject to racial bias. Analysis of the
school-to-prison pipeline must take into account both the
high rates of neighborhood crime and the lack of sufficient
educational resources in poor, racially segregated schools.

SCHOOL CRIMES BRING POLICE PRESENCE   11

References

Benbenishty, R., & Astor, R. A. (2005). *School violence in context: Culture, neighborhood, family, school, and gender*. New York, NY: Oxford University Press.

Bennett, P. R. (2011). The relationship between neighborhood racial concentration and verbal ability: An investigation using the institutional resources model. *Social Science Research, 40*(4), 1124–1141. https://doi.org/10.1016/j.ssresearch.2011.04.001

Chen, G. (2008). Communities, students, schools, and school crime. *Urban Education, 43*(3), 301–318. https://doi.org/10.1177/0042085907311791

Crawley, K., & Hirschfield, P. (2018). Examining the school-to-prison pipeline metaphor. In *Oxford Research Encyclopedia of Criminology and Criminal Justice*. Retrieved from http://oxfordre.com/criminology

Deming, D. J. (2011). Better schools, less crime? *The Quarterly Journal of Economics, 126*(4), 2063–2115. https://doi.org/10.1093/qje/qjr036

Fergusson, D., Swain-Campbell, N., & Horwood, J. (2004). How does childhood economic disadvantage lead to crime? *Journal of Child Psychology and Psychiatry, 45*(5), 956–966.

Hellman, D. A., & Beaton, S. (1986). The pattern of violence in urban public schools: The influence of school and community. *Journal of Research in Crime and Delinquency, 23*(2), 102–127. https://doi.org/1177/0022427886023002002

In APA style, the references are listed on a separate page, with a centered heading.

Sources are alphabetized by the author's last name and are formatted with hanging indents.

A DOI is preceded with "https://doi.org/".

A web source

An article from a scholarly journal

APA
31.2

Hirschfield, P. J. (2018). Schools and crime. *Annual Review of Criminology, 1*(1), 149–169. https://doi.org/10.1146/annurev-criminol-032317-092358

Lacoe, J. R. (2014). Unequally safe. *Youth Violence and Juvenile Justice, 13*(2), 143–168. https://doi.org/10.1177/1541204014532659

Robers, S., Kemp, J., Rathbun, A., & Morgan, R. E. (2014). *Indicators of school crime and safety: 2013* (Report No. NCES 2014-042/NCJ 243299). National Center for Education Statistics. Retrieved from https://nces.ed.gov/pubs2014/2014042.pdf

Saltman, K. J. (2018). *The politics of education: A critical introduction*. New York, NY: Routledge.

Skiba, R. J., Arredondo, M. I., & Williams, N. T. (2014). More than a metaphor: The contribution of exclusionary discipline to a school-to-prison pipeline. *Equity & Excellence in Education, 47*(4), 546–564. https://doi.org/10.1080/10665684.2014.958965

Spring, J. H. (2016). *American education*. New York, NY: Routledge.

Welsh, W. N., Greene, J. R., & Jenkins, P. H. (1999). School disorder: The influence of individual, institutional, and community factors. *Criminology, 37*(1), 73–116. https://doi.org/10.1111/j.1745-9125.1999.tb00480.x

32. Use *Chicago* Style

The documentation style described in *The Chicago Manual of Style: The Essential Guide for Writers, Editors, and Publishers*, Seventeenth Edition, is used in the humanities and in some of the social sciences. The *Manual* recommends two systems: an author–date system similar to the APA system (see Chapter 31) and a notes system. This chapter describes and provides models for the notes system.

In the notes system, researchers acknowledge their sources in footnotes or endnotes. Footnotes appear at the bottom of the printed page, whereas endnotes appear at the end of the document. Although a bibliography can be omitted when using the notes system (since all relevant publication information is provided in the notes), the *Manual* encourages authors to provide a bibliography or list of works cited in documents when more than a few sources are cited. For more information about this system, consult *The Chicago Manual of Style*. Information about the manual can also be found at **chicagomanualofstyle.org**.

For an essay formatted in *Chicago* style, turn to page 464.

Directory of *Chicago Style*

**CMS
32.0**

32.1 Cite Sources in the Text of a Document

Chicago uses footnotes or endnotes. Notes can contain both citation information and commentary on the text—that is, notes can also be used to expand on points made in the text. For digital documents such as websites that consist of multiple "pages" of text, footnotes can take the form of links to notes at the end of a "page" or to pop-up windows that display the notes.

The first time you refer to a source in a note, provide complete publication information for the source. In subsequent references, you need to cite only the author's last name, a shortened version of the title, and the page numbers to which you refer (if the source has page numbers). Separate the elements with commas and end with a period. *Chicago* style italicizes titles of books and periodicals.

The following examples illustrate the most common ways of citing sources within the text of your document using the *Chicago* notes system.

1. Numbering Notes should be numbered consecutively throughout your work, beginning with 1.

2. Placement of the Note Numbers in the Text Place the number for a note at the end of the sentence containing the reference after punctuation and outside any parentheses. However, if you are citing the source of material that comes before an em dash (or two hyphens) used to separate parts of a sentence, the note number should precede the dash. Note numbers are set as superscripts.

> Lee and Calandra suggest that the poor organization of online historical documents may impair students' ability to conduct research without guidance.[1]

> Tomlinson points out that the erosion of Fiji's culture was accelerated by both British and Indian immigration[2]—though the two immigrant groups inhabited very different roles and social classes.

3. Placement of Notes You may choose between footnotes, which appear at the bottom of the page containing corresponding note numbers, and endnotes, which appear at the end of the document in a section titled "Notes." Longer works, such as books, typically use endnotes. The choice depends on the expectations of your readers and your preferences. Regardless of placement, notes are numbered consecutively throughout the document. If you use a bibliography, it follows the last page of text or the last page of endnotes. Model notes for various types of sources begin on page 446.

4. Including Page Numbers in a Note Use page numbers whenever you refer to a specific page of a source rather than to the source as a whole. The use of page numbers is required for quotations.

> 4. Rinker Buck, *The Oregon Trail: A New American Journey* (New York: Simon & Schuster, 2016), 92.

5. Cross-Referencing Notes If you are referring to a source identified in a previous note, you can refer to that note instead of repeating the information.

> 5. See note 3 above.

6. Citing the Same Source in Multiple Notes If you refer to the same source in two or more notes, provide a full citation in the first note. In subsequent notes, provide the author's last name, a brief version of the title, and the page number. If you are referring to the same source in two consecutive notes, you can omit the title in the second one.

> 1. Anna Scternshis, *When Sonia Met Boris: An Oral History of Jewish Life under Stalin* (New York: Oxford University Press, 2017), 17.
>
> 2. Scternshis, 131.
>
> . . .
>
> 4. Scternshis, *When Sonia Met Boris*, 219.

7. Citing a Source Quoted in Another Source

7. José María Arguedas, *Obras Completa* (Lima: Editorial Horizonte, 1983), 1:129, quoted in Alberto Flores Galindo et al., *In Search of an Inca: Identity and Utopia in the Andes* (New York: Cambridge University Press, 2010), 199.

32.2 Prepare the Notes and Bibliography

The Chicago Manual of Style provides guidelines for formatting notes and a bibliograpy. If a bibliography is provided, it should contain all works in the notes, except sources such as personal communication and wikis. A bibliography may also contain works that are relevant to but not cited within your document. In print documents and linear documents that are distributed digitally (such as a word-processing file or a newsgroup post), the bibliography appears at the end of the document. In longer documents, a bibliography could be given at the end of each chapter or section. In digital documents that use links, such as a website, the bibliography is often a separate page to which other pages are linked. To see a bibliography in *Chicago* style, go to page 478.

For notes, include the number of the note, indented and not superscripted, followed by these elements:

- author's name (first name first)
- title (followed by the title of the complete work if the source is an article, chapter, or other short work contained in a larger work)
- publisher (for a book) or publication title (for a journal, magazine, or newspaper)
- publication date
- page(s) being cited

For entries in the bibliography, include these elements and format with a hanging indent:

- author's name (last name first)
- title (followed by the title of the complete work if the source is an article, chapter, or other short work contained in a larger work)

- publisher (for a book) or publication title (for a journal, magazine, or newspaper)

- publication date

CMS 32.2

- page(s) (if the source is a shorter work included in a complete work)

Keep in mind that well-known reference works, such as encyclopedias, and all types of personal communication — personal interviews, letters, surveys, email messages, online discussion groups — are cited in a note only. They are not usually included in the works cited list.

Note: For each type of source, a pair of examples is presented in this section: a model note followed by a model bibliography entry.

Books, Conference Proceedings, and Dissertations

8. One Author Use the basic format described in item 4 on page 444. When citing a book, use the information from the title page and the copyright page (on the reverse side of the title page), not from the book's cover or a library catalog.

> 8. Michael Beschloss, *Presidents of War* (New York: Crown, 2018), 604.

> Beschloss, Michael. *Presidents of War*. New York: Crown, 2018.

If the book is found in a digital format, identify the book type (such as "ePub," "PDF e-book," or "Kindle e-book") at the end of the citation. If a DOI (digital object identifier, a unique number assigned to specific content) is provided, include it. If the book was found on the web and a DOI is not available, provide the URL. Place a period after the DOI or URL.

> 9. Craig Adam, *Forensic Evidence in Court: Evaluation and Scientific Opinion* (Winchester, UK: Wiley, 2016), https://doi.org/10.1002/9781119054443.

> Adam, Craig. *Forensic Evidence in Court: Evaluation and Scientific Opinion*. Winchester, UK: Wiley, 2016, PDF e-book. https://doi.org/10.1002/9781119054443.

**CMS
32.2**

9. Two or Three Authors List the authors in the order in which they appear on the title page. In a note, list the first name for each author first. In the bibliography, list the first author's last name first and list the first names for each other author first.

> 9. Neil Steinberg and Sara Bader, *Out of the Wreck I Rise: A Literary Companion to Recovery* (Chicago: University of Chicago Press, 2016), 247.

> Steinberg, Neil, and Sara Bader. *Out of the Wreck I Rise: A Literary Companion to Recovery*. Chicago: University of Chicago Press, 2016.

10. Four or More Authors In a note, give only the first author's name followed by "et al." (Latin for "and others"). In the bibliography, list all the authors that appear on the title page.

> 10. Stephen J. Fichter et al., *Catholic Bishops in the United States: Church Leadership in the Third Millennium* (New York: Oxford University Press, 2019), 188.

> Fichter, Stephen J., Thomas P. Gaunt, Catherine Hoegeman, and Paul M. Perl. *Catholic Bishops in the United States: Church Leadership in the Third Millennium*. New York: Oxford University Press, 2019.

11. Corporate or Group Author Use the corporation or group as the author; it may also be the publisher.

> 11. Human Rights Watch, *World Report of 2015: Events of 2014* (New York: Seven Stories Press, 2015), 11.

> Human Rights Watch. *World Report of 2015: Events of 2014*. New York: Seven Stories Press, 2015.

12. Unknown Author When no author is listed on the title or copyright page, begin the entry with the title of the work. In the bibliography, alphabetize the entry by the first word other than "A," "An," or "The."

> 12. *Letting Ana Go* (New York: Simon Pulse, 2013), 118–20.

> *Letting Ana Go*. New York: Simon Pulse, 2013.

How do I cite books using *Chicago* style?

PLATO AT THE GOOGLEPLEX

Copyright © 2014 by Rebecca Goldstein

All rights reserved. Published in the United States by Pantheon Books, a division of Random House LLC, New York, and in Canada by Random House of Canada Limited, Toronto, Penguin Random House companies.

Pantheon Books and colophon are registered trademarks of Random House LLC.

Owing to limitations of space, permissions to reprint from previously published material are listed following the bibliographical note.

Library of Congress Cataloging-in-Publication Data
Goldstein, Rebecca. [date]
Plato at the Googleplex : why philosophy won't go away / Rebecca Goldstein.
pages cm
Includes bibliographical references.
ISBN 978-0-307-37819-4   eBk ISBN 978-0-307-90888-7-2
1. Plato—Influence. 2. Philosophy—History—21st century.
3. Imaginary conversations. I. Title.
B395.G445 2014 184—dc23   2013502664

www.pantheonbooks.com

Jacket design by Pablo Delcán

Printed in the United States of America
First Edition
2 4 6 8 9 7 5 3 1

CMS 32.2

When citing a book, use the information from the title page and the copyright page (on the reverse of the title page), not from the book's cover or a library catalog. This tutorial gives an example of a *Chicago*-style footnote or endnote.

See pages 446–453 for models for citing books.

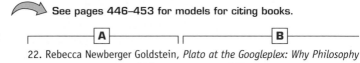

| A | B |

22. Rebecca Newberger Goldstein, *Plato at the Googleplex: Why Philosophy*

| C | D |

Won't Go Away (New York: Pantheon, 2014), 234–36.

A   **The author.** In the note, give the first name first. Follow the last name with a comma.

B   **The title.** Give the full title and subtitle, if any, separated by a colon. Italicize the title and subtitle, capitalizing all major words.

C   **Publication information.** Enclose the city, publisher, and date in parentheses. If more than one city is given, use the first one listed. For a city that may be unfamiliar to your readers or confused with another city, add an abbreviation of the state, country, or province (Cambridge, MA, or Waterloo, ON). Insert a colon. Give the publisher's name. Omit words such as "Inc." and "Co." Include and do not abbreviate terms such as "Books" and "Press." Insert a comma. Give the year of publication, using the most recent copyright year. Close the parentheses and insert a comma.

D   **Inclusive page number(s).** Give the specific page(s) on which you found the information. For numbers 100 and above, give only the last two digits and any other preceding digits if different from the first number (322–28, 599–603).

Bibliography Entry

In the bibliography, give the author's last name first, and separate the elements with periods. Do not enclose the publication information in parentheses.

> Goldstein, Rebecca Newberger. *Plato at the Googleplex: Why Philosophy Won't Go Away*. New York: Pantheon, 2014.

13. Translated Book List the author first and the translator after the title. Use the abbreviation "trans." in a note, but spell out "Translated by" in the bibliography.

> 13. Elena Ferrante, *The Story of the Lost Child*, trans. Ann Goldstein (New York: Europa Editions, 2015), 34.

> Ferrante, Elena. *The Story of the Lost Child*. Translated by Ann Goldstein. New York: Europa Editions, 2015.

14. Edition Other than the First Give edition information after the title.

> 14. Alan Brinkley, *The Unfinished Nation: A Concise History of the American People*, 6th ed. (New York: McGraw-Hill, 2010), 627.

> Brinkley, Alan. *The Unfinished Nation: A Concise History of the American People*. 6th ed. New York: McGraw-Hill, 2010.

15. Untitled Volume in a Multivolume Work In the notes, give the volume number and page number, separated by a colon, for the specific location of the information referred to in your text. In the bibliography, if you have used all the volumes, give the total number of volumes after the title, using the abbreviation "vols." ("2 vols." or "4 vols."). If you have used one volume, give the abbreviation "Vol." and the volume number after the title.

> 15. Fang Hanqi, ed., *A History of Journalism in China* (Singapore: Silkroad Press, 2013), 7:243–49.

> Hanqi, Fang, ed. *A History of Journalism in China*. Vol. 7. Singapore: Silkroad Press, 2013.

16. Titled Volume in a Multivolume Work Give the title of the volume to which you refer, followed by the volume number and the general title for the entire work.

> 16. Rick Atkinson, *The Guns at Last Light: The War in Western Europe, 1944–1945*, vol. 3 of *The Liberation Trilogy* (New York: Henry Holt, 2013), 345–49.

Atkinson, Rick. *The Guns at Last Light: The War in Western Europe, 1944–1945*. Vol. 3 of *The Liberation Trilogy*. New York: Henry Holt, 2013.

CMS 32.2

17. Book in a Series The series name follows the title and is capitalized as a title but is not italicized. If the series numbers its volumes, include that information as well.

17. James Mann, *George W. Bush*, American Presidents Series 43 (New York: Times Books/Henry Holt, 2015), 8.

Mann, James. *George W. Bush*. American Presidents Series 43. New York: Times Books/Henry Holt, 2015.

18. Republished Book Place the original publication date before the publication information for the reprint.

18. James, King of England, *The Political Works of James I*, ed. Charles Howard McIlwain (1918; repr., Whitefish, MT: Kessinger, 2010), 74.

James, King of England. *The Political Works of James I*. Edited by Charles Howard McIlwain. 1918. Reprint, Whitefish, MT: Kessinger, 2010.

19. Author with an Editor List the author at the beginning of the citation and add the editor's name after the title. In notes, use the abbreviation "ed." before the editor's name. In the bibliography, include the phrase "Edited by" before the editor's name.

19. Frederick Douglass, *Narrative of the Life of Frederick Douglass, an American Slave*, ed. Ira Dworkin (New York: Penguin Books, 2014), 114.

Douglass, Frederick. *Narrative of the Life of Frederick Douglass, an American Slave*. Edited by Ira Dworkin. New York: Penguin Books, 2014.

20. Anthology or Collection with an Editor To cite an entire anthology or collection of articles, give the editor(s) before the title of the collection, adding a comma and the abbreviation "ed." or "eds."

20. Ben Marcus, ed., *New American Stories* (New York: Vintage Books, 2015).

Marcus, Ben, ed. *New American Stories*. New York: Vintage Books, 2015.

21. Foreword, Introduction, Preface, or Afterword Give the name of the writer of the foreword, introduction, preface, or afterword followed by the appropriate phrase ("introduction to," "preface to," and so on) before the title of the book. If the writer of the introduction or other part differs from the writer of the book, after the title insert the word "by" and the author's name. In the bibliography, give the inclusive page numbers before the publication data.

21. Martin Stannard, preface to *Muriel Spark: The Biography* (New York: Norton, 2010), xv.

Stannard, Martin. Preface to *Muriel Spark: The Biography*, xv–xxvi. New York: Norton, 2010.

22. Chapter in a Book or Selection in an Anthology Give the author and title (in quotation marks) for the chapter or selection. Then give the title, editor (if any), inclusive page numbers, and publication data for the book or anthology.

22. Saïd Sayrafiezadeh, "Paranoia," in *New American Stories*, ed. Ben Marcus (New York: Vintage Books, 2015), 7.

Sayrafiezadeh, Saïd. "Paranoia." In *New American Stories*, edited by Ben Marcus, 3–29. New York: Vintage Books, 2015.

23. Published Proceedings of a Conference Cite as for an anthology or collection with an editor (see also no. 20 above).

23. Derek McAuley and Simon Peyton-Jones, eds., *Proceedings of the 2010 ACM-BCS Visions of Computer Science Conference* (Swindon, UK: British Informatics Society, 2010), 87.

McAuley, Derek, and Simon Peyton-Jones, eds. *Proceedings of the 2010 ACM-BCS Visions of Computer Science Conference*. Swindon, UK: British Informatics Society, 2010.

CMS 32.2

24. Paper Published in the Proceedings of a Conference Cite as a chapter in an edited book (see also no. 22 above).

24. Dale Miller, "Finding Unity in Computational Logic," in *Proceedings of the 2010 ACM-BCS Visions of Computer Science Conference,* ed. Derek McAuley and Simon Peyton-Jones (Swindon, UK: British Informatics Society, 2010), 2.

Miller, Dale. "Finding Unity in Computational Logic." In *Proceedings of the 2010 ACM-BCS Visions of Computer Science Conference*, edited by Derek McAuley and Simon Peyton-Jones, 1–13. Swindon, UK: British Informatics Society, 2010.

25. Sacred Text Cite sacred texts only within the text of your document. A note should include the book, chapter, and verse but not a page number.

25. Deut. 5:1–21 (New Revised Standard Version).

26. Published Dissertation or Thesis Enclose the title in quotation marks. Insert the phrase "PhD diss." or "master's thesis," followed by the institution that granted the degree and the year. Include the publication number from ProQuest if appropriate.

26. Anthony Colello, "Affirmative Action Bans and Minority Employment: Washington State's Initiative 200" (master's thesis, Georgetown University, 2011), 41–42, ProQuest (AAT 1491319).

Colello, Anthony. "Affirmative Action Bans and Minority Employment: Washington State's Initiative 200." Master's thesis, Georgetown University, 2011. ProQuest (AAT 1491319).

27. Unpublished Dissertation or Thesis Give the author and title, in quotation marks. Then include the phrase "PhD diss." or "master's thesis," information about the institution that granted the degree, and the date.

CMS
32.2

27. Joshua Glenn Iddings, "Writing at One Appalachian High School" (PhD diss., Purdue University, 2013), 96.

Iddings, Joshua Glenn. "Writing at One Appalachian High School."
PhD diss., Purdue University, 2013.

28. Abstract of a Dissertation or Thesis Provide information as you would for an article in a journal (see also no. 29 below). Add information about Dissertation Abstracts International.

28. Yi Mou, "Social Media and Risk Communication: The Role of Social Networking Sites in Food-Safety Communication," abstract (PhD diss., University of Connecticut, 2012), *Dissertation Abstracts International* 74 (2013).

Mou, Yi. "Social Media and Risk Communication: The Role of Social Networking Sites in Food-Safety Communication." Abstract. PhD diss., University of Connecticut, 2012. *Dissertation Abstracts International* 74 (2013).

Sources in Journals, Magazines, and Newspapers

29. Article in a Journal After the journal title, include the volume number, a comma, and the issue number after the abbreviation "no." (Note that volume and issue numbers are not italicized.) Then give the year. In the note, give the specific page number to which you are referring; in the bibliography, give inclusive page numbers of the entire article.

29. Kate McCoy, "Manifesting Destiny: A Land Education Analysis of Settler Colonialism in Jamestown, Virginia, USA," *Environmental Education Research* 20, no. 1 (2014): 86.

McCoy, Kate. "Manifesting Destiny: A Land Education Analysis of Settler Colonialism in Jamestown, Virginia, USA." *Environmental Education Research* 20, no. 1 (2014): 82–97.

If the article is obtained from a database, follow the publication information with the DOI, a stable URL, or, if neither is available, the name of the database.

**CMS
32.2**

> 30. Chih-yu Shih, "Confronting China in an Assymetric Relationship: The Case of Peace Efficacy in Taiwan." *China Review* 19, no. 1 (2019): 63, Project MUSE.

> Shih, Chih-yu. "Confronting China in an Assymetric Relationship: The Case of Peace Efficacy in Taiwan." *China Review* 19, no. 1 (2019): 57–87. Project MUSE.

If the article is obtained from the web, provide the DOI or, if a DOI is not available, the URL.

> 31. Gary Fields, "Palestinian Landscape in a 'Not-Too-Distant Mirror,'" *Journal of Historical Sociology* 23, no. 2 (2010), https://doi.org/10.1111/j.1467-6443.2010.01373.x.

> Fields, Gary. "Palestinian Landscape in a 'Not-Too-Distant Mirror.'" *Journal of Historical Sociology* 23, no. 2 (2010). https://doi.org/10.1111/j.1467-6443.2010.01373.x.

30. Article in a Monthly Magazine Magazines are cited by their dates rather than by volume and issue.

> 30. Peter Huber, "Better Medicine," *Reason*, March 2014, 25.

> Huber, Peter. "Better Medicine." *Reason*, March 2014, 22–30.

If the article is obtained from the web, provide the DOI or, if a DOI is not available, the URL.

> 30. Kathleen Burk, "America: The Last Empire," *History Today*, January 2019, https://www.historytoday.com/kathleen-burk/america-last-empire.

> Burk, Kathleen. "America: The Last Empire." *History Today*, January 2019. https://www.historytoday.com/kathleen-burk/america-last-empire.

31. Article in a Weekly Magazine Cite like a monthly magazine, but provide the day of publication.

> 31. Marty Makary, "The Cost of Chasing Cancer," *Time*, March 10, 2014, 24.

> Makary, Marty. "The Cost of Chasing Cancer." *Time*, March 10, 2014, 24.

32. Article in a Newspaper If the name of the newspaper does not include the city, insert the city before the name (and italicize it). If an American city is not well known, name the state as well (in parentheses, abbreviated). Identify newspapers from other countries with the city in parentheses (not italicized) after the name of the newspaper.

Eugene (OR) Register-Guard

Sunday Times (London)

Page numbers may be omitted, since separate editions of the same newspaper may place articles differently. If a paper comes out in more than one edition, identify the edition after the date.

> 32. Otis Taylor Jr., "Tax Proposals Hard for Soda Fans to Swallow," *San Francisco Chronicle*, October 13, 2016, Bay Area edition.

> Taylor, Otis, Jr. "Tax Proposals Hard for Soda Fans to Swallow." *San Francisco Chronicle*, October 13, 2016, Bay Area edition.

33. Unsigned Article in a Newspaper or Magazine If no author is given, begin the note with the title of the article; begin the bibliography entry with the title of the periodical.

> 33. "Ayes Straight Ahead," *Boston Globe*, October 14, 2016.

> *Boston Globe*. "Ayes Straight Ahead." October 14, 2016.

34. Letter to the Editor Treat as a newspaper article. If no title is provided, place "Letter to the editor" in the title position.

> 34. James Randi, letter to the editor, *Smithsonian*, October 2016, 73.

> Randi, James. Letter to the editor. *Smithsonian*, October 2016, 73.

How do I cite articles from periodicals using *Chicago* style?

CMS 32.2

CROSS-ENFORCEMENT OF THE FOURTH AMENDMENT

Orin S. Kerr

This Article considers whether government agents can conduct searches or seizures to enforce a different government's law. For example, can federal officers make steps based on state traffic violations? Can state police search for evidence of federal immigration crimes? Lower courts are deeply divided on the answers. The Supreme Court's decisions offer little useful guidance because they rest on doctrinal assumptions that the Court has since squarely rejected. The answer to a fundamental question of Fourth Amendment law — who can enforce what law — is remarkably unclear.

After surveying current law and constitutional history, the Article offers a normative proposal to answer this question. Each government should have the power to control who can enforce its criminal laws. Only searches and seizures by those authorized to act as agents of a sovereign trigger the government interests that justify reasonableness balancing based on those interests. The difficult question is identifying authorization; questions of constitutional structure suggest different defaults for enforcement of federal and state law. Outside the Fourth Amendment, governments can enact statutes that limit how their own officers enforce other laws. The scope of federal power to limit federal enforcement of state law by statute should be broader, however, than the scope of state power to limit state enforcement of federal law.

INTRODUCTION

Imagine you are a state police officer in a state that has decriminalized marijuana possession.¹ You pull over a car for speeding, and you smell marijuana coming from inside the car. Marijuana possession is legal under state law but remains a federal offense.² Can you search the car for evidence of the federal crime even though you are a state officer?³

Next imagine you are a federal immigration agent driving on a state highway.⁴ You spot a van that you have a hunch contains undocumented immigrants. You lack sufficient cause to stop the van to investigate an immigration offense, but you notice that the van is speeding in

Periodicals include journals, magazines, and newspapers. This tutorial gives an example of a *Chicago*-style footnote or endnote for a print journal article. (An example of the bibliography entry for this source is at the bottom of the page.) Models for citing articles from journals and newspapers, both in print and accessed electronically, are on pages 453–458.

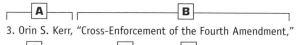

3. Orin S. Kerr, "Cross-Enforcement of the Fourth Amendment,"

Harvard Law Review 132, no. 2 (2018): 478–79.

A **The author.** In the note, give the first name first. Follow the last name with a comma. Separate the names of multiple authors with commas; use the word *and* before the final author's name.

B **The article title.** Give the full title and subtitle, if any, separated by a colon. Put the article title and subtitle in quotation marks, capitalizing all major words.

C **The periodical title.** Italicize the periodical title, and capitalize all major words.

D **Publication information and date.** For journal articles, include the volume and issue number followed by the year in parentheses. Follow with a colon. For monthly magazines, give the month and year. For weekly magazines, include the date of publication (September 6, 2016). Do not abbreviate the month.

E **Specific page number(s).** Give the specific page(s) on which you found the information, unless you are referring to the article as a whole. For numbers 100 and above, give only the last two digits and any other preceding digits if different from the first number (322–28).

Bibliography Entry

In the bibliography, start with the author's last name first, and use inclusive pages for the entire article.

Kerr, Orin S. "Cross-Enforcement of the Fourth Amendment." *Harvard Law Review* 132, no. 2 (2018): 478–79.

How do I cite articles from databases using *Chicago* style?

Libraries subscribe to services such as LexisNexis, ProQuest, InfoTrac, and EBSCOhost, which provide access to databases of digital texts. The databases list publication information, abstracts, and the complete text of documents in a specific subject area, discipline, or profession. This tutorial gives an example of a *Chicago*-style note for a journal article accessed via a database. (An example of the bibliography entry for this source is at the bottom of the page.)

➤ See Chapter 6 for more on searching with databases.

| A | | B | |

1. Jill Lansing, "A New Model of College Choice for Distance Learners,"

| C | | D | E | F |

Journal of Educational Technology Systems 45, no. 3 (2017): 369,

| G | |

https://doi.org/10.1177/0047239516673183.

A **The author.** In the note, give the first name first. Follow the last name with a comma. Separate the names of multiple authors with commas; use the word *and* before the final author's name.

B **The article title.** Give the full title and subtitle, if any, separated by a colon. Put the article title and subtitle in quotation marks, capitalizing all major words.

C **The periodical title.** Italicize the periodical title, and capitalize all major words.

D **The volume number and issue number.** Include the volume number followed by a comma, and then give the abbreviation *no.* and the issue number.

E **The year of publication.** Include the year in parentheses, followed by a colon.

F **The page numbers.** Give the specific page numbers of the reference. (In the bibliography, give the inclusive page numbers.) End with a comma.

G **The DOI, database name, or URL.** If no DOI is available, give the database name or a stable URL.

Bibliography Entry

In the bibliography, give the author's last name first, separate the elements with periods, and give inclusive pages for the entire article.

> Lansing, Jill. "A New Model of College Choice for Distance Learners."
> *Journal of Educational Technology Systems* 45, no. 3 (2017):
> 365–89. https://doi.org/10.1177/0047239516673183.

35. Review Give the author of the review, the review title, if any, and then the words *review of* followed by the title of the work reviewed and the author or editor (for books) or director or performer (for movies, plays, and similar productions).

35. Stephen Holden, "Students Caught in the School Squeeze," review of *Waiting for Superman*, directed by Davis Guggenheim, *New York Times*, September 23, 2010, http://www.nytimes.com/.

Holden, Stephen. "Students Caught in the School Squeeze." Review
    of *Waiting for Superman*, directed by Davis Guggenheim. *New York
    Times*, September 23, 2010. http://www.nytimes.com/.

Reference Works

36. Entry in an Encyclopedia, Dictionary, Thesaurus, Handbook, or Almanac In notes, provide the title of the work (italicized), the edition and its publication date, the abbreviation *s.v.* (for *sub verbo*, or "under the word"), and the title of the entry. *Chicago* does not recommend including reference works such as encyclopedias or dictionaries in the bibliography.

36. *Encyclopaedia Britannica*, 15th ed. (2010), s.v. "Lee, Robert E."

37. Government Publication In general, give the issuing body, and then the title and any other information (such as report numbers) that would help your readers locate the source. Follow with the publication data and the page numbers if relevant. You may abbreviate "Government Printing Office" as GPO.

37. US Senate, Special Committee on Aging, *Social Security: Improvements to Claims Process Could Help People Make Better Informed Decisions about Retirement Benefits* (Washington, DC: GPO, 2016), 7.

US Senate. Special Committee on Aging. *Social Security: Improvements
    to Claims Process Could Help People Make Better Informed Decisions
    about Retirement Benefits*. Washington, DC: GPO, 2016.

38. Pamphlet, Report, or Brochure Cite it as you would a book (see item 8 on p. 446).

> 38. *Facts: Scripps Institution of Oceanography* (San Diego: University of California, 2012), 9.

> *Facts: Scripps Institution of Oceanography*. San Diego: University of California, 2012.

CMS
32.2

Field Sources

39. Personal Interview Give the location and date in a note. Do not include unpublished interviews in the bibliography.

> 39. Christine M. Neuwirth, interview by author, Pittsburgh, March 15, 2019.

40. Letter or Other Personal Communication Do not include personal communications such as letters or phone calls in the bibliography. In a note, give the name of the person with whom you communicated, the form of communication, and the date.

> 40. Megahn McKennan, conversation with author, March 5, 2019.

> 41. Sangita Thakore, letter to author, November 12, 2018.

41. Survey *Chicago* does not specify how to cite unpublished survey results. Cite them in your text as you would a personal communication (see item 40 above).

42. Observation Notes *Chicago* does not specify how to cite observation notes. Cite them in your text as you would a personal communication (see item 40 above).

43. Lecture or Public Address Provide the title, the nature of the speech (such as lecture or keynote address), the name of the organization sponsoring the meeting or lecture, and the location and date it was given.

43. Anna Deavere Smith, "On the Road: A Search for American Character" (lecture, John F. Kennedy Center for the Performing Arts, Washington, DC, April 6, 2015).

Smith, Anna Deavere. "On the Road: A Search for American Character." Lecture presented at John F. Kennedy Center for the Performing Arts, Washington, DC, April 6, 2015.

Media Sources

44. Film or Video Provide the title first, the name of the director, the company, the year it was filmed, and the medium (film, videocassette, DVD).

44. *Won't You Be My Neighbor?,* directed by Morgan Neville (Los Angeles, CA: Tremolo Productions, 2018), DVD.

Won't You Be My Neighbor? Directed by Morgan Neville. Los Angeles, CA: Tremolo Productions, 2018. DVD.

For videos found on the web, provide the sponsoring organization and include the words "video file" after the publication information. Provide the DOI or, if a DOI is not available, the URL. If there is no author's name, list the creator's screen name.

45. GeckoGeekFr, "How to Make a Traditional Origami Crane," video file, 4:02, posted January 6, 2010, https://www.youtube.com/watch?v=jUZaOWibCcs.

GeckoGeekFr. "How to Make a Traditional Origami Crane." Video file, 4:02. Posted January 6, 2010. https://www.youtube.com/watch?v=jUZaOWibCcs.

45. Television or Radio Program *Chicago* does not specify how to cite a television or radio program. Cite as you would a video recording, identifying the medium as "television program," "television broadcast," "radio program," or "radio broadcast."

46. Sound Recording, Audio Clip, or Podcast Give the composer and title of the recording, the performers and conductor, the label, and an identifying number if one is provided.

CMS
32.2

46. Gustav Holst, *The Planets*, Royal Philharmonic Orchestra, conducted by André Previn, recorded April 14–15, 1986, Telarc 80133, compact disc.

Holst, Gustav. *The Planets*. Royal Philharmonic Orchestra. Conducted by André Previn. Recorded April 14–15, 1986. Telarc 80133, compact disc.

For audio clips or podcasts accessed on the web, add the medium, the length (if available), and the DOI or URL after the publication information.

47. Nate DiMeo, "Ida Lewis," Episode 132, September 25, 2018, in *The Memory Palace*, podcast, MP3 audio, 15:20, http://thememorypalace.us/2018/09/ida-lewis/.

DiMeo, Nate. "Ida Lewis." Episode 132, September 25, 2018. *The Memory Palace*. Podcast, MP3 audio, 15:20. http://thememorypalace.us/2018/09/ida-lewis/.

Other Digital Sources

All digital sources should include either a publication date, a revision or "last modified" date, or an access date. After the date, include a DOI or, if the source does not have a DOI, the URL.

47. Nonperiodical Website

47. Abby Mendelson, "Roberto Clemente: A Form of Punishment," Pittsburgh Pirates, MLB.com, May 24, 2013, http://mlb.mlb.com/pit/history/pit_clemente.jsp.

Mendelson, Abby. "Roberto Clemente: A Form of Punishment." Pittsburgh Pirates. MLB.com. May 24, 2013. http://mlb.mlb.com/pit/history/pit_clemente.jsp.

48. Article Posted on a Wiki Cite online postings to wikis in the text but not in the bibliography.

> 48. "Native Americans," Davis Wiki, accessed March 4, 2017, http://daviswiki.org/Native_Americans.

49. Blog Italicize the name of the blog and include the word *blog* in parentheses, if it is not already part of the name.

> 49. Donna Haisty Winchell, "In Arizona, Is It Ethics or Economics?," *Bits: Ideas for Teaching Composition* (blog), March 3, 2014, https://bedfordbits.colostate.edu/index.php/2014/03/03/in-arizona-is-it-ethics-or-economics/.

> Winchell, Donna Haisty. "In Arizona, Is It Ethics or Economics?" *Bits: Ideas for Teaching Composition* (blog), March 3, 2014. https://bedfordbits.colostate.edu/index.php/2014/03/03/in-arizona-is-it-ethics-or-economics/.

50. Email Message *Chicago* recommends that personal communication, including email, not be included in the bibliography, although it can be cited in your text.

> 50. Brysa H. Levy, email message to author, January 4, 2019.

51. Online Posting to a Discussion Group Like email, online postings are considered personal communication and are therefore listed in the text only, not in the bibliography. Include a URL for archived postings.

> 51. Bart Dale, reply to "Which country made best science/technology contribution?," Historum General History Forums, December 15, 2015, http://historum.com/general-history/46089-country-made-best-science-technology-contribution-16.html.

How do I cite works from websites using *Chicago* style?

Scan the website to find as much of the citation information as you can. Remember that the citation information you provide should allow readers to retrace your steps electronically to locate the sources.

CMS 32.2

See pages 461–462 for additional models for citing sources from the web.

> **B**
> 1. "Gun Policy Remains Divisive, But Several Proposals Still Draw Bipartisan
>
> **C** **D**
> Support," Pew Research Center for the People & the Press, Pew Research
>
> **E** **F**
> Center, October 18, 2018, http://www.people-press.org/2018/10/18/gun-
>
> policy-remains-divisive-but-several-proposals-still-draw-bipartisan-support/.

A **The author (not shown).** In the note, give the first name first. Follow the last name with a comma. Separate the names of multiple authors with commas; use the word *and* before the final author's name. If no author is named, begin with the title of the work.

B **The title of the work.** Give the full title and subtitle, if any, separated by a colon. For short works, put the title and subtitle in quotation marks, capitalizing all major words.

C **The name of the website.** Do not italicize the name of the website unless it is the name of a book or periodical.

D **The name of the sponsoring organization.** See the site's footer or "about" page.

E **Date of publication or last modification or access.** If there is no date of publication, include the date the page was last modified or the date on which you accessed the page.

F **The URL.** List the full URL; do not introduce any new hyphens or slashes. End with a period.

Bibliography Entry

In the bibliography, give the author's last name first (or list the sponsor in the author position), and separate the elements with periods.

> Pew Research Center. "Gun Policy Remains Divisive, But Several
> Proposals Still Draw Bipartisan Support." Pew Research Center for
> the People & the Press. October 18, 2018. http://www.people-press.
> org/2018/10/18/gun-policy-remains-divisive-but-several-proposals-
> still-draw-bipartisan-support/.

Chicago-**Style Essay**

CMS
32.2

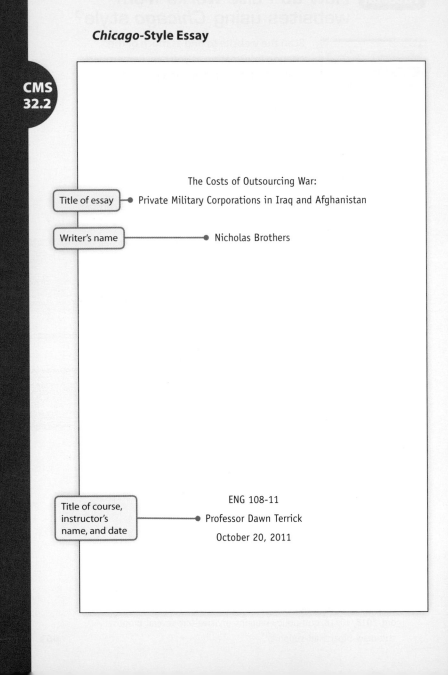

The Costs of Outsourcing War:

Title of essay — Private Military Corporations in Iraq and Afghanistan

Writer's name — Nicholas Brothers

Title of course,
instructor's
name, and date — ENG 108-11

Professor Dawn Terrick

October 20, 2011

CMS
32.2

The Costs of Outsourcing War:
Private Military Corporations in Iraq
and Afghanistan

> Title of essay
> repeated

The United States is considered the preeminent military
power of the world. Yet, it is also a military force that today
cannot get to the battlefield, feed and house its soldiers, or
even protect its bases without the support of a network of
nonstate actors. These organizations are sometimes listed on
stock exchanges worldwide; they have glossy, professional
websites and legions of press agents and lobbyists. They
are private military corporations (PMCs). Their duties range
from cooking and cleaning to planning and even carrying out
covert operations to capture Osama bin Laden. But military
privatization comes at a severe price—not just in terms of
dollars, but also in terms of national security, democratic
ideals, and human lives. By relying heavily on PMCs to carry
out military operations, the US Department of Defense is
undermining its own counterinsurgency efforts in Iraq and
Afghanistan.

> Thesis states
> the writer's
> main point.

Our country's reliance on private military corporations
did not happen overnight, and although the corporatization of
PMCs is relatively new, the idea of privatization is not. From
the time of Alexander the Great to the Napoleonic era, private
soldiers made up the bulk of military forces. Citizen armies

Brothers 3

emerged with the invention of cheap, easy-to-use muskets
in the early nineteenth century. Yet as recently as the Cold
War, US armed forces were traditionally organized, with conventional army, naval, and air units in combat against similar
Soviet units. The idea, of course, was for the military to be
self-sufficient. However, as P. W. Singer explains in his book
Corporate Warriors: The Rise of the Privatized Military Industry,
when the Cold War ended in 1991, the Department of Defense
began closing bases and dissolving or combining units,
setting the stage for the large-scale outsourcing of military
operations.[1] Jonathan Euchner, professor of political science
at Missouri Western State University, explained that the shift
to PMCs must be seen in the context of the overall privatization movement within the US government that began in
1978 under President Jimmy Carter and gained momentum
during the 1980s and 1990s.[2] While the role of PMCs remained
modest throughout the 1990s, new military engagements after
9/11 provided new opportunities for PMCs. As detailed by
investigative journalist Jeremy Scahill in his book *Blackwater:
The Rise of the World's Most Powerful Mercenary Army*, the
War on Terror as prosecuted by the Bush administration
accelerated the privatization of military functions. The new
secretary of defense, Donald Rumsfeld, would codify this
concept, which became known as the Rumsfeld Doctrine.[3] In
this doctrine, a highly mobile infantry force supported by

Information
was
obtained
through an
interview
with an
expert.

The name
of the book
identifies
the source
of the
summarized
information.

Summarized
material

Brothers 4

airstrikes and by contractors would chase Osama bin Laden and al Qaeda in retaliation for the terrorist attacks on the World Trade Center and the Pentagon. The demand for contractors skyrocketed after the invasion of Iraq, with an overextended military needing more and more support as the repeated deployments dragged on for years. Now, the United States is in the final stages of its involvement in one foreign conflict and intractably embroiled in another. The combat mission in Iraq officially ended on August 31, 2010, but, with an insurgency that's growing stronger rather than weaker in Afghanistan, the planned 2011 withdrawal from that theater of war will likely be scaled back.[4]

> First two paragraphs offer background information and history to orient readers.

Today, companies like DynCorp and Blackwater (now Xe Services) are some of the biggest, most diversified PMCs in a crowded market. In a 2007 online chat with the *Washington Post*, Singer, director of the 21st Century Defense Initiative of the Brookings Institution, asserted that at the time there were about 170 firms doing business in Iraq alone.[5] A July 2010 analysis by the Congressional Research Service reported that "contractors make up 54% of the workforce in Iraq and Afghanistan," meaning that contractors slightly outnumbered US soldiers deployed to those countries. More than 13,000 of these contractors are armed.[6] With so many firms and their contractors in play, the dollar amounts involved are unsurprisingly high. The Congressional Budget Office estimated

> The writer introduces a government document as the source of the quoted information.

> A colon (:) is not used when the quoted text is part of the sentence.

> A partial quotation is integrated effectively into the sentence.

**CMS
32.2**

Brothers 5

that the Department of Defense spent $76 billion on

contractors in Iraq between 2003 and 2007.[7] The stagger-

ing cost raises an important question in the mind of any

taxpayer: What are we getting for that money?

As Euchner pointed out, the civilian and military leader-

ship of the United States is attracted to contractors because

they offer streamlined services, with supposedly less bureau-

cracy and fewer regulations. As Erik Prince, the cofounder and

owner of Blackwater/Xe Services, put it, "Our corporate goal is

to do for the national security apparatus what FedEx did to the

postal service."[8] However, critics of PMCs would say that we're

buying the services of mercenaries, since both contractors and

mercenaries are essentially hired guns. Throughout his book,

Scahill provocatively uses "private military corporation" and

"mercenary" as interchangeable terms, underscoring their sim-

ilarities but failing to provide definitions of either. Yet a look

at definitions in Singer's *Corporate Warriors* reveals that PMCs

and traditional mercenaries differ in several key ways. Perhaps

the most important difference is that a private military

corporation is just that: a legal corporate entity[9] (as opposed

to the illegal adventurer or ragtag squad evoked by the word

"mercenary"). Another significant distinction is that PMCs

offer a wide range of services—"training, logistics, support,

operational support, post-conflict resolution," according to the

head of the PMC Sandline[10]—while mercenaries can rarely

The writer poses a question that he will answer in his essay.

An attribution gives context for the quotation.

The writer points out a disagreement between two of his sources.

Brothers 6

do more than engage in combat. However, while PMCs, unlike most mercenaries, are legal, corporate, and diversified in their capabilities, several high-profile abuse cases reveal that it is no wiser to rely on PMCs than on the mercenaries of old.

Numerous examples of abuses, negligence, and outright crimes have taken place since the post-9/11 expansion of the private military industry, and only a handful can be recounted here: A 2002 *Salon* feature details the experiences of the whistleblowers who exposed the sex trafficking that DynCorp International employees, under contract to service helicopters during peacekeeping operations, engaged in while stationed in Bosnia.[11] Scahill writes of the largely underreported involvement of contractors from the San Diego–based Titan Corporation and the Virginia-based CACI in the now infamous torture of Iraqi detainees at the Abu Ghraib prison compound in 2004.[12] And in what has become known as the Nisour Square Massacre, Blackwater employees killed seventeen Iraqi civilians at a busy intersection in Baghdad.[13] These are, of course, only a small sampling of contractor abuses, but they are clearly criminal actions—incidents that can't be explained away as an errant bullet or malfunctioning "smart" bomb.

It might be argued that these abuses are the actions of the individuals hired by a corporation, not part of corporate policy. And it might be further argued that in some of these cases, regular US troops can and have committed

The name of the website is used to identify the source.

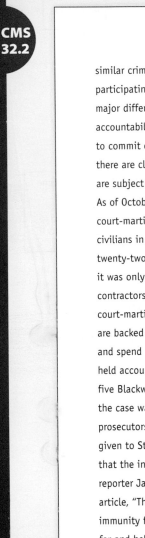

Brothers 7

similar crimes (and in the case of Abu Ghraib, were
participating right along with the contractors). But a
major difference between a contractor and a US soldier is
accountability. While there might exist the same opportunity
to commit crimes between the private and public sectors,
there are clear consequences in place for regular troops, who
are subject to the Uniform Code of Military Justice (UCMJ).
As of October 2010, thirty-four US Army soldiers had been
court-martialed on charges of murder or manslaughter of
civilians in conflict zones in Iraq and Afghanistan, and
twenty-two of those soldiers were convicted.[14] In contrast,
it was only in 2006 that the UCMJ was amended so that
contractors could be charged with criminal actions under the
court-martial system.[15] Unlike regular troops, contractors
are backed by strong money: lobbying groups fight hard
and spend millions to make sure the corporations are not
held accountable.[16] Although charges were brought against
five Blackwater men for the 2007 Nisour Square Massacre,
the case was dismissed when the judge ruled that the
prosecutors could not use statements that the accused had
given to State Department investigators on the condition
that the information could not be applied as evidence. As
reporter James Risen explains in a recent *New York Times*
article, "The Blackwater personnel were given a form of
immunity from prosecution by the people they were working
for and helping to protect."[17] Though the State Department

Brothers 8

has appealed the Nisour Square case, there have yet to be serious legal consequences for these and other contractors who commit crimes.

The atmosphere of lawlessness inherent in battle zones is compounded by the illegal acts of some of these contractors, which, in a low-intensity conflict, may turn citizens into insurgents. The Army Field Manual states that "people who have been maltreated or have had close friends or relatives killed . . . may strike back at their attackers. Security force abuses . . . can be major escalating factors for insurgencies."[18] And, as the Congressional Research Service report points out, Iraqi and Afghan civilians don't always know the difference between a US soldier and a contractor, meaning that, in the minds of the people, the actions of contractors directly reflect on the US military.[19] However, despite the people's inability to tell them apart, contractors and US soldiers have significantly different motivations. By definition, those in the military are serving their commander-in-chief while those hired as contractors are serving a for-profit company. In regards to PMCs' bottom lines, it would actually be advantageous to shoot first and ask questions later, engendering more fear and insecurity and therefore the need for more contracted security guards. This positive feedback loop should not be considered as some elaborate conspiracy; the situation is merely part of the

Attribution indicates the source of the paraphrased information.

Paraphrased information

Source of paraphrased information is provided in a note.

**CMS
32.2**

Brothers 9

culture and nature of profit-motivated actors. It's the reason
why, until the last couple of decades, defense operations
have overwhelmingly been left up to the public, not the
private, sector: ultimately, the motivation of profit is not
necessarily in line with the motivation of national security.

> The writer returns to his original question and asks a more in-depth one.

Given the potential costs in justice and national security,
why hire contractors at all? Ironically, perhaps the most
often cited reason for using private contractors is that
using these corporations saves the taxpayer money since
the government can hire them on an as-need basis and does
not have to pay for contractors' training, health care, or
pensions.[20] Professor Allison Stanger of Middlebury College
challenges this notion in her 2009 book *One Nation under
Contract: The Outsourcing of American Power and the Future
of Foreign Policy* when she points out that nearly all private
contractors previously served in the military, meaning that
many of them are receiving pension payments anyway.
Stanger writes that "the federal government is effectively
paying for the training and retirement of the contractors it
hires, all appearances to the contrary, as well as paying double or triple the daily rate for their services."[21] Therefore the
Department of Defense would actually save taxpayers money
by reversing the trend of privatization.

However, reducing the role of PMCs is very difficult
because the more money the US government spends hiring

**CMS
32.2**

these firms, the more these firms can afford to offer in salary,
and the more soldiers aspire to leave the military to work for
private companies.[22] A brain drain occurs, sapping the strate-
gic and tactical knowledge of the military, thus creating
an increased need for PMCs. Lt. Col. Michael Brothers, who
enlisted in 1981, described this process as one that has been
emotional for many in the armed forces as men and women
in uniform saw their chosen specialties phased out or privatized out from under them.[23] Essentially, PMCs have created
a void, filled it, and re-created the void so they can refill it,
ad infinitum. This makes it increasingly difficult to reverse
the current state of overreliance on PMCs since, according
to the Congressional Research Service report, "many analysts
now believe that DOD [the Department of Defense] is unable
to successfully execute large missions without contractor
support."[24] The vicious cycle of paying for help and then
becoming more helpless makes it imperative that the United
States end its dependence on PMCs as soon as possible.

> Brackets
> clarify the
> abbreviation
> used in the
> original
> quotation.

US citizens should better understand how our military
operations are carried out overseas, since the wars in Iraq
and Afghanistan affect our security, our taxes, and our
consciences as Americans. But we in the polity have not
demanded that contractors paid by the government for
military services be held accountable for their actions, and
neither have we demanded that our leaders recognize

Brothers 11

and address the growing threat to national security PMCs represent. A recent bill called the Stop Outsourcing Security Act, submitted to both houses of Congress by Representative Jan Schakowsky (D-Ill.) in the House and Senator Bernie Sanders (I-Vt.), offers one potential route to intervention. The act would "prohibit the use of private contractors for military, security, law enforcement, intelligence, and armed rescue functions unless the President tells Congress why the military is unable to perform those functions."[25] The passage of this act could be the first step in the process of phasing out the use of private contractors and returning military operations to the public sector. On her website, Schakowsky urges Americans to contact their representatives to cosponsor the legislation and become citizen cosponsors of the Stop Outsourcing Security Act themselves. In the end, we as voters and taxpayers must ask ourselves, who do we want to carry out US defense missions abroad: those accountable to the US military, or those beholden to private corporations? Given the costs in justice and in dollars, it's clear that the US military has come to overrely on PMCs to a point that is dangerous to national security and national interests. This reliance must be reduced, perhaps excised entirely.

> The writer concludes with a strong, clear statement of his position.

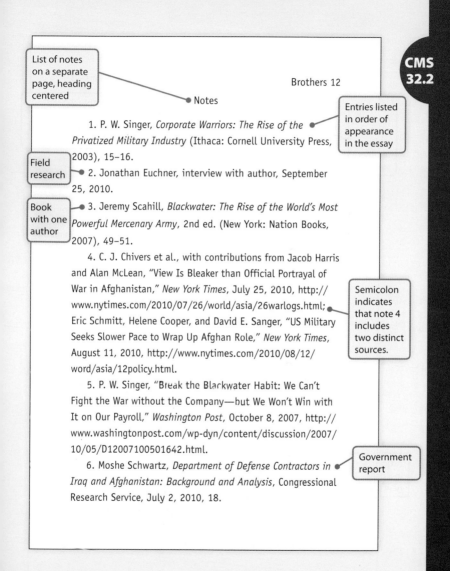

List of notes on a separate page, heading centered

CMS 32.2

Brothers 12

● Notes

Entries listed in order of appearance in the essay

1. P. W. Singer, *Corporate Warriors: The Rise of the Privatized Military Industry* (Ithaca: Cornell University Press, 2003), 15–16.

Field research

● 2. Jonathan Euchner, interview with author, September 25, 2010.

Book with one author

● 3. Jeremy Scahill, *Blackwater: The Rise of the World's Most Powerful Mercenary Army*, 2nd ed. (New York: Nation Books, 2007), 49–51.

4. C. J. Chivers et al., with contributions from Jacob Harris and Alan McLean, "View Is Bleaker than Official Portrayal of War in Afghanistan," *New York Times*, July 25, 2010, http://www.nytimes.com/2010/07/26/world/asia/26warlogs.html; Eric Schmitt, Helene Cooper, and David E. Sanger, "US Military Seeks Slower Pace to Wrap Up Afghan Role," *New York Times*, August 11, 2010, http://www.nytimes.com/2010/08/12/word/asia/12policy.html.

Semicolon indicates that note 4 includes two distinct sources.

5. P. W. Singer, "Break the Blackwater Habit: We Can't Fight the War without the Company—but We Won't Win with It on Our Payroll," *Washington Post*, October 8, 2007, http://www.washingtonpost.com/wp-dyn/content/discussion/2007/10/05/D12007100501642.html.

Government report

6. Moshe Schwartz, *Department of Defense Contractors in Iraq and Afghanistan: Background and Analysis*, Congressional Research Service, July 2, 2010, 18.

CMS 32.2

                                                        Brothers 13

7. Schwartz, 2.

8. Erik Prince speaking at West 2006 conference, January 11, 2006, quoted in Scahill, *Blackwater*, xix.

> A source quoted within another source

> Abbreviated reference to source identified in note 1

9. Singer, *Corporate Warriors*, 46.

10. Andrew Gilligan, "Inside Lt. Col. Spicer's New Model Army," *Sunday Telegraph*, November 24, 1998, quoted in Singer, *Corporate Warriors*, 46.

11. Robert Capps, "Outside the Law," *Salon*, June 26, 2002, http://www.salon.com/2002/06/26/bosnia_4/.

> Article from an online magazine

12. Scahill, *Blackwater*, 221.

13. Charlie Savage, "Judge Drops Charges from Blackwater Deaths in Iraq," *New York Times*, December 31, 2009, http://www.nytimes.com/2010/0101/us/01blackwater.html.

14. Charlie Savage, "Case of Accused Soldiers May Be Worst of 2 Wars," *New York Times*, October 3, 2010, http://www.nytimes.com/2010/10/04/us/04soldiers.html.

15. P. W. Singer, "The Law Catches Up to Private Militaries, Embeds," Brookings Institution, August 25, 2010, http://www.brookings.edu/2007/01/03/the-law-catches-up/.

16. Barry Yeoman, "Soldiers of Good Fortune," *Mother Jones*, May 2003, http://www.motherjones.com/politics/2003/05/soldiers-good-fortune/.

17. James Risen, "Efforts to Prosecute Blackwater Are Collapsing," *New York Times*, October 20, 2010, http://www.nytimes.com/2010/10/21/world/21contractors.html.

> Article in a daily newspaper

18. Department of Defense, *Counterinsurgency*, FM 3–24, December 2006, quoted in Schwartz, *Department of Defense*, 16.

19. Schwartz, 16.

Brothers 14

20. David Isenberg, "Contractors and Cost Effectiveness,"
CATO Institute, December 23, 2009, http://www.cato.org/
publications/commentary/contractors-cost-effectiveness.

21. Allison Stanger, *One Nation under Contract: The Out-sourcing of American Power and the Future of Foreign Policy*
(New Haven, CT: Yale University Press, 2009), 96–97, quoted
in Isenberg, "Contractors and Cost Effectiveness."

22. Robert Young Pelton, *Licensed to Kill: Hired Guns in
the War on Terror* (New York: Three Rivers Press, 2007), 58,
quoted in Scahill, *Blackwater*, 221.

23. Michael Brothers, interview with author, September
20, 2010.

24. Schwartz, *Department of Defense*, 1.

25. Jan Schakowsky, "Contracting," Congresswoman
Jan Schakowsky, last modified October 11, 2010, http://
schakowsky.house.gov/contracting.

Nonperiodical
website

**CMS
32.2**

Bibliography

Capps, Robert. "Outside the Law." *Salon*, June 26, 2002.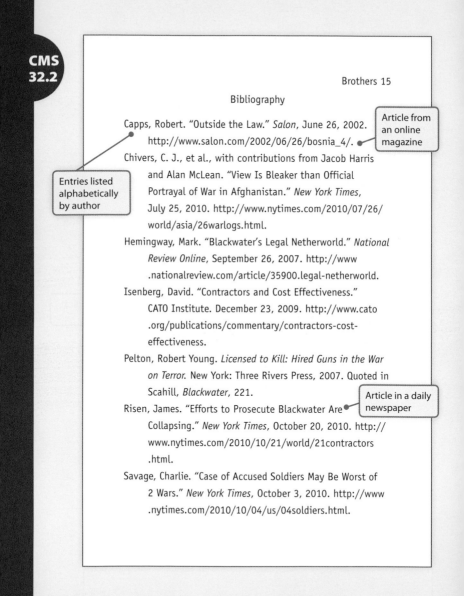

> Article from
> an online
> magazine

    http://www.salon.com/2002/06/26/bosnia_4/.

Chivers, C. J., et al., with contributions from Jacob Harris

> Entries listed
> alphabetically
> by author

    and Alan McLean. "View Is Bleaker than Official

    Portrayal of War in Afghanistan." *New York Times*,

    July 25, 2010. http://www.nytimes.com/2010/07/26/

    world/asia/26warlogs.html.

Hemingway, Mark. "Blackwater's Legal Netherworld." *National

    Review Online*, September 26, 2007. http://www

    .nationalreview.com/article/35900.legal-netherworld.

Isenberg, David. "Contractors and Cost Effectiveness."

    CATO Institute. December 23, 2009. http://www.cato

    .org/publications/commentary/contractors-cost-

    effectiveness.

Pelton, Robert Young. *Licensed to Kill: Hired Guns in the War

    on Terror.* New York: Three Rivers Press, 2007. Quoted in

    Scahill, *Blackwater*, 221.

Risen, James. "Efforts to Prosecute Blackwater Are

> Article in a daily
> newspaper

    Collapsing." *New York Times*, October 20, 2010. http://

    www.nytimes.com/2010/10/21/world/21contractors

    .html.

Savage, Charlie. "Case of Accused Soldiers May Be Worst of

    2 Wars." *New York Times*, October 3, 2010. http://www

    .nytimes.com/2010/10/04/us/04soldiers.html.

**CMS
32.2**

Brothers 16

------. "Judge Drops Charges from Blackwater Deaths in
  Iraq." *New York Times*, December 31, 2009. http://www
  .nytimes.com/2010/01/01/us/01blackwater.html.

Scahill, Jeremy. *Blackwater: The Rise of the World's Most
  Powerful Mercenary Army*. 2nd ed. New York: Nation
  Books, 2007.

Schakowsky, Jan. "Contracting." Congresswoman Jan
  Schakowsky. Last modified October 11, 2010. http://
  schakowsky.house.gov/contracting.

Schmitt, Eric, Helene Cooper, and David E. Sanger. "US
  Military Seeks Slower Pace to Wrap Up Afghan Role."
  New York Times, August 11, 2010. http://www.nytimes
  .com/2010/08/12/world/asia/12policy.html.

Schwartz, Moshe. *Department of Defense Contractors in Iraq
  and Afghanistan: Background and Analysis*. Congressional
  Research Service, July 2, 2010.

Singer, P. W. "Break the Blackwater Habit: We Can't Fight
  the War without the Company—but We Won't Win with
  It on Our Payroll." *Washington Post*, October 8, 2007
  http://www.washingtonpost.com/wp-dyn/content/
  discussion/2007/10/05/D12007100501642.html.

------. *Corporate Warriors: The Rise of the Privatized Military
  Industry*. Ithaca, NY: Cornell University Press, 2003.

------. "The Law Catches Up to Private Militaries, Embeds."
  Brookings Institution. August 25, 2010. http://www
  .brookings.edu/2007/01/03/the-law-catches-up/.

Book with
one author

Nonperiodical
website

Government
report

Dashes
indicate
that
these
sources
are
also by
Singer.

Brothers 17

Stanger, Allison. *One Nation under Contract: The Outsourcing
of American Power and the Future of Foreign Policy.*
New Haven, CT: Yale University Press, 2009. Quoted in
Isenberg, "Contractors and Cost Effectiveness."

Yeoman, Barry. "Soldiers of Good Fortune." *Mother Jones*, May
2003. http://www.motherjones.com/politics/2003/05/
soldiers-goods-fortune/.

33. Use CSE Style

CSE stands for the Council of Science Editors. In this book, CSE style is based on the eighth edition of *Scientific Style and Format: The CSE Manual for Authors, Editors, and Publishers.*

CSE 33.0

CSE style, used primarily in the physical sciences, life sciences, and mathematics, recommends two systems:

- A citation–sequence system, which lists sources in the reference list according to the order in which they appear in the document

- A name–year system, which is similar to the author–date system used by the APA (see Chapter 31)

This chapter describes and provides models for the citation-sequence system. For more information on CSE style, visit the Council of Science Editors website at **councilscienceeditors.org**.

For an essay formatted in CSE style, turn to page 497.

**CSE
33.0**

33.1 Cite Sources in the Text of a Document

The CSE citation–sequence system uses sequential numbers to refer to sources within a document. These numbers, in turn, correspond to numbered entries in the reference list. This approach to citing sources is often less distracting to the reader and saves space within a document.

1. Format and Placement of the Note Sources are cited using superscript numbers or numbers placed in parentheses. Superscript numbers should be formatted in a font one or two points smaller than the body text:

The anomalies in the data[3] call the study's methods into question.

The anomalies in the data (3) call the study's methods into question.

2. Citing a Previously Mentioned Source Use the first number assigned to a source when citing the source for the second time. In the following examples, the author is referring to sources earlier numbered 3, 9, and 22:

The outlying data points[3,9,22] seem to suggest a bias in the methodology.

The outlying data points (3,9,22) seem to suggest a bias in the methodology.

3. Citing a Source within a Source When referring to a source cited in another source, use the phrase *cited in*:

The results[12(cited in 8)] collected in the first month of the study . . .

The results (12 cited in 8) collected in the first month of the study . . .

33.2 Prepare the List of References

CSE style specifies that you document works that are cited in your document or that contributed to your thinking about the document. Cited sources should be identified in a section titled "References," while sources that contributed to your thinking should be given in a section titled "Additional References."

There are, however, two exceptions: personal communication and oral presentations. Personal communication, such as correspondence and interviews, is cited only in the text of your document, using the term *unreferenced* to indicate that it is not found in the reference list:

> . . . this disease has proven to be resistant to antibiotics under specific conditions (2014 letter from Meissner to me; unreferenced, see "Notes").

Typically, information about personal communication is placed in a "Notes" or "Acknowledgments" section. Similarly, oral presentations at conferences that are not available in any form (such as microform, reference database, conference proceedings, or online) should be cited in the text of your document but not included in your reference list.

The *CSE Manual* does not specify the location of the reference list, deferring instead to the formatting guidelines of individual journals in the sciences. In general, however, the reference list appears at the end of print documents and linear documents that are distributed electronically (such as word-processing files or newsgroup posts). In the case of longer documents or documents in which sections of a book (such as chapters) are intended to stand on their own, the reference list might appear at the end of each section or chapter. In digital documents that use links, such as websites, the reference list often is a separate page to which other pages are linked.

To see an example of a CSE-style reference list, turn to page 506.

Books, Conference Proceedings, and Dissertations

4. One Author Give the author's last name and first initial with no comma. Next, include the title, capitalizing only the first word and proper nouns, followed by publication information. Include the state abbreviation in parentheses after the city. If the book was obtained on the web, provide the URL. If a DOI (digital object identifier, a unique number assigned to specific content) is provided, include it. Follow the URL or DOI with a period.

CSE 33.2

> 4. Leonard C. The meat racket: the secret takeover of America's food business. New York (NY): Simon & Schuster; 2014.

5. Two or More Authors List the authors in the order in which they appear on the title page, each of them last name first. (If there are more than ten authors, list the first ten followed by a comma and *et al.*) Note that periods are not used after initials. Separate authors with commas. When using CSE style, abbreviate "United Kingdom" as "GB."

> 5. Willis KJ, McElwain JC. The evolution of plants. 2nd ed. Oxford (GB): Oxford University Press; 2014.

> 6. Gliklich RE, Dreyer NA, editors. Registries for evaluating patient outcomes: a user's guide. 2nd ed. Rockville (MD): Agency for Healthcare Research and Quality; 2010 [accessed 2019 Mar 1]. http://www.ncbi.nlm.nih.gov/books/NBK49444.

6. Corporate or Group Author Identify the organization as the author.

> 6. National Geographic. The national parks: an illustrated history. Washington (DC): National Geographic Society; 2015.

7. Unknown Author Begin with the title.

> 7. Images of Canterbury. Derby (GB): DB Publishing; 2015.

How do I cite books using CSE style?

CSE 33.2

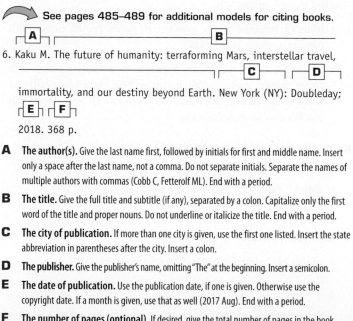

THE FUTURE OF HUMANITY

Copyright © 2018 by Michio Kaku

All rights reserved. Published in the United States by Doubleday, a division of Penguin Random House LLC, New York, and distributed in Canada by Random House of Canada Limited, Toronto.

www.doubleday.com

DOUBLEDAY and the portrayal of an anchor with a dolphin are registered trademarks of Penguin Random House LLC.

Page 325 constitutes an extension of this copyright page.

Book design by Pei Loi Koay
Jacket design by Michael J. Windsor
Jacket images: galaxy © triplstn / Shutterstock, spaceship © DM7 / Shutterstock, planet surface © Kjpargeter / Shutterstock, UFO © Conrad Jay / Stone / Getty Images

ISBN 978-0-385-54276-0
ISBN 978-0-385-54277-7
LCCN 2017046597

Cataloging-in-Publication Data is on file with the Library of Congress.

Manufactured in the United States of America

10 9 8 7 6 5 4 3 2 1

First Edition

When citing a book, use the information from the title page and the copyright page (on the reverse of the title page), not from the book's cover or a library catalog.

➢ **See pages 485–489 for additional models for citing books.**

| A | | B |

6. Kaku M. The future of humanity: terraforming Mars, interstellar travel,

| C | | D |

immortality, and our destiny beyond Earth. New York (NY): Doubleday;

| E | | F |

2018. 368 p.

A **The author(s).** Give the last name first, followed by initials for first and middle name. Insert only a space after the last name, not a comma. Do not separate initials. Separate the names of multiple authors with commas (Cobb C, Fetterolf ML). End with a period.

B **The title.** Give the full title and subtitle (if any), separated by a colon. Capitalize only the first word of the title and proper nouns. Do not underline or italicize the title. End with a period.

C **The city of publication.** If more than one city is given, use the first one listed. Insert the state abbreviation in parentheses after the city. Insert a colon.

D **The publisher.** Give the publisher's name, omitting "The" at the beginning. Insert a semicolon.

E **The date of publication.** Use the publication date, if one is given. Otherwise use the copyright date. If a month is given, use that as well (2017 Aug). End with a period.

F **The number of pages (optional).** If desired, give the total number of pages in the book, followed by "p." (Check with your instructor whether you should include it.)

8. Translated Book Identify the translator after the title, giving the last name first.

> 8. Villani C. Birth of a theorem: a mathematical adventure. DeBevoise M, translator. New York: Farrar, Straus and Giroux; 2015.

9. Book in an Edition Other than the First Note the edition (for instance, "2nd ed." or "New rev. ed.") after the title and with a separating period.

> 9. Roberts N. The holocene: an environmental history. 3rd ed. Oxford (GB): Wiley Blackwell; 2014.

10. Multivolume Work Include the total number of volumes if you are making a reference to all volumes in the work, or "Vol." followed by the specific volume number followed by the title of that volume (if that volume is separately titled).

> 10. Serway RA, Jewett JW. Physics for scientists and engineers. Vol. 5. 9th ed. Pacific Grove (CA): Brooks-Cole; 2013.

11. Authored Book with an Editor Identify the editor(s) before the publication information.

> 11. Einstein A. The cosmic view of Albert Einstein: writings on art, science, and peace. Martin W, Ott M, editors. New York (NY): Sterling Publishing; 2013.

12. Book in a Series Provide the series name and volume, if identified, after the publication year.

> 12. Rosenberg A, Arp B, editors. Philosophy of biology: an anthology. Chichester (GB): Wiley-Blackwell; 2010. (Blackwell philosophy anthologies; vol. 32).

13. Anthology or Collection with an Editor To cite an anthology of essays or a collection of articles, treat the editor's name as you would an author's name but identify with the word *editor*.

> 13. Carlson BM, editor. Stem cell anthology. London (GB): Academic Press; 2010.

14. Chapter in an Edited Book or a Work in an Anthology
List the author and title of the section; then include the word *In*
followed by a colon, the editor's name (last name first followed
by initials) and the word *editor*. Include the book title, place, and
publisher, and note the inclusive pages of the section. Note that
page range numbers are given in full.

CSE
33.2

> 14. Hawks J. Human evolution. In: Losos JB, editor. The Princeton
>   guide to evolution. Princeton (NJ): Princeton University Press;
>   2017. p. 183–188.

15. Foreword, Introduction, Preface, or Afterword If the
part is written by someone other than the author of the book,
treat it as you would a chapter in an edited book (see item 14),
identifying the author or editor of the book before the book title.

> 15. Groopman J. Introduction. In: Cohen J, editor. The best of the best
>   American science writing: ten years of the series. New York (NY):
>   Ecco; 2010. p. ix–xv.

16. Chapter of a Book If you wish to refer to a chapter of
a book, identify the chapter after the book's publication information. End with the inclusive pages of the chapter.

> 16. Cantu R, Hyman M. Concussions and our kids: America's leading
>   expert on how to protect young athletes and keep sports safe.
>   Boston (MA): Houghton Mifflin Harcourt; 2013. Chapter 9, After
>   concussions; p. 127–142.

17. Published Proceedings of a Conference List the editors of the proceedings as authors or, if there are no editors,
begin with the name and year of the conference. Then give
the title of the publication; the date of the conference; the
place of the conference; and the place of publication, publisher,
and date of publication or copyright date.

> 17. Platts H, Barron C, Lundock J, Pearce J, Yoo J, editors. TRAC 2013.
>   Proceedings of the 23rd annual theoretical Roman archaeology
>   conference; 2013; London. Oxford (GB): Oxbow Books; c2014; 160 p.

18. Paper Published in the Proceedings of a Conference
Format the citation as you would a chapter in an edited book.

> 18. Paten B, Diekhans M, Earl D, St. John J, Ma J, Suh BB, Haussler
> D. Cactus graphs for genome comparisons. In: Berger B, editor.
> RECOMB 2010. Research in computational molecular biology, 14th
> annual international conference proceedings; 2010 Apr. 25–28;
> Lisbon, Portugal. Berlin (DE): Springer-Verlag; c2010; p. 410–425.

CSE
33.2

19. Published Dissertation or Thesis Use the general format for
a book, adding the word *dissertation* or *thesis* in square brackets after
the title. Treat the institution granting the degree as the publisher.
If the place is not listed on the dissertation but can be inferred, use
brackets around the place. If the dissertation was obtained on the
web, provide the URL. If a DOI is provided, include it.

> 19. Yang, H. Topics in gravitational-wave science: macroscopic
> quantum mechanics and black hole physics [dissertation].
> Pasadena (CA): California Institute of Technology; 2013; 339 p.
> ProQuest Dissertations and Theses. Ann Arbor (MI): ProQuest;
> c2013. http://search.proquest.com.ezp-prod1.hul.harvard.edu/
> docview/1496774506?accountid=11311.

20. Unpublished Dissertation or Thesis Use the general format for a book, adding the word *dissertation* or *thesis* in square
brackets as a final element of the title. Treat the institution granting the degree as the publisher.

> 20. Wagner KP. A generalized acceptance urn model [dissertation].
> Tampa (FL): University of South Florida; 2010.

Sources in Journals, Magazines, and Newspapers

21. Article in a Journal Abbreviate and capitalize all of the
major words in a journal's title; omit articles, conjunctions, and
prepositions. Follow the specific guidelines in the *CSE Manual*.
A semicolon separates the year and volume number. If there is an
issue number, include it in parentheses, followed by a colon and
the page numbers. There are no spaces between the year, volume
number, and page numbers.

21. Gauthier S, Leuzy A, Racine E, Rosa-Neto P. Diagnosis and management of Alzheimer's disease: past, present and future ethical issues. Prog Neurobiol. 2013;110:102–113.

CSE
33.2

If the article was obtained through a database, give the name of the database, the location and parent company of the database, the date of access, the full URL for the article, and the DOI if one is provided.

22. Chen M, Schlief M, Willows RD, Cai Z-L, Neilan BA, Scheer H. A red-shifted chlorophyll. Science. 2010 Sep 10 [accessed 2014 Feb 1]:1318–1319. Expanded Academic ASAP. Farmington Hills (MI): Thomson Gale; c2010. http://web4.infotrac.galegroup.com. doi:10.1126/science.1191127.

If the article was obtained on the web, provide the access date, the URL, and the DOI, if available.

23. Pitaval A, Tseng Q, Bornens M, Thery M. Cell shape and contractility regulate ciliogenesis in cell cycle—arrested cells. J Cell Biol. 2010 [accessed 2013 Aug 23];191(2):303–312. http://jcb.rupress. org/content/191/2/303.full?sid=d8f7c638-68dc-4082-99a8-ca19a37d72fe.doi:10.1083/jcb.201004003.

22. Article in a Magazine Magazines are not identified by volume. Give only the date (year, month, day for weekly magazines; year and month for monthly magazines). Abbreviate all months to their first three letters.

22. Romero J. Marsquakes could support life deep within the red planet. Sci News. 2016 Sep 28:34–36.

23. Article in a Newspaper Treat newspaper articles as you would magazine articles, identifying their pages by section, page, and column on which they begin (in parentheses). If the article was obtained from the web, provide the access date and the URL.

23. Jalonick MC. Suit says toys in happy meals break the law. Boston Globe. 2010 Jun 23;Sect. B:11 (col. 1).

How do I cite articles from periodicals using CSE style?

NEWS | IN DEPTH

ANCIENT CLIMATE

Sticky glaciers slowed tempo of ice ages

Seafloor cores suggest thickening ice sheets triggered near-collapse of Atlantic currents

By **Paul Voosen**, *in Boston*

About 1 million years ago, one of Earth's most important metronomes mysteriously shifted: Ice ages went from occurring every 40,000 years to every 100,000 years. At the same time, the "conveyor belt" of warming currents in the North Atlantic Ocean slowed sharply. Last week, scientists here at the Goldschmidt Conference presented a clue to these twin mysteries: evidence that

Atlantic is surrounded by ancient crust, whereas the Pacific, thanks to its volcanic Ring of Fire, tilts younger. The neodymium-carrying grit ends up incorporated into the shells of single-celled foraminifera or fish teeth, both of which accumulate over time on the sea floor. Changes in the isotope ratio record the wax and wane of intruding North Atlantic or Pacific waters.

Earlier this decade, the Columbia group tested its approach on two archived sediment cores from the South Atlantic. About

had allowed a thick soil layer to build up on northern landmasses. At first, the soil acted as a grease that caused early ice sheets to collapse before they could thicken much. But repeated glaciations gradually scoured this grit away, and meltwater swept it into the ocean. As the glaciers dug deeper into older rock, the neodymium signal in ocean sediment became more negative. Eventually, the glaciers reached bedrock and began to stick to their base, allowing them to grow thicker—leading to

Periodicals include journals, magazines, and newspapers. This tutorial gives the citation for a print magazine article. Models for citing articles from journals and newspapers, both in print and accessed electronically, are on pages 489–492.

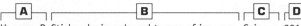

2. Voosen, P. Sticky glaciers slowed tempo of ice ages. Science. 2018; 361(6404):739.

A **The author.** Give the last name first, followed by initials for first and middle names. Insert only a space after the last name, not a comma. Do not separate initials. Separate the names of multiple authors with commas (Cobb C, Fetterolf ML). End with a period.

B **The article title.** Give the full title and subtitle (if any), separated by a colon. Capitalize only the first word of the title and proper nouns. Do not underline or italicize the title. End with a period.

C **The periodical title.** Do not underline or italicize the periodical title. Abbreviate and capitalize all major words, according to the guidelines in the *CSE Manual*. Omit articles, conjunctions, and prepositions, and do not abbreviate one-word titles or one-syllable words in the title. End with a period.

D **The year of publication.** For journal articles, include the year followed by a semicolon. For magazine and newspapers, include the abbreviated month, and if available, the day (2017 Apr 13), followed by a colon.

E **Volume and issue number.** For journal articles, include the volume number followed by the issue number in parentheses, if available, and a colon.

F **Inclusive page number(s).** List the page numbers in full (154–177; 1187–1188). Do not add a space between the colon and the page numbers. End with a period.

24. Kolata G. Stem cell biology and its complications. New York Times. 2010 Aug 24 [accessed 2010 Dec 15]. http://www.nytimes.com/2010/08/25/health/research/25cell.html.

CSE 33.2

24. Unsigned Article in a Newspaper Begin the entry with the title of the article. "Anonymous" is not permitted in CSE style.

24. A mouse to save your wrist and hand. Boston Globe. 2010 Nov 29; Sect. B:8 (col. 3).

Reference Works

25. Encyclopedia, Dictionary, Thesaurus, Handbook, or Almanac Begin with the title of the reference work and information about the edition. Identify the editor, if listed. Provide publisher and publication date.

25. Encyclopedia of climate change. Dutch SI, editor. Pasadena (CA): Salem Press; 2016.

26. Map or Chart Use the name of the area in place of an author. Follow with the title, type of map in brackets (such as physical map or demographic map), place of publication and publisher, and a description of the map. If the map is part of a larger document, such as an atlas, provide publication information for the document and the page number(s) of the map.

26. Netherlands. Independent Dutch breweries [demographic map]. In: The world atlas of beer. London (GB): Octopus Publishing Group; 2012. p. 137. Color.

27. Pamphlet Format entries as you would for a book (see also no. 4 on p. 485).

27. National Alliance on Mental Illness. Depression. Arlington (VA): NAMI, the National Alliance on Mental Illness; 2012.

How do I cite articles from databases using CSE style?

ScienceDirect

Medical Clinics of North America
Volume 101, Issue 1, January 2017, Pages 195-206

What Have We Learned from the Genetics of Hypertension?
Friedrich C. Luft MD PII

Show more

https://doi.org/10.1016/j.mcna.2016.08.015

Keywords
Genetics; Blood pressure; Hypertension; Mendelian; Genomewide association studies

Libraries subscribe to services such as LexisNexis, ProQuest, InfoTrac, and EBSCOhost, which provide access to databases of digital texts. The databases list publication information, abstracts, and the complete text of documents in a specific subject area, discipline, or profession.

CSE 33.2

See Chapter 6 for more on searching with databases.

3. Luft FC. What have we learned from the genetics of hypertension? Med Clin N Am.

2017 [accessed 2019 Apr 24];101(1):195–206. ScienceDirect. Amsterdam (NL):

Elsevier. http://www.sciencedirect.com/science/article/pii/S0025712516373357.

doi:10.1016/j.mcna.2016.08.015.

A   **The author.** Give the last name first, followed by initials for first and middle names. Insert a space after the last name, not a comma. Do not separate initials. Separate the names of multiple authors with commas (Cobb C, Fetterolf ML). End with a period.

B   **The article title.** Give the full title and subtitle (if any), separated by a colon. Capitalize only the first word of the title and proper nouns. Do not underline or italicize the title. End with a period.

C   **The periodical title.** Do not underline or italicize the periodical title. Abbreviate and capitalize all major words, according to the guidelines in the *CSE Manual*. Omit articles, conjunctions, and prepositions. Do not abbreviate one-word titles or one-syllable words in the title. End with a period.

D   **The year of publication.** For journal articles, include the year followed by a semicolon. For magazine and newspapers, include the abbreviated month, and if available, the day (2017 Apr 13), followed by a colon. Follow with the date of access in brackets.

E   **Volume and issue number.** For journal articles, include the volume number followed by the issue number in parentheses, if available, and a colon.

F   **Inclusive page number(s).** List the page numbers in full (154–177; 1187–1188). Do not add a space between the colon and the page numbers. End with a period.

G   **Database, URL, and DOI.** Give the name of the database followed by a period. List the location and parent company of the database. Provide the full URL for the article followed by a period and the DOI, if one is provided. End with a period.

CSE
33.2

Media Sources

28. Film or Video Give the title, and then the type of medium identified in square brackets, followed by individuals listed as authors, editors, performers, conductors, and so on. Identify the producer if different from the publisher. Provide publication information, including a physical description of the medium.

> 28. Great migrations [DVD]. Hamlin D, Serwa C, producers. Washington (DC): National Geographic; 2010. 3 DVDs: 200 min.

29. Television or Radio Program CSE style does not provide guidance on citing television or radio programs. Cite the title of the program, with the medium designated in brackets, followed by information about the series (if any), including individuals such as the producer, writer, director, and the place and date of broadcast at the end.

> 29. Iceman reborn [television program]. Apsell PS, senior executive producer. Nova. New York (NY): Thirteen/WNET; 2016 Feb 17.

30. Sound Recording Cite as you would a film or video recording.

> 30. Howler monkeys: singing into the night [sound recording]. Carroll B, sound recordist. Keene (NH): Belize Bruce; 2013.

Field Sources

31. Personal Interview Treat unpublished interviews as personal communication. Cite them in the text only; do not cite them in the reference list.

32. Personal Letter Cite personal letters as personal communication. Cite them in the text only; do not cite them in the reference list.

33. Lecture or Public Address Like an unpublished paper presented at a meeting, lectures or public addresses are treated as personal communication and are cited only in the text (see p. 489).

How do I cite works from websites using CSE style?

Scan the website to find as much of the citation information as you can. If you cannot find a publication date, provide the date you accessed the website. Remember that the citation information you provide should allow readers to retrace your steps to locate the sources.

See page 496 for additional models for citing sources from the web.

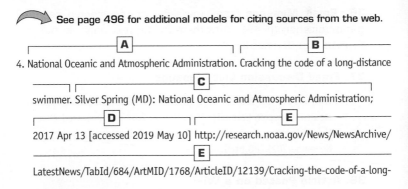

A · **B**

4. National Oceanic and Atmospheric Administration. Cracking the code of a long-distance

C

swimmer. Silver Spring (MD): National Oceanic and Atmospheric Administration;

D · **E**

2017 Apr 13 [accessed 2019 May 10] http://research.noaa.gov/News/NewsArchive/

E

LatestNews/TabId/684/ArtMID/1768/ArticleID/12139/Cracking-the-code-of-a-long-

distance-swimmer.aspx.

A **The author.** Give the name of the organization or author's last name followed by a space and initials for first and middle names. Separate the names of multiple authors with commas (Cobb C, Fetterolf ML). End with a period.

B **The document title.** Give the full title; include the subtitle (if any), preceded by a colon. Capitalize only the first word and proper nouns. Do not underline or italicize the title or subtitle. End with a period.

C **Publisher information.** Give the place of publication followed by a colon, and then the publisher or sponsoring organization followed by a semicolon.

D **Publication date and date of access.** Give the date of publication or the copyright date on the website; if available, include the date of modification or update in brackets. Then give the date of access in brackets. End with a period.

E **The URL.** Give the URL, followed by a period.

Other Digital Sources

34. Website

34. World Health Organization. Geneva (SW): World Health Organization; [updated 2019; accessed 2019 May 4]. http://www.who.int/en/.

35. Document on a Website

35. Strauss G. National Geographic Daily News. Washington (DC): National Geographic Society. Enlisting an army to save a forest. 2016 Oct 5 [accessed 2017 Jan 7]. http://news.nationalgeographic.com/2016/10/erika-cuellar-explorer-moments-rain-forest-South-America/.

36. Email Message Email messages are considered personal communication (p. 494). Cite them in the text only; do not cite them in the reference list.

37. Email Discussion List Message

37. Williams JB. Re: Tomato seed question. In: BIONET. [London (GB); Medical Research Council]; 2010 Nov 1, 7:57 am [accessed 2018 Nov 15]. http://www.bio.net/bionet/mm/plantbio/2010-November/027780.html.

38. Article Posted on a Wiki

38. Epidemic and pandemic spread. In: Influenza [updated 2017 Apr 26; accessed 2017 May 15]. http://en.wikipedia.org/wiki/Influenza#Epidemic_and_pandemic_spread.

39. Entry or Comment on a Blog

39. Bakalar N. Diabetes tied to brain abnormalities. In: Well. 2017 Apr 27 [accessed 2019 May 11]. https://www.nytimes.com/2017/04/27/well/mind/diabetes-tied-to-brain-abnormalities.html.

CSE-Style Essay

> Unnumbered title page includes a descriptive title with all major words capitalized, the student's name, the course name, and the date. All information is centered on the page.

**CSE
33.2**

Promising Advancements in Modern Cancer Treatment

Joshua Woelfle

Biology 597

Professor Diaz

May 3, 2017

CSE 33.2

Page numbering begins on first page of paper body. A short title is included before the page number.

Promising Advancements 1

Chemotherapy is just medieval. It's such a blunt instrument.

We're going to look back on it like we do the dark ages.

— Dr. Eric Topol (Unreferenced, see "Notes")

A source not included in the reference list

Cancer afflicts over a million Americans every year and proves fatal to nearly half of those afflicted. (1) Over the years, scientists have made great strides in understanding the disease, but cancer's widely varied and adaptive nature has made finding a cure nearly impossible. Fortunately, scientists have achieved greater success in controlling cancer, and several promising advancements may soon overtake the traditional treatment options of chemotherapy and radiation. Two of these advancements, anticancer drugs targeting out-of-control cell-growth signaling enzymes and multi-drug resistance (MDR) proteins, may soon relegate the traditional options of chemotherapy and radiation—along with their extremely detrimental side effects—to the past.

Since the 1940s, nonsurgical cancer treatment has consisted almost exclusively of chemotherapy and radiation. These treatments function by destroying rapidly proliferating cells throughout the body and are detrimental to cancer because, by its very definition, cancer is a mass of rapidly dividing invasive cells. Unfortunately, there are a number of other cell types within the body that also divide rapidly, such

Source references are shown in parentheses. Citation-sequence is used, and the sources are numbered in the order they appear in the text.

Promising Advancements 2

as hair, skin, and epithelial cells, all of which suffer the same
fate as cancer cells when these treatments are used. Additionally, chemotherapy causes a vast array of harmful side effects,
including immunosuppression, fatigue and nausea, neurological
disorders, and organ damage (2) which, even if the cancer is
contained, may negatively affect the patient's quality of life.

Despite these harmful side effects, chemotherapeutic
drugs would be a viable option if they were effective at
completely removing cancer from the body. However, the
1997 discovery of cancer stem cells (3) proved that this is
not the case. Cancer stem cells behave in much the same
way as other stem cells, with the ability to differentiate into
various tumor cells as required. This allows cancer stem cells
to adapt as necessary based on environmental conditions,
and often overcome adverse effects caused by treatment.
More detrimentally, cancer stem cells propagate slowly, so
they are not targeted by chemotherapy or radiation. Thus,
there is always the possibility of relapse for patients who
have "successfully" undergone chemotherapy.

Fortunately, alternate options are becoming available
that seem to be more effective than traditional treatments
at removing cancer, while simultaneously eliminating many
of the harsh side effects. At the forefront of these new
treatment options are designer drugs targeting enzyme

> Body of paper is
> double-spaced,
> with one-
> inch margins
> on all sides.
> Paragraphs are
> indented one-
> half inch.

**CSE
33.2**

Promising Advancements 3

proteins whose over activity have been shown to cause cancer. To understand anti-enzyme drug therapy, we must first understand the structure and function of these pro-cancer enzymes. Cancer develops primarily through genetic mutations that alter the body's cellular equilibrium and allow cells to proliferate and migrate without restriction. These requirements, dubbed the "hallmarks of cancer," (4) are required for the successful development of the disease. Specifically, for cancer to arise, it must secure blood supply for growing cells via angiogenesis, allow for unlimited and unrestricted division by manipulating the cell cycle and telo-meres, overcome growth restrictions, prevent cell suicide, and invade surrounding tissue or colonize new sites in the body. These changes require multiple genetic mutations and are regulated by a wide variety of enzymes, many of which are specifically altered in cancer. These specific alterations are the backbone of enzyme directed cancer treatment research.

Enzyme therapy works by targeting and restricting the cancer-specific enzymes required to sustain cancer's develop-ment and longevity. By disabling the mutated enzymes that make the hallmarks of cancer possible, the disease is prevented from further development, as opposed to chemotherapy, which merely destroys already-established cancer cells. Scientists are researching several different enzymes for this therapy.

A source reference is given in parentheses.

Promising Advancements 4

One of these is heparanase, an enzyme that stimulates cell migration. (5) Scientists are also experimenting with a variety of tyrosine kinases that, when mutated, allow unrestricted growth in cancer cells. Of particular note is the recently released drug Gleevec, which targets tyrosine kinase BCR-Abl and is showing positive results in treating leukemia with minimal adverse effects. (6) The success of Gleevec is demonstrative of the power of enzyme inhibitor-based cancer treatment, and many researchers believe the combined power of several enzyme restriction drugs is the next step in cancer treatment. These drugs have the ability to fully restrict tumor growth while allowing patients to maintain a quality of life that is much higher than that of patients undergoing traditional cancer treatments.

Unfortunately, cancer is doing its part to counteract these advances in treatment. Most notably, cancer has begun utilizing the body's own defenses to form resistances to cancer treatment drugs, including enzyme inhibitors. These adaptations, dubbed "multi-drug resistance" cancers, or MDR, can arise through several different mechanisms, each requiring different treatment. The most common and widely understood of these mechanisms is the manipulation of p-glycoprotein (PGP) by cancer cells. Ironically, the body uses PGP as a means of toxin defense. PGP is most commonly

Promising Advancements 5

expressed to protect highly susceptible areas of the body, such as the blood-brain barrier and the testes, and it functions by capturing and expelling toxins from these areas. Some forms of cancer have adapted to express high levels of PGP, which recognizes cancer-targeting drugs (both chemotherapeutic and enzyme inhibitor) as foreign and expels them from the cancer cell, preventing effective treatment. While this adaptation may seem scary enough already, it is compounded by the fact that cancer has also been shown to increase expression of PGP after the initial round of drugs. (7) So even if there was some initial success, the drug's performance will continually decrease in MDR cancers. While PGP mediated drug resistance is the most common form of MDR, it is also the most treatable resistance and can be combated through the use of PGP inhibitors. These inhibitors function precisely as their name implies: by inhibiting the function of PGP throughout the body, thereby preventing cancer cells from expunging drugs and making them susceptible to the same treatments as typical cancers. Previously, researchers criticized this method of overcoming MDR cancer, and rightly so, because delivery of inhibitors was systemic, resulting in crippled toxin defense systems throughout the body. However, recent research suggests that PGP inhibitors can be altered for both direct delivery to cancerous cells and

Promising Advancements 6

increased cancer cell specificity. (8) When these alterations are perfected, PGP mediated MDR will become a negligible issue in cancer treatment since it can be countered with no foreseeable side effects.

Aside from PGP-assisted resistance, the most prevalent forms of multi-drug resistance are those mediated by tumor-suppressor and oncogenic mutations. These resistances commonly operate via the same principles as PGP, by expelling cytotoxic drugs from the cancerous cell before they can cause harm. However, they are the result of mutations in a variety of different genes, which makes treatment of these various MDR mutations very difficult. So while research is being conducted on developing drugs to inhibit the protein responsible for some of the more prevalent of these mutations (namely those involving the MRP gene), the most promising option is also the most simplistic: rather than disable resistances, bypass them. Several methods are currently undergoing testing that utilize this simple concept to combat MDR cancer in vastly different ways. The first, which is being tested by various pharmaceutical companies, involves overloading tumor cells with anticancer (cytotoxic) drugs that are rapidly absorbed and fast acting. This process allows the drugs to act before the cancer cell can expunge a substantial amount, effectively negating the resistance mechanisms of the cell.

**CSE
33.2**

Promising Advancements 7

While this method does serve to counter MDR mechanisms, its shortcomings are the same as those of traditional cancer treatment options: the possible side effects are very detrimental. Because this method most often utilizes typical cytotoxic drugs (and at a higher dosage), the patient is exposed to the negative effects of whichever drug is being administered. Therefore, this method will remain only situationally viable until researchers can develop a sufficiently fast-acting and rapidly absorbed drug that does not pose the risks of currently available compounds.

In contrast to the above method, which utilizes traditional drugs in nontraditional doses to bypass resistance, research being led by Victor Keute and Thomas Efferth aims to use nontraditional compounds that actively bypass cancer cell resistance, rather than just overloading it. Keute and Efferth are examining the active compounds in African medicinal plants for cytotoxic effects. They have identified at least four different compounds in the benzophenone family that exhibit cytotoxic properties and, surprisingly, these compounds seem able to destroy drug-resistant cancer cells just as easily as they can destroy nonresistant cells. (9) This research is still in its infancy, so while thorough clinical trials to examine the viability and potential side effects of these compounds have not yet been conducted, the outlook of this research is very promising.

Promising Advancements 8

Many billions of dollars are spent annually on cancer research. Even so, chemotherapy and radiation have remained the dominant treatment options for more than six decades, in spite of their often severe side effects. These outdated methods have done their part to lower the mortality rate of cancer patients, but at an often substantial cost to their quality of life. Fortunately, recently developed enzyme inhibitor-based drugs, which show great promise in combating the disease with much less substantial side effects, seem poised to replace chemotherapy as the preferred cancer treatment option. Additionally, researchers are in the process of developing several different methods to combat multi-drug resistance in cancer to deal with this ever-increasing complication. If proven successful, these combined options could revolutionize the world of cancer treatment, providing hope to the millions afflicted and bringing us one step closer to removing cancer from the list of most fatal diseases worldwide.

**CSE
33.2**

The reference list is titled "References" and begins on a new page.

Promising Advancements 9

References

The reference list is not alphabetical. Sources are numbered and listed in the order in which they appear in the document.

1. National Cancer Institute. SEER stat fact sheets: all sites. Bethesda (MD): National Cancer Institute; 2013 [accessed 2017 Jan 9]. http://seer.cancer.gov/statfacts/html/all.html.

2. Stanford Medicine Cancer Institute. Chemotherapy drugs and side effects. Stanford (CA): Stanford Medicine; 2014 [accessed 2017 Jan 21]. http://cancer.stanford.edu/information/cancertreatment/methods/chemotherapy.html.

3. Bonnet D, Dick JE. Human acute myeloid leukemia is organized as a hierarchy that originates from a primitive hematopoietic cell. Nature Med. 1997;3(7):730–737.

4. Hanahan D, Weinberg RA. Hallmarks of cancer: the next generation. Cell. 2011;144(5):646–674.

5. Seppa N. Keeping cells under control: enzyme suppression inhibits cancer spread. Sci News. 2004 Aug 28:134.

6. Pray L. Gleevec: the breakthrough in cancer treatment. Nat Ed. 2008;1(1):37. http://www.nature.com/scitable/topicpage/gleevec-the-breakthrough-in-cancer-treatment-565.

7. Ichihashi N, Kitajima Y. Chemotherapy induces or increases expression of multidrug resistance-associated protein in malignant melanoma cells. Br J Dermatol. 2001 Apr [accessed 2017 Jan 8];144(4):745–750. PubMed. Bethesda (MD): Nat Cent for Biotechnol Inf; c2001. http://www.ncbi.nlm.nih.gov/pubmed/11298532.

8. Kanghui Y, Jifeng W, Xun L. Recent advances in research on P-glycoprotein inhibitors. BioSci Trends. 2008 [accessed 2014 8 Jan];2(4):137–146. http://www.biosciencetrends.com/action/downloaddoc.php?docid=141.

Titles of books and periodicals are neither underlined nor italicized. All major words in the titles of periodicals are capitalized. For all other sources, only initial words of the main title and proper nouns and adjectives are capitalized.

CSE
33.2

Promising Advancements 10

9. Gutierrez D. African medicinal plants may stop tumor
growth from multi-drug resistant cancers: research. Natural
News. 2013 Jun 26 [accessed 2017 Jan 9]. http://www
.naturalnews.com/040947_cancer_treatment_african_
plants_medicinal_herbs.html.

The writer included
a list of additional
resources, in
alphabetical order,
that were consulted
but not cited in the
paper.

Additional References

DeVita VT Jr, Chu E. A history of cancer chemotherapy.
Cancer Res. 2008;68(21):8643–8653. PubMed.
Bethesda (MD): Nat Cent for Biotechnol Inf; c2008.
http://www.ncbi.nlm.nih.gov/pubmed/18974103.

Mukherjee S. The emperor of all maladies: a biography of
cancer. 2010. New York (NY): Scribner; 2010.

Persidis A. Cancer multidrug resistance. Nat Biotech.
1999;17:94–95. http://www.nature.com/nbt/journal/
v18/n10s/full/nbt1000_IT18.html.

Szakacs G, Paterson JK, Ludwig JA, Booth-Genthe C,
Gottesman MM. Targeting multidrug resistance in
cancer. Nat Rev Drug Discov. 2006;5(3):219–234.

Thomas H, Coley H. Overcoming multidrug resistance in
cancer: an update on the clinical strategy of inhibiting
P-glycoprotein. Cancer Control. 2003;10(2):159–165.

Notes

Topol E. Quote taken from a 2013 genetics symposium in
San Diego.

Notes include unreferenced
sources, such as the quote
shown here.

Frequently Confused, Misused, and Abused Words

A *pitfall* is, of course, a danger or difficulty that's not necessarily easy to recognize. The words given in this section present well-known, common pitfalls. For a more complete understanding of any of the words or phrases on the list, please check a dictionary.

accept, except. *Accept* is a verb meaning "consent" or "agree." *Except* means "apart from" or "other than."

affect, effect. Except in a few special cases, *affect* is a verb meaning "change," and *effect* is a noun meaning "result."

all ready, already. *Already* is the form that means "before now."

all right, alright. The spelling *alright* is too informal for academic writing. Use *all right*.

all together, altogether. *Altogether* is the form that means "completely" or "on the whole."

a lot. Too informal for academic writing. Where you do use *a lot*, write it as two words, as shown.

alright. See *all right*.

among, between. Use *among* when referring to three or more, and *between* for two.

amount, number, quantity. Use *amount* for things that can't be counted, like water and coffee grounds. Use *number* for countable things, like bottles and cups. Use *quantity* for either.

anyone, any one. *Anyone* is for people, *any one* is for either people or things. Both forms are singular (p. 293, Sec. 25.1).

as. Use *as* or *as if*, not *like*, when what follows it contains a verb: *Do as I say. He acted as if he didn't care.* As can also mean either "when" or "because." Do not use it in ways that will leave readers wondering which sense you intended.

bad, badly. See p. 325, Sec. 27.3.

beside, besides. *Beside* means "next to." *Besides* means "in addition to" or "moreover."

between. See *among*.

bring, take. Use *bring* for motion toward you or toward the focus of the action. Use *take* for motion away from you or from the focus. Either *He brought her a gift* or *He took her a gift* can be correct, depending on the focus of the passage.

cite, site, sight. To *cite* is to quote and/or present a reference. To *site* is to locate; a *site* is a location. A *sight* is something to see.

complement, compliment. A *complement* completes something. A *compliment* is praise.

conscience, conscious. *Conscience* is moral feeling. *Conscious* means "aware."

could care less. Too informal for academic writing.

could of. Incorrect. Write *could have* instead.

data. Often plural in formal writing: *The data are incomplete.*

different from, different than. Use *different from* wherever possible.

each. See p. 293, Sec. 25.1.

effect. See *affect*.

either. See p. 293, Sec. 25.1.

everyday, every day. *Everyday* is an adjective that means "daily" or "ordinary": an *everyday* outfit. *Every day* is an adverb that means "each day": I wear a watch *every day*.

everyone, every one. *Everyone* refers to people. *Every one* means "each one" and may refer to people or things. Both forms are singular (p. 293, Sec. 25.1).

except. See *accept*.

farther, further. Use *farther* for physical distance. Use *further* to mean "in addition" or "additional."

fewer, less. Use *fewer* for things that can be counted, like books and buildings. Use *less* for amounts of things that cannot be counted, like information and food.

firstly. Pretentious. Write *first* instead.

former, latter. Use these words to indicate which of two things you are referring to. For more than two, use *first*, *second*, etc., and *last*.

further. See *farther*.

good, well. See p. 325, Sec. 27.3.

he. See p. 272, Sec. 24.1, for avoiding sexist language. See box on p. 274, Sec. 24.1, regarding gendered pronouns.

imply, infer. To *imply* is to suggest. To *infer* is to deduce or conclude.

into, in to. *Into* is for entering: *He went into the library.* In other senses, use *in to*: *He went in to visit a friend.*

irregardless. Incorrect. Write *regardless* instead.

is when, is where. Too informal for academic writing. Revise the sentence.

its, it's. See p. 344, Sec. 28.4.

kind of, sort of. In contexts like *kind of a good idea* and *sort of a strange request*, too informal for academic writing. Delete.

latter. See *former*.

lay, lie. When the verb takes an object, use *lay* (past tense *laid*): *She laid the book on the table.* Without an object, use *lie* (past tense *lay*, past participle *lain*): *The cat lies in her basket.*

lead, led. *Lead* is both a metal and the present tense of a verb meaning "guide." *Led* is the past tense and past participle of this verb.

lend, loan. In academic writing, use *lend* (past tense *lent*) as a verb, *loan* as a noun.

less. See *fewer*.

lie. See *lay*.

like. See *as*.

literally. Means what it applies to is factual and not a figure of speech. In sentences like *We were literally climbing the walls*, delete it.

loose, lose. *Loose*, an adjective, is the opposite of "tight" or "confined." *Lose* is a verb.

maybe, may be. *Maybe* means "possibly." *May be* is a verb form.

may of, might of, must of. Incorrect. Write *may have, might have*, or *must have* instead.

myself and other **-self pronouns.** See p. 312, Sec. 26.1.

neither. See p. 293, Sec. 25.1.

number. See *amount*.

off of, outside of. Delete *of* whenever possible.

precede, proceed. *Precede* means "go before." *Proceed* means "begin" or "continue."

pretty. In the sense of "somewhat," as in *pretty close*, too informal for academic writing.

principal, principle. *Principal* is a noun meaning "leader" or "sum of money" and an adjective meaning "main." *Principle* is a noun meaning "rule" or "basis."

proceed. See *precede*.

quantity. See *amount*.

quotation, quote. In academic writing, use *quotation* as a noun and *quote* as a verb.

raise, rise. When the verb takes an object, use *raise*: *They raised the flag*. Without an object, use *rise* (past tense *rose*, past participle *risen*): *The sun rose*.

real, really. In the sense of "very," too informal for academic writing.

reason . . . is because, reason why. Redundant. Write *the reason is that* or simply *why* instead.

respectfully, respectively. *Respectfully* has to do with showing respect. *Respectively* means "separately and in the order mentioned": *Gabriela and Roger earned an A and a B, respectively*.

rise. See *raise*.

secondly. See *firstly*.

set, sit. When the verb takes an object, use *set* (past tense and past participle *set*): *He set his backpack down*. Without an object, use *sit* (past tense and past participle *sit*): *The backpack sits on the floor*.

should of. Incorrect. Write *should have* instead.

sight, site. See *cite*.

since. This word can mean either "because" or "after." Do not use it in ways that will leave readers wondering which sense you intended.

sit. See *set*.

sort of. See *kind of*.

suppose to. Incorrect. Write *supposed to* instead.

take. See *bring*.

than, then. Use *than* in comparisons and *then* in reference to time.

that, which, who. For *that* versus *which*, see p. 333, Sec. 28.1. Use *that* for things and *who* for people.

their, there, they're. *Their* is a possessive adjective (p. 344, Sec. 28.4): *Their ideas are interesting*. *There* is an adverb having to do with location and, sometimes, a placeholder for the subject of a sentence (p. 237, Sec. 20.1). *They're* is a contraction (p. 342, Sec. 28.4) for *they are*.

then. When describing a sequence of actions, it's unnecessary to specify *then* before each action. Also see *than*.

toward, towards. Use *toward*.

try and. Write *try to* instead.

unique. This word means "one of a kind," not merely "unusual."

use to. Incorrect. Write *used to* instead.

well. See p. 325, Sec. 27.3.

where. Do not use *where* you could use *that* instead.

which. See p. 243, Sec. 21.3. For *that* versus *which*, see p. 333, Sec. 28.1.

while. This word can mean either "at the same time as," "whereas," or "although." Do not use it in ways that will leave readers wondering which sense you intended.

who. See *that*.

who, whom. See p. 310, Sec. 26.1.

who's, whose. *Who's* is a contraction of *who is* or *who has*: *Who's there? Whose* is a possessive adjective: *Whose book is this? The person whose book it is left it behind.*

would of. Incorrect. Write *would have* instead.

you. See p. 319, Sec. 26.3.

your, you're. *Your* is a possessive adjective: *Your help was invaluable. You're* is a contraction (p. 342, Sec. 28.4) of "you are": *You're welcome.*

When you find yourself puzzling over other pairs of words—for instance, *dependence* and *dependency*—a dictionary can help you. If it gives entries for both versions, either one is correct. If it has one entry in which the variants are separated by *or* (*ax* or *axe*), it's telling you that it's fine to use either one. If it has one entry in which the variants are separated by *also* (*adviser*, also *advisor*), it's telling you that the first word or spelling is more common and therefore preferred.

Glossary of Terms

acronym *(mechanics)*. An abbreviation typically formed from the first letters of words and usually pronounced as a word (*AIDS, NASCAR*) (p. 358, Sec. 29.3).

active reading *(composing processes)*. Reading in a way that involves interacting with the text, for example by highlighting or underlining passages, writing notes in the margins of a document, or questioning the author's ideas (p. 31, Sec. 3.3).

active voice *(grammar)*. Use of a verb so that its subject is the actor (They *walked* the dog), as opposed to being acted upon (The dog *was walked*) (p. 279, Sec. 24.2).

adjective *(part of speech)*. A word that modifies or describes a noun or pronoun (an *excited* dog) (p. 322, Sec. 27.1).

adverb *(part of speech)*. A word modifying a verb, an adjective, or another adverb (a *surprisingly* excited dog) (p. 324, Sec. 27.2).

advocate *(rhetoric)*. A role (p. 7, Sec. 1.2) adopted by writers who seek to convince, persuade, or mediate a dispute among readers (p. 7, Sec. 1.2).

alignment *(genre and design)*. The horizontal arrangement of text and illustrations on a page (p. 77, Sec. 5.3).

alternative subjects *(grammar)*. Subjects connected by *or* or *nor* (the *band* or the *instruments*) (p. 290, Sec. 25.1)

amplification *(rhetoric)*. Providing information to expand on a point (p. 205, Sec. 15.8).

annotated bibliography *(genre and design)*. A bibliography that includes a brief note about each source (pp. 47, Sec. 4.3, and 100, Genre Design Gallery). See also *list of works cited, reference list,* and *working bibliography.*

antecedent *(grammar)*. The noun to which a pronoun refers (*Bingo* was his name) (p. 314, Sec. 26.2).

APA style *(research)*. The documentation system created by the American Psychological Association (p. 402, Chapter 31).

appeal *(rhetoric)*. How a writer shows the connection between a reason and evidence (p. 66, Sec. 4.8).

article *(part of speech)*. A, an, or the (p. 327, Sec. 27.5).

attributive noun *(grammar)*. A noun being used as an adjective (a *dog* bed) (p. 344, Sec. 28.4).

audience *(rhetoric)*. The readers or listeners addressed by a writer or speaker (p. 8, Sec. 1.2).

base form *(grammar)*. A verb form with no ending and no other changes that would signal tense or mood (*walk, eat, drink*) (p. 288, Sec. 25.1).

blog post *(genre and design)*. An entry in a blog (p. 99, Genre Design Gallery, G.7).

Boolean search *(research)*. A search for sources that specifies whether keywords or phrases *can, must,* or *must not* appear in the results (p. 106, Sec. 6.1).

borders *(genre and design)*. Lines or boxes that surround text or illustrations (p. 77, Sec. 5.3).

brackets *(punctuation)*. A symbol, in practice almost always square brackets ([these]), rather than curly brackets ({these}). In quotations, brackets set off words that have been added to or changed from the original (p. 144, Sec. 9.2). Elsewhere, they set off parenthetical elements within text that is already in parentheses (p. 352, Sec. 28.5).

brainstorming *(composing processes)*. Generating a list of ideas (p. 18, Sec. 2.1).

Chicago style *(research)*. The documentation system described in the *Chicago Manual of Style* (p. 443, Chapter 32).

clause *(grammar)*. See *main clause, subordinate clause.*

clustering *(composing processes)*. Generating ideas by drawing lines between groups of related terms or phrases (p. 19, Sec. 2.1).

collective noun *(grammar)*. Refers to a group of people or things as a whole and is usually treated as singular (The *team* plays well together) (p. 294, Sec. 25.1).

color *(genre and design)*. Used to set a mood, call attention to information, or signal the function of parts of a document (p. 79, Sec. 5.3).

comma splice *(grammar)*. A mistake in which two independent clauses are joined by nothing more than a comma (*She ran ahead of me, I followed*) (p. 250, Sec. 22.2).

common knowledge *(rhetoric)*. Information that is widely known (*Washington, D.C., is the capital of the United States*) (p. 158, Sec. 10.2).

comparative adjective *(grammar)*. Compares two things using an -er ending or an adverb (*longer; more interesting*) (p. 326, Sec. 27.4).

complex sentence *(grammar)*. Contains one or more subordinate clauses in addition to a main clause (*Ancient grains, which have become fashionable food ingredients, are genetically much the same as their ancestors were millennia ago*) (p. 242, Sec. 21.3).

compound complex sentence *(grammar)*. Contains more than one main clause and one or more subordinate clauses (p. 245, Sec. 21.4).

compound sentence *(grammar)*. Contains two or more main clauses (*Bulgur is considered an ancient grain, and so is the "pseudocereal" quinoa*) (p. 240, Sec. 21.2).

compound subject *(grammar)*. Two or more things that make up the subject of a sentence (*Sociology and psychology* examine different aspects of the human experience) (p. 289, Sec. 25.1).

conclusion *(rhetoric)*. The end of a document; usually used to reinforce its main point (p. 214, Chapter 17).

conjunction *(part of speech)*. A word used to join other words or clauses. See *coordinating conjunction, subordinating conjunction*.

content curation tools *(research)*. Tools used to create and share collections of sources (p. 135, Sec. 8.2).

context *(rhetoric)*. The factors—potentially including social relationships, culture, history, discipline, physical surroundings, and technology—that shape the reading, writing, and viewing of a document (p. 8, Sec. 1.2).

coordinating conjunction *(grammar)*. *And, but, for, nor, or, so,* or *yet,* each of which joins words and clauses on a roughly equal basis (*I didn't see the movie, nor did I watch the TV series*) (p. 241, Sec. 21.2).

correspondence *(research)*. A form of field research (p. 115, Sec. 6.3) involving the exchange of letters or messages (p. 121, Sec. 6.3).

counterargument *(rhetoric)*. An argument that has been or might be offered in response to an argument (p. 67, Sec. 4.8).

count noun *(grammar)*. Names something that is being counted or could be (We'd like three *bottles* of water, please) (p. 295, Sec. 25.1).

critical attitude *(composing processes)*. When reading critically, approaching a source in a questioning or skeptical frame of mind (p. 29, Sec. 3.1).

critical reading *(composing processes)*. Reading with a purpose (p. 29, Chapter 3).

CSE style *(research)*. The documentation system created by the Council of Science Editors (p. 481, Chapter 33).

dangling modifier *(grammar)*. A word or phrase that seems to modify a word other than the one intended (Mandy saw the book *walking out of class*) (p. 263, Sec. 23.3).

dangling preposition *(grammar)*. An awkward construction in which a clause unnecessarily ends with a preposition (What time does the class last *until*?) (p. 264, Sec. 23.3).

database *(research)*. A digital collection of records and information; library databases supply publication information and brief descriptions of the information in a source (p. 109, Sec. 6.1).

dependent clause *(grammar)*. See *subordinate clause*.

design *(genre and design)*. The use of elements such as fonts, illustrations, color, and borders to affect a reader's understanding of and reaction to a document (p. 72, Chapter 5).

design principles *(genre and design)*. A set of guidelines—including balance, emphasis, placement, repetition, and consistency—that, if followed, can help writers achieve their goals (p. 72, Sec. 5.1).

dialogue *(rhetoric)*. Spoken exchanges between people in a story (p. 42, Sec. 4.1).

documenting sources *(research).* Identifying sources of information, ideas, and arguments in the text of a document and in a works cited or references list (p. 136, Sec. 8.3).

DOI *(research).* Digital object identifier, a unique number assigned to a document (p. 372, Sec. 30.2).

drafting *(composing processes).* Writing a document; usually involving multiple versions that build on each other (first draft, second draft . . . final draft) (p. 11, Sec. 1.3).

editing *(composing processes).* Assessing and improving the effectiveness, accuracy, and appropriateness of the words and sentences in a document (p. 229, Chapter 19).

editing strategies *(composing processes).* Processes, such as reading carefully, marking a document, and seeking feedback, that are used in editing (p. 232, Sec. 19.2).

ellipsis marks *(punctuation).* Three or four spaced periods in a row, used to indicate omission, especially in a quotation (*whose broad stripes and bright stars . . . were so gallantly streaming*), or trailing off (p. 353, Sec. 28.5).

em dash *(punctuation).* A dash about as long as a capital M is wide, used in text for breaks in thought (box on p. 350, Sec. 28.5).

en dash *(punctuation).* A dash about as long as a capital N is wide, used for various mechanical purposes (box on p. 350, Sec. 28.5).

entertainer *(rhetoric).* A role (p. 7, Sec 1.2) adopted by writers who seek to amuse readers (p. 7, Sec 1.2).

evaluation *(composing processes).* Considering the suitability of a source for a writing project, with attention to the following (p. 125, Sec. 7.3):

　　author. The purpose, qualifications, and background of the source's creator (p. 126, Sec. 7.3).

　　comprehensiveness. The extent to which a source provides a complete and balanced view of a topic (p. 128, Sec. 7.3).

　　evidence. Information offered to support an author's reasoning (p. 126, Sec. 7.3).

genre. The extent to which a source shares the organization, design, and writing conventions of similar types of documents (p. 128, Sec. 7.3).

publisher. The purpose and biases of the source's distributor (p. 127, Sec. 7.3).

relevance. The extent to which a source provides information you can use in your writing project (p. 125, Sec. 7.3).

timeliness. A source's publication date (p. 127, Sec. 7.3).

evaluator *(rhetoric).* A role (p. 7, Sec 1.2) adopted by writers who seek to help readers reach an informed, well-reasoned understanding of a subject's worth or effectiveness (p. 7, Sec 1.2).

evidence *(rhetoric).* Information—such as details, facts, personal observations, and expert opinions—used to support assertions and help readers understand a point (p. 171, Sec. 12.2).

exact phrase search *(research).* Search (p. 105, Sec. 6.1) conducted on a phrase, usually specified in a search field or by enclosing the phrase in quotation marks (p. 106, Sec. 6.1).

feedback *(composing processes).* Responses and advice offered to a writer on a draft of a document (p. 15, Sec. 1.4).

field research *(research).* Collecting information through methods including interviews, observation, surveys, and correspondence (p. 172, Sec. 12.2).

figure of speech *(rhetoric).* A word or phrase whose meaning or form differs from or embellishes what it says on the surface (*a dog's breakfast*; *dismal and disconsolate in the darkness*) (p. 282, Sec. 24.2).

first person *(grammar).* Writing whose subject or explicit focus is *I* or *we* (p. 288, Sec. 25.1).

font *(genre and design).* A set of characters, letters, and symbols that share a distinctive design. Examples include Helvetica, Courier, and Times New Roman (p. 77, Sec. 5.3).

formal outline *(composing processes).* An outline (p. 185, Sec. 13.2) that uses numbers and/or letters to organize the elements in a draft (p. 189, Sec. 13.2).

freewriting *(composing processes).* Generating ideas by writing quickly and without editing (p. 18, Sec. 2.1).

gender *(grammar)*. A characteristic of pronouns, which may be masculine (*he*), feminine (*she*), or neutral (*I, you, it, we, they*) (p. 309, Sec. 26.1).

genre *(genre and design)*. Categories of documents, such as academic essays and opinion columns, that have been developed to help writers accomplish a general purpose, such as informing readers or presenting an argument (p. 10, Sec. 1.2).

gerund *(part of speech)*. A verbal functioning as a noun (Sometimes *writing* is fun) (p. 237, Sec. 20.1).

government search sites *(research)*. Web search sites that focus on government documents (p. 111, Sec. 6.1).

illustration *(genre and design)*. Materials such as photographs, videos, charts, graphs, and tables that expand on or visually demonstrate points made in the text of a document (p. 82, Sec. 5.3).

imperative mood *(grammar)*. The verb form used in commands and similar expressions, without an expressed subject (*Don't forget!*) (p. 304, Sec. 25.3).

indefinite pronoun *(grammar)*. A word like *anyone, each, others,* or *something* that refers to unspecific people or things (p. 293, Sec. 25.1).

independent clause. See *main clause*.

indicative mood *(grammar)*. The verb forms that indicate or express facts, seeming facts, and the like (they *reviewed* the evidence; she *will join* the team soon) (p. 304, Sec. 25.3).

indirect question *(grammar)*. A question that is conveyed in reported speech (p. 269, Sec. 23.5).

infographic *(genre and design)*. A type of document that provides a visual representation of a set of facts or data (p. 96, Genre Design Gallery, G.6).

informal outline *(composing processes)*. An outline (p. 187, Sec. 13.2) that provides a brief sketch of the sequence of elements in a draft (p. 191, Sec. 13.2).

informative article *(genre and design)*. A type of document that provides information about a subject. Informative articles appear in newspapers, magazines, scholarly and professional journals, and websites, among other sources (p. 43, Sec. 4.2).

inquirer *(rhetoric)*. A role (p. 7, Sec 1.2) adopted by writers who seek to share new knowledge with readers (p. 7, Sec 1.2).

intentional plagiarism *(composing processes)*. Deliberately copying material from a source, creating fake citations, closely paraphrasing extended passages from a source, or purchasing a document and passing it off as original work, among other forms of academic misconduct (p. 155, Sec. 10.1).

interpreter *(rhetoric)*. A role (p. 7, Sec 1.2) adopted by writers who seek to analyze and explain the origins, qualities, significance, or potential impact of an idea, event, or issue.

interview *(research)*. A form of field research (p. 115, Sec. 6.3) in which one person seeks information from another via spoken or written conversation.

in-text citation *(research)*. Providing information about the source of material in the text of a document, usually in the form of a parenthetical citation or a note (p. 139, Sec. 9.1).

introduction *(rhetoric)*. The beginning of a document; usually used to present its main point (p. 207, Chapter 16).

issue *(rhetoric)*. A point of disagreement, uncertainty, concern, or curiosity that is being discussed by communities of readers and writers (p. 63, Sec. 4.8).

jargon *(rhetoric)*. Specialized language used almost exclusively by a particular subset of speakers and writers (*Dentate nucleus atrophy* was more severe when *frataxin* was very low). In the right contexts it can express information concisely, and in the wrong ones it can puzzle and annoy readers (p. 271, Sec. 24.1).

keyword *(research)*. A word entered in a search form (p. 105, Sec. 6.1).

knowledge inventory *(composing processes)*. An assessment of what a writer knows about a subject (p. 156, Sec. 10.2).

library catalog *(research)*. A database (p. 109, Sec. 6.1) that provides information about the print and digital materials in a library's collection (p. 107, Sec. 6.1).

library stacks *(research)*. Shelves that house a library's collection of books and other bound publications (p. 113, Sec. 6.2).

limiting modifier *(grammar)*. A word like *almost*, *hardly*, or *only*, which may need to be carefully placed so that it does not seem to modify a word other than the one intended (p. 260, Sec. 23.2).

line spacing *(genre and design)*. The amount of vertical space between lines of text (p. 77, Sec. 5.3).

list of works cited *(research)*. A list of sources used in a document, typically alphabetized by author or title, that appears at the end of a document (p. 136, Sec. 8.3; p. 139, Sec. 9.1).

logical fallacy *(rhetoric)*. An error in logic that, if recognized, can undermine readers' willingness to accept an argument (p. 68, Sec. 4.8).

main clause *(grammar)*. A series of words, usually containing a subject and a verb, that expresses a complete thought, though other, attached clauses may add to or modify its meaning (*Quinoa suddenly became popular*) (p. 240, Sec. 21.1).

main point *(rhetoric)*. Often expressed as a thesis statement, the main point is the most important claim made by the writer of a document (p. 165, Chapter 11).

map *(composing processes)*. A visual representation of the sequence in which reasons and evidence will appear in a document (p. 185, Sec. 13.2).

mapping *(composing processes)*. Generating ideas by showing the relationships between terms and concepts or terms and phrases using lines, circles, boxes, or other graphic elements (p. 19, Sec. 2.1).

marking *(composing processes)*. During critical reading, highlighting or underlining or otherwise calling attention to important passages in a text (p. 31, Sec. 3.3).

mass (noncount) noun *(grammar)*. Names something being considered as a whole that cannot be, or is not being, counted (The *water* is cold) (p. 295, Sec. 25.1).

mechanics, sentence *(mechanics)*. The use of capitalization, italics, abbreviations, and acronyms (p. 354, Chapter 29).

media search sites *(research)*. Web search sites that focus on specific types of media such as videos or images (p. 112, Sec. 6.1).

meta search sites *(research)*. Web search sites, such as MetaCrawler, that gather and present results from other search sites (p. 111, Sec. 6.1).

mixed metaphor *(rhetoric)*. An awkward combination of unrelated figures of speech (*He's comparing apples and oranges, so that dog won't hunt*) (p. 285, Sec. 24.2).

modifier *(grammar)*. An adjective, attributive noun, adverb, or a phrase that serves one of these functions, any of which affects the meaning of another element in the sentence (p. 260, Sec. 23.2).

multimedia presentation *(genre and design)*. A presentation made with slides, such as those created in PowerPoint or Keynote (p. 53, Sec. 4.5).

multimodal essay *(genre and design)*. An essay that combines text with images, animation, sound, and/or video to establish a line of argument and support the writer's points (p. 90, Genre Design Gallery, G.3).

negation *(grammar)*. Giving a phrase or sentence negative force, usually with *not*, *don't*, *never*, or a subject such as *no one* or *nothing* (p. 265, Sec. 23.4).

news search sites *(research)*. Web search sites that focus on recent news (p. 111, Sec. 6.1).

noncount noun *(grammar)*. See *mass noun*.

notes *(research)*. Records of information from sources, typically including quotations, paraphrases, summaries, and plans for composing a document (p. 36, Sec. 3.3).

noun *(part of speech)*. A word identifying a person, place, or thing (*farmer, cornfield, agriculture*).

noun complement *(grammar)*. In a sentence, a noun that is being equated with the subject (Her major is *economics*) (p. 292, Sec. 25.1).

noun phrase *(grammar)*. A series of words that together function as a noun (a *complicated but, in the end, deeply fascinating writing assignment*).

number *(grammar)*. Whether a noun, noun phrase, or verb is singular or plural (p. 288, Sec. 25.1).

object *(grammar)*. A noun, noun phrase, or pronoun that is either acted on by a subject (I paid my *bills*) or "governed" by a preposition (The money was in my *account*) (p. 292, Sec. 25.1).

object pronoun *(grammar)*. A pronoun in the right form, or case, to be used as an object: *me, you, him, her, it, us,* or *them* (p. 308, Sec. 26.1).

observation *(research)*. A form of field research (p. 115, Sec. 6.3) in which the researcher views activity in a particular setting (p. 116, Sec. 6.3).

observer *(rhetoric)*. A role (p. 7, Sec 1.2) adopted by writers who seek to share reflections on an individual, event, object, idea, or issue (p. 7, Sec 1.2).

open question *(grammar)*. A question that has many more possible answers than yes or no (*Why do you believe that?*) (p. 268, Sec. 23.5).

organizing pattern *(composing processes)*. Principles—such as chronology, cause/effect, or strengths/weaknesses—for arranging the ideas in a document (p. 183, Sec. 13.1).

outline *(composing processes)*. A textual representation of the sequence in which reasons and evidence will appear in a document (p. 187, Sec. 13.2).

Oxford comma. See *serial comma*.

page layout *(genre and design)*. The arrangement of design elements—such as text and images—on a page (p. 79, Sec. 5.3).

paragraph *(composing processes)*. One or more sentences set off as a distinct unit of text, often by an indented first line or extra line spacing (p. 192, Sec. 14.2).

parallelism *(rhetoric)*. Putting similar ideas or elements of a sentence in similar form (*Composing* music, *cooking* meals for friends, and *going* for long walks are three of my favorite things to do) (p. 253, Sec. 23.1).

paraphrase *(research)*. A restatement in the writer's own words of a passage from a source (p. 146, Sec. 9.3).

passive voice *(grammar)*. Use of a verb so that its subject is acted upon (Mistakes *were made*), as opposed to being the actor (Somebody *made* mistakes) (p. 279, Sec. 24.2).

peer review *(composing processes)*. The process of seeking feedback on a draft from another writer, often a classmate, friend, or family member (p. 14, Sec. 1.4).

periodicals *(research)*. Publications—such as magazines, journals, or newspapers—published at regular intervals (p. 113, Sec. 6.2).

periodicals room *(research)*. Area within a library that contains magazines, journals, newspapers, and other periodical literature (p. 114, Sec. 6.2).

person. See *first person, second person, third person*.

phrasal verb *(grammar)*. A verb whose meaning takes more than one word to convey (Let's go to the gym and *work out*) (p. 291, Sec. 25.1).

phrase *(grammar)*. A series of words intended to be understood as a unit. See also *noun phrase, prepositional phrase* (p. 239, Sec. 20.3).

plagiarism *(research)*. The unacknowledged use of material from a source or the presentation of another writer's work as your own (p. 153, Sec. 10.1).

plural *(grammar)*. The word forms used for more than one (*crocodiles; they waddle*) (p. 288, Sec. 25.1).

point of view *(rhetoric)*. The perspective taken by the writer, such as first person (*I, me, we*) or third person (*he, she, they*) (p. 288, Sec. 25.1).

position *(rhetoric)*. The stance a writer takes on an issue (p. 165, Sec. 11.1).

position statement *(rhetoric)*. A written expression of a writer's position on an issue, usually early in a writing project (p. 166, Sec. 11.2).

possessive *(grammar)*. A form of nouns, pronouns, and adjectives that indicates possession or a similar relationship (my *brother's* book, the book is not *mine, my* brother) (p. 342, Sec. 28.4).

predicate *(grammar)*. In a sentence, a verb and the elements attached to it, often including an object or a noun complement (Almost any writing *can be thought of as telling a story*).

preposition *(part of speech)*. A word that expresses a relationship between a noun—the preposition's object, which usually follows the preposition—and another element in the sentence (They wondered *about* humans' place *in* the universe) (p. 249, Sec. 22.1).

prepositional phrase *(grammar)*. A preposition, its object, and related words (They felt humble *under the starry sky*) (p. 249, Sec. 22.1).

prewriting *(composing processes)*. Work, such as generating ideas, conducted prior to writing the first draft of a document (p. 18, Sec. 2.1).

primary source *(research)*. An original source, such as a work of literature or a video recording of an event (p. 32, Sec. 3.3).

problem definition *(rhetoric)*. A statement of the nature, scope, and effects of a problem (p. 210, Sec. 16.2).

problem solver *(rhetoric)*. A role (p. 7, Sec 1.2) adopted by writers who seek to make progress on understanding and developing a solution to a problem (p. 7, Sec 1.2).

pronoun *(part of speech)*. A word standing in for a noun or phrase that appears nearby in the text, usually before the pronoun (The researchers believed *they* had discovered something *that* was puzzling to *them*) (p. 243, Sec. 21.3; p. 308, Sec. 26.1). Alternatively, a word naming an unspecific person or thing (*No one* had ever reported *anything* like it before) (p. 293, Sec. 25.1).

proposal *(genre and design)*. A type of document that presents a plan to carry out an activity (p. 58, Sec. 4.7).

purpose *(rhetoric)*. What a writer seeks to accomplish by writing a document; what a reader hopes to accomplish by reading a document (p. 6, Sec. 1.2).

qualification *(rhetoric)*. An observation used to narrow the scope of a statement (p. 205, Sec. 15.8). See also *amplification*.

quotation *(research)*. A direct, attributed copy of a passage from a source (p. 142, Sec. 9.2).

readers *(rhetoric)*. The audience for a written document (p. 8, Sec. 1.2).

reason *(rhetoric)*. A claim made in support of a main point (p. 171, Sec. 12.1).

redundancy *(rhetoric)*. Undesirable repetition of an idea (Many of the *new innovations* came out of her lab; she herself developed *a total of five*) (p. 284, Sec. 24.2).

reference list *(research)*. A list of sources used in a document, typically alphabetized by author or title, that appears at the end of a document (p. 136, Sec. 8.3).

reference search sites *(research)*. Web search sites that present results from dictionaries, encyclopedias, and other reference resources (p. 111, Sec. 6.1).

reflective essay *(genre and design)*. An essay in which a writer shares observations about a subject (p. 39, Sec. 4.1).

reflexive pronoun *(grammar)*. A pronoun that refers to the subject of the clause (The puppy shook *himself* off) (p. 312, Sec. 26.1).

relative clause *(grammar)*. A subordinate clause that attaches to another clause with a relative pronoun, such as *that, which,* or *who* (The book *that she checked out of the library* is missing) (p. 242, Sec. 21.3).

relative pronoun *(grammar)*. The word *that* (in certain senses), *which, who, whoever, whom, whomever,* or *whose,* used as the subject or object of a relative clause (p. 243, Sec. 21.3).

reporter *(rhetoric)*. A role (p. 7, Sec 1.2) adopted by writers who seek to help readers become aware of the facts and ideas central to a written conversation (p. 6, Sec 1.2).

research ethics *(research)*. A writer's obligation to respect the work of other writers by acknowledging sources; accurately and fairly representing information, ideas, and arguments made in those sources; and documenting sources (p. 156, Sec. 10.2).

research question *(research)*. A question that guides a writer's search for information about a subject; also known as a *writing question* (p. 23, Sec. 2.3).

revising *(composing processes)*. Rethinking and re-envisioning what has been written (p. 221, Chapter 18).

revision strategies *(composing processes)*. Processes, such as saving multiple drafts, highlighting reasons and evidence, and challenging your assumptions, that are used in revising (p. 225, Sec. 18.2).

rhetorical situation *(rhetoric)*. The setting in which writers and readers communicate with one another; also known as a *writing situation* (p. 6, Sec. 1.2).

role *(rhetoric)*. A relationship a writer adopts toward readers, such as *advocate, reporter,* or *observer* (p. 7, Sec 1.2).

role-playing *(composing processes)*. Adopting a persona, such as a devil's advocate or doubting Thomas, as you respond to another writer's ideas or draft (p. 13, Sec. 1.4).

rules *(genre and design)*. Lines that appear above or below a passage of text (p. 79, Sec. 5.3).

run-on sentence *(grammar)*. This is a run-on sentence it has three sentences jammed together into one with no punctuation run-ons are universally condemned as bad writing (p. 250, Sec. 22.2).

search *(research)*. The process of locating sources (p. 105, Sec. 6.1).

advanced search. Searching databases, library catalogs, and the web using Boolean operators, limits, and special characters (p. 106, Sec. 6.1).

basic search. Searching databases, library catalogs, and the web for documents that contain a specific word or phrase in the subject, title, text, or, in the case of databases, other parts of a database record (p. 107, Sec. 6.1).

secondary source *(research)*. A source that contains information about a primary source, such as a critical essay about a work of literature (p. 32, Sec. 3.3).

second person *(grammar)*. Writing in which the subject or explicit focus is *you*, singular or plural (p. 288, Sec. 25.1).

self-plagiarism *(research)*. The reuse of a document written by the writer (p. 155, Sec. 10.1).

sentence *(grammar)*. A series of words that is complete in itself, generally containing a subject (a noun or pronoun) and a verb, and usually other elements as well (p. 236, Chapter 20).

sentence fragment *(grammar)*. A mistake in which a series of words that is not a complete sentence is treated as if it were one (*Whoever seems most qualified*) (p. 246, Chapter 22).

sentence mechanics. See *mechanics, sentence.*

sentence starter *(composing processes)*. Generating ideas by "filling in the blanks" in a sentence (p. 21, Sec. 2.1).

serial comma *(punctuation)*. The optional comma that may appear before the last element of a series of three or more things (bacon, lettuce, and tomato) (p. 334, Sec. 28.1 and the box on p. 337, Sec. 28.1).

shading *(genre and design)*. The use of color behind a passage of text, most often to call attention to the passage or signal its function in the document (p. 79, Sec. 5.3).

sic *(research)*. Used in brackets to show an error in a quotation from a source (In his second term, President Oboma [sic] argued that . . .) (p. 144, Sec. 9.2).

singular *(grammar)*. The word forms used for one of something (*alligator; it dozes*) (p. 288, Sec. 25.1).

skimming *(composing processes)*. Reading a document quickly (and partially) to gain an overview of its content and structure (p. 31, Sec. 3.3).

source *(research)*. A document that provides information, ideas, or arguments used in another document (p. 9, Sec. 1.2).

source evaluation *(composing process)*. See *evaluation*.

special operators *(research)*. Symbols used to conduct advanced web searches (p. 106, Sec. 6.1).

spelling, grammar, and style tools *(composing processes)*. Tools available in word processing programs to check spelling, grammar, and style (p. 232, Sec. 19.2).

stable URL *(research)*. A URL (universal resource locator, also known as a web address) that can be used to locate a document found in a database search without logging back into the database (p. 372, Sec. 30.2).

subject *(grammar)*. The noun, pronoun, or phrase that a clause is about (p. 236, Sec. 20.1).

subject complement *(grammar)*. Something that is being equated with the subject of a clause (He is a *fool*; he is *foolish*). It may be a noun, pronoun, or adjective. When the complement is a pronoun, it should be a subject pronoun (p. 313, Sec. 26.1).

subject pronoun *(grammar)*. A pronoun in the right form, or case, to be used as a subject: *I, you, he, she, it, we,* or *they* (p. 308, Sec. 26.1).

subjunctive mood *(grammar)*. The verb forms that indicate or express untrue conditions, wishes, and the like (if pigs *could fly*) (p. 304, Sec. 25.3).

subordinate clause *(grammar)*. A series of words that includes a subject and a verb but that cannot stand on its own as a sentence without modification (*what so proudly we hail; that our flag was still there*) (p. 242, Sec. 21.3).

subordinating conjunction *(grammar)*. Words such as *after, although, because, unless, whether,* and *who,* which join words and clauses in a way that directs the focus of the sentence elsewhere (*After it happens, no one will be able to reverse the damage*) (p. 243, Sec. 21.3).

summary *(research)*. A concise statement of information in a source (p. 148, Sec. 9.4).

superlative adjective *(grammar)*. Compares three or more things using an -*est* ending or an adverb (*shortest*, *least boring*) (p. 326, Sec. 27.4).

survey *(research)*. A form of field research (p. 115, Sec. 6.3) in which information is collected through a questionnaire (p. 118, Sec. 6.3).

tag question *(grammar)*. A question appended to a sentence, usually intended to confirm information the writer thinks is correct (You believe that, *don't you?*) (p. 266, Sec. 23.5).

thesis statement *(composing processes)*. A formal statement of a writer's main idea or position on an issue (p. 165, Chapter 11).

they **or** *them* **as singular** *(grammar)*. A debatable but increasingly common usage (Anyone might think *they* know what to do) (box on p. 274, Sec. 24.1).

third person *(grammar)*. Writing in which the explicit subject or focus is other than *I*, the author, or *you*, the reader (p. 288, Sec. 25.1).

topic *(rhetoric)*. The subject addressed in a document (p. 18, Sec. 2.1).

transition *(rhetoric)*. A word, phrase, or sentence signaling a change in the author's line of thought (p. 192, Sec. 14.1).

transition words *(rhetoric)*. Words like *however* and *nevertheless*, and phrases like *all the same* and *to be sure*, that signal that the author's line of thought is taking a turn and help readers understand the relationships among sentences, paragraphs, and sections of a document (p. 257, Sec. 23.2).

unintentional plagiarism *(research)*. The act of engaging in plagiarism without intending to do so; often the result of taking notes poorly or failing to use notes properly (p. 154, Sec. 10.1).

verb *(part of speech)*. A word that describes an action, state, or occurrence (I *ran*; I *felt* so free; it *improved* my mood) (p. 238, Sec. 20.2).

verbal *(part of speech)*. A verb form being used as another part of speech, usually either a noun (*Speaking* is different from *writing*; *To speak* before the council is an honor) or an adjective (a *speaking* part in the play) (p. 248, Sec. 22.1).

verb tense *(grammar)*. The form of a verb that tells the reader whether to interpret the action as past, present, or future (he *studied*, he *studies*, he *will study*), and as continuing (he *is studying*) or not (p. 296, Sec. 25.2).

web clipping tools *(research)*. Tools used to collect and organize information from web pages (p. 135, Sec. 8.2).

web search sites *(research)*. Websites, such as Google and Bing, that help you search for information on websites and many social media sites (p. 110, Sec. 6.1).

wikis *(research)*. Websites, such as Wikipedia, that are intended to be edited and revised by their readers (p. 130, Sec. 7.3).

wildcard *(research)*. A symbol that stands in for one or more letters or numbers in advanced searches of databases, library catalogs, and the web (p. 106, Sec. 6.1).

working bibliography *(research)*. A running list of sources that have been collected in the course of working on a writing project (p. 136, Sec. 8.3).

writing processes *(composing processes)*. The composing processes writers engage in as they plan, draft, revise, and edit a document (p. 10, Sec. 1.3).

writing question *(research)*. A question that guides a writer's search for information about a subject; also known as a research question (p. 23, Sec. 2.3).

writing situation *(rhetoric)*. The setting in which writers and readers communicate with one another; also known as a rhetorical situation (p. 6, Sec. 1.2).

written conversation *(rhetoric)*. An exchange of information, ideas, and arguments among readers and writers who share an interest in a particular subject or issue (p. 5, Sec. 1.1).

Index

Sentence Guides for Academic Writers

Being a college student means being a college writer. No matter what field you are studying, your instructors will ask you to make sense of what you are learning through writing. When you work on writing assignments in college, you are, in most cases, being asked to write for an academic audience.

Writing academically means thinking academically—asking a lot of questions, digging into the ideas of others, and entering into scholarly debates and academic conversations. As a college writer, you will be asked to read different kinds of texts; understand and evaluate authors' ideas, arguments, and methods; and contribute your own ideas. In this way, you will join a number of important academic conversations.

What does it mean to be part of an *academic conversation?* Well, think of it this way: You and your friends may have an ongoing debate about the best film trilogy of all time. During your conversations with one another, you analyze the details of the films, introduce points you want your friends to consider, listen to their ideas, and perhaps cite what the critics have said about a particular trilogy. This kind of conversation is not unlike what happens in academic writing—except for the topics you'll address, such as the best public policy for a social problem or the most promising new theory in treating disease.

If you are uncertain about what academic writing *sounds like* or if you're not sure you're any good at it, this section of *In Conversation* offers guidance for you at the sentence level. It helps answer questions such as these:

How can I present the ideas of others in a way that demonstrates my understanding of the conversation?

How can I agree with someone but add a new idea?

How can I disagree with another writer without seeming, well, rude?

How can I make clear in my writing which ideas are mine and which ideas are someone else's?

The following sections offer sentence guides for you to use and adapt to your own writing situations. As in all writing that you do, you will have to think about your purpose (reason for writing), your role, and your audience (readers) before knowing which guides will be most appropriate for a particular piece of writing or for a certain part of your essay.

The guides are organized to help you present background information, the views and claims of others, and your own views and claims—all in the context of your purpose, role, and audience.

Academic writers present information and others' views

When you write in academic situations, you may be asked to spend some time giving background information for or setting a context for your main idea or argument. This often requires you to present or summarize what is known or what has already been said in relation to the question you are asking in your writing.

SG1   Presenting what is known or assumed

When you write, you will sometimes need to present something that is known, such as a specific fact or a statistic. The following structures are useful when you are providing background information.

As we know from history, _____.

X has shown that _____.

Research by X and Y suggests that _____.

According to X, _____ percent of _____ are/favor _____.

In other situations, you may need to present information that is assumed or that is conventional wisdom.

People often believe that _____.

Conventional wisdom leads us to believe _____.

Many Americans share the idea that _____.

_____ is a widely held belief.

To challenge an assumption or a widely held belief, you have to acknowledge it first. Doing so lets your readers believe that you are placing your ideas in an appropriate context.

Although many people are led to believe X, there is significant benefit to considering the merits of Y.

College students tend to believe that _____, when, in fact, the opposite is much more likely the case.

SG2 Presenting others' views

As a writer, you build your own *ethos,* or credibility, by fairly and accurately representing the views of others. As an academic writer, you will be expected to demonstrate your understanding of a text by summarizing the views or arguments of its author(s). To do so, you can use language such as the following.

X argues that _____.

X emphasizes the need for _____.

In this important article, X and Y claim _____.

X endorses _____ because _____.

X and Y have recently criticized the idea that _____.

_____, according to X, is the most critical cause of _____.

Although you will create your own variations of these sentences as you draft and revise, the guides can be useful tools for thinking through how best to present another writer's claim or finding clearly and concisely.

SG3 Presenting direct quotations

When the exact words of a source are important for accuracy, authority, emphasis, or flavor, you will want to use a direct quotation. Ordinarily, you will present direct quotations with language of your own that suggests how you are using the source.

X characterizes the problem this way: " . . . "

According to X, _____ is defined as " . . . "

" . . . ," explains X.

X argues strongly in favor of the policy, pointing out that " . . . "

NOTE: You will generally cite direct quotations according to the documentation style your readers expect. MLA style, often used in English and in other humanities courses, recommends using the author name paired with a page number, if there is one. APA style, used in most social sciences, requires the year of publication generally after the mention of the source, with page numbers after the quoted material. In *Chicago* style, used in history and in some humanities courses, and in CSE style, often used in the sciences, writers use superscript numbers (like this[6]) to refer readers to footnotes or endnotes. In-text citations, like the ones shown below, refer readers to entries in the works cited or reference list.

MLA   Lazarín argues that our overreliance on testing in K-12 schools "does not put students first" (20).

APA   Lazarín (2014) argued that our overreliance on testing in K-12 schools "does not put students first." (p. 20)

Chicago   Lazarín argues that our overreliance on testing in K-12 schools
and CSE   "does not put students first."[6]

Many writers use direct quotations to advance an argument of their own:

Standardized testing makes it easier for administrators to measure student performance, but it may not be the best way to measure it. Too much testing wears students out and communicates the idea that recall is the most important skill we want them to develop. Even education policy advisor Melissa Lazarín argues that our overreliance on testing in K-12 schools "does not put students first" (20).

Student writer's idea

Source's idea

SG4 Presenting alternative views

Most debates, whether they are scholarly or popular, are complex—often with more than two sides to an issue. Sometimes you will have to synthesize the views of multiple participants in the debate before you introduce your own ideas.

> On the one hand, X reports that _____, but on the other hand, Y insists that _____.
>
> Even though X endorses the policy, Y refers to it as " . . . "
>
> X, however, isn't convinced and instead argues _____ _____.
>
> X and Y have supported the theory in the past, but new research by Z suggests that _____.

ACADEMIC WRITERS PRESENT THEIR OWN VIEWS

When you write for an academic audience, you should demonstrate that you are familiar with the views of others who are asking the same kinds of questions as you are. Much writing that is done for academic purposes asks you to put your arguments in the context of existing arguments—in a way asking you to connect the known to the new.

When you are asked to write a summary or an informative text, your own views and arguments are generally not called for. However, much of the writing you will be assigned to do in college asks you to take a persuasive stance and present a reasoned argument—at times in response to a single source, and at other times in response to multiple sources.

SG5 Presenting your own views: agreement and extension

Sometimes you agree with the author of a source.

> X's argument is convincing because _____.
>
> Because X's approach is so _____, it is the best way to _____.
>
> X makes an important point when she says _____.

Other times you agree with the author of a source but want to extend the point or go a bit deeper in your own investigation. In a way, you acknowledge what other writers have contributed, but then you move the conversation along with a related comment or finding.

X's proposal for _____ is indeed worth considering. Going one step further, _____.

X makes the claim that _____. By extension, isn't it also true, then, that _____?

_____ has been adequately explained by X. Now, let's move beyond that idea and ask whether _____.

SG6 Presenting your own views: queries and skepticism

It can be intimidating to be asked to respond to the work of another writer, especially if that writer is a well-known scholar or expert or even just a frequent voice in a particular debate. College-level writing asks you to be skeptical, however, and approach academic questions as an investigator. It is ok to doubt, to question, to challenge—because the end result is often new knowledge or a new understanding about a subject.

Couldn't it also be argued that _____?

But is everyone willing to agree that this is the case?

While X insists that _____ is so, he is perhaps asking the wrong question to begin with.

The claims that X and Y have made, while intelligent and well meaning, leave many unconvinced because they have failed to consider _____.

SG7   Presenting your own views: disagreement or correction

Sometimes, you'll find that the only response you have to a text or to an author is complete disagreement.

> X's claims about _____ are misguided.

> X presents a long metaphor comparing _____ to _____; in the end, the comparison is unconvincing because _____.

It can be tempting to disregard a source completely if you detect a piece of information that strikes you as false or that you know to be untrue.

> Although X reports that _____, recent studies indicate that is not the case.

> While X and Y insist that _____ is so, an examination of their figures shows that thay have made an important miscalculation.

A note about using first-person "I"

Some disciplines look favorably upon the use of the first-person "I" in academic writing. Others do not and instead stick to using third person. If you are given a writing assignment for a class, you are better off asking your instructor what he or she prefers or reading through any samples given than *guessing* what might be expected.

First person (I, me, my, we, us, our)

> I question Heddinger's methods and small sample size.

> Harnessing children's technology obsession in the classroom is, I believe, the key to improving learning.

> Lanza's interpretation focuses on circle imagery as symbolic of the family; my analysis leads me in a different direction entirely.

> We would, in fact, benefit from looser laws about farming on our personal property.

(continued)

Third person (names and other nouns)

Heddinger's methods and small sample size are questionable.

Harnessing children's technology obsession in the classroom is the key to improving learning.

Lanza's interpretation focuses on circle imagery as symbolic of the family; other readers' analyses may point in a different direction entirely.

Many Americans would, in fact, benefit from looser laws about farming on personal property.

You may feel as if not being able to use "I" in an essay in which you present your ideas about a topic is unfair or will lead to weaker statements. Know that you can make a strong argument even if you write in the third person. Third-person writing allows you to sound more assertive, credible, and academic.

SG8 Presenting and countering objections to your argument

Effective writers know that their arguments are stronger when they anticipate objections that others might make.

Some will object to this proposal on the grounds that _____.

Not everyone will embrace _____; they may argue instead that _____.

Countering, or responding to, opposing voices fairly and respectfully strengthens your writing and your *ethos*, or credibility.

X and Y might contend that this interpretation is faulty; however, _____.

Most _____ believe that there is too much risk in this approach. But what they have failed to take into consideration is _____.

ACADEMIC WRITERS PERSUADE BY PUTTING IT ALL TOGETHER

Readers of academic writing often want to know what's at stake in a particular debate or text. They want to know why it is that they should care and that they should keep reading. Aside from crafting individual sentences, you must, of course, keep the bigger picture in mind as you attempt to persuade, inform, evaluate, or analyze.

SG9 Presenting stakeholders

When you write, you may be doing so as a member of a group affected by the conversation you have entered. For example, you may be among the thousands of students in your state whose level of debt may change as a result of new laws about financing a college education. In this case, you are a *stakeholder* in the matter. In other words, you have an interest in the matter as a person who could be affected by the outcome of a decision. On the other hand, you may be writing as an investigator of a topic that interests you but that you aren't directly connected with. You may be persuading your audience on behalf of a group of interested stakeholders—a group of which you yourself are not a member.

You can give your writing some teeth if you make it clear who is being affected by the conversation about the issue and the decisions that have or will be made about the issue. The groups of stakeholders are highlighted in the following sentences.

Viewers of Kurosawa's films may not agree with X that

_____.

The research will come as a surprise to parents of children with Type 1 diabetes.

X's claims have the power to offend potentially every low-wage earner in the state.

Marathoners might want to reconsider their training regimen if stories such as those told by X and Y are validated by the medical community.

SG10 Presenting the "so what"

Readers will read your document if they feel as if you're either addressing something that matters to them or addressing something that matters very much to you (or to us all). Good writing often hooks readers with a sense of urgency—a serious response to a reader's "so what?"

Having a frank discussion about _____ now will put us in a far better position to deal with _____ in the future. If we are unwilling or unable to do so, we risk _____.

Such a breakthrough will affect _____ in three significant ways.

It is easy to believe that the stakes aren't high enough to be alarming; in fact, _____ will be affected by _____.

Widespread disapproval of and censorship of such fiction/films/art will mean _____ for us in the future. Culture should represent

_____.

_____ could bring about unprecedented opportunities for _____ to participate in _____, something never seen before.

New experimentation in _____ could allow scientists to investigate _____ in ways they couldn't have imagined _____ years ago.

SG11 Presenting the players and positions in a debate

Some disciplines ask writers to compose a review of the literature as a part of a larger project—or sometimes as a free-standing assignment. In a review of the literature, the writer sets forth a research question, summarizes the key sources that have addressed the question, puts the current research in the context of other voices in the conversation, and identifies any gaps in the research.

Writing that presents a debate, its players, and their positions can often be lengthy. What follows, however, can give you the sense of the flow of ideas and turns in such a piece of writing.

_____ affects more than 30 percent of children in America, and signs point to a worsening situation in years to come because of A, B, and C. Solutions to the problem have eluded even the sharpest policy minds and brightest researchers. In an important 2016 study, W found that _____, which pointed to more problems than solutions. [. . .] Research by X and Y made strides in our understanding of _____ but still didn't offer specific strategies for children and families struggling to _____. [. . .] When Z rejected both the methods and the findings of X and Y, arguing that _____, policymakers and health care experts were optimistic. [. . .] Too much discussion of _____, however, and too little discussion of _____, may lead us to solutions that are ultimately too expensive to sustain.

Writer states the problem.

Writer summarizes the views of others on the topic.

Writer presents her view in the context of current research.

Appendix

Verbs matter   Using a variety of verbs in your sentences can add strength and clarity as you present others' views and your own views.

WHEN YOU WANT TO PRESENT A VIEW FAIRLY NEUTRALLY

acknowledges	observes
adds	points out
admits	reports
comments	suggest
contends	writes
notes	

X points out that the plan had unintended outcomes.

WHEN YOU WANT TO PRESENT A STRONGER VIEW

argues	emphasizes
asserts	insists
declares	

Y argues in favor of a ban on ____ _____, but Z insists the plan is misguided.

WHEN YOU WANT TO SHOW AGREEMENT

agrees

confirms

endorses

For a number of reasons, it is smart to endorse X's position.

WHEN YOU WANT TO SHOW CONTRAST OR DISAGREEMENT

compares

denies

disputes

refutes

rejects

The town must come together and reject X's claims that _____ is in the best interest of the citizens.

WHEN YOU WANT TO ANTICIPATE AN OBJECTION

admits

acknowledges

concedes

Y admits that closer study of _____, with a much larger sample size, is necessary for _____.

Common Revision Symbols and Notations

abbr	abbreviation, **29.3**		**tense**	incorrect verb tense, **25.2**
agr	agreement, **25.1, 26.2**			
awk	awkward		**tr**	transpose
cap	capitalize, **29.1**		**trans**	transition needed, **23.2**
case	incorrect case, **25.3**			
cit	citation needed, **9.1**		**wc**	word choice, **24.1, 24.2**
cliché	cliché, **24.2**		**ww**	wrong word, **24.1**
conc	conclusion, **17.1, 17.2**		^	insert
cs	comma splice, **22.2**		⅃	delete
dm	dangling modifier, **23.3**		¶	paragraph, **14.2**
ex	example needed, **15.7**		//	parallelism, **23.1**
frag	sentence fragment, **22.1**		.	period, **28.2**
			,	comma, **28.1**
inc	incomplete		?	question mark, **28.2**
ital	italics, **29.2**		!	exclamation point, **28.2**
jarg	jargon, **24.1**			
lc	lowercase, **29.1**		;	semicolon, **28.5**
mm	misplaced modifier, **23.3**		:	colon, **28.5**
			'	apostrophe, **28.4**
pass	passive voice, **24.2**		" "	quotation marks, **28.3**
ref	pronoun reference, **26.3**			
			( ) [ ]	parentheses, brackets, **28.5**
run-on	run-on sentence, **22.2**			
sexist	sexist language, **24.1**		. . .	ellipsis marks, **28.5**
slang	slang, **24.1**		⌒	close up
sp	spelling, **19.1**		#	space

DETAILED CONTENTS